Wake Up

Words of wisdom to transform your life

SRINIVAS

Contents

Part 2. Learning & Understanding

Part 4. Action & Behavior

Part 5. Personal Growth & Transformation

Part 6. Problems & Challenges

Part 7. Relationships & Social Dynamics

Part 8. Social & Global Issues

Part 9. Values & Morality

Part 14. Purpose & Direction

Part 15. Time & Experience

Part 16. Deception & Illusion

Foreword

Following the success of *"**Be the Best Version of Yourself**"*, Srinivas returns with **Wake Up**—a profound exploration of the unconscious patterns that shape our lives. While his first book focused on self-improvement and personal transformation, **Wake Up** delves deeper, questioning the very foundation of our thoughts, beliefs, and conditioned existence. It is not just a guide to better living but an invitation to awaken—to see life beyond the illusions we have accepted as truth.

Structured as a journey from fundamental awareness to higher consciousness, this book carefully dismantles the mental constructs that keep us trapped in cycles of fear, conflict, and limitation. Each chapter invites deep inquiry, encouraging the reader to observe, question, and ultimately free the mind from its conditioning. Unlike conventional self-help books that offer solutions within the same framework of thought, *Wake Up* challenges the reader to transcend thought itself—to see with a clarity untouched by past influences.

With his distinctive voice, Srinivas once again delivers wisdom in its purest form—not as an authority, but as a fellow traveler on the path of inquiry. His words do not dictate; they liberate. This book is not about adding more knowledge but about shedding illusions. If *"**Be the Best Version of Yourself**"* was a step toward transformation, *"Wake Up"* is the leap toward true freedom. Read it not just with the mind, but with awareness—because awakening is not in the words, but in living.

Preface

Wake Up is not just another book; it is an invitation to question, observe, and see life with absolute clarity. It is a journey from the depths of conditioning to the heights of awareness, from illusion to truth. Unlike conventional self-help books that offer methods and techniques for self-improvement, this book challenges the very foundation of our thought processes, urging the reader to move beyond knowledge and into direct perception.

This book follows a structured progression, beginning with the nature of thought and mental processes and advancing toward deeper inquiries into consciousness, freedom, and higher states of awareness. Each chapter is designed to dissolve illusions, to strip away the layers of conditioning that have shaped our perceptions. The aim is not to provide answers but to create the space for true insight—because real transformation does not come from acquiring more knowledge, but from seeing through the limitations of the mind itself.

Having previously explored personal growth in **Be the Best Version of Yourself**, I now invite you to go deeper with **Wake Up**. This book is not about improvement but about awakening—not about becoming better, but about seeing what is. It requires no belief, no following, no authority—only an open mind and an earnest willingness to observe. Read it with awareness, engage with it fully, and let the journey unfold—not just in thought, but in living.

Introduction

Humans have evolved over centuries, transforming physically, adapting to environments, and advancing in technology. We have built civilizations, explored the depths of science, and created systems that govern our lives. But amidst all this progress, have we truly changed inwardly? Psychologically, are we any different from our ancestors, or do we still carry the same patterns of fear, aggression, greed, and division? Do we continue to behave like animals—driven by survival instincts, reacting without awareness, and endlessly caught in conflict?

This book is not about refining the existing framework but about breaking free from it entirely and questioning the very foundation of our thoughts, emotions, and conditioned behaviors. *Wake Up* invites you to observe yourself without distortion, to see beyond the illusions of self-created identities, beliefs, and fears. Have we genuinely evolved in our consciousness, or are we trapped in the same cycles of suffering, only wrapped in modernity? To seek truth, one must first see clearly—without bias, without fear, and without the burden of past conditioning.

True change is not a matter of time, effort, or accumulation of knowledge. It begins when we deeply understand ourselves. Through this journey, *Wake Up* will not provide answers but will guide you toward asking the right questions—questions that can free the mind from its mechanical repetition, its illusions, and its limitations. The challenge is not to evolve outwardly but to awaken inwardly. Are you ready to *Wake Up*?

WAKE UP

1. Thought &
Mental Process

WAKE UP

WAKE UP

1. Brain

Brain: The Physical Instrument of Perception and Storage

The brain is a powerful tool that helps us think, remember, and survive. It learns from past experiences and uses memory to make sense of the world. However, this process can also limit how we see reality because the brain does not perceive things directly—it filters everything through what it already knows. To feel safe, it follows patterns and routines, which can create habits that make life predictable but also restrict new ways of thinking. It divides and categorizes everything, labeling things as good or bad, mine or yours, which prevents us from seeing life as a whole. The brain also keeps us stuck in the past or worrying about the future, making it difficult to stay fully aware in the present moment.

Many of our struggles come from identifying too much with the brain's thoughts and memories. We often believe our thoughts are the truth, even though they are just interpretations of reality. We attach ourselves to our past experiences and let them define who we are, even though the self is constantly changing. Instead of experiencing life directly, we rely on knowledge, which can be useful but is not the same as true understanding. We also fear the unknown and resist change because the brain prefers what is familiar. This leads to overthinking—constantly planning, analyzing, and remembering—without truly observing what is happening right now.

To free ourselves from these limitations, we need to use the brain as a tool rather than letting it control us. Thought is necessary for daily life, but it should not dominate our perception. Instead of identifying with every thought, we can simply observe them as they arise and let them go. By living in the present rather than being trapped in past memories or future worries, we can experience true awareness. Silence and clarity come naturally when we stop forcing the mind to be still. A mind that understands the limits of thought does not reject it but knows when to use it wisely. In this way, we can live with intelligence, act with awareness, and move through life without fear or confusion.

2. Mind

Mind: The Field of Thought, Awareness, and Illusion

The mind is the movement of thought, memory, perception, and awareness, responsible for understanding, reacting, feeling, remembering, and imagining. It can function mechanically, following conditioned responses, or with deep intelligence, operating through pure awareness. When conditioned, the mind limits perception, interpreting the world through past knowledge and personal bias. However, when it operates with clarity and awareness, the mind transcends its conditioning and connects with the present moment, free from distortion.

The structure of the mind can be divided into three layers: the conscious mind, the subconscious mind, and the silent mind. The conscious mind is the active part, where we analyze, reason, and respond based on knowledge, beliefs, habits, and thinking patterns. The subconscious mind holds the stored memories, experiences, and conditioning that influence unconscious behavior, including past fears, desires, and emotions. Beyond thought, the silent mind exists as a state of natural quietness when thought stills, allowing for pure awareness to emerge free from conflict or distractions.

The mind becomes conditioned through various factors such as education, societal influences, personal experiences, fear, desire, and comparison. This conditioning creates limitations, leading to distorted perceptions of reality and inner conflict. A mind caught in this cycle continuously seeks more—whether it be pleasure, success, or security—leading to dissatisfaction. True freedom arises when the mind is observed without judgment, when thought is seen as a tool rather than a master, and when the illusion of the 'self' as an accumulation of past experiences dissolves. In this freedom, the mind operates from pure awareness, unburdened by conditioning, and acts with intelligence, clarity, and love.

3. Memory

Memory: The Past That Shapes the Present

Memory is the stored accumulation of experiences, knowledge, and impressions from the past. It is essential for practical living—learning skills, recalling information, and functioning efficiently. However, psychological memory, which includes emotional attachments, fears, and personal narratives, shapes perception and often prevents direct contact with the present. Thought, being entirely based on memory, is never truly new but always conditioned by past experiences. This means that our reactions, beliefs, and interpretations of reality are shaped by what has been rather than what is. The sense of 'self' is also built on memory—without past experiences, relationships, and personal stories, the psychological 'I' as we know it would not exist. While practical memory is necessary for daily functioning, psychological memory creates attachments, regrets, fears, and comparisons that limit perception and disturb the mind.

Memory distorts perception by making us see the present through the lens of past experiences rather than with fresh awareness. Instead of meeting life as it unfolds, we react based on conditioning, making our responses mechanical. This also strengthens psychological time, where the past influences expectations for the future, sustaining anxiety, regret, and longing. People cling to memory because they believe it defines their identity, fearing that without it, they would cease to exist as a 'self.' Memory provides a false sense of security, making the mind hold onto familiar experiences even though life is always changing. Emotional attachments, whether to people, places, or achievements, are reinforced through memory, creating suffering when change occurs. Painful past experiences also continue to affect the present, as memory keeps old wounds alive. Additionally, society conditions us to preserve collective memory through traditions, beliefs, and cultural identities, reinforcing continuity while limiting new understanding.

Freedom from psychological memory does not mean rejecting memory but seeing its limitations. The past exists only as a mental record—it has no reality in the now. Understanding this distinction reduces attachment to memory. One can use memory for practical purposes without allowing it to control emotions and perceptions. Observing memory without identifying with it weakens its grip, making past experiences just mental processes rather than fixed aspects of identity. Letting go of hurt and regret allows for healing, as holding onto emotional pain only prolongs suffering. A mind free from psychological memory does not live in past sorrow or future longing but remains fully attentive to the present. In this state, there is no need to recall, compare, or interpret—only direct experience. Memory, while essential for functioning, becomes a burden when it dominates psychological life. A mind free from its weight does not escape the past but sees it without distortion, allowing fresh perception, clarity, and deep awareness.

4. Thought

Thought: The Ever-Moving Stream of the Known

Thought is the product of memory, experience, and accumulated knowledge. It is essential for practical life, allowing us to communicate, solve problems, and navigate the world. However, thought is always based on the past, as it arises from what has already been learned. While it can project into the future, it remains limited by previous experiences. This makes thought useful for technical and functional tasks but problematic when it dominates our psychological existence. When thought tries to understand emotions, relationships, or truth, it creates conflict, illusion, and misunderstanding because it operates through comparison, categorization, and conditioning.

The nature of thought leads to several psychological challenges. Thought creates the sense of "self" by attaching to memories, beliefs, and identities, reinforcing a feeling of separation from others. It generates psychological time by constantly recalling the past or imagining the future, rarely staying in the present. Thought also sustains fear and suffering by remembering painful experiences or worrying about what may happen. It seeks security in relationships, beliefs, and attachments, even though life is constantly changing. In doing so, thought creates the illusion of permanence and resists the reality of impermanence, leading to inner conflict and emotional distress.

To move beyond the limitations of thought, one must observe it without identifying with it. Thought cannot be controlled by force, as any effort to suppress it is itself another form of thought. Instead, awareness of thought—watching it arise and pass without reacting—allows the mind to see its limitations.

When the mind is fully present and attentive, thought naturally quiets down, creating space for direct perception beyond memory and conditioning. In this silence, intelligence, creativity, and insight emerge, free from the constraints of thought. True understanding is not a product of thought but arises when the mind is still, allowing reality to be seen as it is.

5. Thinking

Thinking: The Process That Binds and Liberates

Thinking is the movement of thought, shaped by memory, experience, and conditioning. It is essential for solving problems, communicating, and organizing daily life. However, thinking is always limited by the past because it operates from stored knowledge. While useful for practical matters, it cannot fully understand deeper aspects of life such as love, fear, or truth. We often rely on thinking because it gives a false sense of control, making us believe that by analyzing and planning, we can predict and shape life. Yet, life remains unpredictable, and excessive thinking often leads to confusion rather than clarity. From childhood, we are conditioned to believe that intelligence is thinking, but true intelligence may lie beyond the limits of thought.

The limitations of thinking become clear when we see how it divides life into past, present, and future, creating psychological time. This leads to regret over the past, fear of the future, and constant seeking of security. Thought also fragments reality, analyzing and categorizing rather than perceiving things as a whole. When we look at something, we often see our idea of it rather than the thing itself. Thought interferes with direct perception, turning experiences into mere concepts. Since thought is always old, based on memory, it can never truly encounter something new. This makes it ineffective in understanding the deeper dimensions of life.

To live without being trapped by thought, one must observe it without judgment or identification. When thought is seen clearly, without trying to suppress or control it, its hold weakens. Thought is necessary for practical tasks, but does it need to dictate our inner world? A silent mind is not one that forces thought to stop, but one that is fully aware, allowing thought to slow down naturally. In this awareness, there is space for direct perception and a deeper intelligence beyond thinking. True understanding does not come from analyzing with thought but from seeing reality without distortion. In the stillness beyond thought, there is freedom, clarity, and a profound insight that thought alone can never reach.

6. Chattering

Chattering: The Restless Noise That Clouds the Mind

Chattering is the endless movement of thought, whether spoken aloud or running silently within the mind. It is the restless flow of words, opinions, judgments, and inner dialogues that keep the mind constantly occupied. A mind caught in chattering is never truly quiet, never deeply attentive—it is always engaged with itself, reacting, interpreting, and repeating patterns without fresh inquiry. Chattering is not real thinking; it is a conditioned response, a mechanical loop of past experiences and beliefs. This constant noise prevents deep listening and clear perception, making it impossible to observe reality as it is. Instead of seeing directly, a chattering mind filters everything through pre-existing conclusions, distorting understanding.

The habit of chattering arises from various psychological needs. Many people fear silence because it forces them to confront themselves, making them uncomfortable with inner emptiness or unresolved emotions. Society reinforces the belief that verbal expression equals intelligence, encouraging people to talk excessively without real clarity. Chattering also becomes a form of psychological dependence—people talk compulsively to feel connected, validated, or important, avoiding inward reflection. Thought, conditioned to keep moving, struggles to be still, and this mental restlessness manifests as endless speech or internal monologues. Insecurity further fuels chattering, as excessive talking often serves as a defense mechanism to mask vulnerability, loneliness, or the fear of not being heard.

To be free from chattering, one must observe it without resistance. Suppressing thought only creates struggle, whereas simply watching its movement reveals its nature and allows it to slow down naturally. Silence is not emptiness—it is full of depth and intelligence. A quiet mind listens without reacting, speaks only when necessary, and is not compelled to fill every moment with words or mental noise. Instead of forcing the mind to be silent, one can watch its chattering without involvement, letting stillness arise effortlessly. In this natural silence, perception becomes clear, action is precise, and the mind is free from unnecessary conflict. True intelligence is not in constant talking—it is in deep awareness, where words arise from understanding rather than compulsion.

7. Intellect

Intellect: The Sharp Blade Without Depth

Intellect is the ability to analyze, reason, compare, and accumulate knowledge. It functions through thought and memory, solving problems based on past experiences. While intellect is essential for practical tasks such as science, technology, and daily decision-making, it is limited in understanding deeper aspects of life, such as relationships, love, and truth. Intellect operates within the boundaries of what is already known, meaning it can never perceive something truly new. It categorizes and divides, reinforcing separation between people, ideas, and beliefs, leading to conflict. Though it can describe emotions and concepts, it cannot directly experience them, making it insufficient for understanding the immeasurable aspects of existence.

The limitations of intellect become apparent when it mistakes theories, philosophies, and ideologies for reality. Intellectual constructs do not bring actual transformation—only direct experience does. The intellect also strengthens the sense of self, reinforcing pride, ambition, and psychological conflict. It operates mechanically, processing information in a structured way, but lacks the depth of intelligence, which is fluid, holistic, and free from distortion. Intelligence is not separate from love, compassion, and awareness; it sees things as they are, without interference from past conditioning. While intellect divides and analyzes, intelligence perceives reality as a whole, acting with clarity and understanding.

To move beyond intellect and awaken intelligence, one must observe thought without being trapped in it. Seeing how the intellect creates division and conflict allows for awareness beyond its conditioning. Relying on knowledge for practical tasks is necessary, but psychological understanding requires direct perception rather than accumulated learning. A deeply intelligent mind does not seek immediate conclusions but remains attentive and silent, allowing truth to reveal itself naturally. Problems created by thought cannot be solved by more thought—true intelligence acts instantly, without confusion or hesitation. When intellect is used rightly, without mistaking it for the totality of understanding, there is clarity, wisdom, and effortless action.

8. Intelligence

Intelligence: The Light of Perception Beyond Thought

Intelligence is not the mere accumulation of knowledge, nor is it the ability to analyze or reason logically. It is the capacity to perceive reality as it is, without distortion from fear, belief, or conditioning. While knowledge is useful for practical matters, it is always limited to the past and functions mechanically through memory. True intelligence, on the other hand, is dynamic, free, and capable of seeing beyond accumulated information. It does not seek security in authority or belief but arises naturally in a mind that is open, sensitive, and deeply aware. Intelligence is not separate from life—it moves with clarity, without conflict, and acts from direct understanding rather than conditioned thought.

Several factors prevent intelligence from fully operating. Fear keeps the mind trapped in seeking psychological security, making it incapable of fresh perception. Society, religion, and education condition individuals to accept ideas without questioning, limiting their ability to see beyond what they have been taught. Dependence on authority dulls intelligence, as people look to external sources for truth rather than discovering it for themselves. Additionally, a mind filled with prejudice and belief interprets everything through its conditioning, preventing it from seeing clearly. The conflict between 'what is' and 'what should be' further creates inner division, leading to confusion and contradiction. Intelligence, however, is choiceless awareness—it does not struggle to become something; it simply sees, and in that clarity, action is immediate and natural.

To awaken intelligence, one must observe without judgment, allowing thoughts, emotions, and reactions to be seen without labeling them as right or wrong. Understanding fear dissolves its hold, freeing the mind from its limitations. Letting go of beliefs and conclusions opens perception, allowing intelligence to act without distortion. True intelligence operates in total attention— when one is fully present, without distraction, awareness itself becomes intelligence in action. In a mind free from conditioning, self-interest, and fear, intelligence flows effortlessly, bringing deep clarity, sensitivity, and a profound harmony with life.

9. Understanding

Understanding: Seeing Without the Distortion of the Self

Understanding is not the accumulation of knowledge, intellectual analysis, or the acceptance of beliefs—it is the direct perception of truth. It does not arise from opinions, conclusions, or effort, but from a mind that is completely attentive. True understanding is instantaneous; it does not develop over time or through study.

The struggle to understand comes from our reliance on thought, which is always based on memory and past experience. Since thought is limited by conditioning, it cannot fully grasp something beyond its own past conclusions. Furthermore, understanding is blocked by prejudice, expectations, and the habit of seeking authority for answers rather than discovering truth firsthand. When desire or fear influences perception, the mind distorts reality, preventing real understanding.

The nature of true understanding is immediate, not gradual. One does not need time to see something clearly—understanding happens in an instant, just as one immediately knows that fire burns upon touching it. Thought may analyze, compare, and remember, but true insight comes only when the mind is silent. When one sees a truth deeply, action follows naturally—there is no need for discipline or practice. For example, if one truly understands that attachment leads to suffering, detachment is not something to be forced—it happens instantly. Understanding is also beyond psychological time; it is not gained through effort, study, or discipline but through direct perception in the present moment.

To cultivate understanding, one must observe without seeking conclusions. Instead of trying to understand through effort, can one simply watch without expecting an answer? Understanding arises when the mind is quiet, not when it is searching. Dropping the burden of knowledge allows perception to be fresh, unfiltered by past conclusions. When the mind is fully attentive to 'what is,' reality is seen directly, without distortion. Living with an open mind, free from preconceived ideas, allows understanding to flow naturally. True understanding is like light—it instantly dispels darkness without struggle. In this clarity, there is no need to seek understanding—it happens effortlessly when the mind is silent, open, and free.

10. Clarity

Clarity: The Mind That Sees Without Conflict

Clarity is the ability to see things as they are, without the interference of thought, belief, or desire. It is not intellectual sharpness or analysis but direct perception without distortion. A clear mind is like a still lake—reflecting reality without effort, without being clouded by personal bias. However, clarity is often absent because thought, conditioned by past experiences and memories, interferes with perception. When we look at life through the filter of thought, we do not see reality—we see our conditioning. Additionally, desire and fear distort perception by making us see only what we want or avoid what we fear, leading to self-deception. Psychological time—living in the past or anticipating the future—further confuses the mind, as clarity exists only in the present. Dependence on authority also prevents clear seeing, as truth cannot be borrowed from books, traditions, or teachers—it must be seen firsthand.

True clarity is not an achievement but the absence of confusion. A mind that seeks clarity often creates more confusion because the effort to "be clear" itself becomes a struggle. Clarity arises naturally when the mind is silent, free from judgments, comparisons, and opinions. The weight of past experiences and conditioning clouds perception—when this weight is dropped, the mind sees sharply, directly, and effortlessly. Clarity is also free from effort; one cannot force it to appear, just as one does not try to "see" upon waking in the morning—it happens naturally. A restless mind clouds perception, whereas a still mind allows clarity to emerge on its own.

To come upon clarity, one must observe without interference—can one look at a tree, a person, or an emotion without labeling, analyzing, or interpreting? The moment one sees without mental interference, there is clarity. Being fully present, rather than lost in psychological time, also allows perception to be undistorted. Striving for clarity prevents it; when psychological effort ceases, clarity arises on its own. Thought, when left to settle naturally through deep awareness, no longer clouds perception. In this effortless clarity, action is right, perception is true, and life is lived fully, without inner conflict.

11. Perception

Perception: Seeing Without the Distortion of the Past

Perception is the process of how we interpret and understand reality, influenced by our sensory experiences and psychological conditioning. It can either be clear and direct or distorted by past memories, beliefs, fears, and societal conditioning. True perception involves seeing things as they are, without the interference of thought. Sensory perception is the immediate experience through our senses, like seeing a tree without labeling or analyzing it. Psychological perception, on the other hand, is influenced by our previous experiences, beliefs, and expectations, which can distort the reality we see.

The distortion in perception arises due to the influence of past knowledge, where we interpret the present through previous experiences. For example, if someone hurt us in the past, we might continue to see them through that lens of memory. Our beliefs and cultural conditioning also shape how we perceive the world, causing us to view things through the filters of what we have been taught. Fear and desire further influence perception, often making us see what we want to see or fear, rather than what is actually there. Additionally, the separation between the observer and the observed creates a division that hinders complete understanding, as the mind creates a distinction between "me" and "what I observe."

True perception is when we see without the past interfering, without judgment or comparison. It requires total attention in the present moment, where there is no division between the observer and the observed. In this state, perception is clear, direct, and without distortion. When the mind is silent and thought does not intervene, we can experience reality in its purest form. A mind free from judgment and the interference of thought sees the world with clarity, understanding, and intelligence, leading to actions that reflect true insight and love.

12. Perspective

Perspective: The Lens That Shapes Perception and Limits Truth

Perspective is the way the mind interprets reality based on experience, conditioning, and belief. It arises from thought, memory, and personal bias, shaping how one sees the world. A mind caught in perspective clings to a fixed view, while a mind that understands deeply sees beyond all perspectives. People see the world not as it is, but as they have been taught to see it, and a mind that recognizes its conditioning is already beginning to see more clearly. A narrow perspective creates division, prejudice, and misunderstanding, while a broad perspective allows flexibility, intelligence, and deeper insight. What one calls 'truth' is often just their perspective of it, and true understanding exists beyond perspective, in direct perception. When one believes their view is the only correct one, conflict arises, while a mind that sees multiple perspectives without attachment does not argue—it understands.

Society teaches individuals to accept certain ideas as absolute, reinforcing the belief that their perspective is the truth. A questioning mind does not hold onto perspectives—it seeks direct understanding. People define themselves by their opinions, making them difficult to change, but when one is free from self-identification, perspective loses its rigidity. The unknown is uncomfortable, so the mind clings to familiar viewpoints, yet truth exists beyond comfort—it requires letting go of assumptions. Many believe their perspective is more valid than others, justifying division and superiority, while a mind free from comparison does not see perspectives as 'right' or 'wrong'—it sees them as different. People believe having a strong viewpoint means they are wise, yet true wisdom is not in holding a perspective—it is in seeing through all perspectives.

When one realizes their view is shaped by conditioning, its hold weakens, allowing a free mind to see without the filter of past experiences. True observation happens when the mind is silent, not interpreting, and without immediately forming an opinion. When one stops arguing for a viewpoint, there is space for deeper understanding, and a mind that does not defend itself is open, fluid, and free. No perspective captures the whole of reality, and true insight happens when one sees beyond the limits of personal perception. A free mind does not cling to perspectives—it moves with direct understanding. This does not mean one has no views, but that views do not become prisons.

Perspective is shaped by conditioning, memory, and thought, making it an interpretation rather than an absolute truth. Many struggle with perspective because they attach their identity to it, defend it, and fear seeing beyond it, but true understanding is not in holding a view—it is in seeing without limitation. In this freedom, perspective is no longer a boundary—it becomes a tool, used when needed, but never mistaken for the whole truth, allowing perception to be fresh, clear, and limitless.

13. Rationality

Rationality: The Logic That Can Mislead or Liberate

Rationality is the ability to think logically, analyze, and reason based on facts and structured thought. It plays a crucial role in decision-making, problem-solving, and scientific inquiry, forming the foundation of systematic understanding. However, a mind that depends solely on rationality risks becoming rigid and mechanical, unable to perceive beyond the limits of logic. Rational thought is structured, drawing conclusions by organizing and comparing information, but it is always based on past knowledge and memory. This makes rationality useful for practical matters, yet limited when it comes to understanding the deeper aspects of life, such as love, consciousness, and truth. When rationality is used as a tool rather than a total approach to life, it brings clarity. But when it becomes the sole method of understanding, it prevents deeper insights that exist beyond thought.

The overvaluation of rationality stems from society's belief that logical thinking is the highest form of intelligence. Schools and institutions prioritize reason, equating it with intelligence while ignoring perception beyond analysis. Rationality provides a sense of control, making life feel predictable, but existence itself often defies logic. Emotions, relationships, and reality cannot always be understood through structured reasoning alone. The mind clings to logic to avoid uncertainty, fearing what cannot be explained. However, truth is not always logical—it often exists beyond words and measurable concepts. The rational mind also falls into the trap of rationalization, justifying fears, desires, and conditioning through intellectual arguments, mistaking clever reasoning for truth.

To use rationality without being confined by it, one must see it as a tool rather than a master. Logic is essential for practical matters but should not dominate one's perception of life. True intelligence moves beyond thought, recognizing that rational analysis is always rooted in past knowledge, while direct perception is immediate and fresh. Observing life without filtering everything through logic allows for deeper clarity and understanding. Sensitivity and awareness must complement rationality; otherwise, thought becomes cold and detached. A truly intelligent mind does not reject rationality but also does not rely on it exclusively. It moves freely between reason and insight, embracing both logic and perception without being trapped by either. In this balance, there is no conflict—only deep intelligence, clarity, and freedom.

14. Ideology

Ideology: The Framework That Divides and Conditions

Ideology is a structured system of beliefs that shapes how we think, act, and interpret the world. It can be political, religious, philosophical, or personal, offering a sense of certainty and direction. People often adopt ideologies because they provide psychological security in an unpredictable world. Fixed beliefs create a comforting structure, making life feel more stable. Additionally, it is easier to follow a system than to question deeply, and most people inherit their beliefs rather than discovering truth through their own perception. The ego also finds identity in ideology, leading individuals to defend their beliefs as if they were defending themselves. Society further reinforces ideological conditioning through education, religion, and political systems, teaching people to conform rather than to investigate freely.

However, ideology creates serious limitations. It distorts perception, making people see the world through the filter of their beliefs rather than as it truly is. When facts contradict an ideology, they are often ignored or rejected. Ideologies also divide people, causing conflict, hostility, and even war, as each system claims to be the only "right" one. Moreover, ideology prevents direct understanding by replacing inquiry with repetitive ideas borrowed from books, leaders, or traditions. It strengthens psychological dependence, as people look to ideologies for guidance instead of relying on their own clarity. When the mind is conditioned by ideology, it cannot respond to life freely—it only reacts according to predetermined patterns.

To live without ideology, one must see that all ideologies are secondhand knowledge, inherited rather than discovered. Truth is not found in a belief system but in direct observation of life. If one can look at the world without categorizing events as "right" or "wrong" based on an ideology, perception becomes clear and undistorted. Letting go of psychological identification with labels—whether religious, political, or social—frees the mind from division. Instead of seeking security in beliefs, one can remain in a state of constant inquiry, questioning everything without seeking conclusions. In this freedom, there is no need for ideology because truth is not in thought—it is in direct perception, beyond all mental constructs.

15. Ideas

Ideas: The Seed of Thought That Shapes Action

An idea is a mental construct, a formulation of thought based on memory and past experience. It is not reality itself but a representation created by the mind to interpret the world. While ideas are useful in science, technology, and communication, they become a limitation when applied to understanding life. Every idea is rooted in the past, shaped by previous experiences, and when we perceive life through ideas, we see it through a filter rather than as it is. Ideas also provide a sense of psychological security, making us feel safe within structured beliefs, but this security is often an illusion rather than truth. Furthermore, ideas divide people by creating rigid ideological, political, and religious boundaries, leading to conflict rather than unity.

Living through ideas creates several problems. We often mistake the idea of something for the thing itself—for example, describing love does not mean experiencing love. Thought creates an ideal of how things should be, leading to an inner struggle when reality does not match expectations. This gap between "what is" and "what should be" becomes a source of frustration and suffering. Additionally, ideologies condition the mind, shaping perception according to learned beliefs rather than allowing for fresh observation. The ego identifies with ideas, reinforcing a false sense of self. When someone challenges our ideas, we feel personally attacked, as if our identity depends on defending them. This attachment to ideas keeps the mind trapped in conditioning and prevents direct understanding.

To live without the burden of ideas, one must see their nature without rejecting them. Ideas are necessary for practical life, but they should not interfere with perception. Can one observe life without past conclusions shaping the experience? Seeing without the filter of thought allows for direct perception, free from distortion. Understanding does not come from accumulated knowledge but from deep awareness. A mind that is free from psychological conclusions does not cling to beliefs or reject them—it simply observes, learns, and acts with clarity. True wisdom is not in collecting ideas but in moving beyond them, seeing life as it is rather than through the limitations of thought.

16. Ideals

Ideals: The Imaginary Perfection That Creates Conflict

Ideals are mental projections of perfection—how one should be, how society should function, or how the world ought to be. They are often presented as moral, spiritual, or political goals, shaping a standard to strive toward. While they may seem to provide direction and meaning, ideals create a division between reality and aspiration. We assume that striving toward an ideal leads to self-improvement, yet has any ideal truly transformed human nature, or has it only created further division? Instead of addressing 'what is,' ideals often serve as an escape, a way to avoid facing suffering and imperfection directly. Society, religion, and politics condition us to accept ideals, teaching us to conform to an imagined state of goodness, success, or enlightenment rather than encouraging true self-understanding.

The pursuit of ideals leads to inner conflict. There is always a gap between 'what is' and 'what should be,' creating frustration, guilt, and psychological struggle. A mind that is preoccupied with becoming something does not fully understand itself as it is. Every ideal is a product of the past, shaped by memory and cultural conditioning, and projected into the future, preventing one from seeing life clearly in the present. On a larger scale, ideals divide societies—nations, religions, and political ideologies clash over conflicting visions of what should be. This endless battle over ideals has led to war, oppression, and social fragmentation, yet we continue to believe that a better future will emerge from the very ideals that create division.

To live without ideals is not to become passive but to act with intelligence and clarity. Seeing that ideals are illusions created by thought allows one to observe life without comparing it to an imagined perfection. A truly perceptive mind does not need an ideal to act rightly; it responds directly to each situation as it unfolds. Love, morality, and wisdom do not come from ideals but from deep understanding. True transformation is not in chasing an ideal but in fully meeting 'what is' without resistance. Where there are no ideals, there is no inner struggle—only clarity, direct perception, and the possibility of real change.

17. Imagination

Imagination: The Power That Transforms or Deceives

Imagination is the mind's ability to create, visualize, and project beyond immediate experience. It draws from memory, knowledge, and the unknown, shaping visions of the future and interpretations of the past. This creative force can be used for innovation and artistic expression, allowing one to explore possibilities beyond the ordinary. However, imagination also has the potential to distort reality, leading to illusions and psychological escape. When used without awareness, it creates a false world that disconnects the mind from what is. The challenge lies in understanding whether imagination is serving as a tool for discovery or as a means of avoiding reality.

The nature of imagination is deeply tied to thought and memory. Every imagined scenario is built from past experiences, meaning even the most seemingly original ideas are variations of what has already been stored in the mind. Imagination can expand thought when used freely, but when conditioned by beliefs, fears, or desires, it reinforces illusions. It creates psychological time, making the mind dwell in future hopes or anxieties while also reshaping past memories into something different from reality. This cycle of projection prevents one from fully engaging with the present moment, leading to inner conflict between 'what is' and 'what should be.'

To use imagination wisely, one must recognize that it is not reality but a mental projection. When seen clearly, imagination loses its power to create illusions. It remains useful for creativity, problem-solving, and exploration but ceases to be an escape from the present. Observing how the mind constructs mental images allows one to break the cycle of false hopes and fears. A mind free from dependence on imagination does not reject it but uses it consciously, without mistaking it for truth. In this awareness, imagination becomes a source of deep intelligence, rooted in clarity rather than illusion, enhancing perception rather than distorting it.

18. Creativity

Creativity: The Expression Beyond the Known

Creativity is not merely artistic skill, invention, or talent—it is the ability to see, act, and think beyond memory and conditioning. It is not the repetition or modification of what already exists but the emergence of something entirely new. True creativity arises when the mind is free—when thought does not interfere with direct perception. However, creativity is rare because thought, which functions from past experiences, dominates our thinking. Since thought is always old, can something truly original ever come from it? Society and education further restrict creativity by training individuals to conform to systems and follow structured patterns, limiting their ability to think freely. Fear of failure and criticism prevents creative expression, while the desire for success turns creativity into a mechanical process driven by achievement rather than exploration.

Real creativity requires freedom from the known. To create something new, one must move beyond past knowledge and conditioning. The most profound insights come not from effort but from a silent mind that is open and receptive. A mind that fears cannot take risks, and without risk, there is no discovery. Creativity also demands the absence of imitation—skillful copying is not true creation. When one relies on patterns and past experiences, they are merely reshaping what already exists rather than giving birth to something new. To be truly creative, one must step into the unknown, unafraid and unattached to results.

To awaken creativity, one must observe deeply, free from the interference of thought. Can one look at a tree, a sunset, or a person without filtering the experience through past knowledge? Creativity flourishes in such direct perception. It does not come from seeking inspiration but from allowing it to emerge naturally in a still mind. When one acts without fear of failure, there is freedom to experiment, play, and explore. Creativity is not just about painting, writing, or inventing—it is a way of living, meeting each moment as if for the first time. A truly creative mind is not driven by effort or ambition but is alive, fresh, and limitless, where every thought and action becomes an expression of pure creation.

19. Creation

Creation: The New That Emerges in Silence

Creation is the birth of something entirely new, untouched by memory, imitation, or conditioning. It is not the result of modification or invention but a spontaneous movement beyond thought. True creation does not come from effort, accumulation, or ambition—it arises when the mind is silent and free. Most creative acts are based on past knowledge and experience, merely rearranging the old into new forms. But real creation is not repetition—it is an insight so fresh that it cannot be traced back to previous conditioning. A mind burdened with beliefs, ambitions, and opinions only produces variations of what it already knows, while true creation happens only when the mind is free from the past.

The struggle to create stems from dependence on knowledge, fear of the unknown, and the desire for recognition. Society conditions us to believe that creativity is a product of expertise and accumulated skill, but real creation arises from a mind unburdened by what it knows. Fear blocks true creativity because the mind clings to familiar patterns, avoiding the risk of stepping into the unknown. Ambition and the pursuit of success make creativity mechanical, driven by external goals rather than pure expression. Thought itself, which functions through memory, cannot create—it only imitates and modifies. When the mind measures itself against others, seeking comparison and validation, originality is lost.

To create without effort, one must understand that creativity is not an achievement but a natural movement. The urge to 'be creative' is itself a limitation, for when one stops trying, creativity flows freely. True creation happens in the present moment, without the pressure of producing a result. Fear and the need for psychological security prevent authentic expression, but when one lets go of the need for perfection, creation simply unfolds. A silent mind, free from fixed ideas and conclusions, is the birthplace of the truly new. In this state, creation is not a controlled act but a limitless unfolding, beyond past and future, where the energy of being itself expresses something profoundly original.

20. Concentration

Concentration: The Narrow Focus That Limits or Frees

Concentration is the act of directing attention to a specific object, task, or thought while excluding everything else. It is often mistaken for deep awareness, but in reality, it is a narrowing of perception. A mind that is concentrating may be sharp and efficient, but it is also rigid and exclusive, operating with effort and resistance. To concentrate means to force attention on one thing while blocking out distractions, creating mental strain and fatigue. While concentration is useful for technical tasks and skill development, it is not conducive to understanding life as a whole. The effort to concentrate divides the mind, as it struggles between what it wants to focus on and what it seeks to suppress, reinforcing conflict and tension.

The dependence on concentration arises from societal conditioning and the belief that focus equals intelligence. From childhood, people are trained to concentrate in school and work, equating it with discipline and success. However, true intelligence does not come from narrowing perception but from expanding awareness. The mind believes it can control distraction through concentration, yet distraction exists only when there is effort to focus. A truly attentive mind does not fight thoughts or suppress distractions—it flows naturally, without resistance. Creativity and deep understanding do not emerge from strained focus but from an open, relaxed mind capable of perceiving the whole.

To move beyond concentration, one must see that effortful focus is a form of exclusion. Awareness does not require force—it simply observes without resistance. Instead of trying to fix thought on one point, allowing thought to move freely enables natural attention. True awareness does not hold onto a single object; it is fully present, seeing everything without fragmentation. The idea of a 'controller' who must focus is an illusion—when effort ceases, attention flows effortlessly. Experiencing the present moment without expectation allows for complete engagement without the struggle of forced focus. A mind free from the limitations of concentration is not scattered but deeply perceptive, alive to the totality of life without resistance or effort.

21. Conditioning

Conditioning: The Invisible Chains of the Mind

Conditioning is the psychological process through which the mind is shaped by past experiences, cultural influences, education, religion, and social norms. It dictates how we think, feel, and respond to life, often without our awareness. A conditioned mind does not perceive reality as it is but sees through the lens of past experiences and beliefs, preventing fresh perception. From birth, we are conditioned by family, society, and institutions that define what is good or bad, what to believe, and how to behave. Fear plays a significant role in conditioning, as we conform to authority—religious, political, or parental— without question. Education further reinforces this by training the mind to memorize and conform rather than to think freely. Repetition of thoughts and behaviors strengthens conditioning, making reactions automatic rather than conscious.

The effects of conditioning are profound. It limits perception, preventing us from seeing beyond inherited beliefs. For example, if one is conditioned to believe a particular ideology is the absolute truth, all other perspectives are dismissed without inquiry. Conditioning also creates division and conflict, as national, religious, and ideological identities separate people, leading to prejudice and violence. Instead of seeing humanity as one, conditioned minds categorize people into rigid groups—"I am Indian, you are American"; "I am Hindu, you are Muslim"— fostering division. Moreover, conditioning destroys freedom and intelligence by making the mind follow patterns rather than question them. A conditioned mind depends on external authority for psychological security, leading to fear of the unknown and resistance to change.

Freedom from conditioning is possible through awareness, not resistance. The first step is to observe thoughts, reactions, and behaviors without judgment, seeing how they arise from conditioning. Rather than forcing change, one must question every belief and assumption—"Why do I believe this?" "Is it true, or have I been taught to accept it?" True intelligence is not shaped by conditioning but by direct perception. Looking at people, situations, and emotions without interpreting them through past experiences allows for fresh perception. Living with awareness instead of habit ensures that actions are conscious, not mechanical. Conditioning is the accumulated past controlling the present, but a mind that sees its conditioning without resistance begins to unravel it naturally. True intelligence is the ability to see without filters, act without fear, and live without psychological dependence.

22. Assumptions

Assumptions: The Unquestioned Thoughts That Shape Reality

Assumptions are unquestioned beliefs or conclusions that the mind accepts as truth without direct observation. They arise from past experiences, cultural conditioning, social influences, and personal biases, shaping how one interprets the world. A mind operating through assumptions functions mechanically, filtering reality through pre-existing ideas rather than seeing things as they truly are. Assumptions are often based on incomplete knowledge, as the mind fills in gaps with ideas that seem reasonable but may not be true. This prevents deep inquiry and leads to accepting falsehoods as facts. They also create psychological and social barriers—when one assumes they know another person's motives or character, they stop truly listening, leading to misunderstanding, prejudice, and division.

The reliance on assumptions stems from the mind's tendency to seek efficiency and avoid uncertainty. While assumptions help process information quickly, they also limit deeper understanding. People cling to assumptions because they provide a sense of predictability, making life feel more stable. Society reinforces assumptions through cultural, religious, and political conditioning, discouraging questioning and encouraging conformity. Additionally, individuals attach their identity to their assumptions, defending them as part of their self-image. Past experiences further shape assumptions, but since every new moment is different, relying on past conclusions prevents one from perceiving the present clearly.

Freedom from assumptions comes not by rejecting them outright but by seeing their nature. When one realizes that assumptions are not reality, their influence weakens. Observing thought without immediately believing it allows the mind to break free from blind acceptance. True questioning does not seek confirmation but remains open-ended, free from the need to reinforce existing beliefs. Meeting each moment without preconceived ideas enables fresh perception, unfiltered by past conditioning. Listening and observing without interpretation prevent misunderstandings and allow for direct awareness. A mind free from assumptions does not interpret mechanically—it sees life as it is, without barriers, distortion, or false certainty. In this clarity, intelligence moves effortlessly, and perception becomes truly alive.

23. Belief

Belief: The Acceptance That Replaces Direct Seeing

Belief is the acceptance of something as true without direct understanding or verification. It is often shaped by cultural conditioning, religious upbringing, social influence, and personal experience. While beliefs provide structure to thought and behavior, they also limit the ability to see reality clearly. The mind clings to belief out of fear and the need for psychological security—uncertainty is unsettling, so belief offers a sense of comfort. From childhood, people are conditioned to conform to religious, political, and societal beliefs, making questioning difficult. Beliefs also create a sense of identity, providing meaning and belonging through associations with a nation, religion, or ideology. Instead of questioning and observing for themselves, many rely on belief systems to interpret reality, avoiding direct inquiry and deeper self-discovery.

The attachment to belief creates significant psychological and societal problems. Belief divides people, as religious, political, and ideological attachments lead to conflict, wars, and social tensions. Instead of perceiving reality as it is, people see through the filter of belief, distorting truth and reinforcing illusion. Clinging to belief limits freedom and intelligence, as true intelligence requires questioning, not blind acceptance. The ego further strengthens itself through belief, identifying with ideologies and seeking validation by defending them. This creates resistance to change, as belief becomes intertwined with one's sense of self. A mind trapped in belief is incapable of deep understanding because it relies on preconceived ideas rather than direct perception.

Living without belief does not mean rejecting everything, but rather seeing without preconception. Instead of accepting beliefs, one can observe reality directly, with an open mind free from conditioning. True learning comes not from accepting second-hand knowledge but from seeing clearly for oneself. A mind free from belief does not seek security in ideology, religion, or authority; instead, it faces life as it is, without distortion or fear. Living with awareness, without attachment to belief, allows for exploration, learning, and true understanding. Real freedom is not found in holding onto beliefs, but in the ability to perceive directly, inquire deeply, and move through life without the limitations of conditioned thought.

24. Conclusions

Conclusions: The End of Inquiry and the Birth of Stagnation

A conclusion is a fixed idea or belief that the mind arrives at after reasoning, experience, or conditioning. It becomes a psychological certainty—a position from which we think, act, and judge. While conclusions create the illusion of understanding, they often prevent further discovery. The mind craves certainty, seeking conclusions to feel psychologically secure, yet true security is not found in fixed ideas but in openness to the unknown. We depend on knowledge and past experiences to shape conclusions, but does the past ever fully explain the present, which is always new? Society and education condition us to form opinions, take positions, and defend beliefs, reinforcing rigidity rather than encouraging fresh perception. Over time, we begin to define ourselves by our conclusions, mistaking accumulated beliefs for identity.

The problems with conclusions are many. The moment the mind says, "I know," inquiry stops. Truth is not static—it unfolds continuously, beyond the boundaries of any fixed position. Holding onto conclusions creates conflict, as people argue and defend opposing views, further dividing themselves. Since conclusions arise from past experiences, they limit perception, preventing one from seeing the present clearly. Psychological rigidity sets in when the mind clings to conclusions, making it incapable of fresh insight. Intelligence, however, is found in openness—the ability to meet each moment without the weight of prior judgments.

To live without conclusions is to remain in a state of inquiry. Seeing that all conclusions are based on the past naturally loosens their grip on the mind. Can one question without rushing to find an answer? True inquiry has no end—it remains open, without seeking finality. The present moment is always fresh— can one meet it without carrying the filter of past conclusions? In pure observation, there is no conclusion, only direct perception. Action does not require certainty, only clarity. A free mind moves without rigidity, responding to life with intelligence, without the burden of fixed beliefs. In this state, there is no psychological stagnation—only freedom to see, to learn, and to engage with life without distortion.

25. Judgment

Judgment: The Barrier That Separates Perception from Truth

Judgment is the act of evaluating, labeling, or condemning based on past experiences, conditioning, or comparison. Unlike simple observation, judgment categorizes people, situations, and oneself as good or bad, right or wrong. This mental process creates psychological distance, preventing direct perception and strengthening division. The mind judges because it seeks security, simplifying complex realities to feel safe in fixed conclusions. However, labeling does not bring real understanding—it limits awareness. Society conditions us to evaluate people based on status, intelligence, appearance, or belief, reinforcing bias and separation. The ego thrives on comparison, using judgment to elevate itself and feel superior. Judgment also gives a false sense of control, making us believe we understand others when, in reality, it only reinforces illusion.

The habit of judgment creates several psychological and relational problems. It prevents true understanding by filtering perception through the past, making it impossible to see things as they are. When we judge ourselves, we create inner conflict between 'what is' and 'what should be,' leading to guilt, frustration, and self-doubt. Judgment also strengthens separation between people, creating distance instead of connection. True relationships exist only in the absence of judgment, where awareness replaces bias. Additionally, judgment is a product of psychological conditioning, shaped by inherited beliefs, social norms, and personal biases. A mind caught in judgment does not act freely—it reacts automatically, trapped in past conditioning.

To live without judgment, one must observe without labeling. Can one see a person, a situation, or oneself without immediately categorizing it as good or bad? The moment observation happens without judgment, the mind is free to understand. Judgment is always from the past, shaped by memory and conditioning—true awareness meets each moment freshly, without bringing past conclusions into it. Instead of saying, "This is wrong," can one simply watch, listen, and understand? Awareness allows right action to arise naturally, without interference. When the psychological 'judge' within dissolves, there is no division, no conflict—only clarity. A mind free from judgment listens without resistance, sees without distortion, and acts with intelligence. In this state, there is deep compassion, understanding, and the ability to meet life as it is.

26. Stupidity

Stupidity: The Blindness Created by Ignorance and Conditioning

Stupidity is not merely a lack of intelligence, but the unwillingness or inability to see things as they are. It arises from conditioning, arrogance, blind belief, and the absence of deep questioning. A mind caught in stupidity clings to illusions, while a mind that understands deeply moves with clarity and awareness. One may have vast information but still be blind to truth, for real intelligence is not in accumulation—it is in deep perception. A mind that assumes it already knows stops learning, while true intelligence questions continuously, never assuming final answers. People follow traditions, authorities, and ideologies without questioning, remaining trapped in ignorance. A rigid mind clings to past beliefs, fearing the unknown, but intelligence is the ability to adapt, to see freshly, without resistance.

A mind that refuses to understand others reacts with prejudice, fear, and hostility, strengthening barriers rather than dissolving them. Society teaches compliance, not inquiry, training the mind to follow rather than to see beyond imposed beliefs. People cling to their opinions, unwilling to say, 'I don't know,' yet true wisdom begins when one sees their own ignorance clearly. The ego seeks definite answers, fearing uncertainty, but reality is ever-changing—intelligence moves with it, while stupidity resists it. Knowing facts does not mean one understands life, for true wisdom is not found in words or books but in direct perception. Anger, fear, and desire distort clear thinking, and a mind ruled by emotion reacts blindly, without intelligence.

Many believe intelligence is genetic, but it is shaped by awareness. A mind that watches itself can always awaken from ignorance. Intelligence is not in agreeing or disagreeing—it is in questioning, for a mind that inquires deeply is never trapped in stupidity. When one reacts from anger, fear, or bias, stupidity takes over, yet seeing without reaction brings clarity. The wise do not pretend to know everything—admitting ignorance is the first step to understanding. A mechanical mind follows patterns without thinking, while true intelligence moves with full attention, never acting blindly. Stupidity is not about intelligence—it is about the inability or refusal to see things as they are. Many remain trapped in stupidity due to conditioning, arrogance, fear, and blind belief, mistaking knowledge for wisdom. A mind free from stupidity does not act from habit, does not cling to certainty, and does not react from fear—it sees, moves, and responds with clarity, without distortion. In this freedom, stupidity dissolves—not through force or effort, but because awareness leaves no room for ignorance to exist.

27. Contradiction

Contradiction: The Inner Division That Breeds Conflict

Contradiction arises when there is an internal conflict between opposing desires, beliefs, or actions. It is the struggle between 'what is' and 'what should be,' between thought and reality, and between different aspects of the self. This inner division creates confusion, suffering, and a constant state of unrest. The mind, shaped by past conditioning, holds onto ideals that often contradict present reality. When life does not align with these ideals, frustration and struggle emerge. Additionally, the self is a collection of conflicting desires—one part craves security while another longs for freedom, one seeks success while another desires peace. These contradictions tear the mind apart, making it restless and indecisive. Thought itself is a source of contradiction, as it demands happiness while carrying sorrow, or insists on fearlessness while fear persists. Social conditioning further deepens this conflict by promoting opposing values—teaching humility while encouraging ambition, advocating peace while fostering competition.

The consequences of contradiction are far-reaching. Inner conflict prevents clarity and presence, leaving the mind divided and distracted. This division leads to hypocrisy, where one believes in love but acts from fear, or speaks of peace while fostering inner turmoil. A mind in contradiction is weakened, hesitating between opposing forces, unable to act with decisiveness. This internal struggle wastes energy, as thought moves in endless cycles of comparison, doubt, and resistance instead of engaging directly with reality. Instead of bringing understanding, contradiction locks the mind in a pattern of continuous effort, seeking resolution but only creating further division.

Freedom from contradiction comes not through resistance or attempts at resolution, but through deep observation. The very effort to escape contradiction creates another layer of conflict. Instead of seeking to become something different, one can simply see 'what is' without judgment. The root of contradiction is comparison—measuring reality against an ideal. When one stops comparing, contradiction loses its hold. Observing thought without identifying with it allows the mind to see its own divisions clearly, and in that awareness, struggle dissolves naturally. A mind free from contradiction acts with total attention, without hesitation or internal debate. In this clarity, action is effortless, intelligence operates without division, and life is lived without conflict or struggle.

28. Abstraction

Abstraction: The Thought That Distances from Reality

Abstraction is the mental process of moving away from direct experience by creating concepts, ideas, and representations. While useful for intellectual understanding and practical communication, abstraction becomes a limitation when mistaken for truth. A mind caught in abstraction perceives life through thought rather than direct observation. Instead of seeing 'what is,' it constructs theories, models, and images, distancing itself from actual experience. Thought relies on abstraction to create language, symbols, and structured knowledge, but truth cannot be captured through ideas alone—it must be directly perceived.

Since all concepts are shaped by past experiences, a mind living in abstraction filters reality through memory, preventing fresh perception.

The reliance on abstraction leads to psychological illusions, where ideals like 'love,' 'justice,' or 'freedom' exist more as concepts than as lived realities. People attach themselves to these abstractions, often ignoring contradictions in actual life. Identification with religious, political, or ideological abstractions creates division and conflict, making individuals interact based on opposing beliefs rather than as human beings. Society reinforces this tendency through education, belief systems, and traditions, conditioning the mind to function in abstract terms. Abstractions provide psychological comfort, offering a sense of security and predictability. However, they also prevent direct engagement with reality, making it easier to discuss 'love' or 'peace' than to embody them in daily life.

Freedom from abstraction does not mean rejecting all concepts but seeing their limits. Recognizing that an idea is never the reality it represents allows the mind to stop seeking truth in concepts. Observation without immediate labeling or definition enables clear perception, free from mental distortions. Instead of holding onto ideals, one can act with awareness and compassion in the present moment. Truth is beyond mental representation; it cannot be grasped through analysis but only understood through direct experience. A mind that is fully aware does not escape into concepts but moves with life as it unfolds, seeing without the filter of abstraction. In this clarity, every moment is fresh, every experience is whole, and life is met as it is—without distortion, without illusion, and without the need for conceptual security.

29. Words

Words: The Symbols That Define and Distort Reality

Words are symbols used to communicate thoughts, express emotions, and convey meaning. They arise from the mind's need to categorize, define, and share experiences, yet they are not reality itself—only representations of it. A mind caught in words believes in their absolute meaning, mistaking descriptions for direct experience. The word "water" is not the actual substance, just as reading about love is not the same as feeling it. Words, shaped by culture, history, and conditioning, carry different meanings for different people, limiting true understanding. While they can reveal deep truths, they can also distort reality when used carelessly, creating division, misunderstanding, and illusion.

The limitations of words become evident when they reinforce conditioned thinking. Thought uses words to divide and categorize—'mine' and 'yours,' 'good' and 'bad'—creating conflict and psychological barriers. People become attached to words, defending religious texts, political ideologies, or personal opinions as if they were ultimate truths. This attachment strengthens identity, making one argue over meanings rather than perceiving beyond them. Many also rely on words for security, seeking comfort in philosophies or beliefs instead of directly observing life. Moreover, words are often used to fill silence, escape discomfort, or impress others, masking the depth that exists beyond verbal expression.

To use words without being trapped by them, one must see them as tools rather than truths. Language is essential for communication, but it is limited—it cannot capture the infinite complexity of existence. Understanding this prevents unnecessary attachment to words, allowing them to be used with clarity and purpose. Deep listening goes beyond language, perceiving silence, emotion, and intention rather than just the spoken word. Speaking only when necessary ensures that words serve truth rather than illusion. A mind that lives in awareness rather than verbal constructs sees beyond words, perceiving reality directly. In this freedom, words are no longer barriers but become precise expressions of understanding—used with awareness, without excess, and without distortion.

30. Analysis

Analysis: The Fragmentation of Truth Through Thought

Analysis is the process of breaking down thoughts, emotions, or situations into parts to understand them. It is a function of thought, relying on memory, past experiences, and comparison. While useful in science and problem-solving, does analysis bring clarity in understanding oneself? Society teaches that analyzing emotions, behavior, or the past leads to insight, but does breaking something into pieces reveal the whole, or does it only create more fragmentation? The mind, conditioned to seek causes and explanations, believes that identifying the source of fear or insecurity will resolve it. However, does finding a cause remove the problem, or does it merely keep the mind occupied in endless self-examination? Analysis creates the illusion of control, making one believe that dissecting emotions can bring mastery over them. Yet, since analysis is based on past knowledge, can something new ever be discovered through the old?

The problems with psychological analysis arise from its nature as a movement of thought. The more one analyzes, the more thought divides, compares, and speculates, keeping the mind trapped in mental activity rather than clear perception. Analysis also strengthens the division between the 'observer' and the 'observed'—one part of the mind examines another, creating conflict. But is the observer truly separate from the thing being analyzed, or are they the same movement of thought? True understanding is immediate, not the result of intellectual dissection. When one sees fire, awareness is instant—it does not require analysis. Likewise, emotions like fear or anger can be fully perceived in the moment, without needing to be broken down. However, the habit of analysis prevents direct perception. Instead of experiencing an emotion completely, thought intervenes with questions—"Why am I angry?" "What caused it?"—moving away from direct awareness.

Understanding without analysis comes through silent observation. Can one watch a thought, an emotion, or a reaction without labeling, dividing, or interfering? In this stillness, understanding happens naturally, without effort. Thought, which creates psychological problems, cannot solve them through further analysis. True transformation occurs when thought stops interfering and insight replaces intellectual dissection. Insight is not the product of breaking things down but the direct perception of truth. When one deeply sees that comparison leads to suffering, analysis is unnecessary—the pattern ends instantly. Living without carrying the past into the present frees the mind from the cycle of self-examination. Analysis may be useful in technical matters, but in understanding oneself, it creates more division and mental noise. A mind that observes without analyzing sees truth instantly—without struggle, without fragmentation. In this deep seeing, there is no need for analysis, because understanding is whole, immediate, and free.

31. Conformity

Conformity: The Fearful Surrender to Collective Thought

Conformity is the act of following societal norms, traditions, and expectations without question. It arises from fear—fear of rejection, isolation, or standing alone. A conforming mind suppresses its own intelligence, choosing security over truth. Society conditions individuals to fit into predefined roles, discouraging questioning and independent thought. In this state, the mind stops exploring, discovering, and truly understanding. Conformity creates psychological dependence, making people follow religions, ideologies, and traditions out of habit rather than insight. This dependence prevents true freedom, as one relies on external validation instead of direct perception. The fear of being different breeds mediocrity, as a mind that constantly seeks approval loses the ability to see truth for itself.

The reasons for conformity are deeply rooted in human psychology and social conditioning. The need for security makes people believe that following the majority brings safety, yet true security is found in understanding, not imitation. From childhood, individuals are taught to obey, fit in, and avoid questioning authority—defying this conditioning often results in social exclusion. Institutions such as religions, governments, and cultures reinforce fixed patterns of thought, making it difficult to break free from tradition. The desire for acceptance and recognition further strengthens conformity, as people fear losing approval. In this way, societal expectations become a psychological prison, keeping individuals trapped in repetitive patterns instead of allowing them to live with intelligence and originality.

To live without conformity, one must first observe it without resistance or justification. Seeing how one conforms without reacting against it brings awareness, and true freedom comes from understanding, not blind rebellion. Acting without seeking approval or rejection allows for action based on intelligence, not societal expectations. Questioning every tradition, belief, and authority prevents the mind from falling into conditioned patterns—nothing should be accepted as truth without deep inquiry. Being alone, if necessary, does not mean isolation but freedom from conditioning. Truth is rarely found in the majority; it is discovered in clarity, direct perception, and a mind unburdened by social expectations. A mind free from conformity does not blindly follow or oppose—it understands, and in that understanding, there is true freedom.

32. Dreams

Dreams: The Projections of Thought That Shape Illusion and Desire

Dreams are mental images, desires, and fantasies that arise from memory, conditioning, and the unconscious mind. They appear in sleep as reflections of thought and in waking life as ambitions, hopes, and imagined realities. A mind caught in dreams seeks escape, fulfillment, or psychological comfort, while a mind that understands deeply sees the limitation of dreams and moves beyond them. The mind projects its fears, desires, and memories into images, whether in sleep or in daydreams, for a dream is not separate from thought—it is thought continuing without external limitation. Many dream of success, love, or a perfect future to avoid present dissatisfaction, yet a mind that is fully awake does not seek refuge in dreams—it sees life as it is. The content of dreams—whether ambition, nightmares, or fantasy—is shaped by past experiences, and when one understands how thought conditions perception, attachment to dreams weakens.

People become attached to their dreams, believing them to be their future reality, yet true awareness sees that dreams are only mental images, not real life. Many dream of a better life because they resist what is happening now, but a mind that does not escape sees clearly, without illusion. Society teaches that having dreams is essential for progress, yet true freedom exists when one acts from understanding, not from imagined desires. When one invests emotion into dreams, fear of failure arises, but a mind free from attachment does not fear loss—it moves with reality, not against it. People think dreams are necessary for purpose and motivation, yet true meaning is not found in imagined futures—it is discovered in deep awareness. The dreaming mind lives in the future, imagining what could be instead of seeing what is, and true clarity exists when one is fully in the present, free from imagined outcomes.

Thought creates dreams based on past experience and future desires, and a mind that sees this no longer clings to imagined realities. Many use dreams to avoid dissatisfaction with the present, yet true freedom is not in dreaming—it is in facing reality without resistance. When one watches dreams as they arise, they lose their hold over the mind, for awareness sees thought as movement, not as truth. People believe achieving their dreams will bring happiness, yet happiness is not in the future—it exists only in full presence. The mind that does not seek fulfillment through dreams is already free, for true intelligence acts without expectation, without psychological time. Dreams are projections of thought, shaped by memory, desire, and conditioning, creating a psychological escape from reality. Many struggle with dreams because they attach their happiness and purpose to them, believing their fulfillment will bring meaning, but true freedom is in seeing that all dreams are mental constructs. A mind free from the illusion of dreams does not seek fulfillment in the future—it acts fully in the present, without expectation, without disappointment. In this freedom, dreams lose their grip—not because one rejects them, but because there is no longer a mind seeking escape—only deep awareness, clear perception, and effortless action.

WAKE UP

WAKE UP

2. Learning & Understanding

WAKE UP

WAKE UP

33. Education

Education: Conditioning or Awakening?

Education is meant to awaken intelligence, creativity, and understanding, yet it has largely become a system of conditioning. Instead of encouraging free thought, deep inquiry, and a true understanding of life, education often teaches conformity—what to think rather than how to think. A child enters school with curiosity and openness, but the system conditions them to accept authority, memorize facts, and compete for success. True education is not about accumulating knowledge alone but about learning to observe, inquire, and understand deeply. It should cultivate awareness and sensitivity, not just prepare individuals for jobs and societal roles. However, modern education has largely become a means of fitting individuals into a structured system rather than helping them explore life with intelligence and clarity.

The problems within the education system are deeply ingrained. Schools emphasize competition, exams, and ambition, creating insecurity and fear of failure. Fear stifles curiosity, making learning mechanical rather than an organic process of discovery. Instead of fostering inquiry, students are taught obedience—accepting authority and following rules without question. Memorization is mistaken for intelligence, reducing learning to repetition rather than deep understanding. Moreover, education focuses solely on external knowledge while ignoring emotional and psychological well-being. It does not teach self-awareness, how to deal with emotions, or how to understand relationships. As a result, students become highly skilled in academic subjects but lack the ability to navigate life with intelligence and insight.

True education must go beyond mere knowledge—it must teach how to observe, question, and understand without bias. Learning is not just about receiving answers but about developing the capacity to ask deep questions about oneself, society, and existence. Education must bring freedom, not fear, for a mind burdened by anxiety cannot think clearly. Real learning happens in an atmosphere without pressure, comparison, or ambition—only curiosity and interest. Learning must also extend beyond books, embracing nature, relationships, silence, and direct experience. The purpose of education is not merely a career but a deep understanding of life. An educated person is not defined by degrees but by their ability to live without fear, observe without judgment, and love without attachment. Today's education system trains the mind to conform, but true education awakens intelligence, freedom, and deep inquiry—teaching not just facts, but how to live fully, with awareness, love, and insight.

34. Knowledge

Knowledge: The Weight of the Known

Knowledge is the accumulated experience, memory, and information stored in the brain. It is essential for practical life—science, language, skills, and technology all rely on it. Without knowledge, we could not function efficiently in daily activities. However, knowledge becomes a limitation when it is used to understand psychological and existential truths. All knowledge belongs to the past—there is no knowledge of the unknown. The moment something is learned, it becomes part of memory, no longer fresh or new. The brain records experiences and categorizes them, and thought then uses this stored knowledge to react, analyze, and respond. While practical knowledge must be accumulated and refined, problems arise when knowledge is relied upon to understand oneself, relationships, or truth. For example, a person who has been hurt in the past may approach new relationships through the filter of that pain, preventing fresh perception.

The limitations of knowledge become evident when it is applied beyond practical matters. Knowledge is mechanical and repetitive—it functions like a machine, repeating what has been learned, unable to go beyond itself. It also creates the illusion of the 'self,' reinforcing the ego as a collection of memories, experiences, and labels. The 'I' is nothing but accumulated knowledge of past experiences, yet we mistake this mental construct for our identity. Furthermore, knowledge conditions the mind, creating division through religious, national, and ideological identities. A person taught that their religion or belief system is the only truth cannot see beyond their conditioning. Most significantly, knowledge cannot touch the timeless—love, beauty, truth, and intelligence cannot be stored or carried forward as knowledge. They must be perceived anew in each moment, for no amount of reading about love equals the actual experience of love.

To be free from the limitations of knowledge, one must use it without psychological dependence. While knowledge is necessary for technical and functional tasks, it should not shape identity or perception. Recognizing a road from memory is practical; judging a person based on past experiences is limiting. Observation must happen without the filter of past knowledge—seeing people, emotions, and situations without projecting past experiences allows for fresh perception. A mind that is free from accumulated conclusions is open to direct experience, without seeking security in what it already knows. Truth is not found in books or beliefs but must be discovered moment to moment. Knowledge is essential for practical living, but it becomes a barrier when applied to psychological and existential matters. True intelligence arises when one sees beyond knowledge, understanding that accumulated experience cannot touch the living truth of the present. When the mind is silent and free from the past, it perceives reality as it is—without the distortion of knowledge.

35. Accumulation

Accumulation: The Mind's Obsession with More

Accumulation is not merely the gathering of material possessions but also the psychological collection of experiences, knowledge, beliefs, and attachments. It is the mind's attempt to secure itself by holding onto the past, believing that accumulation brings stability and protection. Whether through wealth, relationships, or knowledge, we assume that having 'more' will provide security. Yet, can true security exist in what can be lost? The self is built on accumulation—memories, achievements, and beliefs shape our identity, making us fear what would happen if we let go. Society further conditions us to measure life by possession, equating success with material wealth, power, and recognition. This conditioning leads to a fear of emptiness, as letting go of accumulation feels like losing something. But is emptiness something to fear, or is it the space in which real freedom exists?

The problems with accumulation are deeply psychological. Holding onto experiences, hurts, and ambitions creates a heavy burden, weighing down the mind. Can one live without carrying this psychological weight? Accumulation prevents newness, as a mind full of past knowledge and conclusions cannot see freshly. True perception requires freedom from the known, yet accumulation binds us to past experiences, limiting our ability to meet life as it is. Additionally, the fear of losing what we have gathered—whether status, possessions, or relationships—leads to anxiety, possessiveness, and insecurity. The 'I' feels real because it clings to these accumulated experiences, strengthening the illusion of self. But is the self anything more than a collection of past thoughts?

Living without accumulation is not about rejecting material necessities but about seeing the illusion of psychological possession. Understanding that inner accumulation creates division and suffering allows for freedom from it. Letting go of the idea that knowledge leads to wisdom is essential—true intelligence is not in gathering information but in deep awareness. Can one fully experience each moment without storing it as a memory to carry forward? When an experience ends completely in the moment, the mind remains light, unburdened. True freedom is found in not owning, not holding, not clinging. A mind without accumulation is not empty in a negative sense—it is vast, limitless, and open. Where there is no accumulation, there is no fear—only deep freedom, limitless awareness, and the ability to meet life with total presence.

36. Schools

Schools: Factories of Conformity or Gateways to Understanding?

Schools are institutions designed to educate, transmit knowledge, and prepare individuals for society. They function within a structured system of exams, grades, discipline, and authority, shaping young minds to fit into predetermined roles. However, do schools truly educate, or do they condition students to conform to society's expectations? While they provide academic and practical knowledge necessary for functioning in the world, they often neglect self-awareness, intelligence, and a deeper understanding of life. Education is commonly seen as a path to success, where children are conditioned to believe that grades, degrees, and achievements define their worth. This leads to competition, stress, and the pursuit of security through knowledge rather than true learning. Schools enforce discipline and structure, instilling obedience, yet does obedience lead to intelligence, or does it suppress independent thought? Parents and society demand standardized education, expecting schools to prepare children for jobs and financial security. But is life only about earning a livelihood, or is there something deeper to understand?

The structure of schools creates several limitations. From an early age, children are taught what to think rather than how to think, leading to conformity rather than creativity. Questioning and free exploration are often discouraged in favor of memorization and rigid curricula. Education becomes a system of competition, where students are trained to compare, achieve, and outperform others. But does true intelligence emerge through competition, or through inquiry and exploration? Memorization is prioritized over insight, reinforcing the accumulation of knowledge rather than wisdom. Real learning is not about collecting facts but about perceiving life as a whole. Furthermore, schools create fear—fear of failure, of exams, of not succeeding in the system. Can a mind that is afraid ever learn freely? Fear stifles curiosity and prevents true discovery, reducing education to a mechanical process of repetition.

Real learning must go beyond institutionalized education. Schools provide technical knowledge, but true education lies in understanding oneself and observing life directly. Can one learn deeply not just from textbooks but by watching nature, relationships, and the movement of thought? A school that teaches only conformity does not nurture intelligence—it produces conditioned minds that accept without questioning. Education should foster awareness, sensitivity, and independent thinking rather than blind acceptance. Understanding is not measured by exams but by the ability to perceive life with clarity. A truly educated person is not one who has memorized facts but one who questions, explores, and thinks independently. Schools today function more like factories for producing workers than spaces for awakening intelligence. Can there be a school where learning is about discovery, not repetition? True education is not about passing exams but about understanding oneself and the world. Learning is not confined to classrooms—it is present in every moment of life, in deep observation, and in seeing reality without distortion. Only when education is free from fear, competition, and mechanical repetition can true intelligence flourish.

37. Teaching

Teaching: Imparting Information or Awakening Intelligence?

Teaching is not merely the transfer of knowledge but the awakening of intelligence and perception. It is not about authority, repetition, or conditioning—it is about exploration and discovery. A true teacher does not impose ideas but helps the student see clearly for themselves. Teaching must go beyond the accumulation of facts, for information alone does not bring wisdom. Can education help a student think freely, question deeply, and see without bias? True teaching is not about making students conform but about awakening their ability to observe, inquire, and understand. A good teacher learns while teaching— if teaching is merely the act of giving answers, it becomes mechanical. Real teaching involves guiding students to understand their own minds, helping them observe thought, fear, and attachment without distortion.

However, education often fails because it focuses on memory rather than understanding. Schools prioritize facts and exams but rarely teach students how to think critically or perceive life deeply. Many teachers impose beliefs—whether ideological, religious, or nationalistic—shaping students within a framework rather than encouraging inquiry. Fear and comparison further destroy true learning, as competition creates anxiety rather than intelligence. When the teacher-student relationship is based on control, free exploration is lost. A real teacher is not an authority figure but a guide and a friend, helping students discover truth rather than follow instructions.

True teaching must be free from conditioning. A teacher who is free from fear, ambition, and prejudice teaches without effort—

not through words alone, but by example. Can students learn more from how a teacher lives than from what they say? Teaching should encourage questioning rather than mere acceptance—if a student simply believes, they have not truly learned. Education must also address the whole human being, not just academics but emotions, relationships, and self-awareness. Teaching should be a dialogue, not a one-way process—when students and teachers explore together without rigid conclusions, learning becomes a shared journey. Teaching is not about control, repetition, or authority but about awakening intelligence. A real teacher does not create followers but free individuals. The best education is not about passing exams but about understanding life deeply.

38. Questioning

Questioning: The Key to Breaking Mental Barriers

Questioning is the act of deeply inquiring into life, not to seek confirmation of what we already believe but to uncover truth. It is not intellectual curiosity or the pursuit of ready-made answers—it is the passion to understand reality without distortion. Without questioning, the mind remains trapped in conditioning, shaped by society, education, religion, and personal experience. True questioning breaks through inherited beliefs, allowing one to think independently. Intelligence is not in memorizing answers but in asking the right questions without seeking comfort. A mind that does not question functions mechanically, following patterns without understanding. Moreover, questioning prevents psychological dependence on external authorities—truth cannot be handed down by religious, political, or ideological figures; it must be discovered firsthand through deep inquiry.

However, questioning is often met with fear and resistance. People fear losing security, as questioning one's beliefs, traditions, and identity may create uncertainty. But is security in belief real, or just a mental illusion? Society discourages deep questioning because it threatens established structures—challenging authority can lead to social rejection. Additionally, the mind seeks easy answers, avoiding the discomfort of uncertainty. True questioning requires patience, attention, and the willingness to live without immediate conclusions. Perhaps the greatest fear is facing oneself completely—questioning not only external ideas but also personal emotions, attachments, and fears. It demands absolute honesty, stripping away illusions and exposing reality as it is.

To question rightly, one must do so without seeking immediate conclusions. The moment an answer is found, inquiry stops. Can one question without the desire to settle on an idea or belief? True questioning is not about rejecting everything but about seeing without bias—looking at oneself and society without defense, justification, or escape. Every assumption must be examined, no matter how sacred, for truth is not found in acceptance but in direct discovery. A mind that allows a question to remain open does not rush toward answers but lets inquiry reveal its depth. Sometimes, the question itself is more important than the answer. Questioning is the foundation of true intelligence and freedom. A mind that does not question is trapped in conditioning, blindly following patterns without understanding. True questioning is fearless—it does not seek comfort, authority, or easy solutions. When questioning is alive, the mind is free—free to see, free to learn, and free to discover truth beyond all illusion.

39. Inquiry

Inquiry: The Pathway to Truth Beyond Belief

Inquiry is the act of questioning deeply, not to find fixed answers, but to understand. It is not an intellectual debate or the accumulation of knowledge but a direct exploration of truth. True inquiry has no authority, no assumption, and no direction—it is free, open, and without motive. From childhood, we are conditioned to accept beliefs, traditions, and societal norms without question. Inquiry breaks through this conditioning, challenging all inherited ideas. It prevents psychological dependence on authority, for truth cannot be found in books, teachers, or ideologies—it must be discovered firsthand through deep questioning. A questioning mind is alive, never stagnant or mechanical. The deeper one inquires, the sharper, more sensitive, and more perceptive the mind becomes. Without inquiry, the mind remains trapped in conditioning, repeating the past. True freedom is not rebellion but the absence of blind acceptance.

However, inquiry is often feared and resisted. To question deeply means facing the possibility that what we believe may be false, and the mind seeks certainty and comfort, making it reluctant to question its assumptions. Psychological illusions—beliefs, identities, and traditions—offer security, but do they provide truth, or just attachment to comforting ideas? Society, culture, and institutions discourage deep questioning to maintain control, fearing minds that think freely. A deeply inquiring mind does not conform—it stands alone, questioning everything, including its own conditioning. Most people prefer to belong rather than to question, making true inquiry a rare and courageous act.

To inquire rightly, one must question without seeking a conclusion. The moment an answer is reached, inquiry ends. True inquiry requires absolute honesty—can one look at oneself, at life, without justifying, defending, or escaping? Inquiry should not be an occasional activity but a state of mind applied to every moment of life. Can one question every reaction, every belief, every assumption without resistance? Thought, rooted in the past, can only analyze and interpret, but true inquiry must go beyond thought, into silent perception. Inquiry is the foundation of a truly free mind—it does not conform, follow, or accept blindly. When inquiry is alive, the mind is never caught in illusion; it remains fresh, always questioning, and open to truth.

40. The Art of Learning

The Art of Learning: Discovering Without Accumulation

The art of learning is not about accumulating knowledge or memorizing facts but about maintaining a state of continuous observation, discovery, and openness to the new. A mind that truly learns does not hold onto past conclusions—it is free, flexible, and always questioning. However, most people mistake knowledge for learning, believing that once they "know" something, inquiry is no longer needed. Knowledge is stored information, but learning is a living process that requires an ever-fresh mind. Society, education, and belief systems condition individuals to accept what to think rather than how to observe, limiting true learning. Fear of being wrong further blocks learning, as the mind resists anything that challenges its identity and beliefs. Additionally, competition and comparison turn learning into a race for achievement, stripping away the joy of deep understanding.

True learning is an ongoing, moment-to-moment process that happens in every interaction and experience. It is not confined to schools or books but is present in daily life when one is attentive and open. A mind that learns is not distracted or mechanical—it is fully present, making learning deep and effortless. Most people acquire knowledge about the external world but never examine their own thoughts, fears, and conditioning. Without self-knowledge, learning remains superficial. True learning also requires humility—a mind that is proud of what it knows cannot learn, as it is already full. When one realizes that there is never an endpoint to learning, the mind becomes free to explore without limitation.

To live in a state of learning, one must observe without forming immediate conclusions. The moment a conclusion is made, learning stops. Can one look at a problem or oneself without rushing to judge or decide? True learning also requires unlearning—letting go of false knowledge and seeing with fresh eyes. Life itself is the greatest teacher, offering lessons through every relationship and challenge. A truly learning mind does not depend solely on books or teachers but learns from everything, without bias. Learning must also be free, not driven by goals such as degrees, recognition, or power. When learning is pursued for a reward, it becomes mechanical rather than joyful. The art of learning keeps the mind alive, open, and inquiring. In a mind that is always learning, there is no stagnation, no finality—only the endless beauty of discovery, where learning and living are one.

41. The Art of Listening

The Art of Listening: Hearing Without the Noise of the Mind

The art of listening is the ability to hear fully, without interpreting, judging, or reacting. It is not merely the recognition of words and sounds but a state of complete attention in which the mind is silent and fully receptive. True listening is not selective—it does not filter out what is unpleasant or disagreeable but remains open to everything as it is. However, we rarely listen in this way because thought interferes, forming responses and judgments before the speaker has even finished. Instead of listening with fresh attention, we hear through the filter of memory, past experiences, and conditioning. The ego seeks to reinforce its own ideas, accepting what aligns with its beliefs and rejecting what does not. This selective listening prevents real understanding. Moreover, distraction and mental noise—worries, plans, and self-talk—block deep listening, making it impossible to be fully present.

True listening happens when there is no judgment, comparison, or psychological resistance. Can one listen without labeling the speaker as right or wrong, without measuring their words against past knowledge? Listening is not just an auditory process but an act that involves the whole mind—hearing not only the words but the silences, the emotions, and the meaning beyond words. The 'self' listens with an agenda—to defend, to argue, or to prove a point. But can one listen without bringing the 'I' into it—simply hearing without reaction? In such listening, there is no separation, no mental barrier—only deep connection. To truly listen is an act of love, a complete giving of attention without distraction or expectation.

The art of listening can be cultivated through deep awareness. Being fully present means giving complete attention when someone speaks, without drifting into thought. Can one listen, not just to words, but to the rustling of leaves, the sound of water, the silence between sounds? Listening to nature, to silence, and to the space between sounds brings a different quality of awareness. Listening inwardly is equally important—can one hear one's own thoughts, fears, and emotions without judgment or suppression? Self-knowledge begins when one listens inwardly without interference. True listening is free from expectation; the moment we listen to gain something, listening is already distorted. The art of listening is the art of complete attention, where the mind is silent, open, and free from judgment. A mind that listens without distortion hears truth—not just in words, but beyond them. In such listening, there is no 'listener'—only listening, only a profound connection with life as it unfolds.

42. The Art of Looking

The Art of Looking: Seeing Without the Past Distorting the Present

The art of looking is the ability to see life, oneself, and the world without the interference of thought, memory, or judgment. It is not intellectual observation or analysis but pure perception. True looking is not limited to the eyes—it is an act of deep awareness, where the mind is completely silent and fully attentive. However, we rarely see things as they truly are because thought interferes with perception. Instead of looking at a person, a situation, or an object directly, we project our opinions, fears, and expectations onto them. From childhood, we are conditioned to analyze, compare, and categorize everything, preventing fresh perception. The ego further distorts vision by seeking confirmation of its existing beliefs, making us see only what aligns with our conditioning. Moreover, distraction and mental noise—constant thinking, planning, and remembering—block deep seeing, keeping the mind restless and preoccupied.

True looking requires freedom from these distortions. Can one look at a tree, a person, or a thought without naming, comparing, or interpreting? The moment thought does not interfere, perception is pure. We often look to reach a conclusion, to find an answer, or to reinforce what we already believe. But can one observe without seeking an outcome—just seeing, without expectation? When looking happens with total attention, there is no division between the observer and the observed. In this state, there is only seeing—not a 'self' that is looking. True looking is not a means to an end; the moment one looks to gain insight, knowledge, or peace, the act of looking is already distorted. Pure perception is complete in itself—it requires no purpose beyond the act of seeing.

To cultivate the art of looking, one must observe without judgment or resistance. When a thought or emotion arises, can one watch it without suppressing or justifying it? The moment one observes without resistance, the mind becomes clear. Looking at everything as if seeing it for the first time allows for fresh perception, unburdened by past knowledge. Can one look at a flower, a person, or the sky without assuming they are already known? True looking happens only when one is fully present, undistracted by thought. This also applies to self-observation—can one watch one's own emotions, fears, and thoughts without trying to control or avoid them? Self-knowledge comes not from effort but from observing oneself as one is, without distortion. The art of looking is the art of seeing without interference, where the mind is free from conditioning and the weight of the past. In this deep looking, reality reveals itself—not through thought but through direct perception, in the living moment.

43. Observer

Observer: The Illusion of the Separate Watcher

The observer is the sense of 'I' that watches, evaluates, and reacts to experience, creating the illusion of separation between the thinker and thought, the experiencer and experience. A mind caught in the observer believes it is distinct from what it perceives, leading to inner conflict and duality. The observer is merely the accumulation of past experiences—memory, knowledge, and conditioning—filtering every perception through the lens of past conclusions, preventing fresh seeing. This division sustains psychological struggle; when one says, 'I am angry,' there is an assumption that the 'I' is separate from the anger. But is there truly an observer apart from the emotion, or is the observer the observed? Thought constructs this observer as a fixed, independent entity, yet if thought ceases, where is the observer? It exists only in psychological time, constantly judging the present based on the past and projecting into the future. But when time ceases—when one is fully present—does the observer remain at all?

We believe in the observer because we have been conditioned to see ourselves as separate from our thoughts, emotions, and actions. From childhood, we are taught that 'you' are different from your inner experiences, reinforcing the illusion of an independent observer. The mind seeks control over its inner world, wanting to transform fear into courage, confusion into clarity, but this effort to control thought is thought fighting itself, deepening inner division. The fear of losing the sense of self further strengthens the illusion of an observer—if it is not separate, what happens to 'me'? We also assume that awareness requires an observer, but does awareness need an 'I' to exist, or does it simply function without division? Thought craves stability and creates the observer as a reference point, but this center is an illusion—it has no reality beyond thought.

To see without an observer is to realize that the observer is the observed. Anger, fear, and desire are not separate from 'you'— they are you. When this is understood, the division dissolves. True observation happens without judgment or control; the moment one tries to modify what is observed, the observer re-emerges. Letting go of psychological time allows perception to be whole—without a past conditioning the present or a future being projected. Thought arises and passes—does it need an 'I' to manage it? When there is no identification with thought, awareness is effortless. A mind without an observer does not create a false center—it simply sees. In this seeing, there is no duality—no separate observer and observed, only the direct experience of life. In this awareness, struggle ends, time ceases, and what remains is clarity, depth, and wholeness—without an observer, without a center, without division.

44. Observation

Observation: Perceiving Without Judgment or Conclusion

Observation is the act of seeing directly, without interference from thought, past experience, or judgment. It is not analysis, evaluation, or conclusion—it is pure perception. True observation is the foundation of understanding, allowing reality to reveal itself without distortion. However, we struggle to observe clearly because the mind is conditioned to interpret rather than see. Instead of simply looking, we immediately analyze, compare, or label, preventing direct perception. Past experiences further cloud observation, as we see through the filter of memory—expecting, fearing, or desiring certain outcomes. Even when observing ourselves, the ego interferes, turning observation into judgment—'I am good,' 'I am bad,' 'I should change.' But can one observe without bringing the 'I' into it, without trying to alter what is seen? Society reinforces the habit of seeking conclusions, looking for answers rather than watching without expectation.

True observation requires a state of awareness free from judgment and comparison. Can one look at a tree, a person, or a thought without labeling or measuring it? Observation is not passive—it is an intense state of attention, where there is no distraction or distortion. It is not one part of the mind watching another, but simply seeing without the interference of the past. In such observation, understanding is immediate—when one observes fear, anger, or conditioning without resistance, there is clarity. In that clarity, the very thing observed begins to dissolve. But observation is often blocked by effort—if one observes with the desire to fix, improve, or suppress, one is not truly observing.

Can one watch without motive, without trying to achieve a result? True observation is complete in itself, with no goal—it is being fully present with 'what is,' without escaping into past or future.

The art of observation is seeing without distortion, without interference from thought. A mind that truly observes is not caught in past conditioning but remains free, present, and fully aware. True understanding does not come from effort, analysis, or judgment—it happens instantly when there is pure observation. When the mind is silent and attentive, there is no need to 'do' anything—seeing itself brings transformation. The false drops away the moment it is seen clearly. In this observation, the self-created divisions, fears, and illusions of the mind dissolve, leaving only clarity, silence, and deep intelligence.

45. Introspection

Introspection: The Art of Seeing Oneself Without Distortion

Introspection is the deep observation of one's thoughts, emotions, and motives without judgment or justification. It arises when the mind is still, alert, and willing to see itself clearly. A mind caught in introspection as an analysis tries to explain itself, while a mind that understands deeply simply observes. Many approach introspection by analyzing past actions or searching for explanations, yet true introspection is immediate—seeing thought as it arises, without delay. The mind often justifies or excuses its own behavior, avoiding truth, but true self-awareness happens when one sees without filtering through personal bias.

People either criticize or defend themselves when looking inward, yet a mind that does not judge sees itself with complete clarity. Many look inward to improve or fix their flaws, yet change that comes from conflict is not real transformation— seeing deeply brings effortless change.

The ego wants to maintain its self-image, avoiding uncomfortable truths, yet true introspection requires the courage to see without escaping. Some try to introspect as a routine, turning it into a method, but deep observation happens naturally when the mind is awake. Society teaches people to focus on external success, not inner clarity, keeping them disconnected from themselves. People believe they 'are' their thoughts, making introspection difficult, but true seeing happens when one realizes thought is separate from the observer. Many seek conclusions about themselves rather than simply watching their mind, yet real introspection does not seek answers—it allows truth to reveal itself. A mind that never looks inward remains a prisoner of its own habits and conditioning, while a mind that observes without resistance dissolves inner confusion effortlessly.

A mind that is alert naturally looks within, without force. When one stops seeking methods, introspection happens on its own. Many try to shape their thoughts while introspecting, yet true introspection watches thought without interference. The mind wants to find definite answers—'Why am I like this?'—but deep introspection is not about answers, it is about seeing clearly. True self-awareness exists only now, not in past regrets or future worries, for a mind rooted in the present sees itself without distortion. Many turn introspection into self-judgment, creating inner conflict, yet a mind that observes without division sees truth effortlessly. Introspection is not about self-improvement, judgment, or analysis—it is the art of observing oneself without distortion. Many struggle with introspection because they seek answers, avoid self-truth, or make it a forced process, but true introspection happens effortlessly in a mind that is fully aware. A mind free from self-deception, resistance, and judgment does not need to try to introspect—it simply watches, understands, and moves beyond illusion. In this freedom, introspection is no longer a burden—it becomes the silent, effortless seeing of the mind as it is, without interference, without avoidance, in complete clarity.

46. Interpretation

Interpretation: The Filter That Distorts Reality

Interpretation is the process of assigning meaning to events, words, or experiences based on one's conditioning, beliefs, and knowledge. It arises from memory, cultural influences, personal bias, and psychological conditioning. A mind caught in interpretation sees reality through its own filters, while a mind that understands deeply perceives without distortion. The mind interprets based on what it has known, not what is actually present, making perception incomplete. True perception exists when one sees without projecting the past onto the present. Two people hear the same words but interpret them differently, leading to misunderstanding and conflict. A mind free from interpretation listens without distortion, allowing understanding beyond words.

People believe their interpretation is reality, yet it is only their version of it. Truth is beyond interpretation—it is direct perception, without mental interference. Thought interprets based on what it knows, but knowledge is always incomplete, meaning perception is never whole when filtered through thought. Instead of seeing, the mind labels, categorizes, and judges, preventing direct experience. From childhood, we are conditioned to analyze, label, and judge experiences, making it difficult to perceive without mental interference. The mind wants certainty, so it holds onto fixed meanings, yet reality is ever-changing—rigid interpretation prevents deep understanding. Instead of seeing reality, people twist facts to fit their worldview, defending interpretations rather than being open to truth.

The mind instantly reacts with interpretation, yet is it necessary? When one watches this process, interpretation loses its grip. Can one see a tree, a person, or a word without interpreting? When one looks without projecting, perception is pure. The mind seeks meaning in everything, but does reality need interpretation, or does it simply exist? People listen to confirm what they already believe, yet true listening happens when the mind is silent, without a personal filter. Thought will always interpret, but does one have to follow it? A free mind sees thought as a movement, not as absolute truth. Interpretation is the mind's attempt to make sense of reality, but it often distorts rather than reveals truth. Many struggle with interpretation because they are conditioned to rely on thought, seek security in explanations, and justify their beliefs. True understanding comes not from adding meaning but from seeing clearly, without interference from past knowledge or bias. A mind free from the burden of interpretation does not project, does not react, and does not impose meaning—it simply observes, moves, and understands without distortion. In this freedom, interpretation dissolves—not because one forces it away, but because there is no longer a mind seeking to shape reality—only pure perception, beyond words, beyond thought, beyond interpretation.

47. Language

Language: The Trap of Words and the Illusion of Meaning

Language is a tool for communication, allowing us to express thoughts, emotions, and experiences. It shapes perception, influencing how we think and relate to the world. While essential for daily life, language also creates division, misunderstanding, and limitation. Words are symbols, not reality itself, yet we often mistake them for truth. The way we speak reflects cultural, religious, and national identities, reinforcing conditioned thought. Different languages separate people, strengthening notions of nationality and division. Labels such as 'Hindu,' 'Muslim,' 'Christian,' or 'American' impose identities that limit true understanding. Moreover, language can be manipulated to deceive, justify violence, or assert power, as seen in political and religious institutions that condition minds through carefully crafted words.

The limitations of language are significant. Words distort direct experience—the word 'tree' is not the actual tree but a representation. When we name something, we often stop observing it directly, relying on the mental image rather than perceiving reality. Language also strengthens the illusion of identity and ego—phrases like 'my country,' 'my belief,' or 'my experience' reinforce psychological separation. Judgment through words further divides perception; calling something 'good' or 'bad' imposes conditioned meaning, preventing pure observation. The search for truth cannot be captured in words—philosophies, scriptures, and teachings can describe truth, but they are not truth itself. Reality exists beyond verbal expression and must be directly perceived, not merely spoken or written about.

To use language without being limited by it, one must understand that the word is not the thing. Recognizing language as a tool prevents attachment to words, allowing the mind to see reality as it is. Communication can be free from division and bias when language is used with awareness, without reinforcing labels or authority. Thought constantly verbalizes experience, shaping perception, but silent observation reveals a reality beyond words and concepts. No philosophy or teaching can fully express truth—it must be directly seen. Language is necessary for communication, but it also conditions thought and creates division. Understanding its limitations brings clarity, allowing perception beyond words. A mind free from verbal conditioning sees the world without distortion, moving beyond the boundaries of language into direct awareness.

48. Scriptures

Scriptures: Wisdom Captured or Thought Imprisoned?

Scriptures are written records of spiritual, philosophical, and moral teachings, often regarded as sacred. They arise from human experience, insight, and interpretation over generations. A mind that engages with scriptures can either use them as a guide for reflection and understanding or become bound by them, mistaking words for truth. Scriptures contain wisdom but are shaped by the time, culture, and context in which they were written. While they may offer valuable insights, truth itself is not found in words—it must be directly perceived. Some find inspiration in scriptures, using them for self-inquiry, while others turn them into rigid doctrines, preventing questioning and independent thought. Since interpretations vary based on individual conditioning and belief, scriptures often become a source of contradiction, division, and even conflict. They can serve as both a means of liberation and a tool for control, depending on how they are approached.

People depend on scriptures for many reasons. They seek security in written words, finding comfort in structured beliefs that provide certainty. However, this security can prevent deep questioning, leading to blind acceptance. Many mistake words for direct experience, believing that reading about truth is the same as seeing it for oneself. From childhood, people are conditioned to respect sacred texts as ultimate truth, making questioning feel like disloyalty or rebellion. Additionally, scriptures offer moral and spiritual guidance, helping individuals define what is right and wrong. Yet, truth is not found in fixed rules—it must be understood in the present moment, beyond dogma. The fear of facing life without external guidance further reinforces dependence on scriptures. Without them, one must rely on their own clarity and perception, which requires deep awareness rather than reliance on written teachings.

To use scriptures without being bound by them, one must see that they are words, not truth itself. Words can describe the path, but they are not the path—truth is living, moving, and beyond written records. Engaging with scriptures should not mean blind acceptance or rejection but intelligent inquiry. Many either follow scriptures rigidly or reject them entirely; true intelligence questions without prejudice. Instead of seeking final answers, one can use scriptures as a means of exploration, reflecting on their meaning rather than clinging to conclusions. Different religions have different sacred texts, often leading to division, yet truth is not exclusive to any one scripture—it exists beyond all separations. One who truly sees does not need scriptures to confirm their understanding. When the mind is fully awake, words become secondary. Scriptures are records of past wisdom, but they are not truth itself—they are only pointers. A mind that uses them for inquiry, not rigid belief, remains free to explore truth beyond words. In this freedom, scriptures are neither worshipped nor discarded—they are seen as tools, useful but not ultimate, pointing toward something that can only be understood through direct awareness and deep inquiry.

49. Philosophy

Philosophy: The Love of Wisdom or the Prison of Thought?

Philosophy is the exploration of fundamental questions about existence, knowledge, reality, and truth. It arises from the human need to understand life beyond immediate experience. However, a mind engaged in philosophy can either use it for deep inquiry or become trapped in intellectual abstraction. Many approach philosophy as theoretical knowledge, but its true purpose is direct understanding. A deeply questioning mind is philosophical even without formal study. Some use philosophy as a tool for freeing themselves from illusions, while others cling to it rigidly, turning it into ideology. Questioning opens the mind to new possibilities, but attachment to philosophical schools merely replaces one belief with another. Since philosophy exists in words, it can only describe truth but never fully capture it. A mind that depends on words and theories risks missing the direct perception of reality. Philosophy is meaningless if it remains an intellectual pursuit rather than a way of seeing and living.

People turn to philosophy for many reasons. The mind seeks answers to life's uncertainty, craving structure in an unpredictable world. However, while philosophy offers ideas, ideas are not reality. Many seek philosophy to understand themselves and the world, but true understanding comes not through concepts but through direct awareness. The mind also fears living without a framework of meaning, using philosophy for psychological security rather than exploration. Religion, culture, and education condition individuals to seek truth in established systems, yet truth is beyond all systems. Many assume that deep thinking alone leads to understanding, but thought is always shaped by past experience and knowledge, limiting perception. When philosophy becomes a mental refuge rather than a tool for inquiry, it no longer serves its true purpose.

To engage with philosophy without being bound by it, one must see that philosophy is only a tool, not an ultimate truth. Ideas may guide exploration, but they are not reality itself. A mind free from attachment to philosophy can use it without being trapped by it. Questioning should be free of the need for comfort—many turn to philosophy to feel secure rather than to see clearly, but true questioning has no goal; it simply seeks to understand. Observation of life must be direct, not secondhand—books may offer insight, but direct experience is the only real teacher. Philosophy should not become an escape from reality, as some hide behind complex theories to avoid facing themselves. True philosophy is not about discussing ideas but about seeing life as it is. A free mind moves beyond mental constructs, seeing without labels or frameworks. In this way, philosophy is not merely a system but a living inquiry where truth is not something to be believed but something to be seen, lived, and understood without limitation.

50. Methods and Systems

Methods and Systems: The Cage of the Mind Seeking Security

Methods and systems are structured approaches—whether in spirituality, self-improvement, or knowledge—designed to bring transformation. They promise progress through discipline, repetition, and adherence to rules. However, can any method lead to truth, or does the very act of following a system limit perception? The mind seeks security in structured approaches, creating the illusion that progress is being made. By following a system, one feels a sense of certainty, avoiding the discomfort of facing the unknown. Many believe that truth, enlightenment, or transformation can be reached step by step, yet is truth something that unfolds gradually, or is it seen only in direct perception? Society conditions us to follow authorities and structured paths from childhood, reinforcing dependence on external guidance rather than deep self-inquiry. Methods also promise an end to suffering, providing a structured way to escape inner conflict. But does following a method truly dissolve suffering, or does it create new struggles by reinforcing effort and expectation?

The reliance on methods and systems presents several limitations. Most systems assume that inner change happens gradually, implying that time is required for transformation. But is truth found in time, or does it exist only in the now? A mind that depends on techniques becomes mechanical, repeating prescribed actions rather than acting from awareness. Real freedom is not found in following a method but in direct perception. Furthermore, every system is based on past experiences, traditions, or teachings—can something new be discovered through what is old? A mind caught in a system seeks results rather than seeing clearly, and true understanding does not arise from repetition but from deep, moment-to-moment attention. The search for a structured path itself may be an obstacle, as it diverts attention from the immediacy of awareness.

To live without methods and systems, one must see that no method leads to freedom. Freedom is not an achievement—it is the absence of conditioning. The moment one realizes that no system can bring truth, the search for structured approaches naturally ends. Real awareness does not come through practice or control but through choiceless observation. Can one watch thoughts, emotions, and life itself without imposing a technique? Transformation is not a matter of gradual progress but of perception—when time is no longer a factor, real change happens instantly. Right action does not require a structured path; it arises naturally from clarity. A mind that sees clearly does not follow—it moves with intelligence. Methods and systems offer security but not real understanding. Truth cannot be approached through repetition, practice, or step-by-step progress. A mind free from systems is not in chaos—it moves with deep intelligence and clarity. Where there is no method, there is no struggle—only direct perception, action, and freedom from all illusion.

51. Experience

Experience: The Past That Shapes the Present

Experience is the accumulation of past events, memories, sensations, and knowledge stored in the mind. It enables us to learn practical skills, navigate relationships, and function in the world. However, while experience is useful, does it bring true understanding, or does it limit perception? We define ourselves by our experiences, believing that our past shapes our identity— "I am this because I have been through that." But is identity anything more than a collection of memories? Experience also creates the illusion of knowledge, leading us to believe that because we have encountered something before, we fully understand it. Yet, can past experience ever reveal the totality of the present moment? Thought relies on experience to predict outcomes and make decisions, but can experience truly prepare us for the unknown, or does it only condition us to react based on the past? Many seek more experiences—through travel, relationships, or mystical pursuits—believing that accumulation leads to growth, yet does gathering more experiences lead to wisdom, or merely to more conditioning?

The limitations of experience become apparent when we see how it shapes perception. Experience is always from the past, recorded in memory and influencing future responses. Can we fully see something new if we look at it through the lens of past knowledge? Experience conditions the mind, shaping fears, beliefs, and habitual reactions, limiting the ability to perceive freshly. When we encounter a person, a place, or an idea, we interpret it through what we already know, rather than seeing it as it is. Many assume that wisdom naturally develops through time and experience, but wisdom is not the product of accumulation—it arises when the mind is free from conditioning. If we rely on experience alone, perception remains trapped in the past, never fully meeting the present.

To live without being shaped by experience, one must see that experience, while useful, is not the whole truth. It is necessary for practical life but does not necessarily bring understanding of oneself. Can we use experience without being imprisoned by it? Observing without the filter of the past allows for fresh perception—can one see a person, a tree, or a moment as if for the first time? The past can only repeat itself; it cannot reveal the new. Living in the present requires freedom from dependence on memory, as life is always unfolding now. Experience belongs to time, but direct awareness exists beyond it. True intelligence is not in accumulating experiences but in seeing without the distortion of memory. Where experience ends, perception is fresh—alive, limitless, and free.

52. Experiencing

Experiencing: The Living Moment Untouched by Memory

Experiencing is the direct contact with life as it unfolds, without distortion, without interpretation. It is not shaped by memory, thought, or analysis but occurs when one is fully present with 'what is.' True experiencing happens only when the mind is silent, observing without interference. However, we rarely experience life directly because the mind is conditioned to live in memory and thought. Instead of perceiving the present moment, we compare, recall past experiences, and filter reality through conditioning. For example, when looking at a sunset, instead of just seeing, thought intervenes—"This reminds me of another sunset" or "I must capture this moment"—preventing direct experience. We also experience life through labels, reducing everything to predefined meanings. The moment we name something, whether a tree, an emotion, or a person, we stop truly observing it. Furthermore, fear and desire distort our perception, making us see life not as it is but as we wish or fear it to be. Cultural, religious, and educational conditioning further filters our experience, shaping our responses rather than allowing for fresh perception.

True experiencing is free from the interference of the 'self'—the collection of memories, opinions, and desires that distorts reality. When one experiences without bringing in the 'self,' there is no division between the observer and the experience—only deep perception. Can one look at a flower, a face, or a moment without comparing it to past experiences? When one is completely present, experience is always fresh, always new. Similarly, emotions can be felt without psychological interpretation—sadness, for example, can be experienced without saying, "I am sad," without resistance or escape. In pure experiencing, emotion is simply energy moving through awareness, not something that turns into suffering. A mind conditioned to seek new experiences for pleasure or excitement often misses the richness of the present. Can one experience without wanting more, without chasing or escaping—just being fully with what is?

To experience life fully, one must observe without naming or comparing. The moment something is labeled, it is reduced to a concept rather than directly perceived. Seeing a tree, a face, or a cloud as if for the first time allows experience to remain fresh. True experiencing happens only in the present—not in the past, not in the future. When attention is total, there is no separate 'I' experiencing—there is only experience itself. Letting go of psychological time—where thought moves between past and future—allows for deeper awareness. Instead of holding onto pleasant experiences or avoiding painful ones, one can simply be with what is. A noisy mind, filled with thoughts, judgments, and expectations, cannot experience purely. In stillness, every sound, movement, and feeling is fully alive, without distortion. True experiencing is not through thought, memory, or desire—it is in full presence, without division. A mind free from labels, past conditioning, and future seeking is a mind that experiences life in its totality. In this state, there is no separate observer—only awareness, deep and limitless, where life is truly seen, felt, and understood.

53. Intuition

Intuition: The Immediate Perception Beyond Thought and Analysis

Intuition is the direct understanding of something without reliance on logic, analysis, or past experience. It arises from deep awareness, sensitivity, and a mind that is free from conditioning. A mind caught in intuition as a mystical ability seeks to develop it, while a mind that understands deeply sees it as natural, effortless perception. Thought is based on memory, calculation, and logic, while intuition sees immediately, without the need for reasoning. Many confuse intuition with emotional impulse or biological instinct, yet true intuition is beyond emotion and thought—it is pure perception. A restless mind, filled with opinions and conclusions, cannot be intuitive, for true intuition arises only when there is inner stillness. Thought moves in time—recalling the past, anticipating the future—whereas intuition exists only in the now, without reference to past knowledge. Many believe intuition is a personal gift, but it is not 'mine' or 'yours'—it arises when the mind is free from self-centered movement.

Society teaches that logic and reason are the only ways to know, yet deep insight is not found through analysis—it happens instantly. The mind seeks certainty, proof, and validation, but intuition is not provable—it simply is. Many mistake emotions for intuition, yet emotions are reactive, shaped by personal conditioning, whereas intuition is clear and detached. People hesitate to trust their intuition because it cannot be explained, yet truth is not always explainable—it is to be seen, not reasoned. Some seek techniques to 'increase' intuition, yet intuition is not cultivated—it is present when thought is quiet. The more one relies on thought, the less intuitive they become, for intuition functions naturally when perception is free from mental interference. Many think their desires are intuitive 'messages,' yet true intuition is not based on personal wants—it is neutral and clear.

When one is fully aware, intuition is already there—seeking to 'develop' it only strengthens mental effort. Intuition does not require validation, and trying to prove it weakens it. A mind that trusts its perception does not hesitate, nor does it filter through thought, for seeing without interpretation allows intuition to function naturally. A mind that seeks intuition makes it into a goal, blocking its natural flow. True intuition arises without effort, without expectation. Intuition is not a mystical gift or a skill to develop—it is the natural intelligence of a mind that sees without interference from thought. Many struggle with intuition because they depend on logic, seek certainty, or confuse it with emotion, but real intuition is not effort—it is the effortless movement of perception. A mind free from conditioning, hesitation, and mental noise does not try to be intuitive—it simply is, perceiving directly, without division, without delay. In this freedom, intuition is no longer something mysterious—it is the natural clarity of a mind that moves in the present, fully alive, fully aware, beyond thought, beyond doubt.

54. Innocence

Innocence: The Mind Unscarred by Time

Innocence is not ignorance, nor is it naïveté—it is the state of a mind unburdened by conditioning, untouched by psychological residue. It is the ability to see without distortion, to live without the weight of accumulated experience. True innocence is not something to be cultivated—it exists naturally when the mind is free. However, innocence is often lost as we accumulate knowledge, beliefs, and experiences that shape our perceptions. From childhood, we gather fears, conclusions, and memories that create mental patterns, preventing fresh observation. Psychological time further burdens the mind—past regrets and future anxieties take away the simplicity of direct experience. The ego, built through comparison and achievement, hardens the mind, making it self-centered rather than open. Society and culture impose ideas of morality, success, and identity, replacing spontaneous perception with conditioned responses.

The loss of innocence has profound effects. A mind that is not innocent becomes cynical and fearful, weighed down by disappointment and distrust. The freshness of perception is replaced by calculation and expectation. Society often mistakes innocence for weakness, valuing cleverness, ambition, and knowledge instead. But is true innocence a sign of ignorance, or does it indicate the highest form of intelligence? Without innocence, relationships are shaped by past hurts, fears, and attachments rather than genuine affection. A calculating mind approaches life through expectation, never truly open to love. Innocence allows for a direct relationship with life, free from the corruption of knowledge, comparison, and desire.

To live with innocence is to be free from psychological residue. Innocence is not about forgetting the past but about living without being shaped by it. When the mind lets go of conclusions, it meets life anew. True perception requires seeing without naming, listening without interpreting. Innocence exists only when the mind is not occupied with past and future, when it is completely present. A mind that is fully attentive, without seeking or resisting, is free. This innocence is not childish—it is the highest form of wisdom. Innocence is not the absence of knowledge but the absence of conditioning. A mind burdened with fear, ambition, and the need to become something is always in conflict—it cannot be innocent. True intelligence lies in this freedom, where perception is pure, unclouded by memory, belief, or comparison. In innocence, life is not a struggle—it is a constant movement of awareness, love, and beauty, untouched by time.

55. Wisdom

Wisdom: The Seeing That Comes Without Accumulation

Wisdom is not the accumulation of knowledge, nor the repetition of ideas—it is the ability to see life clearly, without distortion. It is intelligence that is free from belief, experience, and conditioning. Unlike knowledge, which is gathered over time and stored in memory, wisdom is not something to be acquired—it exists only in the present, when the mind is fully aware. Society often mistakes knowledge for wisdom because it values accumulation over perception. Education teaches us to gather facts, repeat theories, and rely on authority, but can wisdom exist in a mind that merely repeats what it has learned? The ego finds security in knowledge, believing that knowing more makes one wise, but wisdom is not in having answers—it is in the ability to see without illusion. Many mistake belief for understanding, accepting religious, political, or philosophical ideologies as truth. However, belief is secondhand—it is not direct perception. Thought, functioning through analysis and comparison, cannot grasp the whole of life. Wisdom, on the other hand, sees the totality of existence, beyond the limitations of thought.

The nature of true wisdom is the absence of psychological conflict. A wise mind does not struggle between 'what is' and 'what should be'—it sees without resistance, without division. Wisdom exists only in deep awareness, where the mind is fully present, not caught in past knowledge or future expectation. In this state of attention, action becomes natural, effortless, and intelligent. Wisdom is not found in authority or tradition—no teacher, book, or philosophy can give wisdom, as it must be discovered firsthand. Following another may bring comfort, but it will never bring wisdom. True wisdom is humility, not superiority—a wise person does not claim to know everything but remains open to seeing without bias. Wisdom is not about certainty but about the ability to question without seeking rigid conclusions.

To live with wisdom, one must question everything without rushing to conclusions. A wise mind does not seek fixed answers but simply observes deeply. The moment one seeks a conclusion, wisdom is lost. Awareness of thought and its limitations is essential—thought is useful in practical matters but cannot grasp the vastness of life. Can one use thought without being trapped by it? Wisdom arises when the mind is free from psychological fear, as fear distorts perception. A mind that does not cling to beliefs, identities, or ambitions remains open to truth. Understanding happens without effort—wisdom is not the result of struggle but comes naturally when the mind is silent and alert. A wise mind does not chase wisdom—it simply sees without distortion. True wisdom is not knowledge, belief, or authority— it is pure perception, free from conditioning. A wise mind does not struggle or cling but moves with clarity, openness, and deep intelligence. Wisdom cannot be pursued—it arises in a mind that is silent, free, and completely aware. In this state, there is no conflict, no confusion—only deep understanding, beyond words, beyond thought.

56. Technology

Technology: Progress Without Understanding?

Technology is the application of knowledge to create tools, systems, and machines that enhance human capabilities. It has transformed communication, medicine, transportation, and industry, reshaping the way we live. It has brought immense progress—improving efficiency, extending life expectancy, and connecting people across the globe. Machines have reduced physical labor, and instant access to information has revolutionized education, business, and decision-making. Social media has redefined relationships, activism, and cultural exchange. However, while technology has provided comfort and convenience, has it also created new forms of dependence and psychological conflict?

The impact of technology on the mind is profound. Constant reliance on devices weakens deep thinking, making the mind passive and dependent on instant answers rather than direct observation and understanding. Social media fosters the illusion of connection while increasing loneliness, replacing real relationships with virtual interactions. Overstimulation from endless entertainment and information overload keeps the mind restless, diminishing its ability to be silent, reflect, and observe deeply. Technology also fuels comparison and psychological insecurity, as people measure their worth based on online validation, likes, and digital success. This creates a mind trapped in seeking approval rather than understanding itself.

To use technology without becoming psychologically dependent, one must see it as a tool, not an escape. Technology is useful for practical life, but it cannot replace deep awareness and inner clarity. Can one engage with life directly rather than merely through virtual experiences? Nature, human connection, and direct observation hold more value than digital stimulation. Awareness of how technology shapes thought prevents unconscious conditioning—can one use technology without letting it dictate perception? When technology serves intelligence, it remains a tool; when it dominates awareness, it becomes a master. True freedom lies in understanding technology's role without becoming enslaved by it. A mind that sees clearly can use technology efficiently while remaining inwardly free, undistracted, and deeply aware.

WAKE UP

WAKE UP

3. Emotions & Feelings

WAKE UP

WAKE UP

57. Emotions

Emotions: The Movements That Shape Our Inner World

Emotions are responses of the mind and body, arising from thought, memory, and sensation. They include fear, anger, love, joy, sadness, jealousy, and attachment. Most emotions are conditioned reactions, shaped by past experiences, beliefs, and expectations. Thought triggers emotions by recalling past pleasure or pain, creating reactions based on memory. For example, hearing a familiar song may evoke joy or sadness, depending on past associations. Society and upbringing further condition emotions, teaching individuals what to feel and how to react. Certain emotions, such as ambition, are encouraged, while others, like doubt, are suppressed. Emotions create both attachment and conflict, as we cling to pleasurable emotions and avoid painful ones, leading to dependence on external conditions for happiness. Yet, emotions are always changing—no feeling is permanent, but thought continuously revives and sustains emotions, preventing them from naturally fading.

Suffering arises when one clings to or resists emotions. Attachment to positive emotions creates craving, as the mind desires love, pleasure, and happiness to last indefinitely. When these emotions fade, feelings of loss emerge, leading to an endless search for new sources of pleasure. Resistance to negative emotions, such as sadness, anger, and fear, further strengthens them. Suppression or avoidance does not eliminate emotions but keeps them alive in the subconscious. Moreover, emotions create the illusion of the 'self.' The 'I' is a collection of emotional experiences, and we identify with emotions—"I am sad, I am angry, I am happy." But who is this 'I' beyond these shifting emotions? Seeing this illusion is essential to breaking free from emotional turmoil.

Freedom from emotional turmoil does not mean the absence of emotions but the ability to observe them without identification. Instead of saying, "I am angry," one can observe, "There is anger," creating space between awareness and emotion, allowing it to pass naturally. Emotions should not be suppressed, justified, or indulged—simply watched as they arise and fade. The moment one stops controlling emotions, they lose their grip. Thought sustains emotions; a past insult may be over, but reliving it through thought revives anger or hurt. Recognizing this cycle naturally breaks emotional patterns. True freedom comes when happiness is not dependent on people, achievements, or experiences. A mind free from dependence feels deeply but is not controlled by emotions. Emotions are natural movements of thought and sensation, but they become suffering when clung to or resisted. A mind that sees emotions clearly, without reaction or distortion, lives with deep understanding, intelligence, and peace.

58. Feelings

Feelings: The Subtle Currents of the Mind and Heart

Feelings arise from the interaction of sensations, emotions, and thoughts. They include states such as joy, sorrow, love, anger, and fear, shaping our psychological landscape. Feelings in themselves are neither good nor bad—it is our relationship with them that determines whether they bring clarity or confusion. Feelings originate from sensation; a pleasant or unpleasant experience triggers a response in the brain, which thought then interprets, turning it into emotion. Thought sustains and amplifies feelings—when pleasure is experienced, thought remembers and desires its repetition; when pain occurs, thought creates fear and avoidance. The moment thought interferes, feelings lose their spontaneity and become conditioned responses, shaped by past experiences, memories, and psychological conditioning. Instead of perceiving situations as they are, we react through the filter of past emotions, preventing fresh understanding.

The problems arising from feelings stem from attachment, instability, and conflict. Emotional dependence makes us seek security and happiness through people, experiences, or beliefs, leading to fear of loss, jealousy, and attachment. When feelings dominate the mind, they create instability, making us reactive rather than aware, fluctuating between emotional highs and lows that distort perception. Additionally, we often mistake feelings for truth, assuming that our emotional reactions accurately reflect reality. However, feelings are shaped by thought and conditioning, and acting impulsively on them without understanding their nature leads to contradiction and regret. Feelings, though transient, are sustained by thought—clinging to pleasurable emotions and resisting painful ones creates suffering and psychological dependence.

To understand feelings without being controlled by them, one must observe without identification. Instead of saying, "I am sad," one can see sadness as a passing emotion, creating space between awareness and the feeling, preventing attachment. Neither suppressing nor indulging in feelings is necessary— suppression creates inner tension, while indulgence strengthens emotional dependence. Simply watching emotions arise and fade without reaction allows them to pass naturally. Recognizing how thought sustains feelings is key—the emotion itself is momentary, but thought prolongs it by revisiting past experiences or projecting future fears. When this is seen clearly, feelings lose their hold. Living fully in the present prevents emotions from gaining psychological weight—when one is fully attentive, emotions arise but do not create suffering. Feelings are natural but become problematic when thought interferes, creating attachment and inner conflict. A mind that understands feelings observes them with clarity, allowing them to pass without resistance. In this freedom, emotions exist without control or turmoil, and the mind moves with intelligence, love, and deep awareness.

59. Happiness

Happiness: The Fleeting Pursuit That Depends on Circumstance

Happiness is often seen as a state of pleasure, fulfillment, or satisfaction. But is happiness something to be achieved, or does it arise naturally when the mind is free? Most people seek happiness in external things—relationships, wealth, success—believing that fulfillment comes from accumulation or recognition. However, true happiness is not dependent on circumstances; it is not something to be pursued, but rather something that exists when the mind is no longer caught in struggle. The illusion of seeking happiness comes from mistaking it for pleasure. Pleasure is momentary and dependent on external stimuli, leading to desire for repetition, attachment, and eventual disappointment. Similarly, the pursuit of happiness through achievement creates an endless cycle of seeking—when one goal is reached, another desire emerges, preventing lasting contentment. Dependence on relationships for happiness also leads to attachment and fear, as one's well-being becomes tied to others. Many also seek happiness through escape—entertainment, religion, or distractions—but true happiness is not found in avoidance; it is found in deep self-understanding.

We remain unhappy because of desire and comparison. The mind is constantly measuring itself against others, creating dissatisfaction and preventing contentment. Attachment to things, people, or ideas brings fear of loss, leading to anxiety and suffering. Inner conflict further sustains unhappiness—when there is a division between "what is" and "what should be," the mind struggles, creating psychological tension. A mind in conflict cannot be happy—happiness exists in a state of inner harmony. True happiness is not a goal to be attained but a state that arises when the mind is free from struggle. The moment one pursues happiness as an objective, it becomes an idea rather than a reality. Happiness exists in awareness—when one fully lives in the present moment, without fear or expectation, happiness arises naturally. A mind that is free from comparison, desire, and attachment does not seek happiness—it simply is happy.

Living with happiness means ending the pursuit of it. The very act of chasing happiness creates frustration, as it turns happiness into an external objective rather than an inner state. Instead of seeking happiness, can one observe life fully, as it is, without resistance? Happiness exists only in the present—not in past memories or future hopes. When the mind is silent and fully aware, happiness is present. Comparison fuels discontent; letting go of comparison allows one to see life without judgment. Attachment also prevents happiness—depending on people, possessions, or beliefs for happiness creates fear and suffering. True happiness is found in freedom, not in holding on.

Happiness is not in pleasure, success, or relationships—it is in a mind free from conflict and attachment. When there is complete awareness, without struggle, happiness arises naturally. True happiness is not something to seek—it is what remains when the mind is silent, free, and fully present.

60. Joy

Joy: The Effortless State Beyond Desire

Joy is a state of effortless aliveness, free from dependence on external circumstances. It is not pleasure, excitement, or temporary happiness—it is a deep sense of wholeness and clarity. A mind in joy is not seeking, struggling, or escaping—it is simply present, completely alive. Unlike pleasure, which is based on memory and repetition, creating attachment and craving, joy is spontaneous and does not rely on past experiences or future expectations. Fear diminishes the ability to experience life fully, but when fear ceases, joy arises naturally, without effort. Society teaches that happiness comes from success, possessions, or recognition, but true joy has no cause—it is present when the mind is free. A mind caught in struggle, comparison, or ambition cannot know joy. When there is no division between 'what is' and 'what should be,' joy exists effortlessly. Joy is not something to be attained—it is revealed in deep attention to the present. A mind that is fully attentive sees beauty in the smallest moments.

We lose joy when we mistake it for excitement and pleasure. Excitement is temporary and followed by boredom or disappointment, while pleasure creates dependence, making the mind constantly seek more. Desire and ambition replace joy with struggle—the mind believes joy will come in the future through success or fulfillment, but this constant striving prevents the direct experience of joy in the present. Fear and worry block the natural flow of joy, as a fearful mind is preoccupied with security and control. Joy exists only in a mind that is free from psychological burdens. Society further conditions us to believe that happiness must be 'achieved' through wealth, status, or relationships, reinforcing dissatisfaction and making joy seem distant. When the mind seeks joy through external validation—relationships, possessions, or experiences—it becomes fragile, as anything dependent on external factors is temporary.

Living in joy does not require seeking it. Joy is not found through effort—it arises when seeking stops. A mind that is not chasing fulfillment finds joy in simply being. Joy exists when the mind is not caught in past regrets or future desires; in total awareness, there is a quiet sense of completeness. Psychological attachment creates dependency—the need for security, approval, or success prevents freedom. A free mind is joyful because it does not cling to anything. Joy is found in the movement of life—in a flower, a cloud, a moment of silence. When there is no urge to possess or hold onto an experience, joy flows naturally. It does not come from accumulation or achievement—it is simply there when the mind is open. A mind free from fear, conflict, and seeking knows joy without cause. Joy is not the pursuit of pleasure, achievement, or excitement—it is the effortless flow of life itself. When struggle and seeking end, joy arises naturally, without effort or cause. True joy is not personal—it is not 'my' joy or 'your' joy, but the vast energy of life itself. In this joy, there is no desire to hold onto anything—only a deep, unshakable sense of being completely alive.

61. Bliss

Bliss: The Silence That Is Beyond the Self

Bliss is often understood as a state of deep happiness, peace, or spiritual ecstasy. But is bliss just an intense form of pleasure, or is it something beyond all experience? True bliss is not the result of an external event or internal achievement—it is the state of a mind that is completely free. Many believe bliss comes from excitement, pleasure, or deep emotional satisfaction, yet all pleasure is temporary, needing repetition to sustain itself. People seek bliss to avoid pain, conflict, and emptiness, but is bliss something to be pursued, or does it come only when suffering ends naturally? Many associate bliss with meditation, rituals, prayer, or enlightenment, yet if bliss is a goal, is it not just another form of desire?

Any search for bliss creates conflict because the mind is always wanting more. When the mind stops chasing pleasure, stops fearing loss, there is a deep stillness—and in that stillness, bliss exists. True bliss is not a moment of happiness—it is the complete absence of conflict, of the 'self' that desires. A mind burdened with attachment, fear, or craving cannot know bliss, for bliss is not an experience but the absence of resistance. When there is no division within, there is effortless joy—beyond time, beyond thought. Bliss is not something to be remembered or achieved—it is only here, now. When the mind is completely still, not occupied with the past or future, there is bliss without seeking it.

The moment one seeks bliss, they have already moved away from it. Bliss exists only when the mind is not chasing an experience. Effort means struggle, and struggle prevents true bliss. When there is no inner resistance, when one is fully aware without desire, bliss is naturally present. If bliss is something one can "lose," then it was never real to begin with—it was just another form of pleasure. True bliss is untouched by gain or loss. It exists only when the mind is totally in the now, without carrying psychological burdens, without expectation, without clinging to experience. In this freedom, bliss is not something separate from life—it is life itself, untouched by desire, fear, or time.

62. Ecstasy

Ecstasy: The Momentary Dissolution of the 'I'

Ecstasy is not pleasure, excitement, or stimulation—it is the state of being completely free from psychological limitation. It is the dissolution of the 'self,' where there is no separation between the experiencer and the experience. A mind in ecstasy is in total harmony with life, without effort, struggle, or resistance. Unlike pleasure, which depends on repetition, attachment, and stimulation, ecstasy has no cause—it arises naturally when the mind is completely still. Thought functions in time, recalling the past and projecting the future, but ecstasy exists only in the now—outside the movement of psychological time. It occurs when there is no interference of thought, no fragmentation of perception. In this state, everything is seen as it is—without distortion, without expectation. A noisy mind seeking stimulation or excitement cannot experience ecstasy. It is not emotional intensity but the deep stillness where all resistance ends.

We rarely experience ecstasy because we mistake excitement for it. People chase thrills, pleasures, and sensations, believing they will lead to ecstasy. But excitement is temporary, while ecstasy is timeless. The moment one tries to achieve ecstasy, it becomes another object of desire. Ecstasy cannot be pursued—it happens when seeking stops. The 'self' clings to identity and memory, sustaining itself through attachment to the past and fear of the future. When identity dissolves, there is space for ecstasy to arise. Yet, we fear losing control—ecstasy is the total absence of effort and control. A mind conditioned to seek stability resists this state of complete surrender. Dependence on external stimuli for fulfillment also limits ecstasy. Many believe it will come through relationships, achievements, or spiritual practices. But true ecstasy is not caused by anything external—it is the natural state of a mind without division.

Living in ecstasy does not require seeking it. The moment one desires ecstasy, it becomes another object of pursuit. Freedom from desire is the beginning of true ecstasy. Holding onto beliefs, memories, and identities prevents the mind from being empty. When the mind is completely unburdened, ecstasy arises naturally. Thought moves between past and future, missing the intensity of the present. When the mind is fully attentive, ecstasy is the natural state. It is not excitement—it is the immense depth of a silent mind. When one is completely still, without effort, ecstasy is there. The ego is the barrier to ecstasy—it keeps the mind in conflict. When the 'self' is absent, there is only vastness, beauty, and an intensity beyond words. Ecstasy is not pleasure, excitement, or emotional intensity—it is the complete absence of psychological division. The mind seeking ecstasy through experience, thought, or stimulation only moves further from it. When the self dissolves—when there is no attachment, no resistance, no seeking—ecstasy is there effortlessly. A mind that is silent, whole, and fully present moves in ecstasy—not as a fleeting moment, but as a continuous state of deep freedom. In this freedom, life is no longer a struggle—it is a vast, undivided flow of beauty, intelligence, and complete awareness.

63. Calm

Calm: The Stillness That Comes from Understanding

Calm is the state of inner stillness, clarity, and freedom from agitation. It arises not through suppression or discipline but when the mind is free from conflict, fear, and psychological disturbance. A mind caught in calm as a practice tries to force stillness, while a mind that understands deeply is naturally at peace. Many believe calm means stopping thoughts, yet thought is natural—true calm exists when thought flows without resistance or struggle. People try to 'achieve' calm through meditation, control, or suppression, but effort itself creates tension, ensuring that real calm exists only when effort ceases. Relaxation techniques may bring momentary peace, but deep calm is not a practice. A truly calm mind remains still regardless of circumstances, fully present, without past regrets or future anxieties.

Society values excitement, ambition, and constant activity, making calm seem unnatural or unproductive. The mind resists reality, creating struggle, but true calm exists only when one accepts life as it is. Many force themselves to 'stay calm,' yet real calm is not about control—it is about letting go. Seeking calm while fearing failure, loss, or rejection keeps the mind in turbulence, for a free mind has no attachments. Some look for peace in environments, relationships, or rituals, but calm is not found externally—it is the natural state of an undisturbed mind. The more one seeks calm, the more it escapes them, for calm is not something to achieve but something to realize. A restless mind reacts, judges, and struggles, while a calm mind watches, listens, and moves without inner conflict.

Many try to control thoughts, people, and situations to feel calm, yet true calm comes from surrendering control, not strengthening it. Calm exists only now—not in the future, not in the past. A mind that does not chase or regret is always at peace. When one is not attached to results, there is no anxiety, and action becomes effortless. Calm is not about controlling the mind, silencing thought, or escaping from difficulty—it is the effortless stillness that exists when there is no psychological conflict. Many struggle with calm because they chase it as a goal, yet true calm cannot be sought—it is already present when one stops resisting life. A mind free from agitation, attachment, and fear does not 'practice' calm—it simply is, moving without struggle, thinking without conflict, and living without disturbance. In this freedom, calm is no longer something to achieve—it is the natural state of a mind that flows with life, without resistance, without effort, in complete peace.

64. Love

Love: Beyond Attachment, Desire, and Possession

Love is not attachment, possession, or desire—it is something beyond all definitions. Most of what we call love is based on expectation, security, or emotional dependence. True love exists only when there is complete freedom, without fear, without self-interest. We often mistake love for attachment, believing that if we hold onto someone tightly, we love them. But where there is attachment, there is fear—fear of losing, fear of change, fear of being alone. Love that is bound by fear is not love; it is dependency. Similarly, love is not desire or pleasure, which are products of thought and memory. If love is based on pleasure, does it not disappear when pleasure fades? Love is also not duty or responsibility—if love is forced by obligation, is it truly love or merely conditioning?

True love is complete freedom. It does not seek to possess, bind, or control. A mind that truly loves is deeply sensitive—not just to one person, but to all life. This sensitivity is not selective affection but a profound awareness of the interconnectedness of existence. Love is beyond thought, for thought is rooted in memory and conditioning. Love happens only when thought is silent—it is not a conclusion but a living reality. Love has no opposite. If love turns into hate, resentment, or indifference, was it ever love to begin with? True love does not change based on emotions or circumstances—it is not dependent on conditions.

To love truly, one must observe love without defining it. Do not measure or compare love—simply watch how you feel, react, and relate. In silent observation, love reveals itself. Love without seeking anything in return, without expecting approval, comfort, or emotional security. Love that asks for something in return is not love; it is a transaction. Let go of fear and attachment—love is not about holding on, but about giving freedom to yourself and others. Where there is jealousy, control, or need, love cannot exist. Love is only in the present—it is not in past memories or future hopes. When the mind is fully present, fully aware, love flows naturally. Love is not attachment, possession, or emotional craving—it is pure, free, and beyond thought. When the mind is silent, unafraid, and free from desire, love arises without effort. A life lived in love, without division, without expectation, is a life of deep beauty, compassion, and understanding.

65. Compassion

Compassion: The Flowering of True Understanding

Compassion is not merely kindness or sympathy—it is the deep awareness of suffering, both in oneself and in others, without division. It does not arise from duty, morality, or ideology but from direct perception. True compassion is not selective; it does not belong to one person or group but extends to all life. It is not a feeling of superiority, nor is it pity—it is the recognition that there is no separation between oneself and another. Compassion acts not because it is required, but because it is the natural response of a mind that understands suffering deeply. A truly compassionate mind does not seek approval or reward; it does not offer help to feel good about itself. It gives without expectation, without seeking recognition or gratitude.

Compassion is rare because the mind is self-centered, absorbed in its own desires, fears, and ambitions. Where there is self-interest, compassion cannot exist. Society conditions us to divide and compare, to see ourselves as separate based on nationality, religion, race, and belief. Where there is division, there cannot be true compassion. Fear also prevents deep connection—if one allows themselves to feel another's suffering fully, it might disturb their comfort, so they remain detached, offering sympathy without truly understanding. Compassion cannot exist where there is judgment—if one decides who 'deserves' compassion, it is no longer compassion but preference. True compassion has no conditions; it is not based on approval or agreement.

To live with compassion always, one must see suffering without resistance or escape. Instead of avoiding or ignoring suffering, can one look at it fully, without fear? When suffering is seen deeply, compassion arises naturally. Letting go of psychological barriers that divide people is also essential—when one no longer identifies with race, religion, nation, or ideology, compassion flows effortlessly. A mind preoccupied with itself—its ambitions, struggles, and achievements—cannot be compassionate. Can one live without the constant 'me' and 'mine'? Compassion also acts without expectation; it is not an obligation but action born from deep perception. Can one give, help, and love without seeking anything in return? Compassion is not sentimentality or duty—it is the natural flowering of a mind free from division and self-interest. A compassionate mind does not see others through labels—it acts from direct understanding. True compassion is not selective, not judgmental, not self-serving—it is boundless, effortless, and deeply alive. In that state of compassion, there is no 'self' left—only love, only deep action, only the wholeness of life.

66. Kindness

Kindness: The Simplicity That Needs No Reward

Kindness is the spontaneous movement of care, compassion, and understanding toward others. It is not merely an act of generosity but a state of being that arises naturally when there is no self-interest. A mind in kindness does not seek reward, recognition, or validation—it acts out of genuine affection and sensitivity. Many think kindness must be practiced, but forced kindness is not real kindness. True kindness arises naturally when the mind is free from selfish motives. It is not sentimentality; it does not mean being emotionally indulgent or merely pleasing others. Instead, it is rooted in deep understanding and intelligence. When one sees themselves as separate from others, kindness becomes selective. A mind that sees the interconnectedness of life moves in kindness without preference. It is not about being "good" in a moralistic sense; it is simply the absence of self-centeredness. A truly kind mind is not hardened by indifference or distracted by personal gain—it feels deeply but acts wisely, without sentiment or expectation.

We struggle to be kind because we are conditioned to be self-interested. Society teaches competition, ambition, and personal success over care for others, making kindness appear secondary or even weak. Many fear being taken advantage of, believing that others will exploit their generosity. But kindness is not naïve—it is discerning and free from manipulation. Some people are kind only when they expect something in return—praise, loyalty, or reward. This is not kindness but a transaction. A mind that is constantly occupied with its own struggles has little space for kindness. True kindness requires the ability to look beyond oneself. Moreover, many see kindness as a virtue to be cultivated, but when it is practiced as a moral duty, it becomes artificial. Real kindness flows naturally when there is no self-image to maintain.

To be kind without effort, one must see that kindness is not a practice but a state of being. When all self-centered motives drop away, kindness arises effortlessly. It is not something to be developed—it is what remains when the mind is free. True kindness does not expect gratitude or recognition. When one gives without seeking, there is no disappointment or attachment. Kindness flows naturally when one observes life without self-centered thought, seeing suffering, beauty, and struggle with open awareness. A truly kind mind does not have to "try" to be kind—it simply is. Kindness is often blocked by labels, judgments, and biases. When these barriers are dropped, kindness moves without effort. Many are kind to those they like but indifferent to others. True kindness is not selective—it is a response to life itself. Kindness is not a cultivated virtue or a moral obligation—it is the natural expression of a mind free from self-centeredness. Society conditions people to act with personal gain in mind, making real kindness rare. A truly kind mind does not seek recognition, does not act out of duty, and does not discriminate between whom to be kind to. When one sees beyond themselves, beyond psychological barriers and expectations, kindness is not something one must "do"—it simply flows, naturally and effortlessly, as an expression of deep awareness and intelligence.

67. Hope

Hope: The Comforting Illusion That Delays Seeing

Hope is the expectation that the future will bring something better, whether success, happiness, or inner peace. It is often seen as a source of motivation, but is it a real solution or just an escape from 'what is'? Thought creates hope as a way to avoid fully facing the present. When faced with pain, failure, or uncertainty, we turn to hope for psychological comfort, believing that relief will come in the future. But does hope resolve suffering, or does it only postpone its understanding? The mind is conditioned to believe that transformation happens through time—"One day I will be happy, successful, or enlightened." But can real change ever happen through the passage of time, or does it only occur in direct perception now? Hope also prevents direct action—when we rely on hope, we assume change will happen later, which delays real engagement with life as it is. Instead of seeing the truth of a situation, we look forward to something imagined, making hope a subtle form of escape.

The problems with hope lie in its attachment to time. It creates dependency on the future, making the mind live in anticipation, always waiting for something better. This prevents contentment in the present moment. Hope is often born from fear and dissatisfaction—when we hope, we are often afraid of facing things as they are. Instead of being fully with 'what is,' we escape into 'what could be.' Thought moves between past and future, seeking security in imagined outcomes, but is truth found in time, or only in the now? Hope also delays true understanding—rather than directly observing suffering, we project a future where suffering ends. But does avoidance ever bring real resolution? A mind that hopes is a mind that is waiting rather than acting, dreaming rather than perceiving.

To live without hope is not to live in despair, but to see that hope is an illusion. It is just another mental projection, not reality. When this is seen clearly, the need for hope dissolves naturally. Can one act fully, intelligently, without waiting for things to change? True action is immediate, not postponed. Hope looks to the future, but awareness is fully present. A mind in deep attention does not need hope—it sees, understands, and moves with clarity. Instead of hoping for a better life, can one engage fully with life as it is? True peace is found not in imagining a better version of reality but in meeting reality completely, without resistance. Hope is a projection of thought, an escape from facing the present fully. It prevents direct action, creates dependency, and strengthens psychological time. A mind that sees clearly does not need hope—it responds to life fully, without postponement. Where there is no hope, there is no despair—only clarity, intelligence, and freedom in the now.

68. Contentment

Contentment: The Deep Stillness That Comes With Understanding

Contentment is not the satisfaction of desire, but the absence of psychological craving. It arises when the mind is no longer in conflict, no longer seeking fulfillment in external achievements or possessions. A mind caught in contentment as an ideal tries to achieve it, while a mind that understands deeply is content naturally. Many seek contentment in possessions, relationships, or success, yet true contentment is not found through external means—it is the natural state of a mind free from want. A restless mind, caught in ambition, comparison, or dissatisfaction, cannot be content, for when one sees the futility of struggle, contentment emerges without effort. Some fear that contentment means complacency or lack of progress, but true contentment is a state of clarity, where action is not driven by fear or craving. If one seeks contentment as an escape from discontent, it remains a form of conflict. True contentment arises when one understands discontent fully, without resistance.

Society teaches that happiness comes from success, status, and possessions, reinforcing the belief that fulfillment is external. Yet true contentment is independent of circumstances—it is the state of a quiet mind. Many fear that without striving, life will lose meaning, believing that ambition and struggle give purpose, yet struggle only leads to exhaustion, while purpose arises naturally in a content mind. People mistake pleasure, comfort, or temporary satisfaction for contentment, yet pleasure is fleeting— contentment is unshaken by external conditions. The mind is always trying to become something—better, stronger, more knowledgeable—yet when one sees that there is nothing to become, contentment is already there. A mind that wishes for things to be different is always in conflict, while contentment arises when one sees without distortion, without expectation.

If one seeks contentment, it becomes another achievement to chase, yet a mind that stops seeking contentment is already content. When one looks at discontent deeply, without resistance, it dissolves, for contentment is not created—it is revealed when the mind is still. The belief that contentment depends on external success is an illusion, for a free mind is content whether in wealth or poverty, success or failure. The mind that compares itself with others or with an ideal is always dissatisfied, yet contentment is seeing life without measurement, without wanting more. Action that is done for personal gain leads to frustration, while a mind that acts without seeking is content in the very act of living. Contentment is not the result of achievement, accumulation, or effort—it is the natural state of a mind free from conflict and desire. Many struggle with contentment because they seek it as an ideal, pursue fulfillment in external things, or fear that without striving, life has no meaning. A mind that lets go of struggle, comparison, and psychological becoming does not need to seek contentment—it is already present, in the stillness of being. In this freedom, contentment is no longer something to attain—it is the effortless movement of a mind that is fully alive, completely aware, and deeply at peace.

69. Equanimity

Equanimity: The Deep Balance That Exists Beyond Disturbance

Equanimity is the state of inner balance, where neither pleasure nor pain, success nor failure, praise nor criticism disturbs the mind. It arises when one understands the impermanence of all things, letting go of attachment and resistance. A mind caught in equanimity as a practice tries to control emotions, while a mind that understands deeply moves without effort, undisturbed by circumstances. Many mistake equanimity for detachment or emotional numbness, yet true equanimity is full awareness without attachment or reaction. A restless mind is always torn between desire and fear, attachment and aversion, but when one sees that all experiences come and go, equanimity arises naturally. Most people react emotionally to situations, trying to control or resist them, yet a mind that accepts things as they are does not struggle—it moves in harmony with life.

People want to hold onto joy and avoid suffering, yet both pleasure and pain are fleeting—when one accepts this, equanimity arises. The conditioned mind reacts immediately to praise, criticism, gain, or loss, while a mind that watches without reaction remains steady in all situations. Many believe equanimity means 'doing nothing,' but true equanimity is not passivity—it is acting without psychological disturbance. Life is always changing, yet the mind tries to find permanent security in relationships, success, and possessions, reinforcing struggle. When one sees that nothing lasts, equanimity becomes natural. The mind divides experience into good and bad, success and failure, yet equanimity sees beyond these divisions, accepting life as a whole. The moment one lets go of resistance, balance comes effortlessly.

No situation, pleasure, or pain lasts forever—when one realizes this deeply, attachment and fear disappear. A mind that watches thought, emotion, and experience without labeling them remains undisturbed, for true equanimity exists when one no longer divides life into 'good' and 'bad.' Control is an illusion—things happen as they do, regardless of personal will. A mind that stops clinging to control finds deep peace. Anxiety about the future and regret over the past create disturbance, while equanimity exists only in the now, where thought does not divide experience. A person who works only for success is disturbed by failure, but when action is done without seeking reward, equanimity remains unshaken. Equanimity is not about suppression, avoidance, or passivity—it is the natural balance of a mind that sees clearly, without attachment or resistance. Many struggle with equanimity because they seek control, divide life into opposites, and attach to outcomes, yet true equanimity comes when one lets go of all mental divisions. In this freedom, equanimity is no longer a distant ideal—it is the effortless presence of a mind that moves through life without grasping, without resisting, in complete harmony with existence.

70. Desire

Desire: The Flame That Both Burns and Drives

Desire is the strong urge to attain, possess, or experience something. It arises from sensation, is intensified by thought, and leads to action. Desire itself is neither good nor bad, but when misunderstood, it creates conflict, attachment, and suffering. The cycle of desire begins with perception—seeing, hearing, or feeling something pleasurable. The mind registers this pleasure and thought creates an image of repeating the experience. This image intensifies into desire—the longing to have or re-experience pleasure. Desire is always seeking fulfillment, whether through success, recognition, love, wealth, or enlightenment, believing these will bring happiness. But fulfillment is momentary, and the cycle of wanting continues endlessly. Desire creates conflict—when we do not get what we desire, frustration, disappointment, or jealousy follows. Even when desires are fulfilled, fear of loss arises. The mind, driven by desire, is constantly seeking to 'become'—more successful, more spiritual, more powerful—creating an inner struggle between 'what is' and 'what should be.' Desire also strengthens the 'self'—the 'I' is constantly defined by what it desires, leading to attachment to identity, status, and possessions.

Is it possible to be free of desire? Many traditions teach suppression of desire, but this only leads to inner conflict. The key is not to resist desire but to observe it without identification. When one sees how thought creates desire—how memory projects an image of future pleasure—there is an understanding of its movement. Freedom from psychological desire does not mean rejecting all forms of wanting. Practical desires, such as the need for food and shelter, are necessary, but psychological desires—such as the craving for status or validation—create suffering. A mind that sees clearly does not chase illusions of fulfillment. Instead of acting from desire, one acts from intelligence and understanding.

Desire is born from sensation, sustained by thought, and leads to attachment. When misunderstood, it creates conflict, comparison, and suffering. Freedom from desire does not mean suppression but deep awareness of its movement, allowing action without psychological craving. A mind that is free from the endless pursuit of fulfillment does not seek security in pleasure, success, or recognition. It moves without conflict, without struggle, acting from clarity rather than from the restless movement of wanting. Where desire ends, there is deep stillness, a mind that is completely present, no longer caught in the illusion of becoming.

71. Desire and Conflict

Desire and Conflict: The Root of Inner Division

Desire is the movement of thought toward something it wants—whether it is pleasure, achievement, power, or fulfillment. It arises from sensation, memory, and imagination—seeing something, recalling past pleasure, and wanting to repeat or enhance it. Desire itself is not the problem—the conflict begins when desire is divided, resisted, or pursued without understanding. The mind often desires contradictory things at the same time—security and freedom, love and control, pleasure without consequences. This inner division creates struggle, indecision, and suffering. Desire also projects an ideal future ('what should be'), but reality ('what is') may not align with it. This gap between desire and reality leads to frustration, disappointment, and endless effort to 'become' something. The stronger the desire, the greater the fear of not achieving it. The mind clings to what it wants, fearing failure, loss, or imperfection. Comparison and competition arise from desire— seeing others who have what we long for creates jealousy, ambition, and the constant pressure to be 'better.'

Desire moves in a cycle: perception leads to sensation, which thought remembers and turns into desire. Once desire arises, it leads to pursuit, struggle, and potential frustration. If the desire is fulfilled, it only creates new cravings; if blocked, it leads to disappointment and inner conflict. Even when we achieve what we want, we fear losing it, turning pleasure into attachment and attachment into suffering. The pursuit of desire, rather than bringing true satisfaction, keeps the mind restless and divided between wanting and fearing loss. Can one be free from this cycle? Instead of resisting or blindly following desire, one can observe it without reaction. Pure observation allows desire to be seen clearly, without conflict. Every desire is a product of memory—of past experiences seeking repetition. When one sees this, desire loses its psychological grip.

True freedom is not in suppressing desire but in understanding it completely—so that the mind is not controlled by it. Every desire promises happiness, but once fulfilled, it only creates new cravings. Can one live without chasing fulfillment through external things? Physical needs such as food and shelter require action, but psychological desire creates unnecessary struggle. A mind that sees desire clearly, without attachment, acts intelligently—without inner conflict. When one watches desire without resistance or indulgence, it is no longer a source of suffering. A mind that is free from the illusions of desire does not seek happiness in becoming something else—it moves in the present, without struggle, without conflict, completely alive.

72. Passion

Passion: Energy Without Conflict or Contradiction

Passion is an intense energy, a deep fire that drives thought, action, and creativity. It is not mere enthusiasm or excitement but a total intensity of being in what one does. Passion can manifest in love, work, art, or the search for truth. Yet, passion is often misunderstood—many mistake it for desire, obsession, or pleasure. Desire is born from thought, seeking pleasure and fulfillment, while passion is not dependent on personal gain or satisfaction—it is pure energy. Passion flows freely, while obsession is self-centered and possessive. An obsessed mind clings to an idea, person, or goal, leading to suffering. Similarly, passion is not just for pleasure—most people associate it with romance, ambition, or excitement, but true passion exists in a mind that is intensely alive, not seeking escape or gratification.

The nature of true passion is rooted in total attention. When one is completely attentive, without distraction, passion arises—not towards something, but as a state of being fully alive. Passion exists only in freedom; a mind burdened with fear, ambition, or attachment cannot be passionate. Passion flourishes when one is free from psychological baggage. Without passion, love becomes routine, and learning becomes mechanical. True love and deep inquiry require passion without attachment. Passion is also beyond time—most passions are linked to past memories or future goals, but real passion exists in the present moment, without seeking continuity or achievement.

To awaken passion, one must observe without judgment. See how thought interferes, turning passion into desire or ambition—awareness of this process brings clarity. Letting go of psychological fear is essential, as fear blocks passion by creating hesitation and limitation. A fearless mind is naturally passionate about life. Being fully present in everything one does brings passion—not as a means to achieve something, but as an expression of deep attention. Passion that seeks validation is no longer true passion—it becomes ego-driven ambition. True passion burns from within, without expecting anything in return. Passion is the energy of complete attention, free from fear, ambition, or attachment. It is not about achieving but about being intensely alive in the present. A passionate life is one of freedom, creativity, and deep love, untouched by desire or self-interest.

73. Pleasure

Pleasure: The Mind's Endless Chase for More

Pleasure is the feeling of enjoyment, excitement, or satisfaction derived from sensory experiences, achievements, relationships, and memories. It is deeply connected to desire—the longing for repeated enjoyment. Whether through food, success, entertainment, or relationships, pleasure seems to complete us, yet it always leaves behind longing. The mind remembers pleasurable moments and desires their repetition, but pleasure is fleeting, never the same when sought again. Society teaches that happiness comes from achievements, possessions, and experiences, conditioning the mind to chase pleasure as a source of fulfillment. People believe pleasure equals happiness, yet is happiness merely the accumulation of pleasurable moments, or is there something deeper beyond this pursuit?

The more one seeks pleasure, the more one desires, creating a cycle of longing, excitement, and eventual disappointment. When pleasure fades, fear of losing it arises, and its absence creates loneliness, boredom, or frustration. Pleasure, whether physical or psychological, often turns into a craving, leading to dependence on external things for inner satisfaction. It is rooted in the past and future, either as the memory of enjoyment or the anticipation of future satisfaction. True joy, however, is only in the now, existing without dependence on experience. A mind caught in pleasure is constantly seeking, yet never truly content, always moving between moments of satisfaction and the fear of their loss.

Can one enjoy beauty, love, or success without clinging to it? The moment one seeks to hold onto pleasure, suffering begins.

Desire arises when memory recalls pleasure and wants it again, but can one watch this process without being caught in it? Joy is not the opposite of sorrow—it is the absence of psychological seeking. There is nothing wrong with experiencing pleasure, but can one let it pass without longing? A mind free from attachment to pleasure is also free from its inevitable pain. Pleasure is part of life, but when pursued, it turns into craving, dependence, and fear. True happiness is not in chasing pleasure, but in living fully, without the need for repetition or escape. In this freedom, there is joy without seeking, fulfillment without dependence.

74. Excitement

Excitement: The Momentary Escape from Emptiness

Excitement is the surge of energy that arises when the mind anticipates pleasure, success, or new experiences. It is often mistaken for joy, yet it is momentary and dependent on external triggers. A mind caught in excitement seeks to repeat the thrill, creating an endless cycle of stimulation and craving. When excitement fades, restlessness follows, leading to the search for the next moment of intensity. The pursuit of excitement is rarely about the experience itself—it is about the desire for something more, something greater. But can excitement ever bring lasting fulfillment, or is it always a temporary escape from the ordinary?

We believe excitement brings fulfillment, but is it not just temporary pleasure wrapped in anticipation? Excitement thrives on comparison—this experience must be better than the last, the next event must be more thrilling. This constant seeking prevents deep contentment, as the mind is always waiting for the next high. A mind that fears stillness fills itself with stimulation, avoiding the discomfort of silence. But is true aliveness found in endless highs, or in a mind that sees beauty in the ordinary? When excitement is seen for what it is—a momentary rush followed by inevitable decline—it loses its grip, revealing the possibility of a life lived with steady awareness rather than fleeting highs and lows.

To live without dependence on excitement is not to reject pleasure but to understand its transient nature. When one observes excitement without clinging to it, the mind is no longer enslaved by the need for constant stimulation. Awareness brings richness to every moment, without the need for extremes. There is great energy in living fully without chasing artificial intensity. True vitality is not in chasing excitement but in deep presence— where life is neither dull nor chaotic, but effortlessly alive. In this state, every moment holds meaning, not because it is thrilling, but because it is seen with complete attention, without the distortion of seeking.

75. Fear

Fear: The Shadow Cast by Time and Thought

Fear is the anticipation of pain, loss, or danger—whether real or imagined. It arises from past experiences, psychological conditioning, and the mind's constant search for security. A mind caught in fear reacts rather than sees clearly, avoiding, resisting, or fighting what it does not understand. Fear is deeply rooted in psychological time; the mind remembers past pain and projects it into the future, creating anxiety about what might happen rather than responding to what is. In immediate danger, the body reacts instinctively without fear, but psychological fear is different—it is a creation of thought, imagining future suffering. This fear drives avoidance or control, yet both responses only sustain fear rather than end it. The more one runs from fear, the stronger it becomes, shaping choices and actions unconsciously. Fear is also the root of conflict and division, as fear of the unknown fuels prejudice, insecurity, and attachment to authority and belief.

We live in fear because the mind seeks security in an ever-changing world. It clings to financial, emotional, and social stability, but life is uncertain, and this contradiction creates ongoing fear. Society further conditions us to fear failure and judgment, teaching that mistakes are shameful and that approval is necessary. Unfinished psychological pain also sustains fear—past betrayals, losses, and disappointments remain unresolved, projecting themselves into the future. Fear of the unknown, and ultimately of death, drives the mind to seek certainty through beliefs, traditions, and attachments. Many believe fear is necessary for survival, but while physical fear is a natural response to danger, psychological fear distorts perception. Intelligence functions best without fear—it sees danger clearly, without panic.

Freedom from fear begins with seeing it as thought, not reality. Most fears are not about the present but exist only in the mind. When one understands this, fear begins to lose its grip. Avoidance feeds fear, but facing it directly, without resistance, weakens its hold. The need for absolute security is an illusion—life is uncertain, and clinging to guarantees only increases fear. Recognizing that fear protects the ego—its image, attachments, and identity—allows for detachment from its influence. Fear exists in imagined futures, shaped by past experiences; a mind fully in the present is free from its burden. Fear is not ended by suppression or escape but by direct understanding. A mind free from fear does not seek safety in illusions—it moves with life effortlessly, without hesitation, without division, and without the shadow of fear shaping its path.

76. Anger

Anger: The Fire That Burns the Mind and the World

Anger is a sudden surge of intense energy, triggered by frustration, hurt, fear, or opposition. It arises when desires are blocked, expectations are unmet, or when one feels insulted or attacked. Anger is not limited to physical aggression; it also manifests as irritation, resentment, or silent hostility. The root of anger lies in the self—the ego—which reacts when it feels threatened, criticized, or challenged. To protect its identity, beliefs, and attachments, the mind forcefully defends itself. Unfulfilled desires and expectations further fuel anger, as we demand that people, situations, and life conform to our wishes. Beneath anger often lies fear—fear of loss, rejection, failure, or insecurity. Instead of acknowledging these vulnerabilities, the mind masks them with aggression. Anger is also a conditioned response; from childhood, we learn that anger is a means of asserting dominance, control, or authority, reinforcing the habit through social conditioning.

The consequences of anger are deeply disruptive. It creates conflict and division, damaging relationships and strengthening the ego's hold over the mind. A mind consumed by anger loses clarity and reacts impulsively, unable to see truth clearly.

Perception becomes distorted, leading to actions based on emotional blindness rather than understanding. Anger, when repeated, becomes habitual—each reaction deepens the conditioning, making even minor inconveniences trigger irritation. This pattern drains energy, harms the body, and disturbs inner peace, releasing stress hormones and keeping the body in a constant state of tension. The destructive nature of anger extends beyond the self, spreading disharmony and division in relationships and society.

To be free from anger, one must observe it without suppression or justification. Suppressing anger does not remove it, and justifying it only reinforces the pattern. Instead, can one simply watch anger as it arises—seeing how it begins, what it feeds on, and how it fades? Understanding that the 'I' that feels anger is merely a conditioned response weakens its grip. Who is actually angry? Is it not just thought reacting to a challenge? Most people either justify anger or feel guilty for it, but neither approach dissolves it—only deep awareness of its cause allows it to end naturally. Letting go of psychological attachments that create anger—expectations, identities, and beliefs—removes its foundation. A mind that is unattached, free from defensiveness, and unburdened by the past has no reason for anger. In deep inner stillness, anger does not arise, for there is no 'self' to defend, no image to protect. When one lives with total awareness, anger fades—not through control, but through complete understanding. Anger is a conditioned response of the mind, born out of fear, attachment, and ego. A mind that sees anger without resistance is free from its hold—such a mind is silent, clear, and acts from intelligence, not reaction.

77. Hate

Hate: The Deepest Division Created by the Self

Hate is intense aversion, hostility, or resentment toward a person, group, or idea. It arises from fear, hurt, anger, or deep conditioning that strengthens division. More than just an emotion, hate is a form of psychological blindness that distorts perception, making it impossible to see reality as it is. Hate is born from fear and insecurity—when something threatens our beliefs, identity, or sense of security, the mind reacts with resistance and hostility. Often, hate emerges from a sense of powerlessness or vulnerability, creating an illusion of control. Hate is also strengthened by division, as we categorize people by nationality, race, religion, or ideology. Where there is division, there is conflict, and from this conflict, hate arises. Furthermore, hate is fueled by the past; memories of pain, betrayal, or injustice shape our perception of others. But can hate exist if one does not carry the past into the present? Hate also provides a false sense of strength and identity, making one feel justified or superior. Yet, does hate truly make one strong, or does it imprison the mind in conflict and illusion?

The consequences of hate are destructive, both inwardly and outwardly. Hate destroys clarity and understanding—a mind filled with hate cannot see things as they are, as perception is clouded by emotion. Hate creates inner and outer violence, not only in action but also in thought, leading to suffering, aggression, and further division. The ego thrives on opposition— "I am against this, therefore I exist." Hate strengthens the illusion of the 'self,' reinforcing separation from others. However, is the self anything more than a collection of thoughts, memories, and conditioning? Hate also perpetuates a cycle of destruction—one act of hate leads to retaliation, which fuels more hate, continuing endlessly unless broken through deep understanding.

To be free from hate, one must see it without justifying or suppressing it. Instead of acting on hate, can one simply observe it without reaction? The moment one sees hate as it is, without identification, its power weakens. Letting go of the past is essential, as hate often stems from carrying past pain into the present. Can one live without resentment, without allowing memory to shape perception? Hate is a reaction, not reality—when one hates, one sees only what one wants to see, not the whole truth. Stepping back and observing without the filter of hate brings clarity. Where there is deep understanding, hate cannot exist—it survives only in a mind that is unconscious of its own conditioning. A mind that sees deeply, understands fully, and is free from division has no room for hate. Hate is not strength but distortion, blinding the mind and imprisoning the heart. True freedom does not come from suppressing hate but from understanding its roots and dissolving it through awareness. A mind free from hate sees clearly, acts without violence, and moves with deep intelligence and compassion.

78. Anxiety

Anxiety: The Restlessness Born of Psychological Time

Anxiety is the restless movement of thought projecting fear into the future. It arises when the mind anticipates uncertainty, failure, or danger, creating inner tension. A mind caught in anxiety is trapped in psychological time, unable to stay fully present. Fear of the unknown drives anxiety, as the mind seeks security by trying to predict and control the future. However, because the future is always uncertain, this resistance only deepens anxiety. Thought sustains anxiety by creating imagined scenarios, worrying about 'what might happen,' rather than engaging with reality as it is. Desire and comparison further fuel anxiety—the pursuit of success, approval, or security creates tension about the future, while comparison with others reinforces the fear of failure or inadequacy. Anxiety manifests both psychologically and physically, creating stress, restlessness, and bodily discomfort. When fear shapes perception, it clouds judgment, paralyzes action, and leads to impulsive decisions based on insecurity.

We live in anxiety because we depend on the future for happiness. The belief that success or security lies ahead creates worry about achieving it, making the present feel inadequate. Society conditions us to seek stability in careers, relationships, and status, yet nothing in life is permanent—clinging to external security breeds anxiety. Thought, functioning through prediction and fear, anticipates danger even when no immediate threat exists, creating psychological fear. Past experiences of failure or loss reinforce anxiety, as the mind projects past suffering into the future. The mind resists uncertainty instead of seeing it clearly, further intensifying anxiety. Instead of accepting that life is unpredictable, we try to control it, and this struggle generates ongoing worry.

Freedom from anxiety comes not through suppression or control but through understanding. Anxiety is thought, not reality—most fears are projections, not actual threats. Seeing this weakens their grip. Avoidance sustains fear, but when one observes anxiety without resisting it, its power diminishes. The need for absolute security is an illusion—when one stops seeking guarantees in an ever-changing world, the mind becomes free from fear. Psychological dependence on the future must end—happiness is not in what 'might be' but in fully engaging with the present. Anxiety exists when thought clings to past regrets or future worries, but a mind that is completely present has no space for fear. Thought creates time by linking the past to the future, sustaining anxiety. When one stops living in psychological time, anxiety dissolves naturally. Anxiety is not ended by control but by deep awareness. A mind free from anxiety moves with life effortlessly, without hesitation, without conflict. In this awareness, there is no fear—only deep clarity, intelligence, and complete freedom from psychological suffering.

79. Depression

Depression: The Weight of the Past That Clouds the Present

Depression is a psychological state of sorrow, despair, and emptiness that arises from unresolved emotional pain, prolonged disappointment, or a sense of meaninglessness. It traps the mind in the past, preventing it from fully embracing the unfolding present. The nature of depression lies in the accumulation of past pain, where grief, loss, or loneliness are stored, creating a burden that drains the mind and reinforces hopelessness. Depression often manifests through repetitive thought patterns, where the mind continuously revisits past regrets and disappointments, preventing fresh perception and deepening the sense of isolation.

The reasons we sink into depression are complex and rooted in our attachment to past pain and our false search for meaning through external achievements. Society teaches us that fulfillment comes through success, relationships, and desires; when these fall short, we fall into despair, feeling life has no purpose. Depression creates a sense of separation from life and others, amplifying the feeling of being trapped in one's own suffering. Thought processes further fuel this hopelessness, reinforcing the belief that change is impossible. Depression is often perpetuated by resistance to the present, with a longing for the past or hope for the future, which prevents one from fully experiencing and accepting the present moment.

Freedom from depression is not found in suppression or distraction, but in observing the depression itself without judgment or resistance. When one understands that depression is merely thought sustaining past sorrow, it begins to lose its power. Letting go of psychological time, which keeps one trapped in the cycle of past regret and future fear, naturally dissolves depression. True freedom comes from stopping the identification with sorrow, recognizing that depression is not who one truly is. A mind that is fully engaged with life, without seeking an escape or waiting for happiness to return, allows energy and clarity to naturally emerge. In this deep understanding, depression dissolves, and the mind moves freely with life.

80. Frustration

Frustration: The Mind's Struggle Against 'What Is'

Frustration is the psychological resistance that arises when reality does not align with expectation. It is a form of inner tension, a struggle between desire and the limitations imposed by circumstances. The stronger the expectation, the greater the intensity of frustration. The mind desires success, recognition, comfort, or change, but when obstacles arise, resistance builds, leading to irritation, restlessness, and psychological discomfort. Frustration intensifies when one is emotionally attached to an outcome and cannot accept uncertainty. Comparison further strengthens frustration—seeing others achieve what we desire creates feelings of inadequacy. Time also plays a role in frustration, as we impose expectations on how quickly change or achievement should occur. When those expectations are not met, frustration deepens.

The impact of frustration is significant. It clouds clear thinking, making the mind reactive rather than responsive. When frustration dominates, patience and clarity are lost. Some react with aggression, expressing irritation and anger, while others withdraw into passivity or self-pity. Both responses create further inner disturbance. Frustration also generates psychological resistance—the more we fight against it, the more it intensifies. Struggle itself feeds the very problem we wish to dissolve. The mind, caught in frustration, wastes energy, losing focus and balance. Instead of acting with intelligence, it reacts impulsively, reinforcing a cycle of conflict between expectation and reality.

Freedom from frustration is possible when one sees its movement clearly. Awareness of how frustration arises naturally weakens its grip. Instead of resisting frustration, can one observe it without reaction? The mind projects a timeline for success, growth, or change, but when time is no longer a burden, frustration loses its fuel. When action is performed without obsession over results, there is freedom. Can one act fully, without demanding a particular end? A mind free from measuring progress is also free from frustration. Seeing life without the lens of 'better' or 'worse' brings inner ease. Frustration is the result of unfulfilled desire, comparison, and psychological time. A mind that sees its own expectations clearly, without resistance, dissolves frustration naturally. True intelligence acts without struggle, moves without attachment, and exists without the conflict of expectation. Where frustration ends, there is effortless action, deep attention, and complete harmony with life as it is.

81. Grief

Grief: The Pain of Holding on to What Is Gone

Grief is the deep sorrow felt when we lose someone or something we are attached to. It is a reaction to loss, separation, or the realization of impermanence. Grief is not limited to death—it arises when a relationship ends, dreams are broken, or when one feels deeply empty inside. At its core, grief is born from attachment; we hold onto people, memories, and identities for a sense of security. When they are lost, grief arises because we feel that a part of ourselves is missing. However, grief is not sustained by the actual loss but by thought, which continuously replays memories and reinforces sorrow. The mind clings to what was, keeping the pain alive. In grief, one often feels isolated, believing that no one else can fully understand their suffering. This sense of isolation intensifies sorrow, making it difficult to move forward. The fear of letting go also sustains grief—one may believe that moving beyond sorrow means forgetting the one they lost. Yet, love is not in holding on to the past but in understanding the present.

People often handle grief through resistance, escape, or seeking comfort. Some suppress their sorrow, pretending to be strong, but this only buries grief deeper, leading to long-term emotional pain. Others seek distractions—work, entertainment, religion, or substances—to avoid confronting their feelings. However, grief does not disappear; it lingers in the background. Many turn to others for reassurance and consolation, hoping external support will heal them. While comfort can provide temporary relief, no external source can fully remove inner sorrow—it must be understood directly. True healing does not come from avoiding grief but from facing it completely.

To be free from grief, one must observe it without resistance. Instead of escaping, can one simply watch grief as it arises, without suppressing, justifying, or fighting it? The pain of loss is real, but suffering is caused by thought clinging to memory. Seeing this clearly loosens the grip of sorrow. Grief is tied to what was, but life is happening now—when one fully understands the impermanence of all things, suffering dissolves. The fear of letting go is an illusion; love does not exist in memory but as a living reality when the mind is free from sorrow. True healing happens not by forgetting but by seeing deeply, without holding on—allowing love and understanding to remain. Grief is not just pain; it is attachment to the past, sustained by thought. Instead of resisting or escaping, one must observe grief without judgment. In this awareness, sorrow dissolves, and in its place, there is clarity, love, and the deep freedom of understanding.

82. Empathy

Empathy: The Deep Understanding That Transcends the Self

Empathy is the ability to perceive, feel, and understand the emotions of another without distortion, judgment, or self-interest. It arises naturally when the mind is free from ego, comparison, and the desire to impose its own views. A mind caught in empathy as an obligation tries to sympathize, while a mind that understands deeply connects without effort. Many mistake empathy for feeling sorry for someone, yet true empathy is not looking down—it is feeling with, without superiority. When one sees others as separate, understanding is limited, but true empathy arises when the 'self' does not interfere with perception. A mind that judges cannot truly empathize, for it filters others through its own biases. When one sees without opinion, empathy flows naturally, allowing perception beyond thought and reaction.

Society teaches individual success over deep connection, reinforcing the habit of prioritizing the self. A mind focused on 'me' cannot fully understand 'you.' Instead of listening, people project their own emotions onto others, distorting perception. True empathy means seeing without personal bias, not filtering another's experience through one's own. Many avoid empathy because it requires openness, yet real understanding only happens when there is no fear of feeling. Knowing about suffering is not the same as truly feeling another's pain, for true empathy is not intellectual—it is a direct, felt perception. People rush to offer solutions rather than simply listen, but a truly empathetic mind does not try to change—it simply understands, allowing space for connection without force or control.

When ego, judgment, and personal projection fall away, empathy happens naturally. True empathy does not think while listening—it is fully present, without preparing a response. Many intervene out of self-interest rather than true care, but a mind that listens without controlling is deeply empathetic. The moment one labels someone—'weak,' 'wrong,' 'ignorant'—empathy disappears, for seeing without labels brings pure understanding. Empathy is not about becoming overwhelmed by another's pain—it is understanding without being consumed. Many struggle with empathy because they impose their own judgments, fears, and desires onto others, but true empathy comes from awareness, not effort. A mind free from ego, self-projection, and control does not try to be empathetic—it simply understands, without resistance, without barriers. In this freedom, empathy is no longer a technique—it is the effortless connection that arises when one sees life without separation, without fear, in total presence.

83. Sadness

Sadness: The Unspoken Loneliness of the Heart

Sadness is the emotional response to loss, disappointment, or unfulfilled expectations. It arises when the mind clings to something—people, experiences, dreams—and that attachment is broken. A mind caught in sadness resists reality, while a mind that understands sadness moves through it without suffering. When one loses what they love or what they hoped for, sadness arises, yet life is always changing—attachment to what was creates sorrow. The mind compares the past with the present, longing for what was, but when one lives fully in the present, sadness has no place to take root. When one tries to escape sadness or suppress it, it persists, for true healing comes not from avoiding sadness but from understanding it completely. People identify with relationships, success, and dreams—when these are lost, sadness arises, yet identity is fluid, not fixed, and seeing this releases suffering.

The mind wants permanence in a world that is constantly changing, yet when one sees that nothing can be held forever, sadness loses its grip. People seek happiness in relationships, success, and possessions, yet when these are lost, sadness follows—but was the security ever real? Many distract themselves from sadness through entertainment, work, or avoidance, yet true freedom from sadness comes not by running away but by looking at it directly. The mind remembers joy and longs for it to return, yet longing for what was prevents one from seeing what is. One says, 'I am sad,' as though sadness is part of their identity, but sadness is just a passing emotion, not 'you.' Emotions pass like clouds, but when one holds onto sadness, it becomes heavy, while allowing it to flow without resistance lets it dissolve naturally.

Many want to 'fix' sadness, but emotions are not problems— they are passing movements, and when one does not fight sadness, it does not turn into suffering. Sadness is often about what was or what could have been, yet a mind that stays in the present does not cling to emotional pain. Instead of saying, 'I am sad,' simply see that sadness is present—this space between the observer and emotion allows sadness to fade naturally. Many hide from sadness, fearing its depth, but when one experiences it completely, without running, sadness passes like a wave. Life is movement—what was, is gone. When one flows with change instead of resisting it, sadness loses its power. Sadness arises from loss, attachment, and comparison, but it becomes suffering only when one clings to it. Many struggle with sadness because they resist it, escape from it, or make it part of their identity. True freedom from sadness is not suppression—it is complete awareness of it, without resistance, without personal attachment. A mind that does not hold onto the past, does not fight emotions, and does not seek permanence in an impermanent world does not suffer from sadness—it experiences it, allows it, and moves beyond it naturally, in deep understanding, in complete freedom.

84. Sorrow

Sorrow: The Deepest Wound of Humanity

Sorrow is deep psychological pain caused by loss, disappointment, loneliness, or the realization of life's impermanence. It is not merely a personal experience—it is universal, woven into the fabric of human existence. Everyone encounters sorrow through death, failure, rejection, and the suffering of the world. The loss of loved ones creates a deep sense of emptiness, as the mind clings to the past and resists facing life without them. Unfulfilled desires and expectations bring sorrow when life does not unfold as imagined. We seek happiness through people, achievements, and possessions, and when these fail, suffering follows. Loneliness and isolation deepen sorrow, making one feel disconnected, even within relationships. There is also sorrow in witnessing the suffering of humanity—seeing injustice, poverty, war, and cruelty reminds us that pain is not just individual but collective.

Sorrow continues because thought sustains it. The actual moment of loss is brief, but thought revives it by replaying memories, regrets, and what-ifs. The mind clings to sorrow, reinforcing its hold. The desire to escape from sorrow only prolongs it—through entertainment, religion, or distractions, one tries to avoid facing pain, but sorrow remains beneath the surface. Attachment to the past further strengthens sorrow; when the mind resists change, suffering deepens. Instead of allowing life to flow, we hold onto what was, creating an ongoing struggle between reality and desire.

To be free from sorrow, one must observe it without resistance. Instead of suppressing or analyzing it, can one simply watch sorrow as it arises, without trying to change or escape it? True understanding happens only when sorrow is faced fully. Sorrow exists because of attachment to the "I"—the self that wants, fears, and clings. When one deeply understands that the ego is an illusion sustained by thought, sorrow loses its grip. Living fully in the present is key—sorrow exists in psychological time, through regret of the past or fear of the future. When one is completely present, sorrow has no space to take root. Love, when free from attachment, does not bring sorrow. True love is not possession or dependency; it is freedom. Where there is freedom, sorrow does not exist. Sorrow is not just personal; it is the sorrow of all humanity. Instead of escaping from it, one must observe it deeply—only then can it dissolve. A mind free from attachment, fear, and psychological time is free from sorrow. In this freedom, life moves in deep understanding, love, and peace.

85. Hurt

Hurt: The Scars Left by Memory and Experience

Psychological hurt is the pain caused by words, actions, rejection, failure, or loss. It leaves emotional scars, shaping how we think, act, and relate to others. Many of us carry past hurts, allowing them to influence our present relationships—reacting not to what is happening now, but from wounds that remain unhealed. Hurt arises from insults, rejection, and betrayal—when someone criticizes, ignores, or wounds us, the mind records these experiences and replays them, deepening the pain. Expectations and attachments also create hurt—when we seek love, recognition, or respect and they are denied, we feel wounded. The stronger the attachment, the deeper the wound. Comparison and failure further reinforce hurt; when we measure ourselves against others and fall short, feelings of inadequacy emerge. Many of these hurts originate in childhood—parental neglect, school humiliation, or broken relationships shape our self-image, creating lifelong insecurities.

Hurt remains in the mind because thought sustains it. The actual moment of pain is brief, but thought continues to remember and revive it. The mind holds onto past insults, betrayals, and failures, carrying them into the present. Hurt also strengthens the ego—the 'self' is built from experiences, including pain, and holding onto hurt gives the ego a sense of identity, even if it causes suffering. Fear of being hurt again reinforces emotional walls—past wounds create defensiveness, making us cautious in relationships and afraid of future pain. This fear prevents openness, trust, and real connection, keeping the cycle of hurt alive.

To be free from hurt, one must observe pain without identifying with it. Can one see hurt as a movement of thought rather than as "my" pain? The moment one separates from the emotion and simply observes, it begins to dissolve. Hurt is sustained by memory—every time we recall an old wound, we give it new life. Seeing how memory feeds suffering, one can break the habit of replaying past pain. Psychological defenses only reinforce suffering; when we build walls to protect ourselves from pain, we also shut out love and connection. True healing happens when one can be open and vulnerable without fear. Most importantly, one must see that the 'self' that is hurt is an illusion—who is actually hurt? The 'I' that feels wounded is merely a collection of past experiences and self-images. When one sees through the illusion of the ego, there is no one left to be hurt. Hurt is not just an experience but a psychological pattern maintained by thought. When one stops identifying with pain, it naturally fades. Freedom from hurt does not come from avoidance or suppression but from total understanding and awareness. In this clarity, hurt no longer controls the mind, allowing life to be lived with openness, trust, and peace.

86. Loneliness

Loneliness: The Isolation Created by the Ego

Loneliness is a deep psychological feeling of isolation, emptiness, and incompleteness. It is not merely the absence of company—one can be alone without feeling lonely, just as one can be surrounded by people and still experience profound isolation. Loneliness arises when there is a sense of separation between oneself and others, between what one is and what one desires to be. It is rooted in the search for fulfillment through external means—relationships, friendships, social status, and recognition. When these attachments weaken or end, a void is felt, creating a sense of abandonment and incompleteness. Thought reinforces loneliness by creating the idea of a separate self—an 'I' distinct from others, seeking security and belonging. This division between 'me' and 'the world' leads to conflict, fear, and ultimately, loneliness. Dependence on external validation further deepens this feeling—when approval and success are absent, the mind is left facing its own insecurities. Living in the past or future rather than fully engaging with the present also sustains loneliness, as one clings to memories of past relationships or dreams of future companionship, never truly being here, now.

In response to loneliness, people seek various forms of escape. Some look to relationships to fill the void, believing that companionship will remove loneliness. However, when relationships are based on fear of isolation, they become attachments rather than genuine connections. Others turn to distractions—entertainment, work, social media, or travel—keeping themselves occupied to avoid facing inner emptiness. These activities provide temporary relief, but loneliness remains beneath the surface. Many seek comfort in belief systems—religion, ideology, or spiritual communities—hoping to find meaning and connection. Yet belief, while reassuring, does not free one from loneliness; it merely offers psychological security. True freedom from loneliness does not come from external solutions—it requires deep self-understanding.

To be free from loneliness, one must stop escaping and begin to observe it directly. Instead of running from loneliness, can one face it without judgment, without fear? The moment one fully encounters loneliness without resistance, its grip begins to dissolve. Loneliness exists because we perceive ourselves as separate entities, distinct from the whole. But is this 'self' real, or is it merely a bundle of thoughts, memories, and identifications? When one sees that there is no fixed 'I', loneliness fades, replaced by a deep sense of wholeness. Living fully in the present is also key—loneliness is sustained by the mind's movement between past regrets and future hopes. A mind that is completely present, fully attentive, knows no loneliness—because it is not divided. Loneliness is the pain of separation, but aloneness is the freedom to be completely with oneself, without fear, without dependence. In aloneness, there is silence, beauty, and a deep connection with life. Loneliness exists when we seek fulfillment through others, when we escape from ourselves, and when we live in division. True freedom from loneliness comes not from relationships, distractions, or beliefs but from understanding the nature of the self and being completely present. A mind that embraces aloneness, without fear, without attachment, is never lonely—it is whole, free, and in deep communion with life itself.

87. Stress

Stress: The Mind's Resistance to Pressure and Change

Stress is the psychological and physiological tension that arises when the mind is in conflict. It occurs when there is a gap between 'what is' and 'what one desires, expects, or fears.' A mind caught in stress is burdened by pressure, resistance, and the constant struggle to achieve, avoid, or control. The mind feels pressure when it is torn between desire and reality, creating inner conflict that leads to mental and physical strain. Stress arises from the fear of failure, the pressure of meeting expectations, and the insecurity of not being enough. Society conditions individuals to compete, compare, and strive for success, reinforcing stress as a natural response. A mind that resists reality creates friction, and this friction manifests as stress, preventing the free flow of energy.

The overactivity of thought sustains stress, as the mind constantly anticipates, plans, and worries about the future. Thought projects fear into the unknown, making the present moment unbearable. The mind seeks psychological security in an unpredictable world, yet clinging to stability only leads to anxiety. Society glorifies struggle, making stress seem necessary for success, but in reality, stress limits intelligence and clarity. Most stress does not come from real threats but from imagined scenarios created by thought. The desire to control outcomes, people, and situations further amplifies stress, yet life remains uncertain. Stress exists when thought is trapped in past regrets or future worries, for a mind fully in the present has no space for tension.

Can one see that stress is created by thought? The moment one recognizes stress as a mental construction, its grip weakens. Stress thrives on comparison and expectation, yet a mind that does not measure itself against others is free from unnecessary burden. Work can be done with clarity rather than stress—when action is not tied to fear, it becomes effortless. A mind that is fully present does not worry about future results, and when one acts with complete attention, stress disappears naturally. Letting go of the illusion of control brings inner peace, for not everything can be controlled, and life remains uncertain. Stress is not a necessary part of life—it is a conflict created by thought, fear, and the pressure to achieve. A mind free from stress does not struggle with 'what should be'—it moves effortlessly with 'what is.' In this state of awareness, action is not forced—it flows naturally, without tension, without resistance, and without stress.

88. Tensions

Tensions: The Inner Conflict Between Expectation and Reality

Tensions are the psychological and physical states of strain caused by inner conflict, resistance, or external pressure. They arise when the mind is caught between contradictory desires, expectations, or fears, making one feel stretched between 'what is' and 'what should be.' A mind trapped in tension loses clarity, reacting instead of responding, struggling instead of moving with awareness. This internal struggle affects not only mental well-being but also physical health, creating fatigue, stress, and emotional exhaustion. When tension becomes habitual, life feels heavy, and even small obstacles seem overwhelming.

Tensions exist because of our struggle with psychological time—clinging to past regrets, anticipating future worries, and resisting the uncertainty of the present. The mind, conditioned to seek control, perfection, and validation, creates an endless cycle of pressure. Fear, ambition, and social expectations further reinforce this state, making relaxation seem difficult. Physical tension arises from stress, unhealthy habits, and suppressed emotions, while mental tension comes from overthinking, anxiety, and the need to control situations. The more one resists, the more tension grows, as resistance is the very force that strengthens inner strain.

Freedom from tension is not found through escape but through understanding its movement. When one sees that tension is created by resistance, struggle naturally dissolves. Letting go of the illusion of control and dropping expectations lightens the mind, allowing it to move freely. Observing thought without reaction breaks the cycle of over analysis and worry. Tension thrives on psychological time, but when one is fully present, there is no room for unnecessary mental burdens. A mind free from tension acts effortlessly, perceives clearly, and flows with life instead of against it. In this clarity, tension dissolves, leaving behind deep awareness, effortless action, and a profound sense of inner peace.

89. Guilt

Guilt: The Burden That Thought Refuses to Let Go

Guilt is the emotional weight of past actions, mistakes, or failures that the mind holds onto. It arises from social conditioning, moral judgment, and the psychological division between 'what is' and 'what should be.' A mind trapped in guilt is caught in self-punishment, unable to see the present with clarity. The mind replays past mistakes, creating a cycle of self-condemnation that prevents real understanding and change. Guilt is often mistaken for moral responsibility, yet it does not bring transformation—it only sustains inner conflict and reinforces a distorted sense of self.

We hold onto guilt because we believe suffering over our mistakes makes us better or redeems us. Society teaches that guilt is necessary for morality, yet true understanding does not arise from emotional punishment but from clear awareness of one's actions. Fear of judgment, whether from others or oneself, deepens guilt, making it a form of self-inflicted suffering. The mind clings to past mistakes as part of its identity, believing that without guilt, it has not truly learned. In reality, guilt does not correct the past—it only perpetuates emotional turmoil, preventing deep transformation.

Freedom from guilt begins with seeing it for what it is—a conditioned response rather than a necessary weight. Instead of suppressing or justifying guilt, one must observe it without identification. Guilt is not responsibility; responsibility means seeing an action clearly, understanding its consequences, and moving forward without carrying psychological burden. A mind that does not dwell in the past but acts with awareness in the present is free from guilt. True intelligence does not seek redemption through suffering but learns through direct perception, without the need for self-condemnation.

90. Regret

Regret: The Unfinished Business of the Past

Regret is the emotional burden of wishing past actions, choices, or events had been different. It arises from the mind's tendency to compare 'what happened' with 'what should have happened.' A mind caught in regret remains trapped in the past, preventing full engagement with the present. Regret is the mind's conflict with time—thought revisits past events, trying to change them mentally, though they are unchangeable. This conflict creates inner suffering, as the mind resists what is already finished.

Regret sustains psychological division by creating an internal split between 'the one who regrets' and 'the action that was done,' strengthening inner turmoil. It is based on comparison and idealization, where one imagines a better outcome and contrasts it with reality, creating dissatisfaction. Instead of leading to direct learning, regret focuses on self-blame or missed opportunities, blocking insight and clarity. It is ultimately the attachment to memory, keeping painful experiences alive and making the past feel emotionally present.

Why do we hold onto regret? Many believe that regret proves they care, thinking it is necessary for remorse or growth. However, true learning comes through insight, not emotional suffering. Regret also creates the illusion of control—by replaying the past, the mind believes it can somehow alter it, even though this is impossible. Society reinforces guilt, conditioning individuals to hold onto regret rather than move forward with understanding. Additionally, people identify with past mistakes, allowing the ego to define itself through failure. Fear of the present and future keeps the mind anchored in past regrets, serving as an escape from facing new possibilities.

Can one be free from regret? First, it is crucial to see that regret is just a thought, not reality—regret exists only in the mind and has no presence in the now. Observing regret without identifying with it allows it to dissolve naturally. True learning comes from seeing past actions clearly, without self-blame. Dropping comparison between 'what is' and 'what could have been' frees the mind from unnecessary suffering. A mind free from regret lives fully in the present, moving forward with clarity and direct action. Regret is the mind's attempt to alter the past, sustaining psychological conflict and emotional suffering. Real learning comes not through regret but through direct awareness and understanding. A mind unburdened by regret does not carry the weight of the past—it sees, understands, and moves forward with intelligence. In this state, there is no sorrow for what was—only full presence in what is.

91. Jealousy

Jealousy: The Fear of Losing What Was Never Ours

Jealousy is the reaction of the mind when it feels inferior, threatened, or afraid of losing something or someone. It is rooted in comparison, possessiveness, and insecurity. From childhood, we are taught to compare ourselves with others—who is better, more successful, or more attractive? This conditioning creates feelings of inadequacy and breeds jealousy. When we feel we "own" someone or something, jealousy arises at the thought of losing it. The fear that someone else may take what we believe is "ours"—whether it is a person, a title, or recognition— strengthens attachment. Beneath jealousy lies the deep-rooted fear that we are not good enough. When someone else succeeds, it reminds us of our own perceived shortcomings, feeding the ego's need for superiority. The ego thrives on feeling special, and when that image is challenged, jealousy takes hold.

A jealous mind does not see reality clearly—it sees through the lens of insecurity and fear, exaggerating threats and turning small situations into major emotional reactions. This creates conflict in relationships, leading to possessiveness, suspicion, and emotional distance. Instead of love and trust, jealousy fills relationships with fear and control. One who is jealous suffers internally, overthinking and imagining scenarios that may not even exist. Instead of peace, there is anxiety, resentment, and self-doubt. The more we identify with our relationships, achievements, or status, the more jealousy controls us. A free mind does not cling to possession—whether of things or people—because it understands that attachment only strengthens suffering.

Instead of suppressing or justifying jealousy, can one observe it as it arises, without judgment? In seeing clearly, jealousy begins to lose its power. No two people are the same, so why compare? Jealousy exists only when one believes they must compete, must be better than others. Love is not about owning someone—true love has no space for jealousy. Freedom comes when one stops clinging, stops fearing loss, and allows life to flow naturally. Instead of looking to achievements, relationships, or superiority for fulfillment, can one be completely aware, completely present? A mind that is fully attentive, fully alive in the present, has no room for jealousy—it is whole, not seeking. In this freedom, jealousy dissolves—not through suppression, but through deep understanding. A mind free from jealousy is a mind that loves without fear, without control, and without struggle.

92. Envy

Envy: The Measurement That Breeds Bitterness

Envy is the feeling of resentment, discontent, or longing when we see someone having what we desire—whether success, beauty, intelligence, or power. It is born from comparison, where the mind measures itself against others and feels inferior. From childhood, we are taught to compare—who is smarter, wealthier, or more attractive? This habit of psychological measurement ensures that there is always someone "better," creating a sense of lack. The mind, caught in the movement of becoming, is never content with what is; it always seeks to be greater, more successful, or more admired. Society reinforces this by glorifying achievement, wealth, and status, making envy a natural outcome of a mind conditioned to seek external validation.

Envy creates inner conflict, as the mind is constantly torn between "what is" and "what should be." This struggle prevents inner peace and fosters resentment, damaging relationships by breeding bitterness and isolation. Instead of celebrating others' happiness, envy turns their success into a source of frustration. A mind occupied with envy is always looking outward, never inward, preventing true self-understanding. Even if one attains success, there will always be someone "higher," ensuring that envy remains a never-ending cycle. As long as the mind compares, it remains trapped in dissatisfaction, chasing an illusion of completeness that is forever out of reach.

Can one live without psychologically measuring oneself against others? The moment comparison stops, envy begins to fade. Instead of resisting or justifying envy, can one simply observe it as it arises? The more one watches without reaction, the more its power weakens. We believe that by gaining what another has, we will be satisfied, yet real fulfillment is not in external success—it is in deep self-understanding. A mind free from comparison sees beauty in others' success, not rivalry. True intelligence does not compete—it moves in deep awareness. In this freedom, there is no resentment, no struggle—only clarity, joy, and an effortless contentment with life as it is.

93. Discontentment

Discontentment: The Relentless Drive for Something More

Discontentment is the feeling of dissatisfaction, the sense that something is missing in life. It arises from comparison, ambition, and the constant search for fulfillment. A restless mind is always seeking more—more success, pleasure, or purpose—never finding lasting contentment. The mind, caught in the habit of seeking, believes that fulfillment exists in the future, always just out of reach. Yet, does discontentment truly end through acquiring more, or does it only deepen as new desires arise?

At its core, discontentment is born from comparison. The mind measures itself against others, feeling inadequate or incomplete, creating an endless cycle of wanting and striving. It seeks fulfillment in the future, believing happiness will come "one day" through achievement, possessions, or relationships. But this keeps the mind trapped in time, always postponing contentment. Discontentment also creates inner conflict—the division between "what is" and "what should be"—leading to resistance and wasted energy. Desire further intensifies dissatisfaction; when one craving is fulfilled, another arises, continuing the cycle. Thought strengthens this feeling of lack, imagining an ideal state and comparing it to reality, preventing one from seeing that fulfillment is not in the future but in awareness of the present.

Can one be free from discontentment? The key is to observe discontent without trying to escape or change it. Awareness of dissatisfaction, without judgment, allows deep understanding, and when observed fully, discontentment reveals its own illusion. Seeing that no external fulfillment ends discontent weakens the mind's craving for illusions. Letting go of comparison and measurement naturally brings peace, as there is no "better" state to attain. Living completely in the present, without seeking something outside of now, dissolves the restlessness of discontentment. Most importantly, understanding that fulfillment is not an achievement but a state of being ends the search itself—when seeking ends, a deep sense of completeness remains.

94. Boredom

Boredom: The Restlessness of a Mind Seeking Stimulation

Boredom is the mental state of dissatisfaction, restlessness, and lack of interest. It arises when the mind is caught in repetition, seeking stimulation, or resisting the present. A mind trapped in boredom is either escaping into distractions or numbed by habit, unable to see the richness of what is. The mind constantly seeks excitement, avoiding moments that seem 'uninteresting,' and when it does not get what it desires, boredom arises. Life becomes mechanical through routine, making experience feel predictable and dull. A mind that functions in habit loses sensitivity, failing to see the newness in each moment. Conditioned to expect entertainment, purpose, or distraction, the brain falls into boredom when nothing immediate occupies it.

A mind uncomfortable with stillness quickly seeks something to 'fill the gap,' yet true silence is never boring—it is full of awareness. Boredom exists because the mind is either dwelling in past experiences or waiting for future excitement, never fully present. Society conditions us to avoid stillness and constantly 'do something,' reinforcing dependence on external stimulation.

Thought, functioning through comparison, measures the present moment against past pleasurable experiences, making the now seem dull in contrast. Many believe that being 'busy' means being alive, but true aliveness is not in movement—it is in awareness. When nothing externally engages the mind, it must face itself, leading to a craving for distractions. A bored mind sees life through habit, missing its depth and richness.

The feeling of 'nothing interesting happening' is a creation of thought. When one sees boredom as self-created, its hold weakens. Boredom exists only when one is waiting for something more; a mind that is completely attentive sees everything as fresh and new. The mind gets bored when it expects stimulation and does not find it, but when expectation drops, even the simplest things reveal depth. Silence is not empty—it is full of perception and insight. A mind that does not fear stillness is never bored. When one sees without labels, without past references, everything is new. Boredom is not caused by external events but by the mind's resistance to the present. A mind free from boredom does not seek excitement—it finds richness in simply being aware. In this state, there is no dullness—only the endless movement of life, seen with fresh eyes.

95. Dullness

Dullness: The Absence of Attention and Sensitivity

Dullness is not just physical fatigue but the mental heaviness that arises from repetition, habit, and a lack of awareness. A dull mind moves mechanically, repeating patterns without true engagement. It reacts predictably, follows routines blindly, and lacks the sharpness to see beyond its conditioning. Life, when seen through a dull mind, becomes a series of automatic responses rather than a living, dynamic experience. Thought, rooted in memory, limits perception to what is already known, preventing fresh discovery. But is dullness an inevitable state, or is it the result of how the mind has been conditioned?

The mind becomes dull when it falls into habit—repeating the same thoughts, beliefs, and behaviors without question. Habit deadens perception, making every experience seem ordinary and predictable. Fear and the need for psychological security further limit exploration, making the mind rigid and resistant to change. Instead of questioning, it seeks comfort, which gradually leads to stagnation. Sensory overstimulation—through entertainment, distractions, and constant input—also dulls the mind. A mind that is always occupied with external noise loses its natural sensitivity to life. In this state, awareness is dulled, perception is narrowed, and the mind loses its ability to observe with clarity.

A dull mind becomes insensitive—to beauty, to people, to the subtleties of life. It sees but does not truly observe, hears but does not deeply listen. It functions through routine, unable to engage with the depth of the present moment. This lack of freshness leads to boredom, which in turn fuels the search for stimulation. But excitement and escape do not end dullness—they only mask it temporarily. True clarity is not in constant thought but in deep stillness. A mind that is silent, fresh, and completely attentive is never dull. It does not need stimulation to feel alive; it is alive in itself. When dullness ends, life is no longer lived mechanically—it is experienced in its full depth, richness, and beauty, moment by moment.

96. Restlessness

Restlessness: The Inner Agitation That Seeks Escape

Restlessness is the state of inner agitation, where the mind is unable to remain still or content. It arises from psychological discomfort, an unfulfilled desire, or the inability to accept the present moment. A restless mind is constantly seeking—new experiences, distractions, or stimulation—never finding true peace. Thought, caught in movement, fuels this state by anticipating the future or resisting the past, preventing deep stillness. Restlessness is often mistaken for energy, but true energy is not in constant movement; it is in effortless attention and clarity. When the mind is restless, it jumps from one thought to another, unable to focus fully on anything, creating emotional turbulence and dissatisfaction.

Restlessness is sustained by desire, comparison, and fear. The mind, conditioned by society, is taught to chase success, pleasure, and excitement, making stillness appear dull or unproductive. Thought compares the present moment with an idealized future, generating dissatisfaction and the urge to escape. Restlessness is also fueled by fear—fear of emptiness, of being alone, of confronting oneself without distraction. This fear drives the search for stimulation through external means—social interactions, entertainment, ambitions—none of which resolve the underlying disturbance. A restless mind is caught in psychological time, moving between regrets of the past and anticipation of the future, never fully engaged in the now.

Freedom from restlessness does not come through suppression or temporary escapes but through deep awareness of its movement. Observing restlessness without resistance allows it to lose its hold, revealing the mind's tendency to seek fulfillment externally. When one sees that no amount of activity or pursuit will bring lasting peace, the need for seeking naturally diminishes. Attention to the present, without seeking escape, brings a profound stillness that is not forced but effortless. A mind that is no longer chasing, no longer resisting, moves in complete awareness. In this state, restlessness dissolves, leaving behind a presence that is fully alive, deeply silent, and completely at ease.

97. Agitation

Agitation: The Restlessness of an Unquiet Mind

Agitation is the state of mental or emotional disturbance, where the mind is unsettled, restless, and reactive. It arises from unresolved conflict, fear, frustration, and the constant movement of thought seeking security. A mind caught in agitation struggles against discomfort, while a mind that understands deeply remains still even amidst chaos. The mind wants things to go a certain way—when they do not, agitation arises. Resistance strengthens agitation, for a disturbed mind is divided—one part wants calm, while another reacts with frustration. True stillness exists only when there is no inner division. People become agitated when they try to avoid discomfort, uncertainty, or failure, yet trying to escape only intensifies the disturbance. A restless mind makes the body tense, breathing shallow, and actions impulsive, while true clarity exists when the mind is free from agitation, moving with ease.

A mind that is agitated jumps to conclusions, reacts emotionally, and cannot see reality as it is. True perception happens only when the mind is silent and undisturbed. Society teaches people to fix problems quickly rather than to understand them deeply, conditioning the mind to react rather than observe. Agitation arises when one is emotionally attached to outcomes, desperately wanting things to go their way. When one lets go of attachment to results, agitation fades naturally. Many label agitation as 'bad' and try to suppress it, yet resisting it only strengthens it. Thought moves unchecked, filled with worry, regret, and imagination, keeping the mind restless. Instead of seeking stillness, people often turn to distractions—entertainment, work, or conversation—to avoid agitation, yet true freedom is not in escape but in facing it directly.

Agitation is a movement of energy—resisting it creates suffering, while a mind that simply allows it to be does not remain disturbed. Instead of suppressing or reacting, can one just watch agitation? True awareness dissolves disturbance without force. Agitation is often about what 'should have been' or 'what will be,' but a mind fully present has no agitation—it simply moves with life. Many struggle between 'I should do this' and 'I want to do that,' creating inner conflict, while a mind that acts with clarity has no contradiction, no hesitation. Agitation is impulse—when one observes without reaction, disturbance disappears. A mind free from agitation is not dull—it is deeply alive, fully aware. Agitation is not caused by external situations but by the mind's resistance, attachments, and unchecked movement. Many struggle with agitation because they try to suppress, escape, or fight it, yet true freedom comes not from controlling it, but from seeing it clearly. A mind free from agitation does not force stillness—it allows every disturbance to arise, to be observed, and to dissolve naturally. In this freedom, agitation loses its grip—not because one has conquered it, but because there is no longer an 'I' struggling against it—only deep awareness, without resistance, without conflict, in complete peace.

98. Disturbance

Disturbance: The Mind in Conflict with Itself

Disturbance is the state of mental, emotional, or external unrest that disrupts balance and awareness. It arises from fear, desire, unresolved conflicts, and the mind's attachment to certainty. A mind caught in disturbance reacts with anxiety, resistance, or suppression, while a mind that understands deeply moves through disturbance without conflict. The mind seeks stability, but life is always changing, and when one expects permanence, disturbance arises with change. Many fight against their emotions, trying to suppress or control them, yet resistance only strengthens disturbance. Anxiety about the future or regret about the past creates inner restlessness, while living fully in the present weakens its grip. People become disturbed when things do not go as planned, yet true calmness exists when there is no attachment to results. A restless mind distorts reality, reacting emotionally instead of seeing clearly, while a still mind perceives without confusion.

The mind wants to control its environment to feel secure, yet true stability is not in control—it is in understanding. Emotional attachment creates expectations and dependency, but when one lets go, disturbance fades naturally. Most respond to disturbance with immediate emotion—anger, sadness, frustration—yet a mind that simply observes without reacting remains unaffected.

Many seek escape through entertainment, work, or avoidance, but true peace is not in distraction—it is in seeing disturbance fully. One says, 'I am disturbed,' instead of 'Disturbance is present,' making it personal and strengthening its hold. When one does not personalize emotions, they lose their grip, and disturbance passes like a cloud, without resistance.

Disturbance arises naturally, but suffering comes from fighting it. When one does not resist, disturbance moves on its own. Instead of labeling it as 'good' or 'bad,' can one simply watch it? A mind that observes without judgment is already at peace. Many want disturbance to disappear instantly, yet true freedom is allowing it to be, without forcing change. The mind creates disturbance by imagining future problems or past regrets, but when one is fully in the present, it remains undisturbed. Life is movement, and trying to hold onto stability only creates disturbance. True calmness exists when one flows with change, without resistance. Disturbance is not the real problem—it is the resistance, fear, and attachment that make it overwhelming. A mind free from resistance does not fight disturbance—it allows it, watches it, and moves with life, without clinging to stability or fearing change. In this freedom, disturbance is no longer a burden—it is simply another movement of life, passing through, without conflict, without struggle, without leaving a trace.

99. Greed

Greed: The Endless Hunger That Cannot Be Satisfied

Greed is the intense desire for more—more wealth, power, status, knowledge, or experience. It is never satisfied, always wanting, always seeking. Greed is not just about possessions—it is the psychological urge to accumulate, to dominate, to control. We believe that having more will make us happy, secure, and complete, yet no amount of accumulation ever brings lasting fulfillment. Instead, it creates new cravings, keeping the mind in constant pursuit. Fear of poverty, loneliness, and failure drives us to accumulate, believing that security comes from possession. But can greed ever bring real security, or does it only strengthen the fear of loss? Society conditions us to measure success through wealth, power, and achievement, reinforcing greed through comparison and competition. The 'self' seeks to continue, expand, and preserve itself, and greed becomes the mind's way of avoiding its own impermanence.

Greed creates conflict, as nations, corporations, and individuals compete, exploit, and destroy in the pursuit of more. Where there is greed, can there ever be peace? The more one has, the more one fears losing it, leading to anxiety and insecurity. Can one be free if one is constantly protecting what one has? Greed also destroys relationships, turning them into transactions where people are used for personal gain. Love cannot exist where there is greed, for greed seeks possession, while love is free. No amount of success, possessions, or power can satisfy greed; the more one gets, the more one desires. This endless cycle ensures that greed is never-ending, leaving the mind in a state of perpetual dissatisfaction.

Can one observe the movement of greed without judgment, without trying to suppress it? The moment one sees that greed leads only to conflict, its power weakens. Greed exists only where there is attachment—to things, people, or ideas. Can one live without clinging, without seeking possession? A mind that is truly content does not seek more—it is already full. Can one live without waiting for more to bring happiness? When one acts without the motive of gain, work, relationships, and life itself become free, effortless, and full of intelligence. True contentment is not in having more, but in being free from the need for more. A mind that is free from greed does not seek, does not compare—it simply lives, fully and completely, in the present. Where greed ends, love, intelligence, and deep peace begin.

100. Lust

Lust: The Fire That Fades but Never Ends

Lust is the intense craving for physical, emotional, or psychological gratification, often centered around sensual pleasure. It arises from biological impulses, social conditioning, and the psychological need for fulfillment. A mind caught in lust seeks pleasure without awareness, leading to attachment, frustration, and inner conflict. When lust dominates perception, relationships become transactional, and the pursuit of pleasure turns into an endless cycle of craving and dissatisfaction. It blinds the mind to deeper connections, making one chase fleeting excitement instead of true intimacy.

Lust is sustained by thought and memory—past pleasurable experiences are recalled, projected into the future, and repeated through imagination. When one associates happiness with pleasure, lust turns into psychological dependence, leading to seeking, frustration, and fear of loss. Society reinforces this by glorifying sensuality, making people believe that without desire, life is incomplete. Lust also becomes a means of escape from inner emptiness—when one feels emotionally or mentally unfulfilled, pleasure serves as a temporary distraction. But no amount of indulgence can fill the void within; instead, it deepens restlessness and dissatisfaction.

Freedom from lust is not in suppression or indulgence but in deep observation. When one sees how thought sustains desire, its intensity weakens. True freedom comes from neither condemning nor blindly pursuing lust but understanding its movement. Attraction is natural, but when it turns into craving, it becomes bondage. A mind that is fully present enjoys life without turning pleasure into addiction. In this state, passion exists without possession, and desire moves without dominating the mind. In such freedom, relationships are no longer based on need but on deep awareness, respect, and true affection.

101. Satisfaction

Satisfaction: The Temporary Relief That Soon Craves More

Satisfaction is the feeling of contentment that comes when a desire is fulfilled. It may arise from material success, relationships, pleasure, knowledge, or achievement, but is satisfaction ever permanent, or does it always lead to further craving? When we want something and obtain it, there is a momentary relief, yet the mind quickly moves to the next desire. From childhood, we are taught that satisfaction comes from success, wealth, or status, trapping us in a cycle of ambition and momentary contentment. Sensory pleasures bring brief enjoyment, but once they fade, the craving for more returns. We seek emotional satisfaction in relationships, beliefs, and identities, yet when these are threatened, insecurity and dissatisfaction return.

No matter how much one achieves, the mind quickly seeks something new. What satisfies today may bore or frustrate tomorrow. A mind that chases fulfillment is never truly at peace, always moving from one desire to another, believing the next achievement will bring lasting happiness. If one depends on external achievements or relationships for satisfaction, there is fear of losing them. True freedom is not in satisfaction but in a mind that does not need to seek it. Satisfaction is the fulfillment of a particular desire, but contentment is the absence of psychological craving. A content mind does not seek—therefore, it is free from dissatisfaction.

The moment one recognizes that no desire will ever bring permanent fulfillment, the cycle of seeking weakens. Can one live without chasing satisfaction, simply being present with what is? The mind always seeks to "complete" itself through external things, but can one see that wholeness exists only when there is no seeking? True action is not done for satisfaction—it is done out of intelligence and clarity. A mind that acts without expecting fulfillment is always free. Satisfaction is always about the future—"I will be happy when..."—but can one live without postponing happiness, without expecting something to bring it? True freedom is not in achieving satisfaction but in seeing the nature of desire clearly. A mind that no longer seeks satisfaction is a mind that is truly content—free, alive, and deeply at peace.

102. Sensations

Sensations: The Body's Language of Perception

Sensations are the physical and emotional responses experienced through the senses—touch, sight, sound, taste, and smell. They are immediate, direct, and natural, but thought often interferes, giving sensations meaning, attachment, or resistance. Sensations themselves are neither good nor bad; it is the mind's interpretation that creates pleasure, desire, or fear. The nervous system reacts instantly to heat, cold, pain, pleasure, and movement, which is essential for survival. However, does pleasure or pain need psychological attachment? A pleasant sensation, such as music, touch, or taste, creates a memory of pleasure, and the mind seeks to repeat it, leading to craving and attachment. Similarly, the memory of physical or emotional pain creates resistance, making the mind relive past suffering through thought.

The moment one attaches to pleasure, satisfaction is never lasting—there is always a desire for more. Seeking pleasure through food, relationships, or experiences creates dependence on external things, strengthening craving. Conversely, the mind remembers past pain and resists it, even when it is not happening now. Fear of emotional pain blocks sensitivity and openness, making one guarded and reactive. A sensation itself is temporary, but thought prolongs it, turning it into longing or suffering. The taste of food lasts seconds, but the craving for it lasts much longer. This movement of thought prevents direct experiencing of the present, replacing natural awareness with psychological struggle.

Can one feel heat, cold, pain, or pleasure without calling it 'good' or 'bad'? The moment one labels a sensation, thought begins to interfere. Instead of seeking to prolong pleasure or escape discomfort, can one simply observe how sensations arise and fade? This creates freedom from attachment and resistance. Sensations belong to the body, not to the 'self'; can one experience them without saying 'my pleasure, my pain'? When one is completely present, sensations are experienced fully, but they do not dominate the mind. There is no conflict—only deep awareness of 'what is.' Sensations are natural, but when thought clings to them, they create craving, fear, and psychological conflict. True freedom is not in suppressing sensations, but in experiencing them fully without attachment. A mind that sees sensations as they are, without seeking or resisting, lives in complete awareness and deep inner balance.

103. Sensitivity

Sensitivity: The Art of Feeling Without Distortion

Sensitivity is the ability to perceive life fully, to feel deeply, and to be completely aware of oneself and the world without distortion. It is not mere emotional reaction or being easily affected—it is the state of a mind that is awake, attentive, and free from self-centeredness. A sensitive mind sees beauty, understands suffering, and responds with intelligence, without fear or resistance. Yet conditioning dulls the mind, as society teaches conformity, suppression, and the neglect of natural awareness. Education, tradition, and authority train individuals to fit into patterns rather than observe freely. To avoid pain, we build emotional walls, cutting ourselves off from deep feeling, and in resisting suffering, we lose sensitivity. Modern life fills the mind with noise—entertainment, technology, and endless activity—making it difficult for one to be still and truly observe.

A mind occupied with 'me,' 'my problems,' or 'my success' has no space to see others, to feel deeply. Sensitivity arises only when there is freedom from self-interest and psychological noise. To be sensitive is to see, hear, and feel without reacting, comparing, or labeling, allowing perception without the interference of past conditioning. One who is sensitive does not see a tree, a face, or the sky through the filter of thought, but perceives freshly, with full attention. True beauty is experienced when the mind is completely present, not seeking or analyzing. Most people avoid pain, but true sensitivity means being fully present with suffering, without resistance or escape. In deep sensitivity, there is no division between the observer and the feeling—one simply experiences without conflict. Love, in its highest form, is the essence of sensitivity, for it sees another without control, without attachment, without fear.

Can one regain sensitivity? It begins by observing the world, people, and emotions without interpreting them through past conditioning, allowing perception to be free and open. True sensitivity exists only in deep attention to the now—can one listen to the wind, feel the movement of life, without distraction? Sensitivity is lost when the mind is occupied with itself, its desires, fears, and ambitions, but when the self is absent, there is deep connection with life, with others, with truth. A mind weighed down by fear, comparison, and memory becomes dull and insensitive, but when one lives without accumulating emotional burdens, life is seen with extraordinary freshness. Sensitivity is not weakness—it is the highest intelligence, the ability to perceive deeply, love without fear, and respond to life with clarity. A truly sensitive mind is not trapped in self-interest, not occupied with thought—it is open, aware, deeply alive. In this sensitivity, there is beauty, love, and a profound sense of wholeness with life.

WAKE UP

WAKE UP

4. Action & Behavior

WAKE UP

WAKE UP

104. Action

Action: The Movement That Shapes Life

Action is the movement of life, shaping our thoughts, relationships, and interactions with the world. It can arise from deep understanding, free from conditioning, or it can be mechanical, driven by habit, belief, or authority. The nature of action determines whether it leads to clarity and freedom or reinforces struggle and division. When action is spontaneous and unburdened by the past, it is creative and intelligent. But when it is dictated by memory, fear, or ideals, it leads to psychological conflict and fragmentation.

Most action is based on past conditioning—habitual responses shaped by experiences, beliefs, and societal norms. Such action is repetitive, reactive, and limited by the boundaries of memory. Other actions are guided by ideals, driven by a desire to become something or achieve a future goal. This creates a gap between 'what is' and 'what should be,' leading to inner struggle. True action, however, is free from both the past and the imagined future—it arises from direct perception, unclouded by thought. When action flows naturally from deep awareness, it is effortless, immediate, and transformative.

Freedom from conflict in action comes when one sees without interference from the past, without seeking psychological security in the future. A mind that acts out of self-interest or fear creates division, but when there is no psychological center, action is whole and complete. The thinker and the thought, the observer and the observed, are not separate—when this is seen, action becomes effortless, flowing like a river without resistance.

In this state, action is neither reaction nor ambition—it is pure intelligence in motion, without struggle, without contradiction.

105. Action and Idea

Action and Idea: The Conflict Between Thought and Doing

Action is the movement of life, the response to what is, while an idea is a concept, a mental image, or a belief formed by thought. Most actions are not spontaneous but guided by ideas—beliefs, ideologies, and preconceived conclusions. Instead of acting from direct perception, people rely on conditioned thoughts, postponing action, creating inner conflict, and preventing true understanding. A mind caught in ideas acts mechanically, seeking consistency rather than responding with clarity.

Action based on ideas delays and distorts reality. When one sees suffering, the natural impulse is to help, but thought interferes—asking whether it is right, what others will think, or if it aligns with one's principles. By the time thought concludes, the moment for true action is lost. Ideologies and beliefs create contradiction—one may preach kindness but act with hidden self-interest. When action is shaped by conditioning, it becomes repetitive, predictable, and lifeless, lacking the freshness of direct perception. A mind caught in ideas does not see what is but acts from what it thinks should be.

True action is possible only when the mind is free from the burden of ideas. A fully aware mind does not need a guiding belief—it acts with clarity, responding to life as it unfolds. Compassion, for example, is not an idea to be followed but a reality that naturally expresses itself in action. Thought functions in time, remembering, projecting, and planning, but action exists only in the now. Seeing life without the filter of belief, expectation, or past conclusions allows for precise, effortless action. A mind free from ideas acts with intelligence, love, and clarity—without hesitation, without distortion, and without conflict.

106. Action Without Purpose

Action Without Purpose: The Beauty of Effortless Movement

Action without purpose is action that arises naturally, without seeking a result, reward, or fulfillment. It is not driven by desire, ambition, or psychological motives but emerges from direct perception and intelligence. When action is free from attachment to an outcome, it is effortless and complete in itself. A mind acting without purpose does not seek to accumulate, achieve, or prove anything—it simply moves in awareness, without inner conflict.

Most action is conditioned by society, education, and personal ambition, where every effort is measured by its usefulness in terms of success, recognition, or progress. The ego seeks fulfillment through purpose, attaching meaning to work, relationships, and even spiritual practices in the hope of achieving enlightenment, peace, or salvation. Fear of meaninglessness compels the mind to act with a goal, as thought constantly projects into the future, unable to function without an expected result. This dependence on purpose prevents direct perception, making action mechanical and repetitive.

When action is guided by a goal, it creates struggle, as the mind is caught between 'what is' and 'what should be.' True action is complete in itself, not driven by fear or expectation. A flower blooms not for admiration but simply because it flowers. Love, beauty, and truth exist only when there is no motive—when love is free from attachment, beauty is not calculated, and truth is not sought as a means to an end. A mind that acts without purpose is not lost or passive; it is fully alive, deeply aware, and in harmony with life. In this state, action is no longer a means to something—it is life itself, flowing without struggle, without burden, without division.

107. Activity

Activity: The Mind's Need for Constant Occupation

Activity is the movement of thought, action, and effort in daily life—whether physical, mental, or emotional. It includes work, relationships, ambition, entertainment, social engagement, and even inner struggles. Most people believe that constant activity signifies growth, achievement, or fulfillment, but does mere movement bring real understanding? The mind, conditioned to seek occupation, fills every moment with plans, distractions, and pursuits, rarely allowing space for stillness. A life filled with activity may appear meaningful, but if it is driven by habit, fear, or escape, it becomes mechanical rather than transformative.

The mind is always engaged in activity because it fears stillness and emptiness. A quiet mind feels uncomfortable, so it constantly seeks stimulation—through work, entertainment, relationships, or thought itself. Society reinforces this by equating productivity with worth, teaching that success is measured by how much one does rather than how deeply one understands. Even in moments of physical rest, the mind continues moving—analyzing, remembering, anticipating—sustaining inner chatter that prevents true awareness. Activity, when driven by thought, is always conditioned by the past, making action repetitive rather than fresh and intelligent.

Endless activity does not bring clarity; it creates restlessness. A mind caught in movement without understanding is merely occupied, not truly alive. Many use activity as a means to escape their own inner conflicts, engaging in work, causes, or ambitions without real understanding. Constant movement prevents deep observation—one who is always busy never has time to look deeply into life or into oneself. True action arises when the mind is still, fully present, and acts without compulsion. A mind free from the burden of unnecessary activity moves with intelligence, seeing clearly, acting effortlessly, and living without struggle or escape.

108. Habit

Habit: The Unconscious Repetition That Traps the Mind

Habit is the repeated pattern of thought, emotion, and action, operating automatically without awareness. It makes life predictable, reducing the need for constant decision-making. Habits can be physical, such as walking, eating, or driving, or psychological, such as reacting with fear, seeking approval, or following beliefs without question. The mind prefers familiarity, reinforcing habits through repetition, making them feel natural and unquestioned. Over time, habits shape identity, making it seem as though one 'is' their habits rather than merely conditioned by them.

The mind forms habits to create efficiency and reduce effort. What begins as a conscious action becomes automatic through repetition. When a habit brings pleasure or removes discomfort, it strengthens, reinforcing itself through reward. Psychological habits, such as reacting with anger or seeking validation, develop through conditioning—shaped by culture, education, and personal experience. These conditioned responses dictate behavior without conscious choice, limiting direct perception and true freedom.

Habit dulls the mind, making life mechanical and repetitive. Instead of observing each moment freshly, the mind reacts based on conditioned responses, preventing deep understanding. Psychological habits provide an illusion of security, making one cling to routines, traditions, and beliefs out of fear of the unknown. Breaking one habit often leads to replacing it with another, maintaining the same conditioning in a different form. True freedom does not come from replacing habits but from understanding their nature. Awareness of habit, without resistance or effort to change it, weakens its hold naturally. A mind free from habit is awake, sensitive, and fully present, meeting life without the burden of the past.

109. Repetition

Repetition: The Mechanical Cycle That Kills Awareness

Repetition is the constant repeating of thoughts, actions, habits, and beliefs—whether consciously or unconsciously. It exists in daily routines, traditions, rituals, learning, and even relationships. While repetition is useful for practical tasks, such as learning a skill or memorizing facts, does it have a place in deep understanding? When the mind falls into repetitive patterns, it creates a predictable existence that lacks freshness and insight. The mind's reliance on repetition limits its ability to perceive life as it truly is, instead of through the lens of the past.

The mind seeks security in the familiar, clinging to repetitive patterns to avoid the discomfort of the unknown. This desire for predictability traps one in a mechanical existence, dulling sensitivity and awareness. Society and tradition condition individuals to follow routines, beliefs, and social norms without questioning them. As repetition becomes habit, it solidifies into identity, creating a false sense of stability. Furthermore, the mind believes that repetition leads to mastery, but does it truly lead to understanding, or does it merely foster mechanical behavior and shallow responses?

Repetition stifles real connection, especially in relationships, where habitual actions and words make interactions mechanical. True love, is only possible through direct, fresh perception—without the overlay of expectation or memory. In the same way, repetition strengthens fear and conflict, as the mind relives painful memories and anticipates future suffering. True freedom from repetition is found through awareness, not suppression. When one observes repetition without judgment, it naturally dissolves, leaving room for intelligence, creativity, and direct engagement with the present moment.

110. Reaction

Reaction: The Immediate Response Rooted in Conditioning

Reaction is the automatic, conditioned response to external stimuli, driven by past experiences, emotions, and beliefs. It arises without awareness, based on memory, habit, or fear, rather than clear perception. A reactive mind is caught in a cycle of action and response, preventing true understanding and freedom. The mind reacts based on what it has learned, without any fresh observation of the present moment.

The root of reaction lies in conditioning. Thought operates through accumulated knowledge, shaping responses based on previous experiences. When someone insults or praises, the response is immediate because the mind is conditioned to react in a particular way. Every reaction is rooted in memory—whether pleasure or pain—which prevents one from perceiving the present moment with clarity. A reactive mind never truly sees the present as it is but interprets it through past experiences. This creates emotional conflict and strengthens the illusion of a separate self, which constantly defends, attacks, or justifies itself. True intelligence comes when the mind observes without reacting.

We react because we are conditioned to do so from an early age. Society, education, and upbringing train us to respond immediately without questioning. Fear, desire, and psychological identity drive these reactions. The mind feels threatened when challenged, leading to an immediate emotional response. A person identified with beliefs, opinions, or status reacts strongly when questioned. This cycle of reaction sustains the ego and prevents clarity. But living without reaction is possible through observation and awareness. When we observe reactions without justifying or suppressing them, we free ourselves from the patterns of conflict, allowing intelligence to act without interference. True freedom lies in the space between stimulus and response, where clarity and understanding naturally arise.

111. Response

Response: The Conscious Movement Free from Conditioning

A response is how we react to situations, events, or challenges. It can arise from deep awareness or from conditioned thought, fear, and habit. The quality of our response determines whether we act intelligently or merely repeat past patterns. A mind that responds with awareness moves freely, while one driven by conditioning reacts mechanically, unable to perceive the present moment clearly.

Conditioning shapes our responses, as society, religion, culture, and education train us to react in certain ways. We often rely on past experiences and learned patterns rather than fresh observation. Fear influences our reactions by making us defensive, aggressive, or withdrawn, while desire may lead us to seek approval or personal gain in our responses. Thought interferes with direct perception, making us interpret events based on past conclusions, rather than seeing them clearly. The ego further distorts responses, as it acts from a place of self-protection, pride, or attachment, creating conflict and misunderstanding.

A clear response requires inner stillness, not emotional disturbance. When emotional involvement clouds our judgment, our responses become distorted. Desire for a specific outcome further influences our responses, making them less authentic. True response is free from personal motives and comes from being fully present. By observing our reactions without judgment or rush, we create space for intelligence to operate. Letting go of defensiveness and acting without the need for approval or fear of discomfort leads to a genuine response that arises from the present moment, unaffected by past influences.

112. Motive

Motive: The Hidden Force Behind Every Action

Motive is the underlying force behind thought, decision, and action, shaping perception and response to life. It arises from desire, fear, ambition, or conditioning, creating expectations and attachments. A mind driven by motive is never free—it acts with a purpose, seeking fulfillment, security, or recognition. Every action influenced by motive carries an agenda, making it mechanical rather than spontaneous. Thought sustains motive by projecting outcomes, turning action into a means to an end rather than an expression of direct understanding. Whether in relationships, work, or spiritual practice, motive strengthens the illusion of self, reinforcing the idea that action must serve a personal gain. Society further conditions the mind to act for results—success, approval, or achievement—making motive seem necessary in all aspects of life. But does action guided by motive bring clarity, or does it create conflict between 'what is' and 'what should be'?

Motive distorts perception, filtering reality through personal bias. Instead of seeing clearly, the mind sees what it desires or fears, making action reactive rather than intelligent. When action is shaped by a personal motive, it creates psychological struggle—between expectation and reality, between self-interest and the present moment. This conflict breeds frustration when outcomes do not match desires, strengthening disappointment and resistance. Motive also prevents direct action by making it conditional—one acts not for the sake of action itself, but for a future result. Seeking approval, success, or security, people become dependent on external validation, limiting their ability to act freely. A mind that moves with motive is bound by psychological time, always functioning between past experiences and future goals, never fully present. Action without motive, on the other hand, is whole, immediate, and effortless, free from the burden of expectation.

Freedom from motive begins with awareness. Instead of trying to force action to be 'pure,' one must observe how motives arise without judgment. In this deep observation, the need for motive dissolves naturally. Seeing that motive creates dependence on results allows for action that is complete in itself, without attachment. When action is free from expectation, there is total attention, total joy, and total presence. Intelligence moves effortlessly when it is not driven by personal ambition or fear. A mind that no longer seeks psychological rewards acts with clarity and understanding, not for an outcome but because it is the right action in that moment. In this state, there is no struggle, no hesitation—only action that is spontaneous, whole, and deeply alive.

113. Motivation

Motivation: The Drive That Comes from Desire and Fear

Motivation is the internal or external force that pushes one toward action, effort, or achievement. It arises from desire, fear, ambition, or the need for fulfillment. A mind caught in motivation is either energized by clarity or trapped in endless seeking. Many act because they want success, pleasure, or approval, or because they fear failure and rejection. This movement keeps the mind restless, always seeking and never content. Motivation is often sustained by future-oriented thinking, where one believes that a future outcome will bring satisfaction, creating psychological time and anticipation rather than full presence. Some act with natural energy, while others force themselves with struggle, making action lose its flow and intelligence. The mind believes it must 'become' something better—stronger, wiser, more successful—reinforcing the idea that the present is inadequate.

Society trains people to strive for success, making motivation seem necessary, yet this conditioning creates attachment to results rather than the act itself. Without motivation, one fears becoming passive or directionless, yet true movement comes not from external drive, but from deep clarity. Many think struggle is necessary for achievement, believing motivation requires pushing oneself even against natural interest. But real action flows effortlessly when there is deep awareness. When one feels uninspired, they look for external forces to drive them, yet motivation cannot be forced—real energy comes from being fully engaged. Many see themselves as 'driven' or 'unmotivated,' creating self-imposed labels that limit natural movement, turning motivation into a psychological struggle.

Motivation is based on thought projecting an outcome, but when one sees this, they no longer rely on motivation—they simply act. Most wait for motivation before beginning, yet action itself creates energy, making waiting unnecessary. A mind that acts for a result is divided, but when one is fully attentive, motivation is no longer needed—there is only action. Interest naturally brings energy, unlike forced motivation, which creates struggle. When one moves with curiosity and awareness, effort is not needed. The search for motivation keeps the mind in future expectations, yet a mind fully in the now acts effortlessly, without needing external or internal push. Society conditions people to believe motivation is necessary, but real movement comes from clarity, not pressure. A mind that waits for motivation delays action, while a mind that acts without seeking results moves naturally. In this freedom, motivation is no longer a struggle—it is simply the natural flow of energy in a mind that is alive, aware, and unburdened by effort.

114. Imitation

Imitation: The Fear of Standing Alone

Imitation is the act of following, copying, or conforming to an established pattern, authority, or ideal. It arises from conditioning, fear, and the desire for acceptance, making action mechanical rather than intelligent. A mind caught in imitation does not see, question, or create—it merely repeats what has been taught. The tendency to imitate is deeply ingrained from childhood, shaping beliefs, behaviors, and ways of thinking. When one imitates, they do not truly understand but only accept, mistaking repetition for learning.

Imitation is the repetition of the past, absorbing traditions, beliefs, and behaviors from parents, society, and education without direct inquiry. This strengthens psychological dependence on authority—whether religious, political, or social—preventing real freedom. Imitation creates division, as individuals identify with cultural and ideological patterns, leading to separation and conflict. Creativity and intelligence are destroyed when the mind simply follows rather than explores. A mind that imitates does not discover—it only conforms, limiting its capacity to perceive life anew.

Freedom from imitation begins with seeing that imitation is not understanding. Questioning every assumption breaks conditioned patterns, allowing direct perception rather than borrowed knowledge. Letting go of psychological authority enables intelligence to function without dependence on books, traditions, or leaders. Action that is not dictated by the past is possible when the mind observes without conditioning. When one does not fear being different, there is space for true exploration, creativity, and understanding. A mind free from imitation moves with deep awareness, no longer bound by conformity, but acting from fresh perception, alive and original.

115. Initiative

Initiative: The Action That Arises From Clarity, Not Compulsion

Initiative is the spontaneous movement toward action, born from direct perception rather than external pressure or fear. It arises when the mind is free from hesitation, doubt, and the need for validation. A mind caught in initiative as ambition seeks to prove itself, while a mind that understands deeply acts naturally, without force. Many take action impulsively, mistaking movement for initiative, yet true initiative comes from deep clarity, not from restlessness. A hesitant mind is caught between conflicting thoughts, delaying action, but when one sees clearly, initiative happens without inner struggle. People often take initiative to gain approval or success, but true initiative does not seek an outcome—it moves because action is necessary. Many wait for permission, encouragement, or external motivation to act, yet a free mind does not depend on others—it acts from its own understanding.

The mind is conditioned to avoid failure, leading to hesitation, yet true initiative is not about success—it is about movement with intelligence. People postpone action, hoping for certainty and security, yet there is no perfect moment—initiative exists only in the now. Many rely on leaders, systems, or encouragement to take action, yet a mind that understands does not wait—it acts when necessary. Society teaches obedience, making people hesitant to take initiative, but a free mind does not follow blindly—it moves with intelligence. Thought analyzes endlessly—'Should I act or not?'—creating inner conflict, yet when one sees clearly, there is no question—action happens.

Overthinking creates delay, while presence brings immediate action. A mind that is awake does not postpone—it responds instantly.

When one understands what needs to be done, action follows naturally, for a mind without confusion does not hesitate. Fear paralyzes action, making one seek security before acting, but a fearless mind acts without being burdened by self-doubt. Initiative is lost when one seeks permission or recognition, yet a truly independent mind does not ask, 'Should I?'—it simply acts. When one takes initiative only for reward, failure brings hesitation, but true initiative moves freely, without fear of results. Initiative is not about ambition, effort, or proving oneself—it is the natural action that arises when the mind is clear and undisturbed. Many struggle with initiative because they fear failure, overthink, or seek external validation, but true initiative comes when hesitation and dependence drop away. A mind free from fear, self-doubt, and conditioning does not 'try' to take initiative—it acts with intelligence, effortlessly, without seeking permission or reward. In this freedom, initiative is no longer something to cultivate—it is simply the movement of a mind that sees, understands, and responds without hesitation, without resistance, without fear.

116. Ambition

Ambition: The Endless Struggle for Power and Recognition

Ambition is the strong desire to achieve success, power, recognition, or self-improvement. It is driven by comparison, competition, and the urge to 'become' something greater than what one is. Society glorifies ambition, portraying it as essential for progress, yet does ambition bring real happiness, or does it create endless struggle? The mind believes it is incomplete now but will be fulfilled in the future through success, wealth, or achievement. This movement from 'what is' to 'what should be' creates conflict and restlessness. No matter what is achieved, the mind immediately seeks more—higher status, greater recognition, or greater power—ensuring that satisfaction is always temporary, for desire is never-ending.

Ambition thrives on competition, leading to division, jealousy, frustration, and the fear of failure. Nations, religions, and individuals compete for dominance, making ambition a root cause of war, exploitation, and suffering. The 'self' wants to accumulate success, fame, and achievements to feel important, yet the self is merely thought, memory, and identification. What is it trying to improve? Is ambition just another way to reinforce the illusion of the self? The ambitious mind is constantly seeking, yet never at peace, for as long as there is ambition, there is comparison, and where there is comparison, there is always someone 'better,' keeping the cycle of dissatisfaction alive.

The moment one sees that ambition is endless craving without real fulfillment, its hold weakens. Can one act, work, and create without seeking success or recognition? Passion is doing something fully, with love, without seeking a result, while ambition is doing something with the desire for reward and recognition. Can one work with intensity without being driven by ambition? Society teaches us to measure ourselves against others, fueling ambition, yet a mind free from comparison acts out of intelligence, not a desire for superiority. Action that is free from ambition is done in the present, with total attention, whereas the ambitious mind acts for the future, always wanting something later. Ambition creates struggle, division, and an endless cycle of desire and dissatisfaction, but a life without ambition is not passive—it is a life of action without ego, without competition, without craving for success. When ambition ends, there is complete attention to the present, and in that attention, there is deep intelligence, love, and creativity.

117. Craving

Craving: The Hunger That Never Finds Satisfaction

Craving is the intense psychological desire for pleasure, fulfillment, or escape from discomfort. It arises when thought projects an ideal future, seeking satisfaction through external means. A mind caught in craving is never at peace—it is always restless, always seeking more. This movement of seeking creates an illusion of progress, yet no fulfillment ever lasts. Each craving, once fulfilled, gives rise to another, keeping the mind in a continuous state of dissatisfaction. The search for pleasure becomes the center of one's existence, preventing true stillness, clarity, and inner freedom.

Craving is sustained by thought, where desire itself is natural, but craving is desire extended through mental repetition. Thought recalls past pleasures, strengthening the urge to relive them, making the mind dependent on external stimulation. This dependence leads to frustration when desires remain unfulfilled and anxiety when they are attained, as the fear of losing them takes over. Memory fuels craving by storing pleasurable experiences, which thought revives, making the mind chase what was once enjoyed. Society further conditions the mind to seek success, pleasure, and ambition, reinforcing the illusion that fulfillment comes through accumulation. Craving is never satisfied—each achieved desire soon becomes insufficient, keeping the mind trapped in longing.

Freedom from craving begins with seeing that it is a mental habit, not a necessity. The mind is conditioned to seek and chase, but when craving is observed without indulgence, it begins to lose strength. Letting go of the illusion that fulfillment comes through attainment dissolves the endless cycle of seeking. A mind fully present, without seeking the next pleasure, is no longer trapped in craving. When one lives without attachment to pleasure or pain, experience is enjoyed without dependence, and there is no psychological suffering. In this state, there is no seeking—only deep contentment, effortless awareness, and a profound sense of being.

118. Obsession

Obsession: The Fixation That Destroys Clarity

Obsession is the constant repetition of thought, emotion, or desire that consumes the mind. It arises when a particular thought, image, or goal occupies all of consciousness, leaving no room for clarity or balance. This fixation can be centered around a person, an idea, an achievement, or even an ideology. The mind becomes narrow, unable to see beyond this obsession, and this often leads to emotional imbalance, frustration, and suffering. The root of obsession lies in the mind's desire for security and control, attaching itself to one thought or desire in the hope that it will provide fulfillment or stability in an unpredictable world.

The consequences of obsession are far-reaching. It limits perception, reducing the world to just one thought or desire, thus blocking all other forms of understanding. Obsession creates inner conflict, as the mind fears losing what it is fixated on. This fear fuels further attachment, making the obsession stronger. Additionally, obsession diminishes intelligence and freedom, as it makes the mind rigid and mechanical, leaving no space for openness, creativity, or awareness. A person caught in obsession often finds themselves emotionally fragile and dependent on the object of their fixation, whether it be a person, success, or an ideology. This dependency leads to a distorted sense of self, further entrenching the cycle of obsession.

To be free from obsession, one must observe it without judgment or resistance. By fully recognizing the movement of obsessive thoughts and desires, their grip on the mind weakens. It is essential to understand that external objects, people, or beliefs cannot bring lasting fulfillment. True freedom arises when one learns to let thoughts flow naturally without clinging to them. Living with awareness, fully engaged in the present moment, allows obsession to fade, making life open and fluid. Ultimately, freedom from obsession comes from deep awareness and the understanding that attachment only leads to suffering. A mind that is free from obsession moves lightly, with intelligence and clarity, unaffected by the weight of fixed desires or beliefs.

119. Compulsion

Compulsion: The Involuntary Movement of the Conditioned Mind

Compulsion is the urge to act, think, or feel in a certain way, even when one knows it may be unnecessary or harmful. It arises from conditioning, fear, habit, and deep-seated psychological patterns. A mind caught in compulsion is driven by impulse rather than intelligence, acting without true freedom. The force of compulsion often makes one act out of necessity or desire without deeper understanding or conscious decision-making.

Compulsion creates a loss of awareness in action. When one acts compulsively, there is no space between impulse and response. The action becomes mechanical, rather than conscious and intelligent. Repetition strengthens compulsive tendencies—habits, addictions, and routines make it increasingly difficult to break free. The mind becomes conditioned by past actions and continues to seek the same patterns for temporary relief. However, this temporary satisfaction only sustains underlying restlessness, leading to a continuous cycle of desire, fulfillment, and dissatisfaction.

We live with compulsion because we mistake it for passion or necessity. The mind justifies compulsive behaviors as essential, even when they serve only to perpetuate the cycle of craving. Fear of change and uncertainty keeps us anchored in old patterns. Society further conditions us to prioritize compulsive behaviors like ambition and work, making them seem necessary for survival. To be free from compulsion, one must observe it without judgment, allowing awareness to weaken its grip. Understanding that no compulsion brings true fulfillment, and facing the fears behind it, gradually dissolves the cycle. Freedom arises when we create space between impulse and action, living in full awareness rather than in the grip of unconscious patterns.

120. Stimulation

Stimulation: The Search for Excitement That Numbs Sensitivity

Stimulation is the continuous seeking of excitement, pleasure, and mental engagement, either through external or internal means. It can come from entertainment, social media, relationships, ambition, or even intellectual pursuits. The mind, uncomfortable with stillness, constantly seeks stimulation to escape boredom, emptiness, or inner discomfort. This constant craving keeps the mind in a restless state, always searching for something new to fill the void.

The craving for stimulation arises from the fear of psychological emptiness. When there is silence, the mind feels empty, uncertain, or restless. To avoid facing this, it seeks distraction through various activities—whether through entertainment, relationships, or ambitions. From childhood, we are conditioned to associate pleasure with stimulation, and the more we experience pleasure, the more we crave it. However, does this constant pursuit of stimulation bring lasting joy, or is it merely a temporary escape followed by exhaustion and dissatisfaction? Instead of understanding boredom, the mind fills itself with more activity, noise, and stimulation.

The consequences of constant stimulation are significant. The more one depends on it, the less one can be still, observe, or think clearly. Sensitivity to life's subtleties is lost, and true beauty in nature, relationships, and the simple things is missed. A constantly stimulated mind cannot engage in deep understanding or self-reflection, avoiding the roots of its fears and desires. This cycle of seeking pleasure creates craving and conflict, leading to a constant cycle of highs and dissatisfaction. True joy comes from simplicity and awareness, not from the endless search for excitement. A mind free from dependence on stimulation is not dull but alive, aware, and at peace with the present moment.

121. Selfishness

Selfishness: The Isolation Created by Self-Centered Thought

Selfishness is the psychological movement that prioritizes one's own desires, fears, and interests over others. It arises from attachment to the 'self,' reinforcing division, conflict, and isolation. A mind caught in selfishness seeks gain, security, and pleasure without considering the whole. This self-centered movement creates a barrier between individuals, making relationships transactional and limiting true connection. The pursuit of personal satisfaction without awareness of its consequences leads to competition, possessiveness, and emotional detachment. The more one focuses on their own needs, the more isolated they become, creating an endless cycle of craving and loneliness.

The root of selfishness lies in fear and the illusion of a separate self. Thought creates an identity—'me' as distinct from 'you'—making personal interests seem more important than collective well-being. Society reinforces this division, glorifying individual success, status, and ambition. This conditioning makes selfishness appear normal, even necessary. Selfishness often disguises itself under justification, labeled as self-care, practicality, or ambition. Yet, when actions are motivated by personal gain at the expense of others, they remain fundamentally self-centered. This drive to secure one's own pleasure and security leads to inner conflict, possessiveness, and the constant struggle to maintain control over relationships, achievements, and material possessions.

Freedom from selfishness begins with seeing its nature without judgment or justification. When one observes the self-centered movement of thought without defending or condemning it, its hold weakens. Letting go of the psychological need to 'win' or 'dominate' removes the sense of superiority that fuels selfishness. True fulfillment comes from connection, not accumulation—understanding this dissolves the illusion that taking more leads to happiness. A mind free from self-interest acts without seeking personal reward, moving with intelligence, compassion, and a deep sense of wholeness. In this state, selfishness naturally fades, replaced by a profound awareness that life is not separate but interconnected, beyond the narrow confines of the 'self.'

122. Decision

Decision: The Struggle of Thought in Uncertainty

Decision is the process of selecting between alternatives, shaped by thought, analysis, and conditioning. It arises when the mind is uncertain, seeking clarity through comparison and evaluation. A mind that must decide is often in conflict, torn between desire, fear, and past influences. Where there is complete understanding, action is immediate, requiring no decision. Decision exists only in uncertainty, when the mind hesitates between choices, trying to predict outcomes based on past experience.

The struggle of decision-making comes from attachment, fear, and dependency on thought. The mind fears making the wrong choice, seeking the 'best' outcome and creating anxiety. Desire and attachment complicate decisions, as thought is caught between what it wants and what it fears losing. Society reinforces this struggle, presenting endless choices and making the mind restless. Thought, operating through accumulated knowledge, attempts to solve every problem, yet knowledge is always limited. True intelligence is beyond thought—it perceives without the burden of mental comparison.

Freedom from the struggle of decision comes through clarity, not analysis. When perception is clear, action happens without hesitation. Instead of forcing a decision, one can observe the mind's hesitation without rushing toward a conclusion. When fear and psychological attachment are absent, choices lose their weight, and action flows naturally. True freedom is not found in choosing but in seeing without distortion. A mind that is fully aware does not struggle with decisions—understanding arises naturally, and in that understanding, action is effortless, complete, and beyond conflict.

123. Discipline

Discipline: Beyond Control—The Awakening of True Order

Discipline is often understood as control, obedience, or the repetition of actions to achieve mastery. It is either imposed by authority—parents, teachers, or society—or self-imposed through routines and willpower. But is discipline about suppression and conformity, or is there an order that arises naturally from understanding? A mind that follows rigid discipline acts out of fear or ambition, believing that control leads to order. But does control create real order, or does it only strengthen inner conflict?

The need for discipline comes from fear, desire, and dependence on authority. People believe that without discipline, there will be disorder, laziness, or inefficiency. Society teaches that discipline leads to success, whether in career, meditation, or spiritual growth. But repetitive effort strengthens habit rather than bringing real transformation. Dependence on rules and traditions makes one obedient but not truly intelligent. Many assume that self-discipline will bring freedom, yet a mind that is forced, controlled, and conditioned can never be truly free. Discipline as control creates struggle—one tries to be what one is not, leading to frustration and self-contradiction. Mechanical discipline dulls perception, making the mind rigid and insensitive. Suppression does not end disorder—it only hides it, allowing conflict to persist beneath the surface.

True discipline is not forced—it arises from awareness. If one understands distraction, fear, or disorder deeply, unnecessary actions naturally fall away. A mind that is fully aware does not need imposed discipline—it acts with intelligence. When one sees clearly that certain actions lead to confusion, those actions drop away without effort. Where there is understanding, there is natural order—without rules, without struggle. A mind free from patterns and imitation does not need control; it moves with deep clarity. In this state, discipline is not about repetition, suppression, or willpower, but about perceiving reality as it is and acting from that perception.

124. Effort

Effort: The Strain That Blocks Natural Understanding

Effort is the struggle to achieve, change, or overcome something. It exists when there is resistance—when the mind creates a division between the present reality and an ideal or goal. Society conditions us to believe that effort is necessary for success, growth, and transformation. But does struggle truly lead to intelligence, or does it breed more conflict? The urge to become something better, to attain enlightenment, or to free oneself from suffering sustains effort. Thought projects an ideal state and then struggles to reach it, creating an endless cycle of dissatisfaction. Effort exists because of psychological division—when thought sees 'what is' as inadequate and invents a 'what should be.' This conflict fuels resistance, making effort seem necessary.

Effort drains energy by keeping the mind in constant conflict. A mind caught in effort struggles against itself, wasting vitality.

Striving to be something other than what one is prevents true understanding of the present. Transformation does not happen through struggle but through deep perception. The illusion of progress through effort keeps the mind occupied with becoming rather than seeing. The belief in a controller separate from thought sustains internal struggle—"I must control my anger, my fears"—but is the controller different from what it seeks to control? This false division strengthens effort instead of dissolving it.

Freedom from effort comes through awareness, not struggle. Observing without trying to change eliminates the need for effort, allowing understanding to arise naturally. When the mind lets go of ideals and stops striving to 'become' something, transformation happens without resistance. Acting with full awareness, without psychological time or expectation, removes struggle from action. True change is not gradual—it happens in the instant of complete perception. A mind free from division moves without resistance, without conflict, and with total clarity. In such a state, life flows effortlessly, without the burden of effort, allowing intelligence to act in its purest form.

125. Work

Work: The Burden or the Joy of Living?

Work is the action through which we engage with life, whether for survival, creativity, or service. For many, work becomes a repetitive necessity, a means to an end. But when approached with understanding, work transforms into a natural expression of intelligence and skill. A mind that perceives work in its true light does not see it merely as labor but as an integral movement of living. Whether it is earning a living or pursuing passion, the quality of work is determined by the awareness with which it is approached.

Work can be a means of survival or a creative expression of life. For most people, work is simply a way to secure income and stability. However, when done with awareness and purpose, work can become an art, a meaningful engagement that brings joy and satisfaction. Unfortunately, work often becomes a source of psychological struggle. Many people find themselves working out of compulsion, driven by societal expectations or the pressure of ambition. This creates inner conflict, turning what could be a fulfilling activity into a burdensome task. The pursuit of promotions, financial rewards, and recognition often distorts the true meaning of work, reducing it to a transaction rather than an expression of creativity or purpose.

True engagement with work arises when it is done with passion and without the burden of obligation. Society conditions us to work for security, often overlooking the importance of intrinsic interest and understanding. This leads to a mechanical way of living, where work is something separate from the rest of life. The distinction between 'work' and 'pleasure' creates dissatisfaction in both. Work done for the sake of external rewards breeds exhaustion and boredom. However, when work is approached with full attention, without comparison or fear, it becomes effortless. In such a state, work is no longer a task to be completed but a natural flow of expression, seamlessly integrated with the rest of life.

126. Hurry

Hurry: The Restlessness That Prevents Seeing

Hurry is the mental and physical rush to achieve, reach, or complete something, often at the cost of awareness and understanding. It arises from fear, impatience, ambition, and the conditioning that time is always running out. A mind caught in hurry chases the future, while a mind that understands deeply moves with presence and ease. The mind imagines that fulfillment, success, or happiness lies ahead, keeping one in constant movement, never fully present. A hurried mind is distracted, making mistakes and acting without full awareness, while true efficiency comes from calm, focused attention. When one is always rushing, they only skim the surface of life, never allowing deep insight, stillness, or understanding to take root.

The more one hurries, the more they feel there is 'not enough time,' but time is not the problem—restlessness is. People rush to avoid discomfort, to keep busy, and to chase goals, yet true peace exists only when one is fully where they are. Society teaches that faster means better, that success depends on urgency, but real progress is not in speed—it is in depth and clarity. Many hurry because they fear they are 'running out of time,' yet the future is unknown—only the present is real. The mind thinks happiness is in the next achievement, the next goal, the next moment, but when one arrives, it is already rushing to the next thing. Rushing becomes automatic—a way of thinking, not just an action, and a mind that watches this habit begins to move without hurry.

The mind believes urgency is necessary, but when one stops believing in hurry, it loses power. Many rush through tasks but do them poorly, while true efficiency comes when one gives complete attention without rushing. Hurry exists only when one is thinking of the next moment, and when one is fully present, it disappears. The mind creates urgency—"I must do this now!"—but when one watches thought without reacting, they move with ease. Life requires movement, but does it require mental rushing? A still mind can act swiftly, but without the burden of hurry. Many hurry out of fear, ambition, or social conditioning, believing speed leads to success, but true clarity comes only when the mind is not in a rush. In this freedom, hurry disappears—not because one forces slowness, but because there is no longer a mind escaping the present—only awareness, complete and whole.

127. Struggle

Struggle: The Endless Conflict Between 'What Is' and 'What Should Be'

Struggle is the inner and outer conflict between what exists and what we desire, between reality and what we think should be. It manifests as resistance, effort, and psychological suffering. Struggle arises when there is a gap between the present reality and our ideal or expectation. A mind caught in struggle is burdened by inner tension, trying to change or avoid what is, rather than accepting and understanding it.

Struggle is often rooted in the belief that 'what is' is not enough—that life should be different. This desire for change creates internal conflict, as the mind constantly pushes against reality. We are conditioned to believe that success, growth, and transformation can only come through effort, but is this really the case? The more the mind resists what is, the more it fosters tension and dissatisfaction, which only reinforces the struggle. Struggle comes from psychological division, as part of the mind wants something, while another part resists it. This inner conflict makes it impossible to see and act with clarity.

True freedom from struggle does not come from forceful effort, but from accepting reality as it is. A mind that is free from resistance acts effortlessly, moving with understanding and clarity. When one stops fighting against life, action becomes spontaneous, intelligent, and harmonious. Struggle arises from attachment to outcomes, fear of failure, and comparison with others. When we are fully present, without psychological time or expectation, we can act freely and without hesitation. In this space of awareness, life moves effortlessly, and the struggle dissolves naturally.

128. Laziness

Laziness: The Resistance to Observation and Action

Laziness is the reluctance to act, even when action is necessary or beneficial. It is not simply physical tiredness, but the result of psychological resistance, fear, or lack of interest. A mind caught in laziness is not at rest—it is in conflict, seeking escape rather than engagement. True laziness arises from the avoidance of necessary action, stemming from inner struggles rather than physical exhaustion.

Laziness is not just physical inactivity; one can be inactive but fully alert. True laziness occurs when the mind resists necessary action due to boredom, fear, or conditioning. Many avoid tasks because they seem too difficult or because failure feels inevitable. This avoidance breeds procrastination, leading to further inaction. Laziness often emerges from the conflict between "should" and "want," where the mind is torn between duty and desire, draining energy before action even begins. This resistance is strengthened by habit, reinforcing the illusion that avoiding effort is more comfortable than engaging with it.

Laziness is often mistaken for relaxation, but true relaxation is a state of inner peace, whereas laziness involves inner resistance. A lazy mind may feel restless, avoiding action but not truly at ease. The causes of laziness include the belief that action equates to struggle, a lack of interest or purpose in tasks, and being trapped in psychological distractions like entertainment. Fear of failure further prevents action, as does the search for immediate comfort over long-term achievement. Overcoming laziness requires understanding its root causes, such as fear and habit, and acting without psychological pressure. A mind free from these constraints moves effortlessly, with interest and energy, making every action meaningful and natural.

129. Procrastination

Procrastination: The Delay That Strengthens Fear and Doubt

Procrastination is the deliberate delay or avoidance of action despite knowing its necessity. It arises from resistance, fear, mental fatigue, or a desire for temporary comfort. A mind caught in procrastination creates excuses, postpones responsibility, and remains in conflict between "what should be done" and "what is preferred." The mind creates a gap between intention and action, which fosters inner conflict and anxiety.

Procrastination is the conflict between thought and action. Thought forms an ideal of what should be done, but the actual act is delayed due to hesitation or resistance. This conflict leads to guilt, anxiety, and self-judgment. Procrastination is an escape from discomfort, as the mind avoids tasks that seem difficult, uncertain, or demanding, seeking temporary distractions instead. Over time, procrastination strengthens through habit, making even small tasks feel overwhelming. The mind projects these tasks into the future, creating an illusion of more time and keeping one trapped in inaction.

We procrastinate for several reasons—fear of failure or judgment makes action seem risky, while the desire for immediate pleasure over effort drives us to seek distractions. A lack of interest or connection to the task weakens motivation, and the mind often feels overwhelmed by perceived difficulty. The belief in "later" traps the mind in psychological time, preventing full engagement with the present moment. To overcome procrastination, one must see it as a mental habit that delays action. Instead of waiting for motivation, one should engage immediately. By breaking tasks down into smaller steps and living in the present, procrastination loses its grip. A mind free from procrastination does not wait for the "right moment"—it acts now, fully engaged and free from internal resistance.

130. Control

Control: The Illusion of Mastery Over the Self

Control is the attempt to dominate, suppress, or direct thought, emotion, or behavior. It arises from fear, the desire for security, and the pursuit of an ideal. A mind that seeks control is in constant conflict, dividing itself into the 'controller' and the 'controlled.' This division sustains inner struggle, as one part of the mind tries to shape or eliminate another. Society conditions us to believe that control brings discipline and order, but does true order emerge from suppression, or from understanding?

Control creates inner conflict by forcing the mind into opposition with itself. Fear of failure, rejection, or disorder leads to the urge to suppress emotions and thoughts. The desire to 'improve' or 'perfect' oneself strengthens self-discipline, repression, and effort. But a controlled mind, though it may appear disciplined, is not free—it is bound by its own restrictions. Suppression does not resolve the underlying cause of thought or emotion; it merely forces it into hiding, where it continues to shape perception unconsciously. A mind that observes without attempting to control is highly sensitive, intelligent, and capable of direct understanding.

Freedom from control comes through deep awareness, not suppression. Instead of controlling fear, anger, or desire, one can watch them without judgment. When fully observed, they lose their grip naturally. True transformation happens not through willpower but through insight—seeing the nature of thought allows action without resistance. A mind that functions in total attention acts without effort, moving with clarity rather than struggle. Where there is no psychological control, there is no division, no inner conflict—only intelligence operating freely.

131. Resistance

Resistance: The Barrier That Strengthens Conflict

Resistance is the psychological struggle against reality, a refusal to accept things as they are. It manifests as avoidance, suppression, denial, or a constant effort to change thoughts, emotions, or external circumstances. A mind that resists creates division within itself, preventing clarity and direct perception. Resistance is often mistaken for strength and control, but in reality, it leads to conflict, tension, and wasted energy. The mind struggles against emotions, thoughts, and experiences it finds unpleasant, trying to suppress or escape them, yet this only strengthens what it resists. One part of the mind acts as the 'controller,' trying to dominate the 'controlled,' creating inner division and making true understanding impossible. Rooted in fear, resistance arises from the desire to avoid pain, uncertainty, and the unknown, believing that avoidance will bring security.

Constantly fighting against emotions, situations, or people drains the mind of vitality. A mind free from resistance moves with intelligence, responding to life effortlessly. One resists because they believe control brings order, yet forced control only creates suppression, while true order emerges naturally when resistance ends. From childhood, we are conditioned to control discomfort, hide emotions, and conform to expectations, making resistance habitual. The mind clings to the familiar, even when it causes suffering, because change is uncertain. Thought strengthens resistance by categorizing experiences as 'good' or 'bad,' preventing direct perception and making one react rather than observe. Society teaches that resisting challenges, desires, or emotions shows discipline and control, yet real strength comes from deep awareness, not suppression.

Can one observe anger, fear, or pain without trying to change or control them? What is fully seen loses its grip without effort or suppression. A mind that does not defend itself against fear or suffering understands them completely, acting with intelligence. Avoiding pain only prolongs it, while facing it directly brings freedom. The more one fights an emotion, the stronger it becomes. A mind free of resistance acts without inner division, moving with effortless clarity. Practical control is necessary in daily life, but inwardly, wherever there is resistance, there is struggle. True freedom is the absence of psychological resistance, allowing one to meet life fully. When resistance ends, there is deep harmony, freedom, and the ability to perceive reality without distortion, without struggle, and without fear.

132. Suppression

Suppression: The Force That Breeds Inner Rebellion

Suppression is the act of pushing down emotions, desires, thoughts, or impulses out of fear, morality, or social conditioning. It is often mistaken for self-control or discipline, but it is really a form of avoidance. Suppression creates inner conflict because what is denied doesn't disappear—it remains buried, awaiting a chance to resurface. The mind may feel as though it has control, but it only creates a mental pressure that eventually erupts. True freedom and understanding cannot come through suppression, but through accepting and observing what arises without resistance.

The root cause of suppression is the fear of facing oneself completely. Emotions like anger, fear, or sorrow are suppressed because confronting them feels uncomfortable. However, this does not eliminate them—it only hides them temporarily. Society and cultural conditioning further reinforce this tendency, teaching us to suppress what is deemed unacceptable. We often believe that suppressing emotions is a sign of strength or moral superiority, but true strength lies in understanding, not avoidance. Suppressing emotions and desires, therefore, is not a form of control—it is the denial of truth.

Living without suppression requires observing emotions and thoughts without judgment or resistance. When an emotion arises, one must allow it to flow without trying to control or escape it. Suppression is merely avoidance, and real freedom comes from understanding what is, not pushing it away. By observing and understanding emotions as they are, without identification or resistance, the mind becomes free. True transformation comes from seeing and allowing things to dissolve naturally, not through repression or control. A mind free from suppression moves in clarity, with deep awareness, unburdened by conflict or inner division.

133. Adaptability

Adaptability: The Freedom to Move With Change Without Resistance

Adaptability is the ability to adjust to new situations, challenges, and perspectives without inner conflict or fear. It arises when the mind is free from rigid beliefs, attachments, and the need for control. A mind caught in adaptability as a strategy adjusts out of necessity, while a mind that understands deeply flows with change effortlessly. Many mistake adaptability for blind obedience or compromise, yet true adaptability is not submission—it is the ability to respond with clarity. The mind that clings to the past or resists the unknown struggles with change, while a truly adaptable mind sees change as natural and moves with it, not against it. A rigid mind clings to beliefs, habits, and identities, fearing loss of stability, while a flexible mind remains steady, adjusting without attachment.

The mind wants certainty, fearing the unknown, yet control is an illusion—only movement with change brings true stability. Society teaches that success and security come from fixed plans and certainty, yet life itself is uncertain, and true adaptability means embracing this reality. People define themselves by careers, relationships, and beliefs, and when these change, they struggle to adapt, feeling lost. The familiar feels safe, while change brings discomfort, yet growth only happens when one is willing to move beyond the known. Some believe adapting means compromising values, but true adaptability is not about pleasing others—it is about seeing clearly. Resistance to change creates struggle, while adaptation allows smooth transition. A free mind moves without hesitation, without the burden of past conditioning.

Everything moves—seasons change, bodies age, thoughts shift. A mind that does not resist this truth adapts naturally. The more one demands security, the harder it is to adapt, yet when one accepts uncertainty, adaptability happens effortlessly. When one watches thought, belief, and habits without clinging, they adjust easily, for adaptability exists when there is no rigid self-image. Many carry past failures or successes, letting them shape their present actions, but a free mind responds freshly, without being bound by past conditioning. Resistance creates stress, while adaptability brings ease, and a truly adaptable person does not adjust out of fear, but out of deep understanding. Adaptability is not about forcefully changing oneself to fit circumstances—it is the effortless response to life when there is no resistance. A mind free from attachment, self-image, and the need for certainty does not struggle to adapt—it moves fluidly, responding to each moment with intelligence. In this freedom, adaptability is not something one 'tries' to do—it is the natural state of a mind that does not resist life but flows with it, without effort, without conflict.

5. Personal Growth & Transformation

WAKE UP

WAKE UP

134. Becoming

Becoming: The Endless Struggle to Be Something

Becoming is the psychological movement of striving to be something other than what one is. It occurs both externally (through career, status, skills) and psychologically (seeking inner transformation, perfection, or enlightenment). While external becoming can be necessary for growth, such as learning new skills, psychological becoming creates internal conflict and is driven by illusion. The mind is conditioned to believe that it is incomplete and must progress, but this belief creates a constant divide between 'what is' and 'what should be.' This gap fosters struggle and frustration, reinforcing dissatisfaction.

Becoming thrives on psychological time—the belief that fulfillment lies in the future. The mind constantly seeks an ideal state—success, enlightenment, or transformation—at the cost of accepting the present. This striving creates inner tension, as each goal achieved only opens the door to another desire. The pursuit of an ideal perpetuates this cycle, preventing peace and contentment. In truth, the constant urge to become something else strengthens the illusion of the 'self' and reinforces the belief in its inadequacy. True transformation is not found in endless striving, but in direct perception of 'what is' without the desire to change it.

True freedom comes from seeing that becoming is an illusion created by thought, sustained by comparison and fear. The mind conditioned to always seek improvement, validation, or change is never content. Real growth does not come from 'becoming' something else but from understanding the present moment without attachment to past or future. True fulfillment is found not in achieving an ideal, but in being fully present with life as it is, allowing peace and clarity to arise naturally. A mind free from the need to 'become' is whole, complete, and at ease in the present.

135. Success and Failure

Success and Failure: The Illusions That Define Our Worth

Success and failure are mental constructs shaped by societal conditioning, comparison, and personal expectations. Success is often seen as the attainment of a goal, while failure is the lack of it. Both concepts are defined in relation to external standards or achievements, which creates a cycle of measuring oneself against these fluctuating ideals. This cycle traps the mind in seeking approval and fearing inadequacy, preventing true freedom from the influence of societal judgment. These constructs perpetuate psychological conflict, where one constantly oscillates between striving for success and fearing failure.

The concepts of success and failure are deeply rooted in societal conditioning and comparison. Success and failure are not absolute truths but are defined by what society deems valuable at a particular time or place. This external measurement fosters competition, envy, and insecurity. Success creates the fear of losing what one has gained, while failure creates the fear of never attaining success. Both conditions trap individuals in anxiety, preventing them from fully living in the present moment. Instead of fostering real learning or growth, the pursuit of success and the avoidance of failure often blind individuals to the learning inherent in experience itself.

Living without the burden of success and failure begins with understanding that these are constructs created by thought. When one realizes that life is not a competition, but a movement of learning, discovery, and awareness, success and failure lose their grip. A mind free from these concepts acts without fear of outcomes, moving freely in the present moment. True intelligence and fulfillment come from living fully in the now, without comparison or attachment to external results. In this state, there is no need to measure or validate one's existence through achievement—only deep attention to the experience of life itself.

136. Positivity and Negativity

Positivity and Negativity: The Duality That Shapes Perception

Positivity and negativity are two psychological judgments that shape our perception of life. Positivity focuses on what is pleasant, hopeful, or encouraging, while negativity focuses on what is unpleasant, discouraging, or critical. These judgments are rooted in past conditioning, personal desires, and fears. Both positivity and negativity are conditioned responses that the mind uses to react to experiences. Positivity is often encouraged by society as a way to escape difficulties, while negativity arises when expectations are not met. Both are influenced by psychological time: positivity looks forward to a better future, while negativity dwells in past failures or anticipates future suffering.

The mind that sees clearly transcends both positivity and negativity. Wisdom lies beyond this duality, where the mind does not cling to either extreme but simply perceives reality as it is. Forced positivity often suppresses deeper understanding, and resisting negativity only strengthens it. These emotional states are temporary, and one need not identify with them. The mind conditioned to see things in terms of "good" or "bad" is trapped in mental projections. When labels are dropped, reality is seen without distortion, and the mind moves freely, unburdened by judgment.

True freedom arises when one acts without seeking a positive outcome or avoiding a negative one. Intelligence sees without bias, not through the lens of optimism or pessimism. Life is not about making it better or assuming the worst—it is about accepting it as it is. A mind rooted in the present, without mental labels or expectations, responds to life naturally, moving with clarity and understanding. In this freedom, the mind is no longer caught in the pursuit of happiness or the avoidance of suffering but lives fully in the moment, beyond all illusions of duality.

137. Reward and Punishment

Reward and Punishment: The Trap of External Validation

Reward and punishment are mechanisms used to control behavior through external incentives, shaping actions based on the desire for pleasure or the fear of pain. These systems reinforce conformity and obedience, often leading individuals to act not out of genuine understanding, but to achieve rewards or avoid consequences. A mind conditioned by reward and punishment operates mechanically, driven by external validation rather than inner intelligence. This reliance on rewards and punishments creates a cycle of dependency, where the individual seeks validation and avoids discomfort, limiting true freedom and awareness.

The conditioning of reward and punishment begins early in life, where systems like schools, family, and society enforce behavior through incentives and fear. This creates patterns of seeking rewards and avoiding discomfort, which become deeply ingrained in the psyche. While society uses reward and punishment to enforce conformity and control, this approach limits true moral understanding, as it is based on fear and gain rather than insight. The fear of punishment discourages exploration and questioning, leading to a stagnant, conforming mind, while the pursuit of reward often strengthens desire and comparison, creating internal conflict and discontentment.

True freedom comes when the mind is no longer governed by the need for external validation or the fear of punishment. When one acts from understanding rather than seeking approval or fearing consequences, action becomes natural and effortless. By observing fear and desire without reacting to them, the grip of reward and punishment dissolves. The mind becomes free from the constant cycle of craving and suppression, and actions are rooted in clarity, compassion, and a deep connection to life. In this state, there is no psychological dependence on reward or punishment—just a profound sense of freedom and wholeness.

138. Individual

Individual: The Illusion of Separation and Identity

The concept of the individual is commonly understood as a separate entity, a unique being with personal thoughts, experiences, and identity. Society conditions us to believe we are distinct, independent, and must assert our uniqueness. Yet, when examined deeply, is the individual truly separate, or is this merely an illusion created by thought? The mind creates the sense of a distinct self, defined by memories, experiences, and cultural influences, reinforcing the belief in personal separation. But in truth, this idea of individuality is shaped by societal expectations and external conditioning, not by an inherent reality.

The idea of the individual is reinforced by comparison, competition, and the need to assert uniqueness. From childhood, society teaches us to strive for personal success, to be someone special. However, if individuality were genuinely real, would it be so easily shaped by external influences, such as culture, environment, and upbringing? The belief in individualism fosters division, competition, and fear. It strengthens the ego, pushing us further away from understanding the interconnectedness of all existence. This psychological separation creates conflict, not just externally with others, but also internally, as we struggle to maintain the illusion of independence.

In truth, the individual is not separate from the whole of existence. Our emotions, desires, fears, and ambitions are shared human experiences, not personal attributes. The mind creates a division between 'me' and 'you,' but is this division real, or is it just an illusion? True freedom comes from seeing beyond this illusion of separation. When the 'self' is absent—free from conditioning, comparison, and fear—there is a deep understanding that we are part of the whole, not apart from it. True individuality lies not in asserting uniqueness, but in living without the burden of conditioning, acting from intelligence and awareness, and experiencing life fully in the present moment. In this understanding, there is no longer a need to prove oneself, for real freedom is found in the unity of all existence.

139. Individuality

Individuality: The Fearless Expression of One's True Nature

Individuality is the sense of being a unique and separate person, distinct from others, shaped by one's name, culture, education, experiences, and beliefs. It is a psychological construct, a product of thought, that creates a barrier between oneself and humanity. This belief in individuality often leads the mind to perceive itself as distinct from others, reinforcing the sense of separation and conflict. But when examined closely, is individuality truly real, or is it just a mental illusion that limits our perception of oneness with the world?

The desire to feel special and unique drives the clinging to individuality. Society encourages this by promoting achievements, status, and personal identity as a means of validation. The 'self' becomes attached to its uniqueness, seeking importance, recognition, and superiority. When individuality is questioned, fear arises, as the mind worries about losing its sense of self, its identity, and its place in the world. But upon deeper reflection, is the 'self' anything more than a collection of memories and labels? In truth, psychological separation, rather than providing security, creates conflict, division, and competition, as individuals fight for survival, validation, and recognition.

True freedom is not found in the assertion of individuality, but in understanding the conditioning that shapes the self. When one sees the influence of past experiences, beliefs, and societal pressures, the need to cling to an individual identity fades. The realization that the 'self' is not separate from the rest of humanity brings clarity. We all share the same human experiences—pain, joy, fear, and love—yet thought creates the illusion of separation. True uniqueness arises from deep awareness and the freedom from comparison and conditioning. When the psychological 'I' is seen for what it is—a construct of thought—there is no longer a need to prove oneself or compete. In this awareness, there is deep intelligence, love, and a profound connection to life. The search for individuality dissolves, and one finds true freedom in the understanding that we are all part of a greater whole.

140. Opportunity

Opportunity: Seeing Beyond Limitations and Fear

Opportunity is the potential for action, growth, or change that appears in each moment. It is not just an external event but an internal readiness to engage and respond to life as it unfolds. A mind that recognizes opportunity is not simply waiting for favorable conditions but is awake and present, fully aware of what is available in the now. Opportunity exists in the present, not in some distant future, and a mind that postpones action misses the richness of what is right before it.

Many people mistakenly believe that opportunity comes later, but it is always in the present moment. True opportunity is not created but recognized; it requires alertness to see what is already available. Often, opportunities are disguised as challenges or obstacles. The mind, conditioned to resist difficulty, fails to see the potential for growth hidden within those challenges. Moreover, fear and hesitation block the ability to act when an opportunity arises, leading to missed chances and a sense of regret. The greatest opportunities are not necessarily about material gain or success, but about gaining deeper insight and understanding.

We miss opportunities because of conditioned beliefs, fear, and expectations of perfection. The mind is trained to wait for the 'right time,' but the right time is always now. The search for ideal conditions or the avoidance of risk keeps us from seeing the opportunities already in front of us. Additionally, a distracted mind, preoccupied with past regrets or future anxieties, is unable to engage with the present moment. To recognize and seize opportunities, one must live with awareness, free from mental noise and fear, willing to take the first step without waiting for certainty or guarantees. When opportunity is viewed in this way, it becomes a continuous flow of possibilities, not just for success, but for growth and understanding.

141. Patterns

Patterns: The Invisible Structures That Govern Our Lives

Patterns are the repetitive ways in which the mind operates, shaping thought, emotion, and action based on past conditioning. They are formed through repetition and influence from society, culture, and personal experiences. A mind trapped in patterns operates mechanically, unable to perceive or respond to life in a fresh or creative way. The mind clings to these repetitive responses because they provide comfort and predictability, yet this predictability limits freedom and understanding, preventing true engagement with the present moment.

The nature of patterns is rooted in the past; each thought, experience, or emotion leaves an imprint that shapes future responses. This repetition creates a cycle of reactions based on previous experiences rather than direct perception of reality. The mind is often unaware that its responses are shaped by these established patterns, which leads to psychological conditioning. These patterns influence not only practical aspects of life, such as survival and routines but also the deeper psychological aspects, including fear, ambition, and belief systems. Patterns give the illusion of security and control, but in reality, they trap the mind in a narrow, conditioned view, preventing it from experiencing life freely and fully.

To be free from patterns, one must observe them without identifying with them. True freedom comes when the mind stops clinging to past experiences, allowing it to respond to each moment with clarity and fresh awareness. Breaking away from these patterns requires deep awareness, not effort or struggle. Effort to change patterns only reinforces them, whereas seeing them clearly dissolves their power. A mind that lives without reliance on preconceived responses experiences direct perception, free from the confines of habitual thinking. When the mind is free from patterns, it functions with intelligence and creativity, fully engaged with life as it unfolds, not bound by the past but open to the infinite possibilities of the present.

142. Limitation

Limitation: The Boundaries Created by Thought

Limitation, in its essence, is a veil that distorts the pure light of perception, casting shadows over the mind's natural clarity. It is a creation of thought, born from the mental patterns we so blindly inherit and accept. Thought, tethered to memory and past experiences, establishes boundaries, shaping the way we see the world and, more importantly, ourselves. The mind, conditioned by years of belief and societal constructs, clings to these boundaries, creating a false sense of security that locks us into a narrow, constricted existence. It is within these confines that we lose the ability to see beyond what is familiar, comfortable, and known.

The nature of limitation is both insidious and subtle, as it is not always immediately apparent. At times, it manifests as fear—fear of the unknown, fear of failure, and even the fear of freedom itself. These fears create an internal resistance, a defense mechanism that keeps the mind trapped within its self-imposed walls. This resistance, rather than leading to growth or protection, only perpetuates a cycle of stagnation. It prevents the mind from opening itself to new possibilities, new ways of thinking, and new ways of being. In its relentless pursuit of safety and certainty, the mind grows dull, unable to perceive the present moment with the fullness it deserves.

To free oneself from limitation is not merely a matter of 'overcoming' or 'breaking through' the boundaries that encircle the mind. True freedom lies in the deep and quiet understanding of the illusory nature of these limitations. When the mind ceases to identify with its past conditioning, when it relinquishes the constant need for comparison, when it allows itself to be free from the weight of external expectations, it opens itself to the boundless possibilities that lie within. In this space of clarity, the mind becomes not a prisoner of its limitations but an active participant in the ever-expanding unfolding of reality, perceiving life as it truly is, without the filters of fear, habit, and conditioning. Only then does true freedom, and with it, intelligence and clarity, emerge.

143. Leader

Leader: Authority, Influence, and the Burden of Power

A leader is someone who holds authority, guiding others through influence, power, or vision. Leadership arises when people seek direction, security, or solutions from someone outside themselves. This dependency creates a relationship where those who follow the leader lose the ability to think independently, becoming reliant on the leader's decisions and guidance.

Leadership inherently creates division between the leader and the followers. The act of assuming authority establishes a hierarchy, with the leader in control and the followers in a subordinate role.

This division often leads to control and obedience, and in some cases, exploitation. Leaders become symbols, idealized figures that are projected upon, and as a result, they often represent an image rather than a true reality. People tend to follow leaders not just for their wisdom but also to escape from their own confusion and the burden of independent thinking.

People seek leaders because of an inherent fear of standing alone. Without external direction, the mind feels insecure. Society and cultural conditioning also play significant roles, teaching individuals from childhood to respect and follow figures of power. This conditioning often prevents questioning of authority, making dependence on a leader feel natural. However, true wisdom is not found in another; it arises from direct awareness and understanding of reality. When one takes full responsibility for their own understanding, they no longer need to follow leaders. A mind that observes, questions, and takes responsibility is free from dependence, living in complete clarity and intelligence.

144. Inspiration

Inspiration: The Spark That Awakens Inner Movement

Inspiration is the spontaneous energy that arises when the mind is clear, open, and fully present. Unlike motivation, which is driven by effort and the desire for a specific outcome, inspiration flows effortlessly when there is no expectation, ambition, or self-interest. It is not something that can be forced or cultivated, but rather a natural occurrence when one is deeply engaged in the moment, allowing life to move through them without resistance.

Inspiration is a movement of life itself, arising when the mind is free from the clutter of thought, fear, and external pressures.

The nature of inspiration lies beyond intellectual effort or knowledge. While thought can analyze and compare, it cannot create inspiration. True inspiration occurs when the mind is silent and attentive, free from the distractions of psychological time or the urge to control. It is not personal; it is the expression of intelligence and creativity flowing through the individual. Inspiration exists only in the present moment, without the need for planning or future anticipation. When one tries to force inspiration, it slips away, because effort and expectation block the natural flow of creativity.

We often struggle to feel inspired because we seek it with effort, expecting it to come from certain sources or conditions. This pressure and the desire to find inspiration only create mental noise, preventing it from arising. Inspiration is not a result of routine or habit but occurs when the mind is free, observing the present with fresh eyes. It does not depend on external influences like books, music, or people; rather, it is an internal awakening, an insight that emerges when the mind is still. When the search for inspiration ends, it arises naturally, filling every moment with clarity, creativity, and the fullness of life.

145. Confidence

Confidence: The Strength That Comes from Clarity

Confidence is the state of inner clarity and stability, where one acts and thinks with trust, free from external validation or the need to assert oneself. It arises naturally from deep understanding, not from seeking approval or trying to prove one's worth. A mind rooted in true confidence does not fear judgment, nor does it need recognition to affirm its worth. Instead, it moves with clarity, guided by inner insight and awareness. Confidence is not about dominance or superiority; rather, it is a quiet, natural presence that flows effortlessly in any situation.

The nature of confidence lies in its absence of fear and self-doubt. True confidence is not about appearing bold or fearless, but about living without inner conflict or hesitation. It does not depend on others' opinions or praise, as it exists independently of external validation. Confidence is revealed through direct experience and deep understanding, not through mere knowledge or imitation. It is the ability to act from clarity without any division between thought and action. A confident mind moves freely and decisively, unencumbered by hesitation or self-judgment.

Struggling with confidence often arises from societal conditioning—equating confidence with success, achievement, and recognition. Many people seek validation or measure their worth through comparison, leading to insecurity. Fear of being wrong or failing makes them hesitant, further reinforcing the cycle of doubt. However, true confidence does not require comparison, approval, or certainty. It is revealed when fear and self-doubt dissolve, and one acts freely without seeking to prove anything. Confidence is not something to cultivate through effort or imitation; it is naturally present when the mind is free from resistance, fully present, and grounded in understanding.

146. Courage

Courage: Walking Alone Without Fear or Conformity

Courage is not the absence of fear, but the ability to act despite it. It is a state where the mind moves with clarity, strength, and understanding, without being controlled by fear, uncertainty, or opposition. True courage arises from deep awareness and intelligence, not from aggression or blind action. It is a natural response to life's challenges, where the mind is free from hesitation or inner conflict. A mind caught in the image of courage may seek to prove itself, but real courage moves effortlessly, from a place of deep understanding, without the need for validation or approval.

The nature of courage lies in its ability to coexist with fear without being dominated by it. Fear is natural, but true courage is the ability to see fear and act with awareness, not impulsiveness. It is not about overcoming external obstacles, but overcoming the internal battles of self-doubt, insecurity, and conditioning. Courage exists only in the present moment, not in the past or future. It is freedom from the psychological dependence on validation and external approval, where one acts from inner clarity rather than from the desire for recognition or success.

Many struggle with courage because they seek security in approval, certainty, or external reinforcement. The mind often hesitates, fearing failure, rejection, or the unknown. But true courage is not waiting for perfect conditions or eliminating fear—it is acting despite uncertainty and without seeking validation. When the mind is fully aware and free from inner conflict, courage arises naturally. It is not something to attain but a natural state of being, where the mind moves with truth, clarity, and fearlessness. In this state, fear is no longer a barrier, and action is effortless and aligned with understanding.

147. Dedication

Dedication: The Energy That Sustains Meaningful Action

Dedication is the sustained commitment to a task or goal driven by passion, responsibility, or the desire for mastery. It is not about forcing oneself to push through but about being fully engaged in the process itself. A mind dedicated to something acts with clarity and intelligence, moving naturally without being weighed down by the pressure of expectations or external rewards. True dedication arises from within, where one is connected deeply to what they are doing, rather than being motivated by outside forces.

The nature of dedication is rooted in understanding and passion. It is not a mindless repetition or struggle but a genuine, focused involvement in the task. While society often associates dedication with sacrifice or effort, true dedication feels effortless when there is deep passion and clarity. Dedication becomes an obsession only when it is rigid and lacks flexibility. True dedication allows space for growth and change, adapting to new possibilities without losing focus or interest in the task at hand.

Struggling with dedication often arises from external pressures, such as the desire for quick results, recognition, or approval. This external motivation makes dedication feel like a burden, resulting in exhaustion and frustration. When dedication comes from a place of love and inner commitment, it becomes effortless and natural. The key is to act with full presence, free from fear of failure or comparison, and to find joy in the work itself. This allows dedication to flow freely, not as a forced effort but as a deep, engaged experience.

148. Consistency

Consistency: The Balance Between Habit and Awareness

Consistency is the desire for stability, predictability, and uniformity in thought, action, and behavior. It is often praised as a virtue, associated with reliability, steadiness, and discipline. However, does consistency bring truth, or does it create rigidity, preventing real understanding? The mind craves security, seeking predictability to feel in control and avoid uncertainty. Society reinforces this need by valuing those who remain consistent in their beliefs, decisions, and identities, often viewing change as a sign of weakness or hypocrisy. Additionally, people construct a fixed self-image and feel threatened when change challenges their sense of identity. Traditions, routines, and societal expectations further condition individuals to uphold consistency, making life habitual rather than an ongoing inquiry.

However, psychological consistency creates significant limitations. When life is lived through fixed routines and repeated patterns, it becomes mechanical, dull, and resistant to new insights. A mind attached to consistency stops questioning, learning, and seeing freshly. Holding onto a fixed belief, even when reality contradicts it, prevents one from perceiving truth, which is always alive and beyond past conclusions. This rigidity also creates inner conflict—when new understanding arises, yet one clings to past ideas for the sake of consistency, there is a struggle. Moreover, psychological consistency is an illusion; life is in constant motion, and the attempt to maintain a fixed identity or belief structure is an effort to freeze what is naturally changing.

Freedom from the burden of consistency allows for intelligence that is flexible and responsive to each moment. True intelligence does not operate from past conclusions but sees directly, without distortion. Thought, when fluid rather than fixed, enables one to remain open to truth as it unfolds, rather than being bound by old beliefs. A free mind does not need to defend past decisions or maintain an image of itself—it moves effortlessly with awareness, unafraid of change. Psychological consistency may provide a false sense of stability, but real clarity comes from being fully present and responding to life as it is, not as one believes it should be. In intelligence, in truth, in love—there is no need for consistency, only deep understanding that moves in harmony with life, never against it.

149. Progress

Progress: The Movement That Has No Final Destination

Progress is commonly viewed as a journey toward improvement, whether in scientific, technological, or social realms. External progress, such as advancements in medicine, transportation, and communication, is evident. However, true progress in human consciousness remains uncertain. While we have made leaps in technology, has there been any movement in ending the internal conflicts, fears, and divisions that shape our human experience?

We may have advanced externally, but have we truly evolved inwardly to address the suffering, violence, and ignorance that continue to persist?

The assumption that psychological progress mirrors material progress is misleading. While science has changed the external world dramatically, human consciousness—shaped by fear, greed, and division—seems to remain largely the same. We may seek to evolve, becoming wiser, more compassionate, or morally superior, but in essence, this is just the ego seeking to improve itself, reinforcing its limitations. Real transformation, however, is not about becoming something better—it is about seeing through the illusion of 'becoming' and understanding the truth directly, without the filter of time or self-interest.

True progress comes from a deep understanding of life and the dissolution of internal conflict, not from the accumulation of knowledge or achievements. When one stops seeking psychological progress, the mind becomes free, and true transformation occurs. This kind of progress is not measured by external accomplishments but by the freedom from fear, greed, and ambition—creating a mind at peace. Until humanity breaks free from its conditioning and seeks not external validation but inner clarity, progress remains an illusion. True progress is a peaceful mind that can perceive life as it is, in deep awareness, without conflict or division.

150. Achievement

Achievement: The Endless Chase for Recognition

Achievement is the process of attaining goals, whether in personal development, career, or relationships. It is often linked with success, recognition, and the pursuit of progress. While achievement provides a sense of accomplishment, it also fuels an ongoing desire for more, creating a cycle of fulfillment followed by renewed craving. Many believe that achievement brings meaning or security, but in truth, it often leads to further dissatisfaction, reinforcing the need for external validation and recognition.

The pursuit of achievement is driven by societal conditioning, which teaches that success equals self-worth. From childhood, we are encouraged to measure our value based on external accomplishments—be it in wealth, status, or academic success. This creates a mind that equates identity with achievement, often leading to fear of failure or inadequacy when goals are not met. However, true fulfillment is not found in reaching goals but in the awareness of the futility of seeking constant success for self-worth.

To live without the constant pursuit of achievement, one must understand that fulfillment exists in the present, not in future accomplishments. True freedom arises when one can act without seeking rewards or recognition, moving beyond comparison and measurement. In the absence of a need to achieve, life unfolds naturally, with clarity, intelligence, and deep contentment in the now. This freedom allows one to live fully, without the burden of self-measurement or the endless chase for more.

151. Perfection

Perfection: The Ideal That Breeds Conflict

Perfection is the pursuit of an ideal state, an image created by thought that promises flawlessness, completeness, and freedom from imperfection. It arises from the mind's need for order, comparison, and validation, making the mind constantly seek something beyond what is. The very nature of perfection lies in the comparison between what is and what "should be," creating a divide that fuels dissatisfaction. As a result, the mind remains trapped in a cycle of striving, never content with the present moment.

The pursuit of perfection is a mental projection, an illusion created by thought. Perfection does not exist as a fixed reality; it is always an idealized state that the mind believes can be attained. This belief leads to psychological time, where the mind constantly looks forward, thinking it must "become" perfect, which creates struggle and tension. The desire for perfection is rooted in fear—fear of judgment, failure, and imperfection—which leads to a life filled with constant anxiety and dissatisfaction. This chase for an unattainable ideal prevents the mind from fully experiencing the present moment, where true clarity and understanding can arise.

Living without seeking perfection means freeing the mind from comparisons and measurements. When the mind stops seeking an ideal state, it can act freely, without hesitation or self-doubt. Life flows naturally when one accepts imperfection as part of the process, seeing that true fulfillment comes not from achieving an ideal but from fully experiencing life as it is. The freedom from perfection allows the mind to engage with each moment in its entirety, where every experience, even if imperfect, is rich, complete, and alive.

152. Master

Master: The One Who Moves Without the Ego

A master is often seen as someone who possesses great wisdom, skill, or authority, guiding others towards truth, success, or enlightenment. People seek masters, whether in the form of spiritual leaders, political figures, or teachers, believing that they hold the key to understanding or power. However, the concept of mastery itself may be a psychological construct, shaped by the mind's desire for certainty and external validation. The idea of mastery creates an illusion of superiority, but true understanding and wisdom do not come from external authority—they arise from direct perception and self-awareness.

The search for a master is often driven by the mind's need for guidance, security, and certainty. From childhood, we are conditioned to rely on external authority figures—parents, teachers, and religious leaders—believing that their knowledge holds the answers to life's mysteries. This dependency fosters the habit of looking outward for solutions rather than questioning or exploring within. As a result, the search for a master can hinder self-knowledge and personal growth. When we follow a master without inquiry, we risk becoming mechanically reliant on their teachings, rather than developing the intelligence to understand the world for ourselves.

True mastery is not about following or imitating others; it is the ability to see clearly, without distortion or conditioning. A master is not someone who creates followers but one who helps others to think for themselves. True mastery comes from freedom—freedom from the ego, from ambition, and from the need for recognition. It is found in a mind that is free, silent, and aware, one that perceives reality without fear or illusion. The real master is not an external figure but the mind itself, liberated from the constraints of thought, seeking no authority but the clarity of direct perception. Only when we cease the search for an external master do we discover our own inner intelligence and true understanding.

153. Fulfillment

Fulfillment: The Contentment That Lies Beyond Desire

Fulfillment is often seen as the ultimate state of completeness, a moment where one feels satisfied and whole. People chase this sense of fulfillment through relationships, career achievements, possessions, and spiritual pursuits, believing that once they attain these goals, they will feel complete. However, this quest for fulfillment is fleeting, as the sense of satisfaction never lasts. The more one achieves, the more one desires, and the cycle of seeking continues, leaving the mind always in pursuit of something more. Fulfillment, then, is not a permanent state, but rather a constant movement of desire, preventing true contentment.

The pursuit of fulfillment is rooted in the belief that we are incomplete as we are. This creates a deep sense of inner lack, leading to a constant search for something external to fill the emptiness. We are conditioned by society to think that fulfillment is found in achievement or recognition. We look to others, comparing ourselves, and chasing what they have, believing it will satisfy our own desires. However, this external search is always temporary, as once one goal is reached, another one replaces it, and the feeling of fulfillment quickly fades. This creates an endless cycle of seeking, leaving one perpetually unsatisfied.

True fulfillment comes not from external achievements or future hopes, but from an understanding that fulfillment is an illusion created by the mind's desire to constantly seek. When the mind stops chasing fulfillment and simply observes the present moment, it becomes fully content. The need for fulfillment arises from the belief in incompleteness, but when this belief dissolves, peace and contentment arise naturally. Fulfillment is not something to be attained in the future—it is found in living fully in the present, free from the psychological time that creates a sense of lack. When the search for fulfillment ends, true wholeness is experienced, not in becoming, but in simply being.

154. Self-Esteem

Self-Esteem: The Fragile Identity Built on Comparison

Self-esteem is the psychological construct through which we measure our worth, often based on external validation or internal beliefs about ourselves. It is shaped by achievements, opinions, and societal standards that define success, recognition, and status. Society conditions us to associate self-worth with external accomplishments, leading us to either feel superior when successful or inferior when we fall short. But true self-understanding is not found in these comparisons; self-esteem itself is an illusion, a mental image created by thought.

The pursuit of self-esteem arises from the desire for psychological security and acceptance. We crave validation from others, as it helps us feel important and worthy. This need for validation is fueled by comparison—measuring ourselves against others in terms of intelligence, beauty, success, or power. As we constantly evaluate ourselves, we create either feelings of pride or insecurity. This constant evaluation breeds anxiety and pressure to maintain an image, reinforcing the ego and creating division within the mind.

True freedom comes not from having high or low self-esteem, but from seeing self-esteem for what it is—an illusion of thought. When we drop the need to compare ourselves to others, we no longer rely on external validation to determine our worth. A mind that is free from self-esteem does not seek to prove anything but acts from clarity and intelligence. By letting go of the desire to become 'somebody,' we find immense freedom, peace, and natural confidence, fully present and alive without the struggle of self-measurement.

155. Relaxation

Relaxation: The Effortless State of a Mind Without Conflict

Relaxation is the state where both the body and mind are free from tension, effort, and conflict. It is not merely a physical rest but a mental state of complete ease, where there is no struggle or resistance. The mind that is truly relaxed is fully present, without distraction, and free from the constant pressure to achieve or avoid. True relaxation occurs when the mind stops its striving and ceases to measure or compare, allowing it to be at peace in the present moment. It is not a technique to be forced but a natural state that arises when the mind is freed from psychological effort and inner conflict.

The struggle to relax often stems from societal conditioning, where constant activity and productivity are valued over stillness. Many confuse relaxation with laziness or use distractions to escape from their mental restlessness. However, these are not genuine forms of relaxation; they only provide temporary relief while leaving the underlying tension unresolved. True relaxation is the absence of mental and emotional burdens, allowing one to be fully present without the noise of past regrets or future anxieties. It arises when one stops trying to achieve relaxation and simply allows the mind and body to be still, without seeking external stimulation.

Achieving real relaxation requires observing the mind without resistance, allowing thoughts to arise and pass without judgment. It also requires letting go of the psychological time that binds us to the past and future. When we are not constantly fighting against the present moment, relaxation occurs naturally. The body and mind must be in harmony—when the body is free from tension, the mind can follow. True relaxation is not something one can force; it is a state of being that arises when effort ceases, and the mind is free from striving, comparison, and external expectations. In this peaceful state, relaxation is not something to do, but something to experience effortlessly.

WAKE UP

WAKE UP

6. Problems & Challenges

WAKE UP

156. Confusion

Confusion: The Chaos Created by a Divided Mind

Confusion is the state of uncertainty, indecision, and inner conflict, where uncertainty and inner conflict dominate. It arises when the mind is torn between desires, fears, and conditioned beliefs, seeking direction and clarity but finding none. In this state, the mind seeks answers from external sources, hoping that authority, certainty, or guidance will resolve the confusion. However, does seeking external direction truly clear the confusion, or does it perpetuate it by creating dependence and avoiding the root cause?

The source of confusion lies in the conflict between 'what is' and 'what should be.' The mind struggles when reality fails to meet expectations, and instead of accepting what is, it creates a divide, wishing things were different. This is compounded by the habit of seeking the 'right' choice, conditioned by society to believe that the perfect answer exists. The accumulation of conflicting ideas and the fear of making mistakes deepen the confusion, making it harder for the mind to move toward clarity.

The key to ending confusion is not in escaping it through quick decisions or distractions, but by understanding it deeply. Observing confusion without resistance, seeing its root in the movement of thought itself, allows clarity to emerge. When one stops seeking certainty and lets go of the need for choice, right action occurs naturally. True clarity does not come from effort or analysis but from stillness and observation—when the mind is free from judgment and fear, clarity arises effortlessly, bringing freedom from confusion.

157. Conflict

Conflict: The Inner and Outer War That Breeds Suffering

Conflict is the internal and external struggle between opposing desires, beliefs, or emotions. It occurs when there is a division between reality and expectation—between 'what is' and 'what should be'. This division creates tension and suffering, both within the mind and in relationships or societies. Conflict is not just a personal experience; it is ingrained in the way we interact with the world, often arising from comparisons, desires, or our search for security in an impermanent world. It is further fueled by the illusion of the separate self—the idea that 'I' am separate from my emotions, thoughts, and reactions, which leads to internal contradiction and conflict.

Conflict often arises because of our attachment to an ideal or a vision of how we should be, creating a constant division between 'what is' and 'what should be'. We are conditioned to compare ourselves to others, fostering feelings of inferiority or superiority. Our desire for security in a changing world contributes to this conflict, as we try to hold on to fleeting things like relationships, achievements, and beliefs. When reality does not conform to our expectations, frustration arises, and the struggle between thought and reality intensifies. This conflict cannot be suppressed or controlled, as it will only resurface stronger.

True freedom from conflict comes not from suppression but from understanding. Observing conflict deeply, without judgment or escape, allows the mind to see that conflict itself is rooted in thought. The mind that stops comparing, measuring, or seeking to change 'what is' can live without inner division.

When conflict ends, there is clarity, peace, and love. A mind free of conflict acts with intelligence and understanding, not from struggle or fear. In this state, there is no longer the burden of psychological time or the need to 'become' something else—there is only the present moment, free from resistance and filled with awareness.

158. Crisis

Crisis: The Turning Point Where Transformation Begins

A crisis is a moment of disruption, challenge, or conflict that demands a response. It can manifest in many forms—emotional, intellectual, or physical. Whether it's the loss of something significant, the collapse of a societal structure, or personal suffering, crises often force change upon us. The response to a crisis, however, determines whether it leads to transformation or further suffering. While crises may appear as obstacles, they can also serve as opportunities to understand the deeper causes of our fears, conditioning, and attachments. The way we respond, whether through fear and escape or with clarity and presence, dictates the impact of the crisis on our lives.

Crises arise when old structures—whether psychological, societal, or external—fail or no longer serve us. These failures expose the deep-seated conflicts within us, between what we want and what is. They force us to confront our dependency on routines, beliefs, and psychological security. Rather than embracing change, many resist, clinging to the familiar, which only worsens the crisis. However, when we meet a crisis with awareness and understanding, we can dissolve the conflict. We are often conditioned to react through fear, blame, or seeking past solutions that no longer apply. True transformation occurs when we break free from these old patterns and approach the crisis with a fresh perspective, not defined by past beliefs.

In facing crisis without fear or resistance, the mind clears itself of confusion and distraction. Instead of reacting with panic or seeking escape, we engage fully with the present moment, which allows for intelligent action. By seeing a crisis as an opportunity for growth rather than a threat to our stability, we can find freedom and clarity. When we cease to rely on past habits, beliefs, and external validation, we experience true transformation. In such moments, a crisis no longer represents an insurmountable challenge, but a pathway to deeper understanding and personal evolution.

159. Challenge

Challenge: The Test That Reveals Understanding

A challenge is any situation or difficulty that demands a response, whether external, such as problems in relationships or work, or internal, such as fear or confusion. How we approach a challenge determines whether we grow in understanding or remain stuck in old patterns of response. Life is always changing, and challenges arise as part of that natural movement. The mind, in its search for stability, tends to resist challenges, viewing them as uncomfortable or threatening. But challenges also have the potential to reveal our conditioning—our knee-jerk reactions based on past experiences, fears, and beliefs, rather than fresh perception.

The typical response to challenges often involves avoidance or escape. Many distract themselves, use entertainment, or rely on false beliefs to avoid facing the difficulty. Others react emotionally, using fear or aggression, which clouds clear thinking and leads to impulsive decisions. Another common response is trying to solve challenges with old methods or ideas, but this approach often fails, as every challenge is unique. Overthinking can also prevent action, making the challenge seem insurmountable and creating more confusion.

To truly meet a challenge, one must face it without fear or resistance. This means seeing the challenge as it is, without labeling it as good or bad, and dropping the psychological time that causes delay. Instead of relying on past solutions, one must approach each challenge with a fresh perspective, allowing it to reveal the right response naturally. When one observes their inner reactions—such as fear, attachment, or conditioning—without judgment, they begin to awaken intelligence. A challenge, then, becomes an opportunity for growth, clarity, and understanding, leading to a mind that is fully present, alive, and free from the burden of past conclusions.

160. Problems

Problems: The Mind's Invention That Seeks Resolution

A problem arises when there is a conflict between reality, or "what is," and what we desire or expect, which is often referred to as "what should be." This internal struggle creates complexity, and while we may seek a solution, the mind often makes the problem worse. Problems can be practical, such as needing to resolve an issue through action, or psychological, where they are fueled by fear, desire, or conditioning. Psychological problems, in particular, are created by the mind's resistance to the present moment. Instead of accepting reality as it is, we project past fears or future anxieties onto it, making simple situations appear complicated.

The mind often keeps psychological problems alive by overthinking them, analyzing, justifying, or suppressing the situation. The more thought is invested in a problem, the more it grows, as it feeds on the mind's constant rumination. Problems are further intensified by fear and desire, making them seem larger or more pressing than they truly are. For instance, the fear of failure can make a minor issue feel like a crisis. Similarly, the desire for a particular outcome can cloud the mind, preventing clarity and direct action. Instead of addressing a problem, the mind may try to escape it through distractions or by avoiding confrontation with the root cause.

To be free from problems, one must observe them without resistance or judgment. When a problem is seen clearly for what it is—whether real or imagined—its hold on the mind begins to dissipate. The key is understanding the difference between practical problems, which need direct action, and psychological problems, which require understanding. Living without carrying the weight of past problems into the future allows the mind to remain free, clear, and responsive in the present moment. True resolution lies in seeing problems as they are, rather than as the mind imagines them to be. When one stops clinging to the illusion of control or seeking security in problems, the mind becomes unburdened, able to respond with intelligence and clarity.

161. Problems and Escapes

Problems and Escapes: The Endless Cycle of Avoidance

A problem arises when there is a conflict between reality—what "is"—and the idealized expectations of what "should be." It exists when the mind resists accepting reality, and instead of seeing things as they are, it struggles to change or control a situation based on desire or fear. Problems can be practical, which can be resolved through direct action, or psychological, which are created by thought, emotion, and conditioning. Psychological problems often linger because they are not directly confronted and solved, but instead avoided or suppressed, creating a cycle of ongoing conflict.

Escaping from problems is often the mind's first response, as it fears facing uncomfortable truths. The search for quick fixes or distractions—through entertainment, relationships, substances, or even spiritual beliefs—provides temporary relief but does not address the root cause of the issue. Society conditions us to avoid discomfort and seek comfort through external solutions, whether that is through ideologies, status, or pleasures. However, these escapes only serve to deepen the conflict, as the mind does not have the chance to fully understand or address the problem at its core.

Escaping from problems does not make them disappear; in fact, it only allows them to accumulate, silently influencing our thoughts, actions, and emotions. Dependence on these escapes weakens the mind and increases fear and anxiety, as the unresolved issues remain beneath the surface. True freedom from problems is found not in avoidance, but in direct observation and understanding. When we stop seeking comfort and face our problems fully, without resistance, we can dissolve the inner conflict and move forward with clarity, intelligence, and without psychological burden.

162. Mistakes

Mistakes: The Mirror That Reflects Our Blind Spots

A mistake is an action or decision that leads to an unintended or undesirable outcome. It often arises from ignorance, inattention, habit, or misunderstanding. A mind caught in mistakes either learns from them or repeats them due to avoidance or justification. When we see a mistake as an opportunity to understand, it no longer feels like failure, but a natural part of learning. The true danger in mistakes lies not in the mistakes themselves but in how we perceive them. Fear of making mistakes can lead to hesitation and inaction, keeping the mind stuck in a loop of avoidance and uncertainty.

The fear of mistakes is often linked to self-worth, as many people attach their value to success. This pressure to succeed, encouraged by societal expectations, makes mistakes seem dangerous rather than instructive. Instead of learning from mistakes, we are conditioned to avoid them, which only strengthens the fear and prevents natural learning. We tend to justify or hide our mistakes, which only prolongs ignorance. The key to overcoming this fear is to see mistakes as moments of incomplete understanding, rather than personal failures. When we learn to observe our mistakes without judgment or guilt, we create space for genuine learning and growth.

To live without the fear of mistakes, we must separate them from our sense of self. A mistake does not define us—it is merely an event that provides an opportunity to learn and improve. Observing mistakes with honesty and without the need for justification allows us to move forward with clarity. When we act without the fear of failure, we engage more fully with life, learning from every experience. A mind that is free from the burden of fear and guilt no longer hesitates or regrets—it moves with intelligence and deep awareness. In this state, mistakes are not obstacles but stepping stones toward greater understanding and personal growth.

163. Failure

Failure: The Fear That Stifles Growth

Failure is the perception of not meeting an expected outcome. It arises when we compare our actions against predetermined standards of success, and when we don't meet those standards, we label it as failure. However, failure is merely a mental construct—something that exists only in comparison. Without comparison to a goal, failure has no meaning; there is just action and its result. The mind, influenced by thought, creates failure by labeling an experience as falling short. This process keeps us in a cycle of self-doubt, disappointment, and guilt. But failure itself is not a reality—it is a projection of the mind's expectations.

Fear is often at the root of failure. We fear failure because it threatens our self-worth, which has been tied to achievements. This fear can paralyze us, preventing us from taking action, learning, and growing. The mind wants certainty, preferring the predictable over the unknown. When we attach our identity to success, failure feels like an attack on our sense of self. We live in a society that associates success with value, so failure becomes a source of shame. However, when we can view failure not as an end but as an integral part of life's movement, we open ourselves to transformation. Failure can either lead to stagnation or to growth—by seeing it as an opportunity for insight, we can learn and adjust with clarity.

To be free from the burden of failure, we must realize that failure is simply an interpretation of an experience. It is not a final judgment on our worth or abilities. Letting go of the need for success as the only valid outcome allows us to embrace all experiences as valuable. When we act without fear of the result, we no longer tie our self-worth to success or failure. True learning comes from seeing failure as part of life's unfolding, not as something to regret or avoid. A mind that frees itself from psychological measurement and the fear of failure can act fully, without hesitation, and with complete engagement in the present. In this freedom, failure is no longer an obstacle but another step in the ongoing journey of life.

164. Pain

Pain: The Unavoidable Reality of Living

Pain is not merely physical discomfort; it encompasses emotional suffering, such as fear, loss, and disappointment. It arises from attachment, resistance, and unfulfilled desires. Often, we cling to people, experiences, beliefs, and identities, and when they change or are lost, pain surfaces. Psychological pain, unlike physical pain, lingers because we hold onto memories of past hurts, betrayals, or losses, replaying them in our minds. The fear of pain often worsens the experience, creating more suffering. We also bring suffering upon ourselves by having expectations of how life should be, and when reality does not align with those expectations, pain is the result.

Psychological pain shapes how we perceive the world, creating fear and insecurity that influence our actions and decisions. When we identify with our pain, we strengthen the illusion of the 'self'—the belief that we are our suffering. Pain becomes a habit, something we carry from one experience to the next, shaping our responses. However, pain is not something intrinsic to the world—it is a product of our thoughts, memories, and attachments. By seeing pain for what it is, without resistance or avoidance, transformation can occur. Pain, when fully observed, loses its grip over us, and we are no longer trapped by it.

To free ourselves from pain, we must stop resisting it, understand its root causes, and let go of psychological time—living without carrying past hurts into the present. True healing happens when we stop seeking comfort in false escapes, such as distractions, pleasure, or ambition, and instead face our pain directly. Pain is universal—it is not uniquely 'yours.' By seeing it as a part of the human experience rather than a personal burden, it loses its hold over us. In this understanding, pain dissolves, leaving clarity, peace, and freedom. A mind unburdened by the past moves through life with sensitivity, awareness, and a deep sense of being fully alive.

165. Suffering

Suffering: The Resistance to 'What Is'

Suffering is not limited to physical pain; it encompasses deep psychological distress such as fear, loneliness, and inner conflict. It arises from attachment to people, things, and experiences, which we believe will bring lasting happiness. However, when these attachments change or are lost, we experience pain and emptiness. Suffering is further compounded by desires, fears, comparisons, and living in psychological time. The mind constantly dwells on past regrets and future anxieties, making peace in the present elusive. Is suffering an unavoidable part of life, or can it be alleviated?

We suffer because we attach ourselves to fleeting things, such as relationships and possessions, which we believe provide stability and happiness. We also live in pursuit of pleasure and success, but these are temporary, and new desires quickly arise, perpetuating the cycle of suffering. Fear of change, death, and the unknown adds to this suffering, as the mind longs for permanence and stability. The comparison of ourselves to others and the ideal self leads to jealousy, inferiority, and endless striving. When we resist 'what is' and yearn for 'what should be,' suffering is prolonged, keeping us trapped in psychological time.

True freedom from suffering is found in understanding it, not escaping or suppressing it. By observing suffering without resistance and recognizing its root causes—attachment, desire, and psychological time—we begin to dissolve its grip. When we let go of attachment and expectation, and stop seeking psychological security, suffering cannot take root. By living fully in the present, free from the illusions of permanence and self, we can experience a state of deep peace and clarity. In this awareness, suffering loses its power, and life unfolds naturally, without the weight of past or future.

166. Worrying

Worrying: The Futile Movement of Thought Into the Unknown

Worrying is the mind's tendency to project fear into the future, imagining problems that may never materialize. It arises from insecurity, the desire to control the unknown, and a lack of acceptance of life's unpredictability. When we worry, we become caught in a constant mental conflict, unable to rest in the present moment. The mind moves between past fears and future anxieties, never truly engaging with what is. Worry is a form of mental overthinking that drains energy, yet it doesn't lead to action or solutions. It keeps us stuck in a cycle of tension and stress, preventing us from experiencing peace.

The mind often mistakes worrying for preparation, thinking that it will somehow prevent failure or disaster. But in reality, most worries are about things that never happen. Worrying is based on the fear of uncertainty—our minds want control, but life is unpredictable. This resistance to uncertainty only creates more tension, trapping us in a habitual thought pattern. The more we worry, the more the mind becomes conditioned to expect problems. Instead of responding to life with clarity, we are caught in an endless cycle of anxiety.

To be free from worrying, one must see it for what it is—a mental habit that only creates stress and distraction. By living fully in the present, we can let go of the psychological time that keeps worry alive. Accepting uncertainty and embracing the unknown weakens the power of worry, allowing us to focus on what truly matters. When action is needed, we act; when it is not, we let go. In this way, worry no longer dominates our lives. We move through life with clarity and freedom, no longer weighed down by unnecessary fears about the future.

167. Isolation

Isolation: The Loneliness Created by the Self

Isolation is a psychological state that goes beyond physical aloneness; it is the deep sense of separation from others and from life itself. This feeling arises when the mind creates a barrier between 'self' and 'other,' which leads to loneliness, alienation, and inner conflict. The isolation experienced is not necessarily a result of external circumstances but stems from the conditioning of the mind, which fosters disconnection. The mind that isolates itself does so by building walls, seeking safety from vulnerability and emotional pain. However, these very walls also prevent the possibility of true love, understanding, and genuine relationship.

The root of isolation lies in the psychological division that thought creates between "me" and "you," "us" and "them." This illusion of separateness distorts the reality of human connection. While solitude can bring inner peace and fullness, isolation is the feeling of being disconnected, even when surrounded by others. Isolation is further fueled by fear—fear of vulnerability, fear of rejection, and past emotional wounds. These fears cause the mind to withdraw, creating an emotional distance that reinforces the feeling of loneliness. Society, with its emphasis on individualism, competition, and comparison, only exacerbates this isolation, making true connection more difficult.

To free oneself from isolation, it is essential to recognize that it is a creation of thought. The mind labels, categorizes, and separates, and in doing so, it keeps itself disconnected. When one understands this, the illusion of separation begins to dissolve. Letting go of psychological barriers—such as past hurts, beliefs, and rigid identities—creates space for real connection. True relationships require openness and vulnerability, and living without fear of emotional pain allows the mind to experience deep, meaningful connections. Recognizing that you are not separate from life but interconnected with all beings naturally ends isolation. In this understanding, there is no loneliness, only a profound sense of being part of the entire movement of existence.

168. Doubt

Doubt: The Fear of Stepping Into the Unknown

Doubt is the act of questioning accepted beliefs, ideas, or experiences, and it can either open the mind to new understanding or trap it in endless uncertainty. True doubt is not simply skepticism or cynicism; it is the refusal to accept things without understanding. It challenges the mind to break free from conditioning and encourages independent thought. By questioning, we move toward clarity, and the foundation of true intelligence begins with doubt. Without it, the mind remains stagnant, merely repeating what it has been taught, never engaging deeply with the present or reality.

Doubt has the power to free us from psychological dependence, where many rely on external authorities for truth—books, teachers, or traditions. The genuine discovery of truth happens when we stop accepting secondhand knowledge and allow direct perception to take place. While doubt is essential for intelligence, it can also lead to confusion if it is not understood. When doubt arises, it is important to remain open, observing thoughts and beliefs without fear of what may be discovered. True doubt does not seek immediate answers, nor does it rely on easy conclusions. Instead, it is an inquiry that seeks to see clearly, without the burden of needing certainty.

A mind that doubts wisely is one that uses doubt as a tool for understanding, not a source of endless insecurity. It observes without resistance, allowing clarity to emerge when falsehood is discovered. Rather than clinging to uncertainty, the doubting mind moves beyond confusion into insight. Doubt, when applied correctly, leads to freedom—a mind that is free from conditioning, free from illusion, and capable of discovering truth. In this space of true doubt, the mind is not caught in a cycle of hesitation but moves effortlessly toward clarity, understanding, and real intelligence.

169. Insecurity

Insecurity: The Root of Fear and Dependence

Insecurity is the state of uncertainty and vulnerability, often experienced in various areas of life such as relationships, career, or personal self-worth. It arises from the mind's deep-rooted fear of the unknown and the desire for psychological stability. The mind seeks to alleviate insecurity by clinging to external sources of comfort like beliefs, possessions, or achievements, but these are transient and do not offer true security. True stability can only be found within, yet the mind continuously seeks to escape insecurity by attaching to things that seem permanent.

The root of insecurity lies in the mind's resistance to the ever-changing nature of life. As everything around us—relationships, jobs, health, and even emotions—constantly evolves, the mind strives to hold onto something permanent to create a sense of stability. This reliance on external validation through status, money, or relationships only deepens insecurity, as the fear of losing these attachments becomes overwhelming. Furthermore, societal conditioning breeds insecurity by constantly encouraging comparison with others, which leads to anxiety, self-doubt, and unnecessary competition.

To be free from insecurity, one must realize that external security is an illusion. The mind must understand that nothing is permanent, and all attachments, whether to material possessions or relationships, are inherently unstable. Observing insecurity without fleeing from it, and letting go of comparisons and judgments, allows it to weaken naturally. True security lies in a mind that is fully present and aware, free from the need to measure success or seek approval. A mind that understands insecurity does not cling to external sources for comfort—it moves with clarity and inner stability, grounded in awareness rather than attachment.

170. Rejection

Rejection: The Pain of Seeking Acceptance

Rejection is the experience of being denied acceptance, approval, or a sense of belonging. It arises when expectations are not met, whether in relationships, personal ambitions, or societal standards. A mind caught in rejection feels hurt, isolated, or unworthy, and this reinforces its dependence on external validation. The pain of rejection is not inherent in the experience itself but in the mind's resistance to accepting reality as it is. This conflict between expectation and reality creates the emotional wound that is associated with rejection, reinforcing the cycle of hurt and self-doubt.

We fear rejection because we are conditioned from childhood to seek approval as a means of survival and belonging. Many people attach their self-worth to external validation, and when rejection occurs, it triggers feelings of inadequacy and loss. This creates a psychological wound that, over time, shapes the individual's identity and behavior. The ego either becomes defensive or insecure, depending on how rejection is internalized. It either builds walls to protect itself from further hurt or falls into a pattern of self-pity and low self-esteem. Rejection can also become a tool for division, as social structures and relationships often use it to control and manipulate.

True freedom from the pain of rejection comes not from avoiding it but from understanding its nature. When we stop taking rejection personally, it no longer has the power to wound us. Rejection is a reflection of someone else's perspective and says nothing about our inherent worth. By letting go of the need for external validation and observing the pain without identifying with it, we can break the cycle of hurt. Embracing rejection as a moment of insight allows us to see where attachment exists and use it as an opportunity for growth. When we live authentically, free from the fear of exclusion, rejection loses its grip, leaving space for clarity, understanding, and deeper emotional freedom.

171. Enemy

Enemy: The Illusion of Separation and Opposition

An enemy is not an external reality but a mental construct, born from the mind's projections of fear and division. It arises when the mind perceives another as an obstacle, a threat, or someone who opposes its desires, beliefs, or security. This perception creates an illusion of separation, where "us" is pitted against "them," making true understanding impossible. Instead of seeing the person as they are, the mind reacts through past experiences and emotional projections, creating hostility and conflict. This concept of an enemy is perpetuated by societal conditioning, cultural beliefs, and ideological differences, which deepen the divisions between individuals, groups, and nations.

The illusion of an enemy is rooted in psychological division. Thought categorizes people as either allies or adversaries, and this division sustains fear and hostility. The idea of the enemy is not based on any direct threat but on the mind's projection of its insecurities, fears, and past conflicts. Fear, rather than reality, shapes the perception of others as enemies, creating unnecessary conflict and division. The ego thrives on opposition, as it gives the mind a sense of purpose, bolstering its identity. This attachment to the past, through resentment and old wounds, further reinforces the belief in enemies, preventing fresh understanding and real connection.

True freedom comes not from defeating or eliminating enemies but from seeing that they are a product of conditioned thought. When the mind no longer identifies with fear or resentment, the need for an enemy dissolves. By observing without labeling or judgment, one can see others as they are, without the bias of division. Understanding fear, rather than reacting to it, removes the illusion of opposition, allowing the mind to act intelligently and with clarity. In the absence of division, there is no conflict—only peace, as the realization dawns that all enemies are constructs of the mind, and true understanding transcends them.

172. Distraction

Distraction: The Escape That Numbs Awareness

Distraction is the mind's tendency to escape from the present moment, avoiding direct engagement with reality by seeking external stimuli. It manifests in various forms such as entertainment, work, relationships, or even intellectual pursuits. At its core, distraction is a mechanism of avoidance—whether from boredom, inner emptiness, or unresolved emotional discomfort. The mind, when faced with stillness, is compelled to escape because it fears confronting its unresolved issues. In this way, distraction becomes a temporary refuge from the internal conflict that arises when we face our true feelings or thoughts.

The mind seeks distraction for several reasons, primarily to avoid facing itself. Silence or stillness forces the mind to confront its fears, insecurities, and deeper emotions—things the mind would rather not address. Additionally, society conditions us to value busyness, equating constant activity with success and productivity. In this context, a still mind is seen as unproductive. Distraction provides temporary pleasure, but it never resolves the underlying psychological discomfort. The mind is often driven by the desire for stimulation, and without it, it feels uncertain and lost. This is the fear of emptiness, which is only pacified by constantly seeking new distractions.

However, the consequences of living in a state of distraction are profound. A distracted mind fails to engage in deep self-reflection, preventing true understanding or transformation. It remains in a cycle of superficiality, unable to engage in focused thought or genuine perception. Distraction also strengthens the dependency on external factors for happiness—without these distractions, the mind experiences emptiness. True peace comes not through escape, but by allowing the mind to be still and fully present. When the mind is no longer dependent on external stimulation, every moment becomes rich with clarity, awareness, and depth.

173. Disorder

Disorder: The Chaos Born of Inner Division

Disorder arises when the mind is divided, creating confusion, conflict, and psychological turbulence. It occurs when there is a gap between reality and our ideals, creating a constant inner struggle. This inner division leads to fragmentation, where thoughts, emotions, and actions are not in harmony, preventing clarity and direct perception. The mind often seeks external order through control or systems, but these only mask the internal chaos. True resolution comes when the mind ceases to resist, accept division, or escape from itself.

The root of disorder is the conflict between 'what is' and 'what should be,' where ideals and expectations create an ongoing internal contradiction. Thought, based on past experiences and conditioning, continues to carry accumulated fears, desires, and judgments, making life a series of reactions rather than fresh responses. Disordered thinking creates further fragmentation, both internally and externally, contributing to societal conflict, relationships, and global tensions. As long as the mind remains fragmented, disorder persists, and we escape into distractions or attempts to control the situation, which only perpetuate the confusion.

To free oneself from disorder, one must observe it without trying to fix or escape it. The act of observing without interference allows the natural dissolution of confusion. True order is not something that can be achieved through thought; it arises when the mind is silent and free from psychological opposites. This order is not imposed but emerges spontaneously when the mind is fully present, free from fear, resistance, and external dependencies. When disorder is seen clearly and understood, it dissolves, revealing a state of clarity and undivided perception, where life is experienced as it is, without struggle.

174. Disease

Disease: The Disharmony Between Body and Mind

Disease is a disturbance that occurs when the natural balance of the body and mind is disrupted. It can be physical, such as those caused by infections, genetic factors, or lifestyle choices, or psychological, arising from stress, trauma, and suppressed emotions. True health is not simply the absence of disease but an understanding of the root causes of imbalance. Often, our mind's reaction to discomfort, whether mental or physical, plays a significant role in exacerbating disease. Physical ailments are often compounded by psychological stress, which affects the body's ability to heal.

The causes of disease are both internal and external. On the physical level, poor diet, lack of exercise, and environmental toxins weaken the body's defenses, while some diseases are inherited or triggered by uncontrollable factors. Psychological stress, including anxiety, unresolved emotions, and fear, can compromise the immune system and disrupt bodily functions. Suppressed emotions, such as grief or anger, often manifest physically, showing the deep connection between mind and body. Thought patterns that focus on past suffering or future worries can amplify the discomfort, making disease worse.

To reduce the risk of disease, one must live in balance. This includes nourishing the body with healthy food, regular movement, and sufficient rest. The mind should be free from unnecessary tension and worry. By observing illness without fear or resistance, we can approach healing with wisdom and awareness. Healing goes beyond the mere treatment of symptoms; it involves a complete change in lifestyle, attitude, and awareness. True well-being arises when the body is free from toxins, the mind is free from stress, and the heart is free from fear. In such a state, disease loses its power and becomes a signal for deeper understanding and growth, not just a physical challenge to overcome.

7. Relationships & Social Dynamics

WAKE UP

175. Relationships

Relationships: The Mirror That Reflects Who We Are

Relationships are not just the connections we share with others—they are mirrors in which we see ourselves, shaped by our inner states, emotions, and past conditioning. Every interaction, whether it's with family, friends, or a partner, reflects parts of our identity, often revealing conflicts within. When we approach relationships with the intent to fulfill personal needs or expectations, it creates a foundation of dependence and control. These relationships, though initially fulfilling, are often based on attachment and what we gain from others, rather than a deep understanding of one another. True connection comes when we stop viewing relationships as tools for self-validation or security.

We often struggle in relationships because we are conditioned to seek stability through others. Fear of loneliness and the desire for emotional security cause us to cling to relationships, seeking from them what we believe we cannot find within ourselves. Holding onto past hurts and unrealistic expectations distorts our perceptions, leading to resentment and misunderstandings. Many enter relationships with the intent to change or "fix" the other person, rather than seeking to understand them as they are. This desire to change others only reinforces the cycle of control, leaving no space for authentic connection.

To relate without conflict, we must see relationships as mirrors of our own inner world. Each reaction, whether positive or negative, reflects something about ourselves—our fears, attachments, or desires. By letting go of possession, expectation, and the need to control, we create space for real understanding. True love is not about demanding or possessing—it is about complete attention and freedom. When we embrace solitude, free from the fear of being alone, relationships become less about need and more about connection. In this clarity, relationships no longer create conflict—they become opportunities for deep, unfiltered love and understanding.

176. Communication

Communication: The Art of Listening Beyond Words

Communication is the exchange of thoughts, feelings, and meaning between individuals, and it encompasses much more than words alone. It involves gestures, silence, and the ability to listen deeply. However, true communication requires not just the act of expressing oneself, but also the capacity to understand others. A mind that truly communicates is one that listens attentively and responds with clarity, rather than simply speaking or reacting.

The nature of communication is centered on both speaking and listening. Most people listen with the intention of responding, not understanding. True listening requires full attention and a suspension of judgment, allowing one to perceive the deeper meaning behind words. Words, though necessary, are limited tools for conveying meaning, as real understanding transcends language. Silence plays a crucial role in communication, as it creates space for deeper reflection and the exchange of meaning that words alone may not express.

The barriers to effective communication often arise from preoccupations with the self, emotional reactions, assumptions, and excessive speaking. When we respond emotionally or assume we know what others mean, we distort their words and create conflict. Real communication requires not just hearing, but listening with an open mind, free from bias and judgment. To communicate effectively, one must be fully present, speak clearly and with intent, and understand that silence is as important as speech. When communication flows in this way, it becomes an effortless and meaningful exchange that leads to genuine connection and mutual understanding.

177. Speaking

Speaking: Words That Connect or Divide

Speaking is the verbal expression of thought, emotion, and knowledge, and it is a powerful tool for communication. However, it can also distort or conceal the truth. When a mind speaks with awareness, the words used are not just for the sake of expression but carry clarity and depth, conveying truth without distortion. Unfortunately, most of the time, speech is mechanical and unconscious—spoken out of habit or emotion, not full attention. This can lead to misunderstandings, misrepresentations, and missed opportunities for genuine communication.

The nature of speaking involves more than just the words themselves. Words, though essential, are often limited in capturing the full depth of an experience. When speech is driven by emotion, bias, or assumption, it leads to confusion and miscommunication. On the other hand, when one speaks from direct perception and clarity, their words are precise and meaningful. Speaking also involves energy—tone, rhythm, and intention behind the words matter as much as the words themselves. Words can create connection when used consciously, but they can also divide and create conflict when spoken carelessly.

To speak with clarity and intelligence, it is important to observe the urge to speak before acting on it, recognizing that not every thought requires verbal expression. When words are necessary, they should be measured, precise, and free from emotional distortion. A mind that speaks from stillness, presence, and awareness conveys truth without aggression or manipulation. In this way, speech becomes an act of insight, connection, and wisdom, where words are not just sound but the transmission of thought and understanding.

178. Authority

Authority: The Weight of Control and Obedience

Authority, in its various forms, plays a significant role in shaping behavior and perceptions, both externally and internally. External authority, such as governments, laws, and societal norms, is often necessary for maintaining order, while internal authority—stemming from our past experiences, beliefs, and conditioning—can shape our responses, often unconsciously. While authority in practical matters may be useful, it becomes problematic when it limits independent thought, understanding, and self-awareness. This dependence on authority prevents individuals from seeing and experiencing life directly, reducing their capacity for independent inquiry and genuine learning.

The impact of authority is often subtle, conditioning the mind to accept second-hand knowledge without questioning. This acceptance breeds fear, conformity, and psychological dependence, making it difficult for individuals to challenge ideas or beliefs. In situations where authority dictates actions or thoughts, the ability to perceive truth independently becomes clouded. When people follow authority without understanding, they miss the opportunity for true learning, which comes from direct observation and questioning. Blind obedience to established systems can also lead to unnecessary divisions, preventing individuals from exploring deeper, more authentic insights into life and the world.

To break free from the limitations of psychological authority, one must question everything, observe without influence, and not seek security in external systems. True intelligence arises when individuals understand the limitations of their conditioning and knowledge, and instead, approach life with an open mind, free from imposed beliefs or ideologies. Learning and growth happen when the mind is free, actively questioning and discovering new truths. True freedom is found in the ability to question, observe, and discover reality for oneself, rather than relying on authority to define it for us.

179. Superior and Inferior

Superior and Inferior: The False Measure That Divides Humanity

Superior and inferior are judgments based on comparison—whether in intelligence, wealth, status, ability, or appearance. They arise from conditioning, competition, and the mind's habit of measuring itself against others. A mind caught in superiority seeks dominance, while a mind caught in inferiority feels inadequate. A mind that understands deeply moves beyond both. The mind compares—'I am more successful,' or 'I am not as good as them'—but without comparison, would superiority or inferiority even exist? A superior mind fears losing its position, while an inferior mind struggles to 'become better,' creating anxiety, competition, and endless dissatisfaction. Superiority exists only in relation to others—without comparison, it has no meaning. When one sees life without measurement, the struggle to be better dissolves.

The superior mind looks down on others, feeling entitled, while the inferior mind feels unworthy, seeking validation. Both are products of the same illusion—measuring self-worth through comparison. Intelligence, skill, and success vary among individuals, but does that make one 'better' than another? When one stops measuring, all people are simply different, not 'higher' or 'lower.' Society conditions us to measure success, intelligence, beauty, and status, creating insecurity and competition. People attach their identity to achievements, believing their worth is defined by external success, making superiority and inferiority inevitable. The mind clings to superiority out of fear of being unimportant, yet true confidence comes not from being 'better' but from being free of comparison. Superiority gives a false sense of control, while inferiority creates dependence on approval—both illusions that prevent real freedom.

The mind creates measurement—without it, no one is 'better' or 'worse.' A mind that does not compare is free from superiority and inferiority. True confidence is not in being 'above' others but in not needing to compare at all. When one no longer defines themselves by position, all struggle disappears. Can one look at themselves or others without mentally ranking them? True understanding sees differences, but without labeling them as 'better' or 'worse.' The mind that does not seek superiority has no fear of inferiority. When one no longer fears 'not being enough,' they are already free. Society will always rank people, but does one have to participate? A mind free from comparison does not seek to be superior or fear being inferior—it simply is. The ideas of superior and inferior are created by thought's habit of comparison, leading to division, insecurity, and conflict. A mind free from the need to be 'better' and the fear of being 'less' does not engage in competition—it sees all as different, not 'higher' or 'lower.' In this freedom, superiority and inferiority dissolve—not through effort, but because there is no longer a self that needs to compare, to dominate, or to be measured—only deep awareness, without division, without struggle.

180. Following

Following: The Fear of Walking Alone

Following is the act of adopting beliefs, ideologies, or actions based on external authority, rather than through personal understanding. It is a surrender of one's intelligence to traditions, ideologies, or leaders, preventing genuine inquiry. A mind that follows is mechanical and conditioned, unable to perceive truth directly. True insight is not found in imitation but through direct perception and independent thought. As a result, following creates a psychological dependency on external influences, making the individual dependent on others for guidance, approval, and security, thus limiting freedom and growth.

The nature of following stems from imitation, where individuals replicate the paths or beliefs of others without truly discovering them for themselves. Truth cannot be found by simply adhering to the beliefs of others; it must be experienced directly. When a person constantly follows external direction, they limit their ability to think independently, and this dependence weakens their intellectual freedom. Fear and conformity often motivate the act of following, as people seek comfort in certainty provided by authorities, rather than questioning and discovering truth for themselves. The path of following creates psychological dependence, stifling real intelligence and growth.

Living without following requires a shift in perception—one must stop seeking guidance or approval from external sources. To be free from following is to embrace direct perception, questioning authority, and not relying on others for answers. The key is to observe without bias, see beyond conditioning, and act from clarity. True intelligence and freedom arise from understanding, not from conforming to external ideas. Truth cannot be handed to us; it is discovered within through awareness. When the need for comparison or validation fades, there is no longer a need to follow, only to act from understanding.

181. Respect

Respect: The Recognition That Comes Without Demand

Respect is the deep recognition of another's worth, dignity, and individuality. It is not based on authority, tradition, or social norms, but arises naturally from understanding and awareness. A mind that truly respects does not see others through the lens of comparison or hierarchy, but perceives each person as they are, without judgment or the need for superiority. Real respect is not forced or conditional—it flows from a place of genuine appreciation, allowing one to connect deeply without control or division.

We often struggle with respect because society teaches us to respect authority and titles rather than people themselves. We confuse respect with fear, flattery, or the need to please. True respect does not depend on someone's status or on meeting specific expectations—it is the recognition of shared humanity, beyond labels. When one lacks self-respect, it becomes difficult to offer respect to others. Additionally, ego and societal status can often dictate who is deserving of respect, but true respect is reserved for those who demonstrate integrity, wisdom, and understanding, not power or influence.

Living with true respect means seeing others as equals, not as figures to be dominated or idolized. It requires listening fully, without judgment or the need to agree or disagree. Respect arises naturally from understanding, not from obligation or fear of rejection. When the mind is free from comparison, judgment, and the need to conform, respect flows effortlessly in all relationships. True respect does not seek validation, nor does it rely on external factors—it exists as an inherent part of human connection, in every interaction, without the conflict or division that often accompanies it.

182. Respectability

Respectability: The Mask Worn for Social Acceptance

Respectability is the external pursuit of approval, recognition, and social acceptance, often built on conforming to societal norms and expectations. It is driven by the desire to be seen as honorable, successful, and virtuous. People seek respectability to avoid social rejection, gain status, or mask inner insecurities, but in reality, it is an illusion that can prevent true self-understanding and freedom. The fear of losing respect or reputation can lead to dishonesty, hypocrisy, and a shallow existence based on appearances rather than substance.

The desire for respectability is rooted in the need for validation and acceptance from others. It often leads to a cycle of conformity and self-deception, where individuals act according to what society deems respectable rather than what is true or aligned with their authentic selves. Respectability, therefore, becomes a trap—people are conditioned to seek approval and fear judgment, even if it means sacrificing their integrity. It fosters hypocrisy, where one's public image is often disconnected from their private reality, and it limits personal growth by discouraging independent thought and genuine self-expression.

Living without seeking respectability requires stepping away from societal pressures and acting from a place of true understanding. Instead of living to please others or conform to social expectations, one can act from clarity, guided by what is true, intelligent, and authentic. True freedom comes when one stops measuring their worth against external standards and begins to live in alignment with their own values. In this state, there is no need for respectability, as one is already at peace with themselves, living honestly and without fear of judgment.

183. Power

Power: The Desire to Dominate and Control

Power is the ability to control or influence others, situations, or systems, and it is present in many aspects of life, such as politics, business, and even in our personal minds. While power may seem to provide security, stability, and the ability to control outcomes, it often only breeds more fear and insecurity. The desire for power arises from the need for importance and the belief that having control over one's environment or others will lead to lasting happiness. In reality, power often masks deeper insecurities and inner emptiness, with individuals seeking control over others to compensate for their own struggles.

The pursuit of power leads to division and conflict, both internally and externally. It strengthens the ego, fostering a false sense of superiority, and perpetuates fear, manipulation, and control. True love and understanding cannot exist in an environment driven by power, as power breeds submission and oppression. Additionally, the desire for power is insatiable—once power is gained, the need for more arises, creating an endless cycle of craving. This constant striving for control traps the mind in dissatisfaction, preventing real fulfillment and peace.

Living without the desire for power allows for true freedom and strength. When one recognizes that power is an illusion, and that it does not provide lasting security or fulfillment, its hold weakens. A mind that does not seek control over others operates with clarity, intelligence, and compassion. True strength lies not in domination, but in the ability to act with wisdom, sensitivity, and cooperation. In this freedom, there is no need for power—only love, understanding, and the freedom to live fully in the present moment.

184. Influence

Influence: The Subtle Force That Shapes Thought

Influence is the power to shape thought, perception, and behavior, often without conscious awareness. It can come from external sources like society, media, or authority figures, or from internal sources such as past experiences, fears, and desires. A mind that is influenced acts based on absorbed impressions, frequently without recognizing how these forces shape its thoughts and actions. This creates a kind of psychological conditioning, where the mind begins to perceive reality not as it is but through the lens of what it has been taught or conditioned to believe.

The nature of influence can be both conscious and unconscious, with some influences being direct and obvious, while others are subtle and form over time. External influences such as culture and authority can create conformity, while internal influences, often rooted in past experiences, can limit understanding or reinforce fear and prejudice. In some cases, the influence is constructive, encouraging growth and creativity, while in others, it can be limiting, preventing clear perception or true freedom. The challenge lies in recognizing influence and understanding how it shapes our thinking and actions.

To be free from influence is not to reject all external sources or information but to develop the ability to observe and understand them clearly. This requires a mind that is aware of its conditioning and able to question without seeking mere confirmation. When we observe thoughts without immediate reaction or judgment, we begin to see their origins. True freedom comes from acting with awareness and understanding, not from unconscious influence or habitual responses. In this clarity, the mind is no longer controlled by influence; it moves naturally and effortlessly, responding to life with deep intelligence.

185. Manipulation

Manipulation: The Hidden Game of Control

Manipulation is the act of influencing or controlling others for personal gain, often through deception, persuasion, or emotional pressure. It arises from the desire for power, security, or advantage over others. A mind caught in manipulation seeks to control situations and people, while a mind that understands deeply moves without hidden motives. The manipulator seeks control to serve their own needs—whether emotional, financial, or psychological—while true understanding acts without hidden motives or the desire for dominance. People are manipulated through half-truths, exaggerated emotions, or selective facts, yet when one sees manipulation clearly, its influence weakens.

Manipulation can be direct, such as coercion, threats, or deception, or it can be subtle, as seen in guilt-tripping, flattery, and emotional conditioning. Those who manipulate often make others feel dependent on their approval, affection, or authority. A mind that sees through manipulation is independent, not controlled by external influence. Many manipulate because they fear losing power, position, or relationships, but true strength does not need control—it moves with freedom and honesty. People use manipulation to maintain authority in relationships, workplaces, and social structures, yet real influence does not come from control—it comes from truth and clarity.

When one understands the fear behind manipulation, it dissolves. A fearless mind has no need to control others. Many manipulate unconsciously, shaping situations to serve their interests, but a mind that watches itself closely does not deceive. Real freedom exists when one does not seek to shape others' opinions or actions. Manipulation relies on secrecy, half-truths, and persuasion, while a truthful mind communicates openly, without hidden agendas. Many react to being manipulated with anger or defensiveness, but a mind that sees through manipulation is not disturbed by it—it simply does not participate. In this freedom, manipulation dissolves—not because one fights against it, but because there is no longer a need for it—only openness, honesty, and deep understanding remain.

186. Personality

Personality: The Image Crafted by Thought

Personality is the collection of traits, behaviors, habits, and tendencies that shape how we present ourselves to others. It is influenced by culture, upbringing, genetics, and life experiences, but the question arises: is personality something permanent, or is it merely a set of patterns created by thought? Many of us believe our personality defines who we are, providing a sense of stability, but in reality, personality is often a repetitive projection of the past, shaped by societal labels and conditioning.

Personality, often reinforced by society, becomes our identity. We attach ourselves to labels such as introvert or extrovert, creative or logical, which create fixed images of ourselves and make us believe we are unchanging. The ego thrives on these labels, seeking security and consistency. However, this attachment to personality can hinder growth and true self-understanding. Trying to improve or perfect personality traits can lead us to focus on superficial changes rather than understanding the deeper layers of our nature.

Personality, at its core, is a collection of conditioned responses, and as such, it limits true transformation. When we say, "This is just who I am," we close ourselves off from growth. True freedom comes not from changing personality traits, but from realizing that personality is not who we truly are. The moment we stop identifying with our personality and observe it without attachment, we discover that beyond the labels and fixed images lies a space of awareness, creativity, and intelligence that is free from the constraints of ego and conditioning.

187. Comparison

Comparison: The Measure That Breeds Inferiority

Comparison is the act of measuring oneself against another, whether in terms of success, intelligence, appearance, or spiritual attainment. It arises from the desire for recognition, superiority, or a sense of place in the world. The mind, conditioned by society and personal experiences, constantly evaluates itself against others, but this cycle does not bring satisfaction. Rather, it breeds competition, conflict, and insecurity. Through comparison, we either feel superior, leading to arrogance, or inferior, leading to self-doubt. Both conditions reinforce the ego, keeping us trapped in psychological struggle.

The problems with comparison are profound. It prevents true self-awareness by forcing us to see ourselves only in relation to others. This constant measuring of worth, whether to feel better or worse, distorts our perception and obstructs real transformation. Comparison strengthens the ego by reinforcing the notion that identity comes from being "better" or "worse" than someone else. It divides society, encouraging prejudice and conflict as groups, nations, and ideologies compete for superiority. This perpetual cycle of judgment creates disharmony in the world and within the self.

To live without comparison is to break free from the prison of the ego. It requires observing oneself and others without measuring or judging. True freedom is found when we stop striving to become "better" or "more" than others, and simply allow ourselves to be as we are. In the absence of comparison, there is clarity, peace, and freedom. A mind free from comparison operates without conflict, fully present and aware, experiencing life without the distortion of measurement or competition.

188. Attraction

Attraction: The Pull of Desire and Perception

Attraction is the natural pull towards a person, object, idea, or experience, arising from sensory perception, emotional response, memory, and psychological conditioning. While attraction can be a simple instinctual reaction, it often leads to attachment, where the mind seeks fulfillment through external factors. This dependence on what is attractive to us creates inner conflict, as the desire to possess or keep the object of attraction often leads to attachment, insecurity, and suffering.

Attraction is deeply rooted in desire—whether it is for comfort, pleasure, or security. The mind often draws itself to what it believes will fulfill these needs, creating a cycle of longing and attachment. This attraction is also shaped by past experiences, where memories of past pleasure or comfort influence what we find attractive today. The mind's tendency to compare one person, idea, or object to another only strengthens this attraction, creating preferences and desires based on social conditioning or personal history. This leads to the belief that fulfillment comes from the presence of the desired object or person, which ultimately reinforces psychological dependence.

To break free from the attachment that attraction creates, one must understand that true love is not rooted in need, expectation, or the fulfillment of personal desires. By observing attraction without immediately acting on it, the mind can gain clarity. Recognizing the conditioning behind attraction allows the individual to see that its influence weakens, leading to freedom. Living without seeking fulfillment through others enables one to experience attraction without attachment, understanding it as part of life rather than something to possess. This awareness creates freedom, where attraction simply exists without leading to dependency, allowing for true peace and clarity.

189. Agreements

Agreements: The Bonds That Create Order or Conflict

Agreements are the foundational structures that allow societies, relationships, and individuals to function smoothly. They set expectations, create cooperation, and provide stability. However, while agreements can bring order, they also have the potential to limit growth when followed without inquiry. Many agreements, whether social, cultural, or personal, are rooted in tradition, conditioning, and fear. They are often maintained to avoid conflict or to preserve the status quo. However, the blind adherence to such agreements can create conformity and stagnation, preventing the mind from experiencing true freedom and clarity.

People often follow agreements without question due to fear—fear of conflict, rejection, or loss. Social conditioning from an early age teaches us to obey rules, moral codes, and societal expectations. This conditioning makes it difficult to question the relevance or truth of the agreements we follow. Many of these agreements offer a sense of security and stability, but true security comes not from external contracts but from understanding oneself deeply. Furthermore, the collective acceptance of an agreement does not necessarily make it true, as truth must be directly perceived and understood.

True freedom comes not from rejecting all agreements but from discerning which agreements serve clarity and understanding and which ones are born of fear or conditioning. A mind that questions agreements without fear is free to act with intelligence and awareness. When one lives with awareness, agreements are not followed mechanically—they arise naturally, without limitation or conflict. In this freedom, there is no need for blind adherence to tradition or the expectation of others. The mind that acts from clarity and direct perception is able to move in the world, guided by a deep understanding of what is necessary and right.

190. Marriage

Marriage: The Institution of Love or a Framework of Security?

Marriage is often considered a significant social, emotional, and legal bond between two individuals, shaped by cultural, religious, and societal expectations. Beyond its legal aspects, marriage can also become a psychological relationship based on love, companionship, and sometimes emotional dependence. People often marry for various reasons, including societal conditioning, emotional security, sexual fulfillment, and economic or practical benefits. While society views marriage as an essential institution for stability, many individuals also seek companionship and emotional support through marriage, and historically, it provided economic security and status. However, marriage can also become a source of possessiveness, expectation, and disappointment, especially when love turns into attachment or dependency.

The problems in marriage arise when there is possessiveness, unmet expectations, or a loss of love due to routine and emotional dependency. Partners may enter marriage with unrealistic expectations, which, when unmet, lead to conflict. In some cases, the belief that marriage will complete an individual or fill a void results in dissatisfaction, and in extreme cases, divorce. To create a healthy marriage free from conflict, it is crucial to understand that love is not about possession or control. True love in marriage is unconditional, and the relationship should be based on mutual respect, understanding, and freedom. Both partners must be fully present and aware in their relationship, free from past resentment and future expectations, to maintain the vitality and meaning of their bond.

In essence, a marriage that is free from conflict is based on love without attachment, control, or fear. It requires awareness and a willingness to renew love continuously, understanding that relationships are not about completing one another but about sharing life together. When both partners act from love, free from the psychological need for validation or security, marriage becomes a nurturing and supportive bond that fosters growth, freedom, and mutual respect.

191. Attachment

Attachment: The Clinging That Breeds Fear

Attachment is the emotional and psychological bond we form with people, possessions, beliefs, or experiences. It provides a sense of security, yet it also brings fear, conflict, and suffering, as it ties our identity to what is external. While relationships and material things are part of life, attachment distorts them, making them sources of comfort and stability rather than aspects of a more liberated existence. Attachment arises from the fear of loneliness and the desire for security, making us believe that we need something external to complete us. This leads to possessiveness and anxiety when these attachments are threatened.

The consequences of attachment are vast, as it breeds fear of loss and emotional suffering. The more we attach ourselves to something, the more we fear losing it. This fear creates possessiveness, jealousy, and insecurity in relationships. In the process, we lose our freedom, as the mind clings to beliefs and traditions, preventing us from growing or exploring new ideas. Instead of embracing change, attachment leads to resistance, creating stagnation and hindering understanding. When we identify ourselves with what we are attached to, losing these attachments feels like losing part of our identity, deepening the cycle of fear and suffering.

To be free from attachment, one must observe without judgment, understanding that attachment itself creates suffering. Freedom comes not by forcefully detaching but by seeing attachment's true nature—recognizing it as a product of fear and desire for security. True love and relationship can only exist when there is freedom, not dependence. By letting go of the need for external validation and living in the present, we dissolve attachment and its consequences naturally. In this freedom, love, intelligence, and joy are experienced without the burden of fear or possessiveness.

192. Possessiveness

Possessiveness: The Desire to Own Another

Possessiveness is the emotional or psychological desire to hold onto people, things, or ideas, often driven by the need for security and control. It arises from attachment, fear of loss, and the desire to stabilize one's identity through ownership. Whether it involves relationships, material wealth, beliefs, or even experiences, possessiveness limits true freedom by fostering dependency and attachment. It is not only about owning tangible things but also about the need to control and possess aspects of life and others, leading to the illusion of security.

Possessiveness grows out of the fear of losing what we depend on for comfort, identity, and emotional fulfillment. The ego's need for control manifests through possessiveness, which creates emotional attachment and jealousy. Society reinforces this tendency by equating one's value with their possessions, relationships, and status. In an environment where comparison is constant, the desire to hold onto what we have becomes even stronger. At the same time, possessiveness prevents us from living fully in the present, as we hold onto past memories or anxiously cling to future outcomes.

The consequences of possessiveness are far-reaching. It destroys love by turning it into a tool for control, weakening genuine connection and freedom. Jealousy and conflict arise when we try to possess what is not truly ours to own. Possessiveness limits personal growth and change by fostering stagnation, as it resists the natural flow of life. However, freedom from possessiveness comes when we understand the illusion of ownership. When we can let go without fear, we experience true love—unattached and free. Living fully in the present, without clinging to past experiences or future expectations, allows for deep connection and genuine freedom. In this state, possessiveness no longer holds power, and we are free to move through life with clarity and peace.

193. Dependency

Dependency: The Fear of Being Alone

Dependency arises when the mind seeks security, identity, and fulfillment from external sources like relationships, beliefs, or material possessions. This attachment creates fear, as the mind becomes dependent on what it perceives as necessary for stability. When the mind is free from dependency, it operates from inner clarity and strength, not from fear or attachment to external factors. True freedom is found when the mind is no longer bound by these attachments, allowing for a more genuine experience of life.

The root of dependency lies in fear and conditioning, where society teaches us to rely on others for validation and security. We may seek emotional comfort, approval, or even self-worth from external sources, but true freedom comes when one can stand alone, free from this psychological need. A mind that is free of dependency does not seek validation but understands its inherent value. This inner realization allows for deep self-awareness, providing stability from within, instead of relying on the outside world for affirmation.

Living without dependency requires awareness of the attachments that bind us to others or external conditions. When one observes their dependencies without judgment, the mind naturally begins to let go of them. True security is found within, not in external sources, and only through self-awareness can one break free from the cycle of dependency, living with clarity and inner peace. The more one practices this awareness, the more deeply rooted the sense of internal security becomes, fostering true independence and emotional freedom.

194. Expectations

Expectations: The Silent Cause of Disappointment

Expectations are mental projections of how life, people, or situations should unfold, arising from past experiences, societal conditioning, and personal desires. They create an illusion of control, making the mind believe it can shape the future. However, life is inherently uncertain, and when reality does not match expectations, frustration, disappointment, and conflict arise. Society imposes ideals about success, love, and happiness, conditioning individuals to expect specific outcomes. Expectations are also an extension of desire—the mind seeks pleasure, stability, and achievement, projecting an imagined future. When these expectations remain unfulfilled, suffering begins. Additionally, expectations strengthen the illusion of the self, as the ego builds its identity around its desires and attachments. When expectations are unmet, the ego feels wounded, reinforcing feelings of insecurity and dissatisfaction.

Living with expectations leads to several psychological and relational challenges. The stronger the expectation, the greater the pain when it is not fulfilled. This attachment to outcomes prevents one from accepting life as it unfolds. In relationships, expectations become a source of conflict, as people are expected to behave in ways that align with personal desires. When they do not, feelings of betrayal and resentment arise. Expectations also create psychological time, making happiness conditional—"I will be happy when this happens." However, true joy is never in the future; it exists only in the present. Expecting perfection further prevents true understanding, as it causes resistance to seeing things as they are. Reality is neither good nor bad—it simply is. When one expects life to conform to an ideal, one loses the ability to perceive its beauty and depth in the present moment.

To live without expectations, one must see them as mental projections rather than reality. Understanding that expectations exist only in thought weakens their grip on the mind. Instead of hoping for specific outcomes, one can engage fully with the present, meeting life as it unfolds without resistance. Letting go of the illusion of control allows for psychological freedom—true peace is not found in forcing life to fit desires but in embracing it as it is. Acting without attachment to results brings a sense of effortlessness and completeness, allowing one to move through life without inner conflict. Where expectation ends, clarity begins, and in this freedom, life flows naturally, without struggle, without resistance.

195. Compromise

Compromise: The Balancing Act Between Conflict and Peace

Compromise is the act of finding a middle ground between conflicting ideas, desires, or interests. It often emerges in relationships, decision-making, and conflict resolution, where different parties have opposing needs or viewpoints. While compromise can foster harmony and cooperation, it can also betray truth and integrity if not approached with awareness. A mind caught in compromise for convenience may sacrifice core values for the sake of agreement. True understanding, however, enables one to discern when to adapt and when to stand firm, without compromising on essential principles.

Compromise can lead to both positive and negative outcomes. On one hand, it can help resolve conflict, creating peace and mutual understanding. On the other hand, compromising on truth or integrity can lead to dishonesty and internal conflict. Many compromises are made to maintain peace, security, or advantage, yet when driven solely by self-interest, they become manipulative. Some compromises are made voluntarily, while others arise out of fear, pressure, or obligation. The challenge lies in knowing when to compromise and when to hold one's ground. In certain situations, compromising on key values can cause long-term harm, as some truths cannot be sacrificed for convenience.

A mind free from insecurity understands that not all compromises are necessary. It knows when to compromise on less significant matters for the sake of relationships and cooperation, while holding firm on fundamental principles. True compromise comes from deep understanding and thoughtful consideration, not from blind submission to external pressure or the desire to please others. When compromise demands the sacrifice of truth or integrity, it must be rejected. True strength lies in knowing when to stand alone in defense of what is right, without fear or hesitation.

196. Cooperation

Cooperation: Working Together Without Losing Oneself

Cooperation is the natural harmony that arises when individuals act in unity, free from conflict, self-interest, and personal motives. It is not about imitation, compromise, or obedience, but rather a collective action that emerges when people are aligned in their understanding of truth. True cooperation occurs when there is no division, no "us" versus "them." It is effortless, arising from a shared perception of reality, and is not driven by the need for recognition, power, or personal gain. The mind free from ambition and division naturally flows into cooperation without needing force or authority.

We struggle to cooperate because ambition, competition, and fear often create division. Society conditions us to value personal success over mutual effort, and the fear of insecurity makes people cling to groups, beliefs, or ideologies. Authority and obedience are mistakenly equated with cooperation, but real cooperation arises from shared awareness, not compliance. Personal desires and opinions further interfere with unity, turning cooperation into negotiation rather than genuine collective action. Only when people move beyond personal motives and see the shared reality can true cooperation emerge.

To cooperate without conflict, one must see cooperation not as submission but as a natural, intelligent action arising from mutual understanding. It requires letting go of psychological identities and separations, such as nationality, belief systems, or ideologies. When each person is free from the need for reward, recognition, or personal gain, cooperation flows effortlessly. True cooperation is grounded in shared humanity, where individuals understand their interconnectedness. In this state, action is not driven by authority, rules, or negotiation but is a harmonious, collective movement of intelligence and clarity.

197. Arrogance

Arrogance: The Illusion of Superiority Born from the Ego

Arrogance is the exaggerated sense of self-importance, superiority, or entitlement. It arises from insecurity, comparison, and the illusion of knowing more or being better than others. A mind caught in arrogance seeks dominance and validation, while a mind that understands deeply moves with humility and clarity. People who feel inferior often overcompensate by acting superior, yet true confidence does not need arrogance—it exists without the need to prove. The arrogant mind constantly measures itself against others, asking, 'Am I better, smarter, more powerful?' A mind that does not compare has no need for arrogance. Those who believe they 'already know' stop questioning, listening, and evolving, making arrogance a barrier to real learning. A person who looks down on others creates division, making genuine connection impossible. True understanding exists only in equality, not superiority.

People define themselves by what they know, what they own, or what they achieve, and when identity is built on external factors, arrogance follows. Many hide their insecurities behind forced confidence, fearing they will appear weak or unimportant. Yet true confidence does not need to assert itself—it moves naturally. Society teaches people to 'rise above' others rather than grow together, reinforcing arrogance as a sign of success. Some see arrogance as power, believing dominance is necessary, but real strength does not dominate—it understands. Many resist humility, fearing it means lowering themselves, yet humility is not weakness—it is freedom from the need to appear great. Arrogance is an illusion that fails in the face of reality, for life is always larger than the individual—no one is beyond mistakes or learning. A truly wise mind knows its own limitations.

When one understands that arrogance is a cover for insecurity, it loses its foundation. A secure mind does not need to elevate itself. Arrogance exists because the 'self' is attached to thoughts of superiority, yet when one watches thought without attachment, arrogance fades naturally. Without measuring oneself against others, there is no need to feel superior or inferior, for a mind free from comparison is free from arrogance. Arrogance believes it already knows, while humility allows for infinite learning. A truly intelligent mind never stops questioning. The arrogant mind seeks recognition and admiration, but when one no longer needs external approval, arrogance dissolves. Many fall into arrogance by attaching self-worth to knowledge, status, or power, yet real wisdom exists only when one lets go of the need to feel superior. A mind free from arrogance does not seek dominance, does not compare, and does not need validation—it moves with humility, intelligence, and deep awareness. In this freedom, arrogance disappears—not through force or suppression, but because there is no longer an 'I' that needs to prove, to dominate, or to be above others—only a mind that sees clearly, without illusion, without self-importance.

198. Separateness

Separateness: The Illusion That Divides Humanity

Separateness is the belief or perception that we are distinct, isolated, and independent from others, from nature, and from life itself. This feeling arises from thought, identity, and conditioning, which create a false sense of division between individuals, groups, and even nations. The idea of separateness leads to comparisons, conflicts, loneliness, and a continual search for a sense of belonging. The mind's tendency to identify with the 'self' as a distinct entity gives rise to the belief that we are separate from everything else, thus perpetuating this illusion of separation.

The ego is the root of separateness, creating a sense of 'me' and 'you' based on memories, experiences, and beliefs. It then engages in comparison, defense, and division, which prevents a true connection with others. From an early age, society, culture, and religion condition us to believe in belonging to specific groups—be it by nationality, race, or ideology—reinforcing the belief that we are different from those outside these groups. Language and thought further intensify this division, with concepts like "mine" and "yours" making separation appear inevitable. Fear and desire, both rooted in this sense of separateness, deepen the feeling of isolation and cause us to act out of personal gain rather than collective well-being.

The consequences of believing in separateness are far-reaching. It breeds conflict and violence, as seen in wars, religious divides, and nationalism, where one group perceives itself as superior to others. It also results in emotional isolation, even within relationships, because the mind is trapped in the idea of 'me' and 'my experiences.' Comparison and competition thrive in this mindset, fueling insecurity and envy. A lack of sensitivity toward others and nature follows, as we exploit both without realizing that we are all interconnected. To move beyond separateness, one must see that it is a mental construct—created by thought and fear. True freedom comes not from strengthening the 'self' but from realizing that we are all part of a greater whole, experiencing life together, beyond individual separation.

199. Friend

Friend: The Bond That Transcends Need and Expectation

Friendship is a bond of mutual understanding and affection, where there is no desire to control or possess the other. True friendship allows freedom without expectations or obligations. When a relationship becomes possessive or dependent, it ceases to be a true friendship, instead becoming a form of attachment. Real friendship exists when there is no need to validate one another, but rather, when there is a natural flow of connection between individuals. A friend is someone who mirrors our thoughts and actions, helping us see ourselves clearly without reinforcing illusions.

We often seek friendship because of our fear of loneliness or the desire for validation. Society conditions us to believe that happiness depends on relationships, leading us to cling to social bonds. However, attachment creates fear, jealousy, and control. When we depend on friendships for emotional support or to fill a void, we may lose sight of the true nature of the relationship. True friendship is not about filling an emptiness but about sharing understanding and affection freely, without the need for security or validation.

To have friendship without attachment, one must recognize that it is not about ownership or possession. A friend should not be seen as someone who must meet all of our emotional needs. When expectations and demands are dropped, friendships become natural and light. By letting go of psychological dependence and living in the present, we can form deep connections that are not bound by the past or past memories. In this state, friendship becomes a joyful, open, and non-possessive experience, where both individuals can simply enjoy each other's presence without fear or obligation.

200. Loyalty

Loyalty: Faithfulness or the Fear of Change?

Loyalty is a powerful bond that often arises from deep emotional attachment, trust, and the need for belonging. However, it can be distorted by cultural conditioning, fear, and blind obedience, leading to inner conflict and the loss of personal freedom. When loyalty is grounded in love and understanding, it fosters trust and strengthens relationships. But when loyalty is driven by fear or societal expectations, it can blind the mind, preventing clarity and true discernment. Blind loyalty creates division, fosters "us versus them" thinking, and may lead to unquestioning obedience, even when something is unjust or harmful.

People often value loyalty because it offers a sense of security, belonging, and stability. From an early age, we are conditioned by families, schools, and societies to uphold loyalty to traditions, beliefs, and authorities. This conditioning makes questioning loyalty feel like a betrayal, even when it is necessary for truth and growth. However, loyalty should not be about obligation or fear—it should arise from choice, understanding, and commitment to what is right. True loyalty does not require blind devotion, but rather stands by truth, questioning when necessary, and acting with clarity and integrity.

To live with true loyalty, one must not surrender their freedom or intelligence. Loyalty should not be based on attachment to individuals, systems, or authority but should be directed towards truth and justice. By questioning loyalty without fear of betrayal, we can support others without justifying their mistakes. True loyalty exists in relationships built on understanding and honesty, not pressure or obligation. In this state, loyalty becomes a natural expression of trust, freely given without control or fear. It is no longer a duty or an expectation, but a conscious choice rooted in truth and freedom.

201. Trust and Faith

Trust and Faith: The Risk of Belief Without Seeing

Trust and faith are two concepts that often overlap but differ significantly in their nature and origins. Trust is built on understanding, experience, and observation. It grows from real interactions and the alignment of actions with truth. It is dynamic and evolves based on reliable patterns and consistency. On the other hand, faith is belief without evidence or direct proof. It often arises from conditioning, tradition, or hope, and it provides comfort in the unknown. While trust is grounded in reality, faith can sometimes lead to illusion if not questioned or critically examined. Trust creates stability based on reliability, whereas faith often creates psychological security but may also shield one from uncertainty without addressing reality.

People seek trust and faith for different reasons. Trust is sought when we desire practical stability in relationships or situations. It fosters connection and creates reliability, allowing relationships to thrive. Faith, however, often arises from fear of uncertainty and a desire for emotional security. It provides comfort, especially during crises, but it can also prevent questioning and critical thinking. The mind conditioned to follow authority or belief systems may mistakenly confuse hope with reality, relying on faith to guide actions without considering the underlying truth. True security, however, is not found in blind belief or adherence to external figures but in understanding and seeing life as it truly is, without distortion.

To live without blind faith or undue dependence on external sources of security, one must understand that trust arises from clarity and experience. It is not based on assumptions or desires but on what can be directly observed and known. When one questions faith, particularly when it is rooted in inherited beliefs, it becomes possible to see the truth beyond the illusion. True trust is grounded in understanding and deep perception, not in belief or expectation. By letting go of the need for psychological dependence on faith, one can experience the freedom to trust life and relationships based on genuine clarity, not blind acceptance. Trust, rooted in awareness and understanding, enables one to live confidently, without seeking external validation or reassurance.

202. Care

Care: The Sensitivity That Moves Without Self-Interest

Care is not merely an emotional feeling or obligation; it is the ability to pay deep attention, take responsibility, and be sensitive toward life. True care arises when there is no self-interest, fear, or attachment but comes naturally from understanding and compassion. It is not about control or possessiveness but about seeing others clearly, without distortion or expectation. While many confuse care with sentimental attachment, real care is an unconditional presence in the moment, acting with intelligence and sensitivity toward others.

The nature of care involves being fully present, with deep attention and no agenda. Care is not about expecting affection or recognition; it is a natural movement of understanding that does not seek ownership but allows freedom. Care cannot arise from neglect, indifference, or habitual patterns of behavior—it requires complete awareness and sensitivity. When care becomes mechanical or self-centered, it ceases to be real care. Instead, it turns into a transaction or a form of control, preventing true connection and understanding.

To truly care, one must observe without interference or judgment. This means letting go of possessiveness in relationships and being fully present in every interaction. Real care does not seek reward or recognition but flows naturally from understanding and empathy. When one observes life without the distraction of self-interest, care arises effortlessly, free from attachment and expectation. In this state, care is not just a feeling—it is a deep movement of intelligence and compassion, without division, effort, or force.

203. Gratitude

Gratitude: The Joy of Recognizing the Present

Gratitude is the recognition and appreciation of life, relationships, and experiences without expectation or comparison. It arises naturally when the mind is free from desire, dissatisfaction, and the pursuit of 'more.' A mind caught in gratitude as a habit forces thankfulness, while a mind that understands deeply is effortlessly grateful. Many treat gratitude as a practice, but true gratitude is not an effort—it arises when one sees clearly. A mind free from complaints, comparisons, and expectations is naturally grateful. The mind that is always seeking more—more success, more possessions, more experiences—cannot be truly grateful. When one lets go of the need for 'more,' what is already present becomes enough.

People often feel grateful for material wealth, health, or external success, but true gratitude is not tied to what one has—it is the deep appreciation of life itself. The mind compares—'I have more than others,' or 'I have less than others'—but when comparison stops, gratitude arises, not for being 'better off,' but for the simple joy of being. Many are grateful only when things go well, yet true gratitude remains even in difficulty—it is not about external conditions but inner clarity. Society teaches people to focus on what they lack rather than what is already present, keeping the mind in a state of pursuit rather than appreciation. When gratitude is attached to external rewards, it becomes transactional, depending on what one receives rather than on deep understanding. A mind caught in comparison cannot feel gratitude, and when life is taken for granted, the richness of the present is lost.

Can one be grateful without seeking gratitude? A forced gratitude practice is mechanical, but when one truly sees, gratitude flows naturally. When the mind does not chase future happiness, it appreciates the now, and gratitude arises from the simple awareness of being alive. People forget to appreciate what seems ordinary—health, relationships, nature—but true gratitude sees everything as a gift, without labeling it as 'special.' When one expects life to be a certain way, disappointment follows, yet gratitude exists only when there is no expectation. It is not about having more or being better off than others—it is simply the joy of being, without attachment to outcomes. Gratitude is not something to be practiced, forced, or pursued—it arises naturally when the mind is free from craving, comparison, and expectation. In this freedom, gratitude is no longer a concept—it is the effortless recognition of life's abundance, present in every moment, without effort, without seeking, without end.

204. Tradition

Tradition: The Weight of the Past on the Present

Tradition is the passing down of beliefs, customs, and practices from generation to generation, offering a sense of identity, continuity, and security. It often shapes how individuals live their lives and interact with the world. However, while tradition may provide structure and comfort, it can also condition the mind to accept established ideas without questioning them. A mind trapped in tradition follows these practices not because they are true, but because they are familiar, often hindering fresh perception and personal discovery.

People follow tradition primarily for psychological security. It offers a sense of belonging, stability, and familiarity, making it easier to avoid the discomfort of uncertainty. The fear of the unknown often makes individuals cling to old customs, risking the rejection of new ideas in favor of preserving their sense of identity. Additionally, from childhood, society and religion instill the idea that tradition is a virtue, leading individuals to adopt beliefs and practices without ever questioning their truth or relevance. This conditioning creates a false sense of wisdom, assuming that the longevity of tradition equates to its validity.

Living without the psychological weight of tradition means questioning and examining established customs. Truth does not reside in repeated rituals or inherited beliefs but in the ability to see life directly, free from the filter of past conditioning. While practical traditions may serve a purpose, psychological dependence on tradition can keep the mind in bondage. True freedom arises when the mind is open to the new, willing to move with the changing world without clinging to outdated practices. A mind that is free from tradition can engage with life with intelligence, creativity, and clarity, always seeking what is true in the present moment.

205. Society

Society: The Structure That Shapes and Confines

Society is the collective structure formed by human relationships, laws, beliefs, and institutions, deeply influenced by the individuals who compose it. It is shaped through culture, education, and authority, yet it is also a reflection of our inner conditioning—our fears, desires, and conflicts. Rather than being an external entity separate from us, society is a projection of the collective mind. It mirrors the mental states of its individuals, and as such, its problems and divisions are rooted in the way people think and behave.

The formation of society is an extension of human thought. Individuals seek security, recognition, and order, and society builds structures to satisfy these needs, such as governments, religions, and institutions. But these systems often create conformity rather than true freedom. From birth, we are conditioned into societal roles—through beliefs, behavior norms, and moral codes—making it difficult to distinguish whether society is truly just or merely a product of conditioning. Furthermore, society thrives on division and competition—dividing people into nations, races, classes, and ideologies—which leads to conflict and a cycle of comparison, ambition, and struggle. The presence of authority reinforces these divisions, often leading to a lack of true understanding and freedom.

For society to change, individuals must first change. Society is not an external force; it is the sum of its members. If individuals remain trapped in fear, greed, and ambition, society will continue to reflect these traits. True transformation begins with awareness of how deeply we are conditioned by our environment. When individuals question traditions, authority, and beliefs—guided not by rebellion but by intelligence—society begins to shift. True order comes not through laws or external enforcement but through individuals who act with intelligence, free from fear, comparison, and attachment. Only when individuals free their minds from conditioning and division can society truly evolve into something just, peaceful, and intelligent.

206. Social Approval

Social Approval: The Hunger for Acceptance

Social approval is the need for recognition, validation, or acceptance from others. It arises from conditioning, fear of rejection, and the desire to belong. A mind caught in social approval shapes itself to fit expectations, while a mind that understands deeply moves without dependence on others' opinions. People adjust their behavior, speech, and appearance to be accepted, creating a dependence that prevents true individuality and self-awareness. Fear of rejection or judgment makes one conform, even when it is unnecessary. True freedom exists when one does not seek to be liked or accepted. Society conditions individuals to behave according to cultural and social norms, using approval as a tool to manipulate behavior.

When one wants to be authentic but fears disapproval, an inner struggle arises. A free mind acts not for acceptance but from understanding. The same society that praises today may criticize tomorrow, making social approval temporary and conditional. True confidence does not rely on unstable external validation. From childhood, we are taught that being accepted means being good or successful, reinforcing the belief that external validation is necessary. The mind seeks approval to avoid isolation, yet true connection comes from authenticity, not conformity. Many think being liked will bring opportunities and fulfillment, but real success is not in being approved—it is in being true to oneself.

The need for approval is created by thought, not reality, and when one sees this, its power weakens. Most actions are shaped by fear of what others think, but a free mind does not hesitate—it moves without seeking validation. People look to others to confirm if they are right or valuable, yet when one trusts direct perception, approval becomes irrelevant. The need for approval exists because one maintains an image, but a mind without self-image does not seek validation. Approval-seeking creates anxiety and limitation, while acting from understanding makes approval or disapproval lose importance. In this freedom, approval and disapproval become meaningless—what remains is authenticity, intelligence, and action that arises from truth, not from the need to be accepted.

207. Validation

Validation: The Search for Worth in the Eyes of Others

Validation is the desire for recognition, approval, or acceptance from others, often stemming from insecurity, social conditioning, and the need to affirm one's worth. A mind caught in the cycle of seeking validation depends on external opinions and feedback, leading to a fragile sense of self. When validation is sought, it weakens inner freedom, as the mind adjusts its actions to fit others' expectations rather than acting from its own understanding and clarity. This external dependency creates a disconnect from one's authentic self, as the need for approval becomes a constant source of inner conflict.

The nature of validation revolves around the need for confirmation of self-worth. People want reassurance that they are valued, successful, or right in their actions, but this dependence on others for self-esteem makes it unstable. When we base our self-worth on the opinions of others, it becomes a continuous cycle of seeking approval. Validation also thrives on the fear of rejection or being judged as inadequate. This fear drives conformity and suppresses independent thinking, as the mind becomes preoccupied with fitting in rather than expressing truth. As a result, validation ultimately undermines authenticity, preventing individuals from acting freely and without concern for how they are perceived.

Living without seeking validation requires an understanding that true self-worth is independent of external recognition. When one stops acting for approval, their actions become pure and self-contained. True confidence arises from inner clarity, not from the validation of others. By observing the need for validation without reacting to it, a person can break free from its grip. The mind that does not compare itself to others has no need for external validation. In this freedom, life becomes authentic, and self-worth is no longer tied to the opinions of others but grounded in deep understanding and clarity.

208. Praise and Insult

Praise and Insult: The Two Sides of Psychological Dependence

Praise and insult are external judgments that shape our psychological responses, but they have no inherent meaning unless we accept them. Praise offers recognition, approval, and admiration, which the mind clings to for a sense of importance. On the other hand, insult involves rejection or criticism, which creates emotional pain and defensiveness. Both praise and insult stem from others' opinions, and when we depend on these external validations, we enter a cycle of seeking approval and fearing rejection. This cycle limits true understanding and peace, as the mind is forever caught between these polar extremes.

The attachment to praise and the aversion to insult are psychological traps that bind us to others' perceptions of us. We become conditioned to either seek praise or avoid insult, and in doing so, we allow our sense of self-worth to be defined by others. This creates insecurity, as we rely on external validation to feel good about ourselves and fear criticism or exclusion. However, the truth of who we are cannot be defined by praise or insult; these are fleeting, momentary judgments that do not reflect our true nature. By seeing them for what they are—temporary, external reactions—we can begin to free ourselves from their influence.

To live without being affected by praise or insult requires observing them without attachment. When we receive praise, we can enjoy it without craving more; when we face insult, we can observe it without reacting. True freedom comes when we stop seeking validation or fearing criticism. A mind that is not governed by the desire for approval or the fear of rejection moves confidently, grounded in clarity and truth. In this state, there is no need for praise to affirm our worth or insult to diminish it; we are whole, unshaken, and complete in our understanding.

8. Social & Global Issues

WAKE UP

209. Humanity

Humanity: The Shared Consciousness That Binds Us All

Humanity is not merely a collection of individuals but a shared existence, encompassing the collective consciousness of all people. It includes the entire spectrum of human experience— fear, love, ambition, sorrow, and the endless search for meaning. While humanity holds the potential for unity, it often finds itself trapped in cycles of division and conflict. These divisions, fueled by personal identities and ideologies, create barriers between individuals and groups, perpetuating suffering. Humanity's true challenge is recognizing that it is a whole, not a fragmented collection of isolated selves, and moving towards unity through understanding and compassion.

Humanity is in conflict because of psychological divisions that separate individuals based on nationality, religion, race, and ideology. These divisions lead to competition, war, and suffering, as the mind clings to the idea of "us" versus "them." People seek security in external factors such as belief systems, possessions, and social status, but this security is an illusion. The pursuit of material wealth and success, fueled by greed and fear, exacerbates inequality and exploitation, leading to endless dissatisfaction. Moreover, humanity carries the inherited burden of history—wars, prejudices, and conditioned thought patterns that prevent real progress. As long as these patterns remain unexamined, humanity is doomed to repeat them, trapped in the illusion of progress.

The future of humanity is deeply tied to individual change. While societal structures like governments and religions may play a role, true transformation begins in the individual. Society is merely a reflection of the collective consciousness, which is shaped by the minds of individuals. When one sees beyond the psychological labels of nationality, religion, or ideology, division dissipates, and a deeper sense of connection emerges. Security does not lie in external factors or illusions but in understanding and living in harmony with reality. A mind free from the shackles of greed, fear, and division naturally acts with intelligence, compassion, and clarity, leading to a new humanity. The future depends on whether humanity awakens to this truth and transcends the conflict rooted in separateness.

210. Culture

Culture: The Traditions That Shape and Divide

Culture is the accumulation of traditions, beliefs, customs, and knowledge passed down through generations. It shapes language, behavior, values, and identity, significantly influencing how one sees and interacts with the world. While culture provides a sense of belonging and helps preserve human creativity and expression, it also conditions the mind, creating psychological boundaries and reinforcing divisions. This dual nature of culture offers both richness and limitations—offering us a framework for understanding the world while also constraining our perception by defining what is acceptable and valuable.

The nature of culture lies in its ability to both enrich and limit. On one hand, it brings art, music, philosophy, and expressions of human creativity that are vital to human experience. On the other, culture imposes boundaries—defining what is acceptable, moral, and valuable. It creates a psychological separation between 'us' and 'them,' fostering national, religious, and social divisions. A mind deeply conditioned by culture often struggles to see beyond its inherited beliefs, and this conditioning prevents questioning, creating conformity to established norms. Furthermore, culture often reinforces authority and tradition, preventing fresh perception and change as individuals are discouraged from questioning what is considered sacred or established.

Culture can limit freedom by imposing rigid identities and divisions. Labels like nationality, religion, or belief system separate individuals psychologically, fueling conflict and misunderstanding. Breaking away from these norms is often met with rejection, isolation, and criticism, as many prefer the comfort of belonging over the challenge of seeing beyond cultural conditioning. When one follows rituals and customs blindly without understanding, the mind remains trapped in cultural limitations. Thought strengthens this conditioning by operating through memory, reinforcing past traditions and experiences, and distorting reality through the filter of cultural identity. However, by observing culture without attachment or rejection, individuals can step beyond it and move towards freedom. When one is no longer psychologically identified with a culture, it becomes possible to appreciate its beauty while remaining free from its psychological grip.

211. Governance

Governance: Order or the Illusion of Control?

Governance is the system through which societies are organized, and it serves the purpose of maintaining order, ensuring justice, and regulating collective living. While governance is necessary to prevent chaos, its effectiveness depends on whether it truly serves the people or becomes a mechanism for control. A mind caught in authority follows orders blindly, while a mind that seeks understanding questions governance's role and ensures it remains rooted in wisdom and justice. True governance arises when individuals are aware and responsible, creating systems that nurture the well-being of all, not just a select few.

The nature of governance involves both its necessity for social order and its potential for misuse. While governance is essential to prevent disorder and maintain fairness, it often operates through power rather than wisdom. Many systems of governance prioritize control over intelligence, leading to corruption and exploitation. True governance requires not just laws and regulations, but a conscious and aware populace that can challenge injustice and actively participate in ensuring fairness. It is not limited to political systems but extends to how individuals govern themselves and their relationships, creating harmony or division based on awareness and responsibility.

While governance can create structures for justice, it is often marred by corruption, control, and the fear of freedom. People often blindly accept authority, expecting governance to solve all problems without considering their own role in society. This passive dependence weakens the possibility of real change. True governance requires active participation, questioning authority, and an understanding that governance exists to serve, not rule. By eliminating corruption within ourselves and acknowledging the need for flexibility in systems, we can move toward a more just society, where governance adapts to the needs of all people, rather than suppressing them. A free mind creates a system that nurtures fairness and ensures intelligent, ethical governance.

212. Politics

Politics: The Struggle for Power Disguised as Leadership

Politics is the system of governance and power that shapes societal structures and influences decision-making. In its ideal form, politics should focus on justice, public welfare, and leadership; however, it often devolves into a struggle for power and control. At its core, politics mirrors the mind of society—its divisions, struggles, and ambitions. Instead of fostering unity, politics often deepens conflict, and its primary purpose of serving the public can be obscured by manipulation and self-interest. The true challenge lies not in the system itself but in the mental conditioning that supports it.

Politics exists to create social order, resolve conflicts, and distribute resources. However, the pursuit of power often overshadows these noble aims, with individuals and groups using the system to gain control for personal benefit. Ideologies further divide people, creating opposing factions that perpetuate conflict and prevent cooperation. The belief that politics will bring meaningful change is often misguided, as it tends to modify the same cycles of oppression and inequality, rather than addressing their root causes. This cycle of ambition, manipulation, and division creates a political environment where true transformation remains elusive.

The corruption inherent in politics—manifested through manipulation, propaganda, and division—prevents true freedom from emerging. Laws and policies, while necessary for governance, cannot foster the internal order required for justice and peace. True freedom arises from within, not through the control of governments or systems. To move beyond the limitations of politics, individuals must seek to understand the nature of power and free themselves from ideological conditioning. Only through inner transformation can society evolve into a place of true unity, free from fear, greed, and division. In this state of awareness, true change occurs, not through external systems, but through the awakening of individuals.

213. Corruption

Corruption: The Rot That Thrives in Power and Greed

Corruption is not just an issue of political systems, governments, or large institutions—it is a mindset that distorts truth, integrity, and fairness for personal gain. It starts in the mind as a small compromise, often justified by fear, insecurity, or ambition. A person caught in corruption rationalizes dishonesty and manipulation to secure their own advantage, neglecting the consequences on others. While it can be manifested in large-scale political scandals or corporate fraud, corruption also shows up in everyday acts like favoritism, small lies, or using influence for personal benefit. The core of corruption is self-interest—it arises when personal gain becomes more important than fairness or truth.

The persistence of corruption is fueled by societal conditioning and the human desire for success, power, and validation. People are taught to value wealth, status, and power over integrity, leading them to justify dishonest behavior as a means to reach their goals. Many see corruption in others but fail to recognize it in themselves, either through small compromises or rationalized actions. Fear of isolation, failure, or losing power often leads individuals to engage in corruption to protect their interests. However, true change starts not with opposing corruption externally but by examining the corruption within one's own mind and behavior.

To be free from corruption, one must begin by addressing it within themselves. Corruption originates in the mind as thoughts that seek advantage or twist the truth, and when these thoughts are recognized and understood, they naturally dissolve. True integrity is not about avoiding large-scale corruption but living honestly in all aspects, even the smallest actions. A mind free from the desire for power, prestige, or position cannot be corrupted. When one acts from clarity, without fear or self-interest, they live with integrity, and the temptation for corruption fades. True freedom is achieved not by fighting corruption in others but by dissolving it within oneself.

214. Poverty

Poverty: The Failure of Society to Share and Care

Poverty is not just a lack of material resources but also an issue of opportunity, awareness, and systemic inequality. It arises from the imbalances in economic, social, and political structures that create a cycle of deprivation, making it difficult for individuals to break free. Those born into poverty are often trapped, unable to see beyond immediate survival, and may feel powerless due to the systems that limit their opportunities. True poverty also includes mental poverty, where the mind is conditioned to believe in scarcity and lack, preventing growth, creativity, and self-empowerment.

Poverty persists because society often accepts it as a natural consequence of economic inequality. This belief that some must be poor for others to be rich creates a mindset that prevents questioning the systems that maintain poverty. While charity can offer temporary relief, it does not address the root causes of inequality. Welfare systems, in many cases, reinforce dependency rather than fostering independence and empowerment. The rich and powerful often ignore the structural barriers that cause poverty, viewing it instead as a personal failure or a result of laziness, which further perpetuates the cycle.

True freedom from poverty requires a shift in both the external systems and the internal mindset. We must question the social and economic structures that sustain inequality and work toward a more just society where extreme wealth and poverty are not tolerated. Empowering individuals through education, skill-building, and self-sufficiency is key to eliminating poverty. When the mind is free from the conditioning of scarcity, wealth becomes more than just material—it becomes the richness of awareness, intelligence, and the ability to live without fear or limitation.

215. Exploitation

Exploitation: The Manipulation of Others for Self-Gain

Exploitation is the act of using someone or something for one's own benefit, often without regard for their well-being. It exists in economic, social, political, and personal relationships and is rooted in greed, power, and the desire to control or dominate. People exploit to gain wealth, status, or authority, with nations, corporations, and individuals maintaining superiority through domination. The desire for more—money, success, possessions—fuels exploitation, while fear of poverty, failure, or insignificance justifies it. Social and economic systems encourage exploitation, normalizing inequality where the strong benefit at the cost of the weak. Even in personal relationships, exploitation arises when one person manipulates another for love, attention, or security, turning human connections into transactions rather than mutual understanding.

Exploitation creates division and conflict, as those who are exploited eventually resist, leading to tension, rebellion, and instability. Societies built on exploitation suffer from resentment and violence. In personal relationships, when people use each other for gain, there is no real love, only selfish interest, resulting in mistrust and emotional suffering. The one who exploits becomes hardened, insensitive, and blind to their own cruelty, while the one who is exploited loses dignity, freedom, and self-worth. Once exploitation begins, it expands—power seeks more power, wealth seeks more wealth—trapping both the exploiter and the exploited in a cycle of fear, oppression, and injustice.

Can one observe where they use others for personal gain—at work, in relationships, in daily interactions? The moment one sees exploitation without justification, a shift begins. Letting go of the desire to dominate or gain from others allows one to act not from self-interest but from true understanding and respect. Many use others for emotional security, validation, or dependence, yet can one be completely whole within, without needing to use others for fulfillment? A mind free from exploitation does not seek advantage—it moves with intelligence, fairness, and love. When one sees that exploitation leads to suffering for both oneself and others, it naturally ends. A world without exploitation is possible only when there is deep awareness of how we treat others—not as means to an end, but as human beings. A mind free from exploitation acts from love, fairness, and understanding—not from self-interest.

216. Symbols

Symbols: The Images That Define and Divide

Symbols, in their simplest form, are representations—words, images, rituals, and concepts—that stand for something beyond themselves. They are tools for communication, allowing us to convey meaning, but when mistaken for reality, they distort perception. The mind often clings to symbols—whether national flags, religious icons, or political ideologies—creating psychological attachments that can lead to division and conflict.

Rather than directly perceiving truth, we interpret it through symbols, which prevents us from experiencing life as it truly is. Symbols can also be used to manipulate and control, evoking blind loyalty and reinforcing division, often leading to war and discrimination.

The reason we depend on symbols is multifaceted. Firstly, we mistake symbols for truth, believing that religious texts, flags, or ideological concepts hold ultimate reality. But true understanding exists beyond representation—it is in direct perception. Symbols give us a sense of security and identity, providing comfort in the face of uncertainty. Yet, in doing so, they limit our ability to see beyond them. We are conditioned to accept symbols as reality, and through this conditioning, we become attached to the false sense of belonging they provide. We unite under shared symbols, but true unity is not in external representations—it's in genuine human relationships that transcend labels.

To live without being bound by symbols, one must understand that symbols are not the reality they represent. By letting go of psychological identification with symbols—such as nationality, religion, or ideology—one can free themselves from division and conflict. True perception comes from seeing life without translating it into familiar symbols, embracing what is directly before us. Symbols are necessary for practical communication, but they should not define our inner life. When we stop seeking meaning in symbols, we open ourselves to an undistorted perception of life, experiencing it directly with clarity and understanding. In this freedom, there is no need for representation—just pure insight and truth.

217. Identification

Identification: The Psychological Need to Belong

Identification is the process of attaching oneself to a belief, nationality, religion, group, person, or idea. It provides a sense of belonging and psychological security but also leads to division, fear, and conflict. The mind, in its search for stability, clings to labels—"I am this," "I belong to that"—reinforcing the illusion of the 'self.' This identification creates an artificial structure that defines who we believe we are, giving us a sense of continuity and importance. The need for psychological security drives identification, as life's uncertainty makes people seek stability through associations with family, culture, religion, and political beliefs. Without identification, one may fear being nothing, so the mind builds an identity to give itself meaning. The desire to belong and be accepted further strengthens identification, leading to conformity and the fear of questioning. Additionally, identification fortifies the ego—when identity is challenged, people react with fear, anger, and defensiveness, as if their very existence is under attack.

However, identification brings several problems. It creates division and conflict—the moment we say, "I am Hindu," "I am Muslim," "I am Indian," or "I am American," we separate ourselves from others. Wars, religious clashes, and social conflicts arise not from truth but from identification with labels. Identification also prevents direct understanding—when one identifies with a belief, they stop questioning it, defending their conditioning instead of seeing reality clearly. This leads to fear and insecurity, as people attach their self-worth to their status, relationships, and reputation. When these external identities are threatened, they feel lost because they have never questioned whether identity was real in the first place. Furthermore, identification makes the mind rigid, unable to see with freshness. It repeats inherited beliefs rather than discovering truth for itself.

Living without identification requires seeing it as an illusion. If identity is just a construct of memory, belief, and thought, is it real? The moment one sees that identity is not fixed, its hold weakens. Observing without attaching—watching reactions without defending ideas as 'mine'—is the beginning of freedom. One can exist without clinging to nationality, religion, or ideology, simply living as a human being. This does not mean rejecting society but not being psychologically bound by any identity. Action without identification is free, intelligent, and peaceful—it does not come from attachment but from clarity. Identification is the mind's attempt to create security, yet it leads to division, fear, and blindness to truth. The moment one sees through this illusion, there is freedom—freedom to think, to love, and to live without conflict. A mind free from identification does not belong to any group, nation, or belief—it is simply aware, present, and deeply alive.

218. Discrimination

Discrimination: The Prejudice That Creates Superiority and Inferiority

Discrimination is the act of dividing individuals or groups based on perceived differences, such as race, gender, or class. It originates from deep-rooted conditioning, where the mind clings to identity and superiority. This creates an "us vs. them" mentality, fostering separation and conflict. A mind trapped in discrimination cannot see the unity of humanity, while a mind that understands transcends these distinctions, realizing the falseness of separation. In truth, all forms of division are born out of attachment to belief, identity, and the desire for security.

Discrimination is sustained by the identification of the self with groups—whether by race, religion, class, or ideology. This identification leads to exclusion and prejudice, perpetuating societal divisions. These divisions, in turn, fuel exploitation, oppression, and endless struggle, as one group seeks to assert its dominance over another. Fear plays a major role in discrimination, as people cling to their group for safety and reject others as a defense mechanism. Societies justify discrimination as natural or necessary, but true order is based on wholeness and equality, not on artificial distinctions.

The persistence of discrimination arises from a deep-seated desire for identity and belonging, often without questioning the inherited biases. Those who benefit from these divisions defend them, fearing the loss of privilege or power. However, differences in appearance, belief, or background do not equate to superiority or inferiority. True freedom from discrimination begins by seeing that all divisions are illusions, created by thought, not reality. When one frees the mind from labels and no longer identifies with group divisions, discrimination ends naturally, making space for unity and understanding.

219. Divisions

Divisions: The Fragmentation That Breeds Conflict

Division is the mental separation between individuals, ideas, and beliefs that creates conflict. It exists at every level, from nations and religions to social classes, races, and even within our own minds. Though external differences may exist, psychological division is created by thought, which categorizes, compares, and labels. This division leads to endless struggle, isolation, and misunderstanding, fostering an "us vs. them" mentality. The more we identify with a particular group or belief, the more we create a barrier between ourselves and others.

The root of division lies in the mind's desire for security in identity. By identifying with a country, religion, or ideology, we feel stable and protected. However, true security does not come from division but from understanding the oneness of humanity. Thought creates separation by naming and comparing—this leads to competition, jealousy, and the pursuit of superiority. From childhood, we inherit traditions and beliefs that reinforce these divisions. Fear of the unknown strengthens these separations, as we cling to what is familiar and reject what is unfamiliar or different.

The consequences of division are profound. It leads to conflict, as history shows through wars fought over race, religion, and borders. Division also creates psychological isolation, where we feel disconnected from others, unable to trust or connect. Furthermore, division prevents true understanding and love, as a divided mind sees others through labels rather than recognizing their shared humanity. True freedom and peace come when one realizes that division is an illusion created by thought. By letting go of psychological identification with nationality, religion, or ideology, we break down the barriers between ourselves and others, leading to a deeper connection, compassion, and understanding.

220. Nationalism

Nationalism: The Worship of Borders That Separates Humanity

Nationalism is the psychological attachment to a country, a flag, or a group of people, creating an "us vs. them" mentality that divides humanity. It fosters a sense of belonging, security, and identity, but this security is based on illusion. A mind caught in nationalism perceives the world through borders, believing that one's identity is defined by national affiliation. But in reality, this mindset only fuels conflict and separation, as it reinforces differences between groups rather than acknowledging the shared humanity we all possess.

Nationalism is a form of psychological conditioning that is deeply ingrained from childhood. We are taught that we belong to a nation, and this belief is reinforced by cultural, social, and political influences. The sense of ownership over a country is instilled in us, but is this concept of ownership truly real? Nations divide themselves into superior and inferior groups, with each defending its interests and justifying actions like war to protect its sovereignty. However, if every nation pursues its own interests at the cost of others, can true peace ever be achieved? Nationalism thrives on division and fear, often manipulated by leaders to secure power and control.

Breaking free from nationalism requires understanding that humanity is one, beyond the borders of nations. While traditions and cultural symbols might invoke pride, they also reinforce outdated notions of separation. Nationalism binds individuals to the past and cultivates a sense of superiority, yet it fails to offer true security or peace. A mind that is not shackled by national identity can act with intelligence, compassion, and a broader sense of unity with all of humanity. When one sees through the illusion of nationalism, there is no longer a need to belong to a particular nation, only to life itself. True freedom is not in identification with a nation, but in embracing the commonality of human existence, transcending boundaries and labels.

221. Aggression

Aggression: The Outward Expression of Inner Conflict

Aggression is often seen as a sign of strength, but it is more accurately a reaction driven by fear, anger, or insecurity. It arises when we feel threatened—whether in terms of status, control, or emotional well-being. Society glorifies competition, power, and domination, which feeds the impulse to react aggressively. When faced with conflict or hurt, the natural response is often aggression, driven by a desire to protect oneself or assert dominance. However, in reality, aggression rarely addresses the root cause of fear or hurt—it only perpetuates more violence and division, leaving a cycle of unresolved conflict.

The consequences of aggression are far-reaching, extending beyond physical violence into emotional and psychological harm. Aggression breeds retaliation, reinforcing the very hostility it seeks to end. It clouds intelligence, leading to impulsive reactions that prevent true understanding. A mind governed by aggression cannot form deep connections or engage in compassionate dialogue. While aggression is often mistakenly seen as power, it is actually a sign of inner weakness—a lack of clarity or understanding. True strength lies not in domination but in the ability to remain calm, clear, and insightful, responding to challenges with wisdom rather than force.

To be free from aggression, one must first observe it without justifying or suppressing it. Understanding that aggression is not strength is crucial—strength arises from clear understanding and thoughtful action. By letting go of the burdens of past hurts and future fears, one can move beyond aggression and act from a place of clarity. True freedom from aggression means being able to act firmly and wisely without being controlled by anger or the impulse to react. In this state, there is no conflict, only decisive action that is firm, clear, and rooted in intelligence and compassion.

222. Violence

Violence: The Destruction Born from Fear and Division

Violence is more than physical aggression; it encompasses anger, hatred, jealousy, domination, and psychological conflict. It arises when there is division—between individuals, ideologies, nations, or even within ourselves. The mind creates this division by identifying with a belief, group, or identity, leading to the "us vs. them" mentality. This sense of separation breeds aggression, fueling violence in various forms. The underlying causes of violence often stem from fear and insecurity, where we react violently to protect our sense of self or to maintain control over our surroundings. When desires are blocked or unmet, frustration often turns into anger, further contributing to violent behaviors.

Violence manifests in many ways, including physical violence such as war and abuse, as well as subtler forms like verbal and emotional aggression. Verbal violence—through insults, criticism, and gossip—can leave lasting wounds that are more damaging than physical harm. Inner psychological violence occurs when individuals struggle against their own desires, suppress emotions, or experience self-criticism. This internal conflict creates a tension that often spills over into external violence. The root causes of violence are not only external; they are deeply ingrained in the psyche, and healing begins when we confront and address this inner turmoil.

The first step in ending violence is to see it within ourselves. By observing anger, irritation, and jealousy without reacting or justifying these emotions, we begin to dissolve their power. Inner conflict creates violence, and true peace can only arise when the mind ceases to fight against itself. Dropping the need for comparison with others is essential, as comparison breeds frustration and envy, which in turn fuel violence. Ultimately, fear is the root of aggression, and when we understand and dissolve fear through awareness, violence fades naturally. In relationships, love free from possessiveness removes the need for control and jealousy, eliminating the violence they breed. True peace is possible when we end violence within, leading to harmony and understanding in the world around us.

223. War

War: The Ultimate Madness of the Divided Mind

War is not just a physical conflict between nations; it is the outward manifestation of the inner violence within individuals. It exists wherever there is division—whether in politics, religion, economics, or personal relationships. War arises from the minds conditioned by fear, nationalism, ambition, and the desire for security. When people identify with a country, religion, race, or ideology, they create separation, which inevitably breeds conflict and escalates to large-scale violence. The mind's attachment to its identity leads to the justification of war, often under the guise of defending a "right" cause, when in reality, all wars are rooted in the same psychological need for control and division.

The search for power and security plays a significant role in the existence of war. Nations and corporations, driven by a desire for resources and control, view war as a means to gain influence and wealth. However, this search for control leads to more fear, hatred, and retaliation, never providing the security it promises. The economic and political benefits that war brings to a select few further fuel its continuation. From childhood, we are taught that competition, aggression, and dominance are necessary, glorifying those who fight in war. This conditioning, coupled with the acceptance of violence in society, creates a culture where war is seen as honorable and even necessary.

War can only truly end when we understand that it begins in the mind. The divisions we create through identification—whether by nationality, ideology, or religion—are the root causes of war. If we stop creating psychological divisions and live without violence, we will naturally cease to contribute to war. A peaceful society is only possible when individuals are free from psychological violence and conflict. True peace comes when one sees the futility of division and competition. A mind free from fear, greed, and ambition lives in intelligence, peace, and love, and such a mind does not create war.

WAKE UP

WAKE UP

9. Values & Morality

WAKE UP

WAKE UP

224. Values

Values: The Principles That Shape Human Conduct

Values are the principles and guidelines that shape human behavior, decisions, and relationships, often seen as essential for maintaining order and justice in society. However, one must question whether these values arise from genuine understanding or are merely imposed by societal norms, culture, and tradition. While values may offer stability and structure, they can also limit the mind, creating a false sense of security and identity. A mind bound by rigid values may conform without questioning the true essence of right and wrong, rather than acting from a place of deep awareness.

The problem with imposed values is that they create division. Different societies and cultures uphold conflicting values, often leading to conflict and misunderstanding. Clinging to one's values prevents openness, preventing the ability to understand and respect others. Furthermore, values, when fixed, become rigid and prevent true understanding, as they make one react based on preconceived beliefs instead of direct perception. In this way, imposed values can breed hypocrisy, where people pretend to follow moral codes without acting with true intelligence, compassion, and integrity. The result is a morality that is often disconnected from real life and living truth.

True morality and goodness are not based on following predefined values but arise from awareness, intelligence, and compassion in each situation. When one acts out of deep understanding and clarity, morality becomes natural. It is essential to free oneself from the psychological authority of societal, political, or religious values. A mind free from such conditioning does not need a set of values to act justly. Instead, it acts in harmony with the present moment, without fear, without rigidity, and without the need for rules or control. In this freedom, true morality unfolds effortlessly, as it arises directly from clear perception and intelligent action.

225. Morality

Morality: The Codes That Govern Behavior

Morality is often understood as a set of rules, principles, or beliefs about right and wrong, shaped by society, religion, and tradition. It is typically imposed externally through laws, customs, and social expectations. However, one must question whether morality is a matter of blind obedience, or whether it can arise from deep understanding, self-awareness, and clarity. Often, people follow moral codes out of fear of punishment, the need for social approval, or simply because it is ingrained in their upbringing. But is true morality about following rules or about understanding the deeper implications of one's actions?

The problems with imposed morality arise when it is based on fear and external pressure. If one behaves morally only to avoid punishment or to seek a reward, is that true virtue? This kind of morality breeds division, as different cultures and religions possess different moral codes, often leading to judgment, intolerance, and even violence. Additionally, when morality is based solely on rules, it prevents deep understanding and growth. True morality cannot be found in rigid conformity to laws—it must come from intelligence and compassion, arising naturally from clarity and direct perception of what is right.

True morality is not about imitating others or adhering to external rules. It is an expression of deep awareness and understanding. Real morality exists universally, beyond cultural or religious conditioning, and is not dependent on laws or social norms. When one acts out of love, compassion, and intelligence, without personal gain or fear, true morality arises. A mind free from internal conflict, judgment, and contradiction naturally acts with wisdom and clarity. This freedom from inner conflict and attachment to external validation is where true morality lies—not in duty, but in understanding and compassion for others.

226. Ethics

Ethics: The Judgment of Right and Wrong in Action

Ethics is not a rigid set of rules but a reflection of deep understanding about what is right and wrong. While it often stems from social conditioning, personal experiences, and a need for order, true ethics arises from awareness, intelligence, and direct perception. A mind bound by conventional ethical systems may follow them blindly, but a mind that understands sees beyond these constraints, acting with clarity and responsibility. True ethical behavior is not about external rules or enforcement; it emerges from one's inner clarity and awareness of the consequences of their actions.

The nature of ethics is fluid—it evolves with awareness. What is considered ethical in one culture or time may not hold the same weight in another. This reveals the limitations of a fixed ethical system that fails to account for evolving circumstances. When ethics is shaped by fear or social pressure, it becomes distorted, creating conflict, hypocrisy, and division. True ethics transcends this and manifests in daily life, where one's actions, big or small, align with an understanding of humanity and compassion. It is not about condemning others or following rules mechanically but about living with integrity and sensitivity toward the world.

To live ethically without relying on a rigid system, one must move from fear and conformity to a state of true understanding. Ethics becomes natural when it is not just theoretical but applies to real-life relationships and interactions. A mind free from external enforcement of rules acts ethically because it understands the consequences of its actions. In this freedom, ethics flows effortlessly—shaped by clarity, integrity, and a deep connection with life, not by the need for approval, reward, or punishment. It is not the imposition of principles but the natural expression of a compassionate and intelligent mind.

227. Good and Bad

Good and Bad: The Duality Created by Conditioning

Good and bad are mental constructs, often shaped by culture, beliefs, and social conditioning, designed to categorize experiences and behaviors into moral opposites. These concepts arise when the mind compares and judges, creating division between what is deemed acceptable and unacceptable. A mind caught in these labels constantly reacts based on past conditioning, rather than understanding the true essence of the moment. Good and bad exist as judgments, not absolute truths, and are always defined by contrast—one can only call something "good" in relation to something "bad." This comparison creates conflict, perpetuating the cycle of judgment and division.

The nature of good and bad is rooted in the conditioning of thought, influenced by societal and cultural beliefs, and often used as tools of control. Religions, governments, and institutions define good and bad to maintain order and obedience, leading people to act out of fear or conformity. However, good and bad are not fixed—they are dynamic and context-dependent. What is considered "bad" in one situation may, in fact, be necessary in another. This constant labeling and comparing prevent real understanding of human behavior and perpetuate psychological division, where individuals or groups label themselves as "good" and others as "bad," deepening conflict.

Living without the concept of good and bad requires the mind to see beyond these labels and embrace direct perception. When one observes life without judgment, a deeper insight into human nature emerges. True action arises not from moral conditioning but from intelligence and clarity, acting in the moment without fear of moral uncertainty. A mind free from the division of good and bad sees the complexity of life without simplifying it into dualities. This clarity leads to a state where life is no longer divided, and action flows naturally from deep awareness and understanding, free from conflict and distortion.

228. Good and Evil

Good and Evil: The Psychological Division That Breeds Conflict

Good and evil have been conditioned into human consciousness as opposing forces, each defined by cultural, religious, and societal standards. These concepts, often handed down through traditions, shape how we perceive the world and judge actions. However, can good and evil be considered absolute realities, or are they merely constructs created by the mind? In many cases, what one culture or religion deems as good, another might label as evil, reinforcing the idea that good and evil are subjective, ever-changing, and dependent on context. This duality creates a constant psychological conflict within individuals, as they suppress thoughts deemed evil while striving to cultivate what is considered good, often leading to hypocrisy and inner struggle.

The root of this division lies in the concepts of comparison and judgment. We are conditioned to compare ourselves to moral ideals, judging actions as good or bad based on external standards. This mindset keeps us trapped in a cycle of moral assessment, preventing us from understanding ourselves directly and honestly. The idea of good and evil becomes further complicated when we realize that the two are interconnected. As soon as we define good, we inevitably create its opposite—evil. This interdependence suggests that good and evil are not absolute, but are part of a psychological framework created by the mind's tendency to label and categorize experiences. The root of evil, therefore, is ignorance—the inability to see things as they truly are, free from conditioning and self-interest.

True goodness lies beyond this duality. It is not the opposite of evil but exists independently of it. When the mind is free from fear, division, and conditioning, goodness arises naturally from understanding. This shift in perception allows individuals to act from intelligence and love rather than adhering to rigid moral codes. Goodness is an act of clarity, not a rule to be followed. To transcend good and evil, one must see beyond the labels and judgments that divide them. A mind that is free from duality does not need moral struggle—it simply acts rightly because it sees clearly. In this freedom, the concepts of good and evil lose their hold, and true understanding and love naturally guide one's actions.

229. Right and Wrong

Right and Wrong: The Relativity of Moral Judgment

Right and wrong are not universal truths but constructs shaped by culture, beliefs, and personal conditioning. These moral concepts arise when the mind categorizes actions, behaviors, and choices based on inherited or learned standards. A mind caught in the framework of right and wrong constantly judges, compares, and conforms, instead of perceiving situations with intelligence and clarity. This division between right and wrong limits true understanding and prevents fresh insight into complex life situations.

The nature of right and wrong is rooted in conditioned judgments. What is considered "right" in one culture or era may be perceived as "wrong" in another, showing that these concepts are subjective and changeable. The duality of right and wrong creates constant inner conflict as the mind evaluates actions against fixed moral codes. These moral judgments are often used for social control and obedience, where authority figures impose rigid rules. In truth, ethical action arises not from fear of punishment or desire for reward but from awareness of the consequences of one's actions.

Living without the burden of right and wrong requires seeing these concepts as mental constructs. True moral action comes from deep understanding, not from conforming to external rules. When one observes actions without moral judgment, the need for right and wrong fades, and intelligence guides decision-making. A mind free from rigid morality does not react based on imposed labels but acts from clarity and responsibility. In this freedom, there is no division between right and wrong, and the mind operates in harmony with truth, responding directly and wisely to the present moment.

230. Rules & Regulations

Rules & Regulations: The Boundaries That Create Order and Restriction

Rules and regulations are often seen as necessary tools to maintain order and ensure justice within society. They offer structure and guidelines that help people coexist harmoniously. However, when these rules are followed without questioning their underlying purpose, they can become restrictive. True freedom is not found in blind obedience to laws, but in understanding their purpose and applying them with intelligence. A mind that follows rules only out of fear or habit is not free—it is constrained by a system that fails to encourage genuine inquiry or responsibility.

The nature of rules is not fixed; they are shaped by culture, society, and historical context. What is considered just or fair at one point in time may become outdated as collective understanding evolves. Rules must be adaptive, reflecting the changing needs and values of society. When rules are adhered to rigidly, they prevent growth and creativity. True intelligence lies not in mere compliance, but in the ability to question and apply rules in a way that serves the greater good, not just conformity or control.

The struggle with rules often arises from the fear of questioning authority or the perceived consequences of non-compliance. People are conditioned to obey without examining the fairness or relevance of the rules. This fear of standing apart from societal norms prevents personal growth and a deeper understanding of justice. True freedom comes when one is able to live without being bound by rigid rules, yet still act with responsibility and awareness. A mind that is free from fear and blind obedience moves with clarity, applying structure where necessary but not allowing it to control or limit the potential for change and evolution.

231. Justice

Justice: The Pursuit of Fairness in an Unjust World

Justice is the principle of fairness, harmony, and the right distribution of consequences and opportunities. It arises from the need to correct wrongs, ensure equality, and establish order in society. A mind caught in justice as punishment seeks revenge, while a mind that understands justice sees beyond law and retribution to true balance. Many believe justice is about making wrongdoers suffer, but true justice seeks not revenge, but balance and correction. Laws are often created to serve those in power, and justice can be tainted by bias and control. When justice is reduced to retribution, it becomes a cycle of harm, reinforcing divisions rather than resolving conflicts. A legal system may enforce rules, but real justice arises when individuals act with fairness and clarity.

People judge others while justifying their own wrongs. A just mind does not divide—it sees the whole. Justice is not merely a legal system but a state of consciousness. Courts and governments enforce justice through rules, but real justice arises when individuals act with fairness and clarity. Without psychological clarity, justice is merely an extension of power, dictated by conditioned thought rather than a deep sense of responsibility. Many seek justice only when they are harmed, equating it with punishment rather than restoration. True justice does not depend on personal experience; it is impartial and unshaped by influence.

A mind free from hatred, personal attachment, and the desire for retribution does not struggle for justice—it lives justly. Justice is meaningless without compassion, as true justice is not just about laws but about understanding human nature. Without compassion, justice becomes rigid and cruel. True justice does not seek suffering—it restores harmony. It does not act from personal anger but from understanding. A society built on punishment is not truly just; justice must come from individual integrity, not just enforcement. A mind that seeks fairness outside must first find balance within. In this freedom, justice is no longer about right and wrong—it is about wholeness, where action is taken not out of anger, but out of truth, without cruelty, without division, without fear.

232. Purity

Purity: The Mind Uncontaminated by Corruption

Purity is the state of being free from distortion, corruption, and psychological conflict. It arises when the mind is unburdened by fear, attachment, and conditioning. A mind caught in purity as an ideal tries to achieve it through discipline, while a mind that understands deeply sees that purity exists only in direct perception. Many associate purity with moral codes, rituals, or traditions, but true purity is not in action alone—it is in the mind that is free from distortion. Some try to force purity by rejecting thoughts, desires, or emotions, yet suppression only strengthens inner conflict. Real purity is the absence of struggle, not the outcome of restraint.

A divided mind, caught between 'what is' and 'what should be,' is never pure. When there is no inner conflict, the mind moves without corruption. People seek to 'become' pure, believing it is something to be gained, but purity is already present when illusion and conditioning fall away. The mind that is constantly thinking about 'me' and 'mine' is filled with self-interest, and true purity exists only when the ego is not the center of action. Many define purity through rituals, traditions, and codes of conduct, yet real purity is not created by following rules—it is found in deep understanding. The struggle to 'be good' or 'avoid bad' is itself an impurity, for a pure mind does not fight itself—it moves with deep harmony.

The more one tries to 'become' pure, the more impurity remains. When one sees that purity is not created but uncovered, it happens naturally. A mind burdened by belief, fear, or desire cannot be pure, for true purity exists when one is free from inner conditioning. The past distorts perception, making thought impure, but when one sees without the filter of memory, purity exists effortlessly. Purity is not in words, appearance, or rituals—it is in action free from ego. Many seek purity through discipline, religious practice, or suppression, but true purity arises when one sees beyond illusion and conditioning. In this freedom, purity is not an achievement—it is the natural, effortless state of a mind that sees clearly, without struggle, without division, beyond all ideals.

233. Honesty

Honesty: The Courage to See and Speak the Truth

Honesty is the state of being truthful and transparent, without deception or self-deception. It arises when the mind perceives reality without distortion, avoidance, or pretense. When one is caught in dishonesty, there is often a desire to protect one's image, avoid negative consequences, or manipulate others' perceptions. However, true honesty comes from seeing things as they are, without bias or fear of judgment.

Honesty is not just about what is spoken, but about seeing clearly and perceiving life without distortion. One can speak the truth yet still be dishonest if their perception is clouded by self-interest. True honesty starts with oneself—when a person recognizes their own motives and sees through their own biases, dishonesty fades. It is important to note that honesty is not about being harsh or brutal; it is about being sensitive and revealing the truth without causing unnecessary harm. A mind free from fear has no reason to lie, and honesty becomes an effortless state of awareness rather than a forced virtue.

The struggle with honesty often arises from fear—fear of consequences, fear of judgment, or the desire to maintain a particular image. Society conditions individuals to conform, to say what is expected, and to avoid self-confrontation. This leads to self-deception and a selective expression of truth. True honesty, however, is not about rationalizing or explaining, but about observing thoughts without justification and letting go of the need to impress. In this state, honesty arises naturally, without fear or manipulation, and becomes the effortless unfolding of truth in every action and word.

234. Integrity

Integrity: The Alignment of Thought, Word, and Action

Integrity is the state of being whole, undivided, and aligned with truth, where thoughts, words, and actions are in harmony without distortion. It arises when there is no inner conflict, no compromise out of fear or convenience. A mind with integrity does not act to please others or seek external validation; it simply moves in clarity and honesty. Integrity is not a rigid adherence to moral codes but a natural expression of personal truth that comes from deep self-awareness.

The struggle with integrity often arises from the fear of the consequences of truth. Many people compromise their integrity to avoid conflict, rejection, or punishment. Society conditions individuals to prioritize approval over truth, and many rationalize small compromises as necessary or practical. However, every compromise weakens one's clarity and strength. True integrity requires the ability to act honestly without justification, without masks, and without the need for external rewards. It is a state of being that requires no effort when one acts from understanding and inner clarity.

Integrity is not about appearing morally upright to others—it is about being truthful and honest, even when no one is watching. True integrity means living without division between public and private selves, acting consistently in all situations. When one is free from fear, self-deception, and social conditioning, integrity becomes effortless. It is not a moral ideal to strive for but the natural unfolding of truth, where words and actions align perfectly, creating trust and authenticity in every interaction. In this state of freedom, integrity is not a struggle—it is simply the clear expression of who we truly are.

235. Sincerity

Sincerity: The Authenticity That Needs No Pretension

Sincerity is more than just being honest with others—it is about seeing the truth of one's own mind without distortion or self-deception. While many people speak openly or follow societal norms with sincerity, true sincerity involves a deeper level of self-awareness. It is the ability to observe one's thoughts, emotions, and actions without justification or suppression. When thought, feeling, and action align in harmony, sincerity arises naturally, allowing one to act from clarity, not fear or ego.

The challenge with sincerity is that society often encourages insincerity through expectations, masks, and the need for approval. Fear of judgment or desire for acceptance can distort one's sincerity, leading to actions that are not aligned with inner truth. True sincerity requires the courage to act without the need to conform or manipulate perceptions. It is also essential to question one's beliefs and convictions, as attachment to fixed ideas can cloud genuine understanding. Without self-awareness and the ability to question one's own motives, sincerity can easily become a form of blind belief, reinforcing rather than dissolving illusions.

Living with true sincerity means shedding psychological masks and acting from a place of deep understanding. It is the recognition that one's actions and thoughts should be aligned with the present moment, not with past conditioning or future desires. A sincere mind is not driven by fear of loss or the need for validation; it is free to perceive truth as it is. In this clarity, sincerity does not need to be cultivated through effort—it arises naturally when one lives fully aware and without inner contradiction.

236. Responsibility

Responsibility: The Awareness That Extends Beyond the Self

Responsibility is not just about fulfilling duties or obligations—it is a profound awareness of how our actions impact the world. True responsibility emerges from the recognition of our interconnectedness, not from societal or religious imposition. It is not confined to personal matters such as family, work, or nationality; it extends to all of humanity, recognizing our collective role in shaping the world we live in.

Responsibility is not a burden to carry, but a natural outcome of understanding our influence on life. A responsible mind does not act out of compulsion but out of clarity and awareness. True responsibility is not limited to personal interests or boundaries but recognizes the broader impact of our actions on society and the world. Responsibility is free from self-interest—it arises from insight and the ability to see the truth of a situation, not out of fear, ambition, or gain. It is the absence of blind obedience to authority and conformity, acting intelligently from deep understanding.

To live with total responsibility, one must see beyond divisions and understand that the world and oneself are interconnected. Actions should be taken without seeking external validation or recognition—living in truth, not for applause. True responsibility begins with immediate action—no waiting for others to act first or for conditions to improve. It requires independence from external dependency and a deep inner understanding of one's role in shaping the world. Ultimately, responsibility arises from a free mind, not bound by fear or societal conditioning, but guided by clarity, wisdom, and an awareness of the larger picture.

237. Virtue

Virtue: The State of Being Beyond Moral Conditioning

Virtue is often understood as goodness or morality, but is it something that can be cultivated through discipline and imposed rules, or does it naturally arise from deep understanding? True virtue is not about following moral codes or traditions but about living with clarity, intelligence, and freedom from self-interest. It is not a matter of conforming to societal expectations or gaining approval but of acting in accordance with an inner truth that transcends fear and external validation.

The illusion of cultivated virtue arises when society teaches that goodness must be practiced and controlled. But when virtue is forced through discipline or fear of consequences, it loses its true essence. The act of following moral codes out of habit or for reputation does not equate to true virtue. Virtue that arises from fear of punishment or desire for reward is not virtue at all—it is merely self-interest masquerading as goodness.

True virtue exists when there is no self-centeredness. It is the natural expression of love, compassion, and truth when the ego is absent. Virtue is not a distant ideal to strive for in the future but is reflected in how one acts in the present moment, with intelligence and awareness. It is the result of a mind that sees clearly, without distortion, and acts accordingly. When one is free from fear, ambition, and self-interest, virtue arises naturally without effort, without the need for rules or social approval. In this state, virtue is not an aspiration—it is the effortless unfolding of a mind that is deeply awake, clear, and harmonious with life itself.

238. Patience

Patience: Waiting Without Expectation or Resistance

Patience is the ability to remain calm, attentive, and undisturbed in the face of delay, difficulty, or uncertainty. It arises when the mind is not driven by urgency, expectation, or frustration. A mind caught in patience as an effort struggles with waiting, while a mind that understands deeply moves without time-bound restlessness. Many see patience as tolerating discomfort or waiting with effort, yet true patience is effortless—it comes from seeing that nothing in nature is rushed. The mind that lives in expectation—'When will this happen?'—creates impatience, but when one is fully present, patience arises naturally. Impatience is the result of desire clashing with reality, while a patient mind does not fight against what is—it moves with life, not against it.

Society values speed, efficiency, and instant gratification, conditioning people to seek immediate results and making waiting feel unbearable. The mind wants events to unfold according to its desires, yet reality does not follow personal expectations. Many mistake patience for laziness or inaction, but it is deep awareness, not delay. People rush because they want to control situations and outcomes, but control is an illusion—patience comes when one lets go. Impatience exists only when the mind is unsatisfied with now; when one fully embraces the present, patience is no longer needed—it simply is. A truly patient mind does not postpone action—it moves when necessary, without hurry, without hesitation.

The mind says, 'This should be happening faster,' but is that true? When one questions impatience, its hold weakens. True patience exists when one watches, listens, and acts without rushing toward a result. Many fear that if they are patient, they will 'waste time,' yet when one is fully present, there is no wasted time—only deep living. A patient mind does not postpone action—it moves when necessary, without rush. Impatience is impulse—reacting without seeing fully, while awareness brings natural patience. Patience is not about enduring delays or forcing oneself to wait—it is the natural stillness of a mind that does not chase the future. A mind free from urgency, fear, and expectation does not struggle to be patient—it simply moves without rush, without resistance, in full awareness. In this freedom, patience is not something to cultivate—it is already there, in the silent clarity of a mind that does not fight against time but moves in harmony with life itself.

WAKE UP

10. Negation & Absense

WAKE UP

239. Ignorance

Ignorance: The Darkness That Thought Cannot Dispel

Ignorance is not just the lack of knowledge; it is the inability to perceive things as they truly are. A mind steeped in ignorance is often conditioned by society, beliefs, and past experiences, leading to a distorted view of reality. This creates a world where partial truths are mistaken for the whole, and assumptions are defended as facts. Ignorance thrives on blind acceptance, where the mind, unwilling to question or look beyond, clings to familiar beliefs, reinforcing division and conflict. It is in the face of ignorance that fear arises, making change seem threatening and halting true understanding.

The struggle with ignorance stems from the mind's attachment to comfort and certainty. People often mistake memorized information for intelligence, clinging to facts without understanding their deeper meaning. We tend to accept authority without question, fearing the uncertainty that comes with exploration. The mind also divides reality into fragments, simplifying the complexity of life into categories, which only strengthens ignorance. The key to freeing oneself from ignorance is not the accumulation of knowledge, but the willingness to question, to look deeply, and to see things as they are, without distortion or preconceived notions.

True freedom from ignorance requires a shift in how we perceive the world. It begins by seeing that ignorance is not just a lack of information, but the failure to truly see. By questioning everything, including our own thoughts, and by observing without immediately labeling or categorizing, clarity emerges. A mind that does not seek psychological security in fixed beliefs is free to observe reality directly. It is through awareness and deep perception, not blind acceptance or reliance on authority, that ignorance dissolves, allowing truth to shine through naturally. In this state, ignorance is no longer a barrier—it is replaced by intelligence, understanding, and openness.

240. Misunderstanding

Misunderstanding: The Barrier Between Perception and Reality

Misunderstanding arises when reality is distorted by thought, assumption, and emotional interference. It creates a barrier between people, preventing clear communication and fostering conflict. Thought imposes meaning onto situations based on past experiences, shaping perception rather than allowing one to see things as they are. When the mind is caught in misunderstanding, it reacts impulsively, projecting fears, desires, and expectations onto others instead of observing without judgment. This creates an illusion of separation and a cycle of conflict, where relationships suffer and misunderstandings go unchallenged.

The root of misunderstanding lies in psychological projection, where the mind filters reality through preconceived notions. Instead of listening openly, people interpret the world through their past knowledge and emotional responses. Fear and strong emotions further cloud perception, leading to misinterpretations and assumptions. This often occurs in social and cultural contexts, where deeply ingrained beliefs and traditions shape how we see others and ourselves. Misunderstanding, therefore, not only distorts individual perceptions but also perpetuates societal divisions, causing ideological and cultural clashes that hinder genuine understanding.

To live without misunderstanding requires a shift in how we perceive and respond to the world. True understanding emerges when we listen without prejudice, observe without interpretation, and question assumptions. By letting go of psychological defensiveness and the need to protect one's identity or beliefs, the mind becomes clear, free from the distortions that breed misunderstanding. When one sees that all misunderstanding stems from the conditioned mind, clarity follows, allowing for deeper connection, communication, and insight. In this state, the mind moves freely, without confusion or judgment, fostering true intelligence and harmonious relationships.

241. Not Knowing

Not Knowing: The Beginning of True Learning

Not knowing is the state of a mind that is open, free from preconceived ideas, assumptions, and past conditioning. It is not about ignorance, but rather the willingness to approach life with curiosity and without clinging to certainty. In this state, the mind is fresh, ready to explore the world without the limitations of fixed beliefs or the need for validation. True intelligence arises when one is able to see things as they are, without the distortion that comes from the accumulation of knowledge or previous experiences.

The nature of not knowing lies in its freedom from the burden of accumulated knowledge. Knowledge, while practical, can create mental clutter and prevent the mind from perceiving fresh insights. When we approach life without assumptions or conclusions, we make space for deeper understanding and exploration. Not knowing is not confusion or lack of direction; rather, it is the clarity that comes from being fully present and open. It allows the mind to remain flexible, free from the fear of uncertainty, and capable of discovering new truths beyond the confines of past conditioning.

Living in a state of not knowing requires letting go of the need for control and certainty. Our conditioning often pushes us to seek answers quickly, to label and categorize everything we encounter, but true understanding comes when we are willing to observe without rushing to conclusions. In this state, each moment is new, and every experience is an opportunity for discovery. The fear of the unknown dissolves when we realize that not knowing is not a threat but a gateway to deeper perception, intelligence, and insight. When we stop clinging to the need to "know," we open ourselves to the continuous unfolding of life, full of wonder and clarity.

242. Escape

Escape: The Mind's Evasion from 'What Is'

Escape is the mind's attempt to avoid facing reality, often driven by discomfort, fear, or a desire for relief. It manifests through distractions, pleasures, and illusions, whether through entertainment, work, relationships, or belief systems. In avoiding "what is," the mind seeks temporary comfort, but this only postpones deeper understanding and true clarity. Rather than confronting fear, loneliness, or uncertainty, the mind runs from these uncomfortable emotions, creating a cycle of avoidance that reinforces a false sense of security without resolving the underlying issues.

The cycle of escape is sustained by fear and a deep-seated need for external validation or distraction. Society, with its constant emphasis on achievement, success, and entertainment, promotes escapism, making it more difficult to face life with full awareness. People often mistake escape—through pleasure, success, or relationships—as a form of fulfillment. However, these distractions never address the root cause of dissatisfaction. The mind, constantly in motion and seeking the next experience, becomes addicted to this cycle of avoidance, making it harder to break free from the habit of escape and truly face reality.

True freedom from escape comes when the mind is no longer afraid of discomfort or uncertainty. By observing and experiencing "what is" without judgment, suppression, or the need to run away, one begins to see things clearly. Fear, when faced directly, loses its power, and the mind can rest in stillness, where understanding arises naturally. In this state, there is no need to seek relief or avoidance—only the direct perception of life as it is, free from illusions, distractions, and superficial fulfillment.

243. Forgetfulness

Forgetfulness: The Dissolution of Memory and Identity

Forgetfulness is the result of a mind that is not fully present, often rooted in distraction, avoidance, or a lack of attention. It is not simply about memory loss but is a deeper issue related to not giving full attention to the present moment. When one is constantly distracted or preoccupied with the past or future, clarity fades, and important aspects of life are forgotten. A mind that struggles with forgetfulness tends to repeat mistakes, creating a cycle of confusion that prevents growth and understanding. In contrast, true awareness requires one to live fully in the present, where forgetting is no longer a concern because there is no need to remember—it is naturally retained in the mind's clear observation.

The mind's habit of forgetting arises from various psychological and social factors, including fear, discomfort, and the overwhelming flood of information in the modern world. We tend to remember what aligns with our desires, fears, or identity, while everything else fades into the background. Painful memories or truths are often suppressed, and this avoidance creates a deeper form of forgetfulness, where the mind unconsciously ignores what it cannot deal with. Additionally, relying on past knowledge instead of being open to new understanding can reinforce forgetfulness, as the mind clings to what it already knows rather than seeking to see things as they truly are in the moment.

To live without forgetfulness, one must cultivate deep attention and awareness. This involves letting go of mental clutter and distractions that weaken focus, as well as living fully in the present without being consumed by the past or future. When the mind is quiet, free from the need to retain or hold onto information, understanding becomes effortless. Forgetfulness disappears not through forced memory, but through the natural clarity that arises from awareness. A mind that is present in each moment is not burdened by the need to remember—it simply sees and understands, with no struggle and no attachment to time.

244. Distortion

Distortion: The Warping of Truth by Thought

Distortion arises when the mind's perception is clouded by thought, past experiences, and emotional influence. It prevents one from seeing reality as it truly is, instead shaping it based on what the mind wants, fears, or expects. This misperception occurs because thoughts and emotions continuously interfere with direct observation, creating an illusion that replaces truth. Fear amplifies the distortion, making harmless situations appear threatening, while desire fabricates false realities, making one see things through the lens of personal want rather than objective truth. As a result, the mind becomes trapped in an endless cycle of misunderstanding, leading to confusion and inner conflict.

The mind, conditioned by past experiences, beliefs, and societal influences, struggles to see things as they are. Instead, it filters everything through preconceived notions, reinforcing the distortion. This psychological conditioning, while offering a sense of security, limits one's capacity for clear seeing and prevents true understanding. As a result, relationships and perceptions become distorted by the mind's attachment to ideals, comparisons, and expectations. Emotional reactions further cloud judgment, making it even more difficult to perceive reality without interference. The mind becomes attached to beliefs, judgments, and ideals, reinforcing its own distortions, while avoiding the discomfort of seeing things plainly.

To free oneself from distortion, it is necessary to observe without interpreting, questioning one's assumptions, and letting go of attachments to beliefs and ideals. When the mind is quiet and free from emotional influence, it can perceive reality without bias, as it is. True understanding arises when one is aware of how past experiences, beliefs, and emotions shape perception, allowing for clearer, unclouded awareness. Living without comparison or expectation helps one experience the present moment directly, without distorting it to fit personal narratives. In this state of awareness, distortion fades away, and one sees life with clarity and understanding, free from illusion and self-deception.

245. Negation

Negation: The Art of Seeing by Letting Go

Negation is the process of seeing and understanding what is false, allowing it to dissolve naturally without resistance or suppression. It is not an act of rejecting or fighting against something; rather, it is the clarity that arises when the mind deeply perceives and understands the illusion for what it is. This understanding does not come from effort or control, but from complete awareness. True negation occurs when the mind sees something untrue without needing to replace it with an opposite idea or force it out. The false simply drops away when it is seen clearly, and in this process, the mind becomes free.

The necessity of negation arises from the fact that the mind is often conditioned by false beliefs, assumptions, and societal constructs that distort reality. These influences create psychological conflict, where there is a division between "what is" and "what should be." By negating these false beliefs—whether they are about identity, security, or expectations—the mind frees itself from the struggle of contradictions. This process is not about acquiring more knowledge or adding to what is known, but about removing what is not true. In doing so, the mind moves from conflict and confusion to clarity, where truth can be directly perceived.

To live through negation is to embrace the freedom of not clinging to falsehoods, whether they come from fear, time, or dependence on others. Negating the illusions of psychological security, the need to 'become' something, and the authority of secondhand knowledge leads to a mind that is not tied to past conditioning. In this freedom, there is no longer attachment to beliefs, opinions, or the need for validation. The mind, free from the weight of illusions, is open, present, and clear, perceiving life as it truly is. Through negation, clarity arises, and with clarity comes deep, lasting freedom.

246. Solitude

Solitude: The Aloneness That Is Not Loneliness

Solitude is the state of being inwardly whole, free from the need for external validation or distractions. It is not about being isolated or lonely but about being deeply connected with oneself, experiencing a profound sense of completeness. The mind in solitude is fully present, not withdrawn or detached, but completely aware and attentive, observing life without interference or external influence. Solitude provides the space for direct perception, where the mind is not clouded by the noise of social conditioning or personal desires, allowing clarity to emerge naturally.

Fear of solitude often arises from the mind's conditioning to seek company or distraction, avoiding the discomfort of being with oneself. Many are afraid to face their inner contradictions, insecurities, or fears that solitude brings to the surface. However, true solitude is the absence of craving for companionship or validation. It is the freedom to be alone without seeking fulfillment from external sources. In this state, one is not driven by loneliness but experiences inner peace, finding completeness in the stillness of being. Solitude is not an escape from life, but a deep engagement with it, free from the pressures of societal expectations.

A mind that embraces solitude is not isolated; rather, it is deeply aware and in harmony with the present moment. It moves beyond the distractions of daily life and the need for constant external stimulation, allowing for true self-awareness and understanding. Solitude enables a person to observe their thoughts, emotions, and conditioning without judgment or bias, leading to clarity and wisdom. In this state of stillness, the mind is free from fear, and there is no desire to escape or seek fulfillment. The result is a vast sense of freedom and wholeness, where perception is direct, unclouded, and completely aligned with reality.

247. Nothingness

Nothingness: The Space Where True Understanding Blossoms

Nothingness is not a void or absence but the state where the mind is free from all psychological accumulation, where identity, belief, and attachment no longer define existence. It is the dissolution of the "self," the thought-constructed entity that seeks continuity and meaning. Contrary to the common perception of emptiness, nothingness is a space that opens the door to true freedom. It arises when the mind ceases to hold onto past experiences and desires, allowing it to be present without the burden of self, offering a deeper connection with the essence of life itself.

Fear of nothingness arises because the mind clings to the idea of identity, purpose, and continuity. From childhood, we are conditioned to seek security in the self—our names, experiences, roles, and achievements. To the mind, nothingness seems like the loss of everything; however, when we examine this fear, we realize that the "self" is merely a collection of memories and experiences. The belief that life must have meaning also keeps us attached to the notion of purpose. Yet, meaning itself is an illusion created by thought, and when the mind is free from such constructs, there is no longer a need for meaning—it simply is.

True nothingness is the absence of the psychological structure that is built on time, memory, and desire. It is not something to be sought or forced but arises naturally when the mind becomes still and free from the noise of thought. In this state, there is no fear of the unknown because the mind is fully present, not bound by past or future. Nothingness is not a denial of existence but the deep stillness where clarity, intelligence, and freedom emerge. It is in nothingness that the mind discovers its true nature—without conflict, without self, and without struggle. In this profound awareness, the beauty of life unfolds beyond thought, beyond identity, and beyond the limitations of the self.

11. Order & Harmony

WAKE UP

248. Order

Order: The Natural Flow That Emerges Without Control

Order is not something that can be imposed or forced; it arises naturally from deep self-awareness and clarity. It is the state of a mind free from contradiction, where there is no inner conflict, no struggle between what is and what should be. True order is not a set of rules or structures—it is the absence of resistance to life as it is. When the mind is clear and undivided, order is effortlessly present, not because of control or discipline, but because the mind is in harmony with itself and the world around it.

Many seek order through control, routines, and external structures, believing that these will bring stability and security. However, imposed order often leads to rebellion, inner resistance, and conflict, as the mind struggles against what is forced upon it. True order comes from within—it is the result of observing life without judgment or attachment, where the mind is free from the clutter of fear, desires, and memories. When one drops the psychological clutter, clarity arises, and order is naturally restored in every action and thought.

To live in total order, one must see that disorder arises from inner division and contradiction. When the mind is caught in conflict—whether through comparison, attachment, or fear—disorder prevails. But when one lives in the present moment, free from the burden of psychological time, true order manifests effortlessly. Intelligence, not mere discipline, creates harmony in life. In this state, there is no need to control or force order—it arises naturally from deep awareness, allowing one to act with clarity, intelligence, and complete freedom.

249. Harmony

Harmony: The State of Being Without Inner Conflict

Harmony is the natural state of a mind that is free from inner conflict and psychological division. It is not the absence of disturbance but the end of contradiction within the mind. When the mind sees life as a whole, unfragmented by opposing desires or fears, harmony arises effortlessly. True harmony is not something that can be achieved through effort, but something that is revealed when the mind stops resisting and moves freely with life, without imposing external expectations or control.

The root of disharmony lies in inner division, where desires and fears clash, creating tension and struggle. Many seek external conditions to bring inner peace, but true harmony comes from the ability to live fully in the present moment, free from the psychological time that keeps the mind trapped in past regrets and future expectations. By letting go of inner contradictions and psychological resistance, the mind can observe life without the need to impose judgments or force outcomes. Harmony is found when one acts with awareness, accepting the flow of life without resistance or fear, seeing life as one indivisible whole.

In our daily lives, we are conditioned to seek harmony through control, conformity, or the perfect external environment, but true harmony does not come from these sources. It arises naturally when the mind is clear, undivided, and open to the reality of life as it is. When the mind is free from the conflict between 'what is' and 'what should be,' it moves effortlessly with life, responding with intelligence and clarity. Harmony is not an achievement—it is a state of being, one that exists when we let go of internal division and live in the present moment.

250. Peace

Peace: The Silence That Comes from Understanding

Peace is not merely the absence of external conflict or a temporary sense of calm; it is an inner state where the mind is completely still, free from psychological struggle. True peace arises when there is no internal division or contradiction, and the mind is clear of fear, attachment, or desire. It is not something that can be sought or achieved through external means, such as control, effort, or discipline. Rather, peace is found when one deeply understands the nature of thought, emotion, and the division created by the mind itself. The search for peace often perpetuates conflict, as the very act of seeking implies that peace is absent, thus creating a desire or struggle to obtain it.

The reasons we lack peace stem from inner conflict, fear, and attachment. The mind is in constant turmoil, divided between what it desires and what it fears. This division prevents a deep sense of peace, as the mind constantly shifts between contradictory desires, regrets, and worries. Fear, whether of failure, rejection, or death, adds to this restlessness, leading us to seek external security, such as material wealth, relationships, or rigid beliefs. However, these external sources are unstable and cannot provide true peace. Moreover, seeking peace through escape—whether through religion, ideologies, or meditation techniques—often creates more inner struggle, as the mind remains in conflict, desiring an outcome rather than simply being at peace.

True peace comes when we observe our thoughts, emotions, and fears without resistance or judgment. It is the absence of psychological security and the recognition that peace is not dependent on external circumstances. By letting go of attachments, living fully in the present moment, and ceasing the search for peace, we allow peace to arise effortlessly. When the mind is silent, free from the compulsion to seek or avoid, it naturally becomes peaceful. Peace is not an ideal or goal, but the natural state of a mind that has freed itself from psychological noise, allowing for clarity, presence, and deep understanding.

251. Stillness

Stillness: The Mind Untouched by Thought

Stillness is not the mere absence of movement, but a deep, profound silence that comes when the mind is completely free from thought. It is not a state to be forced or practiced; rather, it arises naturally when thought ceases. True stillness is not inactivity or dullness, but a heightened form of intelligence, where the mind operates with complete awareness, unburdened by effort or distraction. This state of stillness allows the mind to perceive reality without distortion, revealing a clarity and depth beyond ordinary understanding.

The mind, however, is rarely still due to its conditioning. From an early age, we are taught to think, solve problems, and remain active, causing the mind to be restless and uncomfortable with silence. Additionally, fear of emptiness and the absence of the ego drives the mind to continuously seek and become, constantly moving towards goals or future achievements. Thought is also addicted to psychological time, moving between the past and the future, never staying in the present. This constant mental activity prevents true stillness from manifesting.

True stillness is not about suppressing thought but about observing the movement of thought without judgment. It occurs when there is no inner struggle or resistance, allowing the mind to be completely present in the moment. In this state, the mind is free from psychological accumulation, no longer burdened by the past or projecting into the future. Stillness is the source of true intelligence and understanding, as it opens the mind to the unknown, beyond experience and conditioning. In that stillness, there is no fear, no division—only pure, undistorted awareness of being fully alive and fully present.

252. Quiet

Quiet: The Space Between Noise and Awareness

Quiet is not simply the absence of external noise; it is a profound stillness of the mind, free from restlessness and internal conflict. True quiet arises naturally when the mind ceases its endless activity, not through force or suppression, but as the mind becomes still, with nothing to resist or control. A quiet mind is fully present and aware, capable of perceiving reality without distortion, and it is this clarity that brings depth to understanding and insight into life.

The nature of quiet lies in its freedom from inner conflict. A mind caught in the struggle between desire and resistance cannot be truly quiet. When the mind accepts "what is" without resistance to "what should be," quietness arises effortlessly. True quiet is not a void but an alert, sensitive awareness—far from being dull, it is the most alive state of the mind, attentive and receptive to the present. Quiet is not created by effort, but emerges when the mind stops trying to force silence, as this very effort is itself noise.

A mind that seeks quietness through constant distraction, fear, or desire for control cannot experience true peace. The struggle to silence thought, or the resistance to inner silence, only reinforces the noise within. Quiet comes naturally when one observes thought without becoming involved, when the need for control is dropped, and when the mind is completely present without running away to past or future. In this quietness, there is no goal, no expectation—only clarity, deep awareness, and an openness to perceive truth directly. When quiet is allowed to exist without effort or interference, it becomes a living state of harmony, where the mind is alive, fully present, and free from all internal division.

253. Beauty

Beauty: Seeing Without the Distortion of the Self

Beauty is not confined to the external world—it is a perception that arises from a mind free from conflict and distortion. It is found in the simplest moments, in a sunset, a work of art, or even in the quiet presence of nature. True beauty comes when the mind is silent, when it is not caught in judgment, comparison, or desire. It exists only when perception is unclouded by thought, allowing one to experience life in its fullness, without the limitations that habitual thinking imposes.

The nature of beauty lies in deep attention, free from distraction or interference. When the mind is fully present and undivided, beauty is felt deeply. It is not the result of comparison or idealized standards—it simply is. Beauty exists not just in the physical realm but in moments of pure awareness, where the mind is quiet and receptive. When we cease to analyze, measure, or categorize, beauty reveals itself in all things, not as an object to possess but as a living experience that can only be truly seen when one is free from the need to control or hold onto it.

To perceive beauty deeply, one must observe without naming or comparing, letting go of the habitual tendencies that limit perception. Beauty is experienced fully when the mind is present in the moment, when there is silence within, and when the observer is free from attachment. A mind that is silent, open, and attentive sees beauty everywhere, not as something separate from life but as an integral part of it. In the absence of conflict, desire, and mental noise, beauty is not a fleeting experience—it becomes the very essence of existence, felt and understood in every moment.

254. Balance

Balance: Walking the Fine Line Between Effort and Effortlessness

Balance is not something we strive for through force or discipline—it emerges naturally when the mind is free from conflict and extremes. Often, we try to control our thoughts, emotions, and actions in an attempt to achieve balance, but true balance is not the result of effort; it is the natural flow that arises when we move with life, not against it. The key to balance is in accepting what is, without resisting or forcing it, allowing life to unfold harmoniously without inner struggle. A balanced mind is one that adapts effortlessly to the constant changes and challenges of life, free from the burden of attachment, fear, or ambition.

We often struggle with balance because we live in a world that encourages extremes—ambition, competition, and the pursuit of more. Society conditions us to strive for success while avoiding failure, to seek pleasure and avoid pain, and in doing so, we create inner turmoil. True balance, however, is not about finding a middle ground between opposites, but about moving beyond them altogether. When we stop attaching ourselves to outcomes and learn to live fully in the present moment, balance arises naturally. It is a state of ease, where there is no resistance to what is, and no need to control the flow of life.

Living in balance means letting go of inner conflict, allowing thoughts and actions to flow in harmony with one another. It is not something that is achieved through external stability or mental rigidity, but through a deep understanding of ourselves and our relationship to life. When we are free from the fear of uncertainty and the need to control outcomes, balance happens effortlessly. True balance is not a state to be attained— it is the natural state of being when the mind is calm, undivided, and fully present. In this state of balance, life flows freely, without conflict or extremes, and we are at peace with ourselves and the world around us.

255. Structure

Structure: The Framework That Can Liberate or Restrict

Structure plays an essential role in bringing order and organization to various aspects of life—whether it's mental, physical, or social. It provides the framework for communication, laws, education, and personal behavior, helping societies and individuals function efficiently. However, when structure becomes rigid and overly fixed, it can limit freedom and understanding. A mind caught in rigid structure often follows rules without question, leading to mechanical behavior rather than intelligent action. True freedom comes when structure is used as a tool, not as an identity, enabling adaptability without attachment.

The human mind, shaped by conditioning, often relies on structured beliefs, ideologies, and identities for security. People find comfort in familiarity and order, but excessive attachment to structure can create psychological prisons. Structure is necessary for stability, but it must be flexible to adapt to new situations. When one clings too strongly to established systems, whether in tradition, law, or personal belief, it prevents growth, creativity, and the ability to see beyond the confines of mental constructs.

The key lies in questioning and evaluating the usefulness of structure, ensuring it serves its purpose without becoming an obstacle to deeper understanding and personal evolution.

To live freely within structure, one must use it intelligently and with flexibility, recognizing its purpose without being trapped by it. Truth and meaning do not reside within fixed systems—they transcend them. A mind that is free from rigid structure moves with intelligence, observing when structure limits rather than facilitates growth. In this state, structure no longer serves as a limitation but as a functional tool, allowing life to flow naturally and harmoniously. When structure is no longer held as an absolute, it becomes an element of understanding, adaptable to each situation without unnecessary resistance or rigidity.

256. Stability

Stability: The Illusion of Security in a Changing World

Stability is often sought externally, through wealth, relationships, or career, but true stability is found within—through inner clarity and the absence of conflict. It arises when the mind is not divided by fear or desire, but instead moves effortlessly with life, unshaken by external conditions. When the mind is free from psychological conflict and fear, stability becomes a natural state. True stability is not about rigidly controlling life or avoiding change, but about seeing clearly, accepting the flow of life, and responding with awareness, without attachment or resistance.

Many struggle with stability because they attach it to external factors or resist the changes that life inevitably brings. A mind that seeks stability through control or routine is vulnerable to uncertainty, as true stability cannot be maintained by rigid structures or predictability. The fear of change creates instability, while the attachment to fixed routines and beliefs strengthens the illusion that stability lies in them. True stability exists when one is open to change, free from psychological attachment, and able to observe thought without being controlled by it. A mind that remains present and engaged with life, without clinging to the past or fearing the future, finds that stability naturally arises.

Living with stability requires letting go of the need for external validation, embracing uncertainty, and remaining grounded in the present moment. Stability is not something that must be reached or forced—it is already within, waiting to be recognized. When the mind is fully present, without reacting to every passing emotion or thought, true stability manifests effortlessly. It is the ability to move with life, fluidly adapting to whatever comes, while maintaining a steady center. In this freedom, stability is no longer a goal to strive for—it is a natural expression of a clear, aware, and undivided mind.

257. Simplicity

Simplicity: The Freedom of a Mind Unburdened by Complexity

Simplicity is not about reducing life to minimalism or stripping away material things—it is an inner state where the mind is free from the clutter of unnecessary thoughts, desires, and attachments. A simple mind is one that perceives life directly, without the weight of expectations, fears, or judgments. When one lives simply, it is not a forced effort to renounce the world, but a natural result of understanding that complexity is born from the mind's need to control, compare, and accumulate. The clarity that comes with simplicity brings freedom from inner conflict, making life more meaningful and fulfilling in its purest form.

The struggle for complexity is often rooted in the mind's desire to feel important or secure. We accumulate knowledge, possessions, and relationships, believing they will give us meaning or happiness. However, this pursuit only leads to exhaustion and confusion. Fear of the unknown, fear of failure, and fear of missing out lead us to build psychological walls—whether in beliefs, ambitions, or attachments. True simplicity, however, arises from the ability to let go of these fears and to live fully in the present, unburdened by the need for control or external validation. A mind that does not chase after desires or cling to the past is naturally at peace, experiencing life in its most vibrant, unfiltered form.

Living simply does not mean eliminating all complexity from life; it means approaching each moment with full attention and awareness. When we stop imposing labels, judgments, or expectations on what we experience, we allow reality to be seen as it is—without distortion. Simplicity is the freedom from psychological time—living without constantly reliving the past or worrying about the future. It is a state of being present, of acting without inner contradiction, where every action is full of clarity and purpose. In simplicity, there is no inner struggle, just a deep understanding that life is best lived in the moment, without the need for complexity.

258. Space

Space: The Vastness That Thought Cannot Contain

Space is not merely the physical void between objects—it represents the vast psychological openness within the mind, free from mental clutter, conflict, and conditioning. This space allows perception to be unrestricted and clear, enabling the mind to move freely without limitation. A mind with space sees life without distortion, reacting to the present moment with intelligence and awareness, not clouded by past experiences or future anxieties. True space arises naturally when the mind is quiet, free from the incessant noise of thought and emotion, and is available for genuine, unimpeded observation.

In the absence of mental clutter, space reveals itself as the foundation for deep awareness and intelligence. Without the constant interference of desires, memories, and fears, the mind becomes receptive to truth and reality. Space does not require effort to create; it is a state of being revealed when unnecessary thoughts and psychological burdens are released. A mind that is filled with fear, ambition, or attachment cannot function with clarity, while a mind with space can think deeply and act without conflict, seeing things as they truly are. The more one creates room for stillness and attention, the more space exists, opening up a world of possibility and insight.

The struggles we face with creating space stem from the mind's tendency to be constantly active—engaged in thought, comparison, and preoccupation with the past or future. Society, with its constant stimulation and demands, exacerbates this overcrowding. The ego, too, resists space, as it thrives on maintaining its importance through thought and identity.

However, true space can only exist when the mind is free from these attachments, when it stops seeking distraction, and when it can observe without judgment or interference. In this state of awareness, the mind becomes spacious, silent, and open, allowing life to unfold naturally, free from the constraints of psychological noise.

259. Unity

Unity: The Realization That Division Is an Illusion

Unity is the natural state of wholeness where there is no division between the observer and the observed. It is not a concept or something to be achieved through external efforts or belief systems, but a state of being where fragmentation ceases. True unity is experienced when there is no sense of separation, when the mind is not divided by its desires, fears, or ideologies. It is beyond the dualities that create conflict and suffering, and it arises naturally when effort, comparison, and the self are no longer present. Unity exists in the silence of thought, in the acceptance of what is, and in the deep awareness that sees life as a whole.

The search for unity often leads us to believe that it can be achieved through systems, agreements, or ideological movements. However, these external solutions only create new divisions, as they often exclude others who do not share the same beliefs or structures. Unity cannot be forced or controlled—it is a state of being that arises when the mind is free from identification and psychological boundaries. The division created by the self, the 'I,' strengthens separation, making it difficult to see that true unity is not the opposite of division but the ending of it. When the self dissolves, and there is no longer an 'I' separating itself from others, unity becomes a natural state.

Living in unity requires the dissolution of the psychological barriers that divide us. When the mind lets go of its attachments to identity, beliefs, and personal desires, unity is present. It is not something that can be achieved by effort or striving, but something that arises effortlessly when we live fully in the present, without comparison or division. Unity is not a mental concept, but a direct perception of wholeness in which the observer and the observed are one. When the mind is completely present, free from the illusion of separation, unity flows naturally, without conflict, without division, and beyond all external distinctions.

260. Comfort

Comfort: The Temporary Refuge That Prevents Transformation

Comfort is often seen as a refuge from life's challenges, offering a sense of security, peace, and stability. It arises from external factors such as possessions, relationships, routines, and beliefs that provide reassurance. However, true comfort is not just about external reassurance but about a deeper inner peace that allows the mind to remain undisturbed regardless of the circumstances. In reality, seeking comfort too eagerly can foster dependency, dull our sensitivity, and prevent us from facing uncomfortable truths about ourselves and life. Rather than providing true security, comfort often becomes a trap that stifles growth and avoids the rawness of reality.

The mind seeks comfort to avoid the uncertainty and unpredictability of life. We fear the unknown and desire stability, which leads us to cling to beliefs, relationships, ideologies, and routines that offer a false sense of permanence. This pursuit of comfort can also be an escape from emotional discomfort—many turn to distractions like entertainment or social activities to avoid facing deep-seated fears or unresolved pain. Society conditions us to believe that happiness lies in external comforts, and we chase pleasure while trying to avoid discomfort. However, this habitual search for comfort keeps us from questioning deeper truths and prevents the kind of transformation that only arises when we step beyond the safe confines of comfort.

To live without the constant pursuit of comfort, one must learn to observe and sit with discomfort rather than seek an escape. True freedom comes not from avoiding discomfort but from understanding it fully. The fear of losing comfort often traps us, but when we realize that comfort does not provide lasting peace, we can begin to find stability in awareness and clarity. Comfort, when seen as a psychological dependence, loses its grip and allows us to engage with life more fully, without fear, attachment, or avoidance. In this state, we become deeply aware and alive, no longer dependent on comfort for security, but grounded in the clarity and understanding that comes from seeing life as it truly is.

261. Security

Security: The Search for Safety in an Impermanent World

Security is often perceived as the key to peace and stability, a psychological state where one feels safe from external threats and uncertainties. People seek security in various forms: financial stability, emotional support, relationships, and ideologies, hoping that these will protect them from the unpredictability of life. However, the pursuit of security often creates more fear, as it is based on the illusion that there is something permanent in a constantly changing world. True security is not found in external possessions or relationships, but in the deep understanding that life is inherently uncertain, and that peace comes from accepting this truth without fear.

The illusion of psychological security arises when we cling to beliefs, identities, and expectations, believing they will provide stability. In relationships, for instance, we often mistake love for ownership, thinking it can guarantee permanence. In reality, love, like all things, is fluid, and the fear of losing it creates attachment and suffering. Similarly, financial success or career achievements, which we believe will protect us, never provide lasting peace. Instead, they often foster anxiety, as the fear of losing what we've gained outweighs any sense of security. The more we seek stability, the more we live in fear of losing it, reinforcing the very insecurity we try to avoid.

True security exists only in the present moment, where the mind is free from attachment to the past or future. When we stop seeking external validation or permanence, we release the anxiety that comes from clinging to the transient. Life moves constantly, and real security is found in understanding this movement—accepting change rather than resisting it. Freedom from attachment is the only true security, as it brings peace regardless of circumstances. A mind that embraces this clarity is not trapped by fear, nor is it dependent on the illusion of control; instead, it rests in the present, fully alive and free from insecurity.

12. Material & Physical World

WAKE UP

WAKE UP

262. Nature

Nature: The Intelligence That Exists Without Conflict

Nature is the vast and interconnected movement of life—trees, rivers, animals, the earth, and the universe itself. It is a constant cycle of birth, growth, decay, and renewal, moving without human interference or ambition. However, human beings often view nature as something external to themselves, something to conquer or use for personal gain. The division between humanity and nature, along with technological advancements and the desire for control, has led to a disconnect, preventing us from truly observing and appreciating nature as an integral part of life.

Nature offers profound lessons about life—its cycles, its freedom from psychological time, its acceptance of change, and its ability to exist without conflict. A flower blooms, a river flows, and a bird flies, all without striving or comparison. In contrast, human beings often live in resistance to change, caught in the illusion of time and striving for an unattainable ideal. The simplicity and stillness of nature can teach us to live more mindfully, without the constant measuring and comparing that often define human existence. When we quiet our minds and observe nature without judgment, we reconnect with the essence of life.

Living in harmony with nature means recognizing that we are not separate from it. The air we breathe, the food we consume, and the very elements that make up our bodies are part of the earth's continuous cycle. To truly live in harmony, we must observe nature with clear eyes, without thought or interference, and refrain from exploiting it for personal gain. By living simply, without excess or greed, and by being present in the stillness of nature, we learn to live not in pursuit of psychological desires, but in deep connection with the earth and all its creatures. In nature's quiet beauty, we find sacredness—not in the structures we create, but in the unspoken, ever-flowing life of the natural world.

263. Environment

Environment: The Reflection of Human Consciousness

The environment is not merely the physical surroundings or natural ecosystems; it encompasses the psychological, social, and cultural realms that influence human existence. It is both an external reality—air, water, and land—and an internal one shaped by our thoughts, beliefs, and relationships. The state of the environment reflects the state of human consciousness. As the external world suffers from pollution, deforestation, and conflict, it is a direct result of the disorder within the human mind. The destruction of nature mirrors the inner turmoil and disconnection humanity experiences, revealing how closely the two are intertwined.

The crisis of the environment stems from human greed, exploitation, and the belief in separation between man and nature. When we view nature as a resource to be controlled and consumed, we deplete and damage it. But as we harm the earth, we harm ourselves, as we are intrinsically connected to the environment. The real solution lies in transforming human consciousness—when the mind becomes free from greed, violence, and competition, the world will no longer need to be exploited. This shift in consciousness will create not just ecological balance, but a deeper, more harmonious relationship between humanity and the earth.

Living in harmony with the environment means recognizing that we are not separate from nature; the air we breathe, the food we eat, and the very existence of our bodies are part of the natural world. True environmental care arises from understanding this deep connection, not from following external rules or policies. By living simply, without excess, and by bringing inner clarity to our actions, we can act in a way that preserves rather than destroys. When one is fully aware of the world around them, from the movement of trees to the wind in the sky, destruction becomes impossible. In this awareness, care for the earth flows naturally, without effort, without conflict, and with deep respect for all life.

264. Matter

Matter: The Form That Appears Solid but Is Ever-Changing

Matter is the physical substance that forms the foundation of all existence, including the body, the mind, and the external world. It is subject to the laws of physics, yet the way we perceive matter is heavily influenced by thought, conditioning, and perception. A mind that sees matter purely as an object, separate from consciousness, misses the deeper relationship between the observer and what is observed. Matter is not merely a collection of physical parts; it is an interconnected movement that reflects life itself. The boundaries between thought and matter blur when we understand that both are part of a unified process.

The true nature of matter is that it is in constant transformation—everything, from atoms to bodies, is in a cycle of birth, decay, and renewal. Our thoughts, too, are a product of the brain, which is itself material, influencing how we perceive the world around us. This connection between matter and thought highlights the limitations of the mind, as thought can only function within the confines of the material world. Yet, the mind yearns for something beyond matter, something immeasurable—truth, beauty, and transcendence—that thought cannot grasp. This desire for the unlimited creates a constant tension between the mind's material limitations and its search for deeper meaning.

To truly understand matter, one must observe it without the filters of preconceived ideas or concepts. The separation between self and the external world is an illusion; both are part of the same movement of existence. By recognizing that thought is limited and by seeing the interconnectedness of all matter, the illusion of separateness dissolves. Freedom comes from letting go of psychological attachment to matter, understanding that all things, including the self, are impermanent. True understanding arises when we perceive matter fully, without the distortion of seeking permanence or escaping into abstraction, allowing us to live in harmony with the reality of the present moment.

265. Energy

Energy: The Movement That Fuels All Existence

Energy is not simply physical vitality; it is the driving force behind thought, emotion, action, and perception. Every action we take—whether working, thinking, or feeling—requires energy. However, we often feel drained or restless because much of our energy is wasted in inner conflict, excessive thinking, and attachment. A mind divided by desires, fears, and expectations constantly uses energy in resistance, rather than flowing with life. When the mind is at ease, when it is not struggling with itself, energy can be fully harnessed, moving effortlessly in the direction of clarity and action.

The nature of true energy is rooted in total attention and presence. When the mind is fully present, energy flows naturally and effortlessly. It is highest when there is no psychological division—when thought, emotion, and action are aligned without contradiction. This state of unity does not demand more doing, but rather a release from resistance. True energy is found in moments of silence, where the mind is quiet yet intensely alive. By letting go of unnecessary thoughts, attachments, and fears, the mind can reclaim its natural vitality, allowing energy to surge in its purest form.

Living with total energy means acting without psychological effort. It is about observing life without interference from constant thinking, labeling, or judging. When the mind is still, energy does not deplete—it awakens. Energy is strongest when one is completely in the present moment, free from the burdens of past memories and future anxieties. By living in the now, without clinging to time or mental distractions, life becomes a flowing expression of vitality, clarity, and deep presence. In this state, action becomes effortless, and life is experienced with intensity, free from struggle and full of vibrant energy.

266. Health

Health: The Harmony Between Body and Mind

Health is not simply the absence of disease but a state of complete well-being where the body, mind, and consciousness function in harmony. It includes physical vitality, mental clarity, emotional balance, and deep self-awareness. True health is inseparable from how one lives, thinks, and acts, where the body's vitality reflects the inner peace and balance one maintains. A healthy life arises not just from external care but from an internal state of understanding, where the mind is calm, clear, and aligned with the needs of the body.

Many struggle with health because we often treat it as merely a physical condition, focusing on diet, exercise, and medicine while ignoring the psychological factors that impact our well-being. Stress, emotional turmoil, and inner conflict take a toll on health, manifesting in both the body and mind. True health requires an integrated approach that includes mental and emotional well-being. Unhealthy habits often stem from psychological conditioning, where the mind's unresolved dissatisfaction drives destructive behaviors. Understanding the root causes of these habits, rather than merely addressing the symptoms, is key to true health.

Health is the natural state of a body that is not abused or burdened by stress, poor nutrition, or toxins. A healthy mind and body are inseparable, and the mind's clarity and peace directly influence the body's energy and function. Living in balance—without extremes—allows health to thrive. True health arises from awareness and understanding, not external fixes. By living in harmony with our body's needs and maintaining mental and emotional balance, health becomes a natural state, effortlessly present in a life free from inner conflict and struggle.

267. Sleep

Sleep: The State Where the Mind Renews or Remains Restless

Sleep is essential for both the body and mind, serving as a time for rest, renewal, and rejuvenation. Physically, it allows the body to repair and restore itself, strengthening the immune system and processing energy. Mentally, it is a time when the mind processes experiences, stores memories, and releases tensions. Deep sleep offers the mind and body a chance to reset, free from the demands of the day, and restores balance within the system. Without sufficient sleep, both mental clarity and physical health deteriorate, making it essential for optimal functioning and well-being.

Many struggle with sleep due to an overactive mind, emotional stress, and unresolved psychological conflict. The constant movement of thought—focused on past regrets or future worries—prevents the mind from relaxing into deep rest. Emotional turbulence, such as unresolved fear or attachment, keeps the mind in a state of agitation, further hindering restful sleep. The overuse of stimulants such as caffeine or excessive screen time also disrupts natural sleep cycles, making it difficult for the nervous system to unwind. A fear of losing consciousness, linked to the ego's attachment to control, may also resist deep rest, preventing the mind from surrendering fully to sleep.

True, restorative sleep arises naturally when the mind is quiet and unburdened. Observing the movement of thought before sleep, without resistance or judgment, allows the mind to ease into rest. Letting go of the need to force sleep, embracing the present moment, and avoiding mental accumulation throughout the day creates an environment for deep relaxation. When the mind is free from unnecessary thought, anxiety, and inner conflict, sleep becomes effortless and peaceful, providing true rest and mental clarity.

268. Sex

Sex: Desire, Attachment, and the Search for Fulfillment

Sex is a natural biological function, deeply embedded in human experience. However, it has often been surrounded by societal and religious beliefs, leading to confusion and conflict. While sex is a powerful energy that influences emotions, relationships, and human behavior, the mind's approach to it often causes issues. When sex becomes attached to guilt, repression, or indulgence, it moves away from its natural expression, becoming either an obsession or something to avoid. These distortions make it harder to understand sex in its true, natural form.

Cultural and religious conditioning has long shaped how people perceive sex, often turning it into a source of guilt or obsession. The repression of sexual expression leads to shame, while glorifying it turns it into a pursuit of pleasure without meaning. In both cases, sex becomes disconnected from its natural beauty and purpose, turning it into either a source of internal conflict or dependency. Furthermore, when sex is used as a means of escape from loneliness, boredom, or stress, it loses its authenticity, becoming an addiction rather than a connection between two individuals.

True understanding of sex comes when one observes it without judgment, guilt, or the need for possession. The natural urges of the body are neither good nor bad, but are often clouded by thought and conditioned beliefs. When one sees how thought sustains desire, especially by repeatedly imagining pleasure, it becomes easier to release obsessive cravings. Love, free from attachment and control, allows sex to become a natural part of life, rather than something sought for fulfillment or as an escape. True freedom in relationships and sex exists when there is understanding, where both individuals can enjoy each other without fear, attachment, or expectation.

269. Money

Money: The Symbol That Controls Human Lives

Money is an essential tool for navigating the modern world, necessary for securing basic needs like food, shelter, and comfort. However, it has evolved beyond a means of exchange into something that governs many people's lives, shaping their values, relationships, and sense of security. A mind consumed by the pursuit of wealth becomes fixated on status, accumulation, and financial security, often mistaking this external success for true peace of mind. In doing so, money transforms from a necessity into an obsession, creating internal division and fear of loss.

The psychological trap of money arises when it becomes equated with self-worth, success, and happiness. Society often links wealth with achievement, and individuals measure their value based on their financial standing, breeding envy, competition, and a sense of inferiority or superiority. This obsession fosters dependence, as people seek security in material possessions and wealth, mistakenly believing that money can provide lasting peace. In reality, no amount of money can address inner insecurity or the fear of life's uncertainties, making financial pursuits ultimately hollow and unfulfilling.

True freedom comes when one sees money for what it is—a practical tool—and not a means of defining personal worth or happiness. A mind that is free from the need for wealth-based validation can earn and live comfortably without succumbing to greed or fear. Real security arises from the understanding that inner peace is not contingent on external circumstances. By living simply and letting go of the psychological burdens of possession and comparison, one can experience a life of intelligence, creativity, and genuine fulfillment, unaffected by the anxieties tied to wealth.

270. Wealth

Wealth: Possession Without True Abundance

Wealth is often seen as the key to security and happiness, yet it is more than just material abundance—it is the accumulation of resources, money, and influence that provide comfort and convenience. However, the pursuit of wealth can easily become an obsession. The more one acquires, the more they seek to protect it, fearing loss, instability, and competition. Society frequently ties one's worth to financial success, creating division between the rich and poor, where wealth serves as both a tool of power and a measure of personal value. But despite its external benefits, wealth cannot guarantee peace or security within; a wealthy person can still be burdened by psychological insecurity, loneliness, and dissatisfaction.

The desire for wealth is deeply ingrained in human nature. We seek it because we believe it will bring security, power, and happiness, and society reinforces this belief by equating wealth with success. People work not out of joy but often out of fear—fear of poverty, fear of being inadequate, and fear of instability. Yet no matter how much wealth is accumulated, it remains incapable of providing lasting peace. True security is found not in possessions but in a mind free from fear, one that lives with awareness and intelligence rather than the pursuit of material gain. The constant chase for more only breeds anxiety and competition, creating a cycle of fear and struggle.

Living with wealth does not mean being possessed by it. When one realizes that wealth is simply a tool, not a measure of self-worth, they can use it wisely without becoming emotionally tied to it. True freedom comes from living simply and not being burdened by excess. Wealth, when shared without attachment or the desire for recognition, flows naturally and does not dominate one's life. Ultimately, true wealth lies not in the accumulation of material goods but in the freedom from attachment, in the ability to use resources with intelligence, and in the recognition that peace comes from within, not from external possessions. A mind free from the pursuit of wealth lives without conflict, without fear, and without the illusion that money equates to happiness.

271. Rich and Poor

Rich and Poor: The Division Created by Society and the Mind

Rich and poor are labels given based on material wealth, social status, or access to opportunities. They arise from economic systems, inherited privilege, and the conditioning that equates wealth with success and poverty with failure. A mind caught in the idea of rich and poor seeks status and security, while a mind that understands deeply sees beyond material comparison. Society defines richness by wealth and possessions, and poverty by the lack of them, yet true wealth is not in material gain—it is in clarity, understanding, and freedom. Many believe money brings happiness, yet wealthy people are often restless, and while poverty is difficult, it does not mean a person is empty or inferior. The rich fear losing what they have, while the poor desire what they lack, strengthening inequality and dissatisfaction.

Society equates success with financial gain, reinforcing the idea that money defines worth, yet a mind that sees clearly does not measure itself by possessions. People define themselves as 'rich' or 'poor,' shaping their self-worth around money, but true identity is not in status, but in the quality of one's awareness. Many chase money, believing it will bring freedom, yet external wealth without inner richness leads only to further craving. The mind seeks comfort, fearing financial instability, but when one understands the impermanence of wealth, fear weakens. Society respects the rich and often neglects the poor, reinforcing class division, yet a truly intelligent mind does not see others through economic status—it sees beyond labels. Comparison strengthens the illusion of rich and poor, making individuals feel superior or inferior, yet when one stops comparing, richness and poverty lose their psychological weight.

A person rich in understanding is free, regardless of material wealth, for when one lets go of attachment to money, richness or poverty loses its hold. Without measuring oneself against others, what does it mean to be 'rich' or 'poor'? A free mind does not seek superiority or feel inferior—it simply exists. Can one look at money and status without labeling them as 'good' or 'bad'? When there is no judgment, one sees the reality of material conditions without attachment. Many believe financial security will bring inner peace, yet true security is not in bank accounts— it is in deep understanding. A mind trapped in wealth seeks more, and a mind trapped in poverty resents what it lacks, yet when one sees clearly, action is not based on greed or self-pity, but on wisdom. The idea of rich and poor is a social division, reinforced by economic inequality and the mind's habit of comparison. Many struggle with these labels because they attach self-worth to financial success or feel trapped by material limitations, yet true wealth is in understanding, not possessions. A mind free from comparison, fear, and attachment does not define itself by money—it moves with clarity, acting intelligently without greed, without envy, without seeking status. In this freedom, richness and poverty are no longer measures of worth—they are simply external conditions, while the real richness exists in a mind that is whole, undivided, and beyond all illusions of superiority and inferiority.

WAKE UP

13. Existence & Reality

WAKE UP

WAKE UP

272. Existence

Existence: The Mystery of Being and Becoming

Existence is not something that can be explained, analyzed, or understood by thought—it simply is. It is the totality of being, the unfolding of life that happens without cause or reason. A mind caught in the effort to define existence will search for answers and meanings, but true existence transcends intellectual grasp. It is not created, controlled, or confined to any framework—it exists as it is, beyond the need for definition or explanation. As the mind struggles to grasp its nature, it can never truly experience existence fully, for it is not in conceptualization, but in direct, unmediated awareness.

The true nature of existence lies in its continuous transformation. Nothing remains static—everything flows, evolves, and changes. The attempt to hold onto permanence is a futile effort, as it creates suffering. Additionally, the mind's division between 'self' and 'existence' is an illusion. The 'I' is not separate from the totality of life—it is part of it. When one realizes that they are not apart from life, but are life itself, the need to define existence disappears. Existence is not bound by time or thought; it exists beyond them, ever-present and eternal, not subject to the limitations of intellectual understanding or the search for purpose.

To live in the fullness of existence is to live without the search for meaning or answers. It is to let go of the desire to define, control, or manipulate life. Existence, in its purest form, needs no purpose—it simply unfolds. The mind that is free from questions, from the desire for meaning, or from the need for security does not escape life—it becomes one with it. This is the freedom that exists beyond struggle, beyond illusion. In that state, existence is not a mystery to be solved—it is the vast, infinite unfolding of life, continuously happening, effortlessly, beyond thought, beyond time, and beyond any attempt to define it.

273. Reality

Reality: The Perception Shaped by the Mind

Reality is the totality of what is, existing beyond thought, belief, and perception. It encompasses everything we experience—the physical world, relationships, the body, the mind—but thought distorts it. Our minds often impose limitations on what we see, shaping our perception based on past experiences and conditioning. The real question is whether reality is something fixed or constantly evolving. As long as we view the world through the lens of thought, we are unable to see it clearly, and in this distortion, we miss the true nature of what is.

Thought, driven by beliefs, desires, and fears, often misrepresents reality. We mistake our beliefs for the truth, applying religious, political, or ideological filters to interpret life. This creates a distorted view of reality where emotions, memories, and projections take precedence over what is truly happening in the present moment. Memory further complicates the situation, as it redefines reality based on past experiences and expectations. When the mind is fragmented by the divisions created by thought, it can never perceive reality as it is. The self, built on the collection of thoughts, memories, and desires, is itself a distortion, making it impossible to fully grasp reality.

To perceive reality without distortion, one must acknowledge the limitations of thought. Thought is always based on memory and experience, and it cannot grasp the whole picture of reality. By seeing without the filters of belief and opinion, and by living fully in the present without being burdened by past memories or future expectations, one can experience reality as it truly is. Reality, in its purest form, is simply what is, unfolding without interference. When the mind quiets, free from judgment and control, reality reveals itself—not as an object to be defined, but as life to be lived fully, without distortion or division. In that clarity, reality can be experienced directly, in its totality and beauty.

274. Actuality

Actuality: Seeing Life as It Is, Not as One Wishes It to Be

Actuality is the raw, undeniable truth of the present moment—what exists here and now, independent of the mind's projections, beliefs, or desires. It is not what we imagine or wish for, but simply what is. However, in our daily lives, we often fail to see actuality clearly because the mind constantly distorts perception through past conditioning, memory, and expectation. Thought interferes with direct perception, filtering the present moment through ideas, fears, and desires, preventing us from truly experiencing what is in front of us.

Living in illusion rather than actuality leads to psychological conflict. When we hold onto beliefs, attachments, or ideas about how things should be, we are caught in a struggle between what is and what should be. Actuality, however, is free from such conflict. It simply exists, and its true perception requires us to stop searching for something beyond the present. This search for truth, meaning, or enlightenment often makes us overlook the simple reality of the moment. We also tend to cling to the past, allowing memories to cloud our ability to see the present clearly, further distancing ourselves from actuality.

To perceive actuality without distortion, one must observe without the interference of thought or labeling. The mind must be fully present, without psychological movement or attachment to past or future. In this state, the need for psychological security through beliefs or conclusions dissolves, revealing reality as it truly is. Actuality is beyond the grasp of thought—it cannot be analyzed or remembered, only directly experienced. In silence and clarity, free from the noise of mental projections, actuality is effortlessly revealed, and we encounter life in its purest form, without division or conflict.

275. Life

Life: The Ever-Changing Flow Beyond Definitions

Life is the ongoing, dynamic flow of existence, encompassing all that is—movement, change, relationship, awareness, joy, and suffering—all happening in the present moment. Yet, many of us are not truly living; instead, we are merely existing, trapped in the cycles of routine, fear, and conditioned responses. We often resist change, clinging to the illusion of permanence, fearing the unknown, and seeking stability in things that are inherently unstable. Life, however, is constantly evolving, and trying to control it only leads to struggle. We also live in psychological time, dwelling on past regrets or future anxieties, thus missing the richness of the present. The search for external meaning through possessions, relationships, and status only leads to temporary fulfillment, followed by dissatisfaction. Society teaches us to strive for more, but in doing so, we may never fully experience the beauty and depth of what is.

True living is about accepting life as it is, without resistance or the need to control it. Life is not a problem to be solved but a reality to be experienced. Our relationship with ourselves, others, and the world is where true living lies. Without awareness in these relationships, we miss life's richness. True living is found in deep observation, where we look at life without judgment, fear, or expectations. Life has no inherent purpose other than to be lived—complete and whole in itself. When we cease seeking external meaning or purpose, life reveals its own beauty and depth, which is beyond what we can conceptualize. To live fully is to embrace the present, to let go of psychological burdens and fully engage with whatever arises in the moment.

The key to living without struggle is accepting the flow of life, not clinging to one part and rejecting another. By being fully present with what is happening now, we realize that the richness of life is not found in thought, memory, or imagination, but in the clarity and awareness of the present moment. When we stop seeking meaning in external achievements or spiritual goals, life reveals its own inherent meaning. Living without psychological burdens—free from past hurts and future fears—allows us to see life as it truly is. In this state of awareness, life is no longer a struggle. It becomes an effortless, complete, and harmonious experience. A mind that is fully awake, present, and unburdened moves with life naturally, living fully without conflict.

276. Death

Death: The End of the Known and the Beginning of the Unknown

Death is often viewed as the cessation of life—the end of the body, the brain, and all physical functions. However, psychologically, death goes beyond this physical ending; it represents the termination of attachment, identity, memory, and the self. While we may intellectually understand death, the fear it evokes often stems from our lack of direct understanding. We fear death because we do not know what lies beyond it, and because it threatens everything we have built up and held onto—our memories, relationships, possessions, and the identities we have crafted. This fear is compounded by the uncertainty of the unknown; we cannot predict what happens after death, whether it is the cessation of all or a continuation of existence in some form.

One can begin to understand death while living by recognizing that death is not separate from life but is intertwined with every moment. To truly understand death is to die to the past every moment—releasing memories, attachments, and the psychological need for continuity. This death is not physical, but a letting go of the mental structures that bind us. Psychological time, the constant stream of "I was," "I am," and "I will be," is rooted in the fear of death. Living completely in the present moment, without clinging to the past or projecting into the future, allows one to move beyond the fear of death. Death is not something to be feared; it is something to be integrated into life, an ongoing process that occurs every time a thought, experience, or identity ends, making space for renewal.

When one frees themselves from the fear of death, they begin to live without attachment. The understanding that everything is temporary eliminates clinging, allowing for a deeper appreciation of each moment. By embracing the beauty of endings, one can see that death is essential for life to flow and evolve. The fear of death often arises from the attachment to a self that is ultimately illusory—when one deeply inquires, they see that the "self" is a collection of memories and identifications, and that there is no "me" that can die. Living without the fear of death opens the possibility for living fully, without hesitation or resistance, in complete presence. In dying to the attachments of time, identity, and the past, one experiences life in its truest, immeasurable form—beyond fear, beyond the known.

277. Mutation

Mutation: The Constant Transformation of Life and Thought

Mutation is not a slow, incremental process of change, but a radical shift in consciousness—a complete transformation of the mind. It is the instant cessation of conditioned responses, allowing something entirely new to emerge. Unlike gradual evolution, mutation is not about improving upon the old; it is about the total ending of the old, the dissolution of past conditioning, and the arrival of a fresh perception. A mind that undergoes mutation does not work through effort or discipline to refine its patterns; it steps out of the constraints of the past and embraces a new reality in its entirety.

The nature of true mutation lies in its immediacy and depth. It is not something that evolves over time or through gradual adjustment, but a sudden and total change. The moment falsehood is seen as false, it drops away instantly. This profound shift requires total awareness—a mind that is silent, clear, and free from fragmentation. When the past is fully let go of, fear dissipates, and the mind enters a state of freedom that allows for complete renewal. Mutation cannot occur in a mind still bound by the past or clinging to psychological time. It arises only when one is present, observing without seeking results, and allowing the transformation to happen naturally.

Living in a state of mutation involves the death of the past—the ending of attachment, belief, and identity. It is not about striving to become something better, but about seeing things as they are, without any desire to change them. Mutation is a process of pure observation and insight, where the mind frees itself from the need to modify or control. A mind that mutates does not remain stuck in patterns or seek improvement; it steps beyond conditioning entirely. In this state, there is no struggle, no division—only freedom, clarity, and the birth of something completely new.

278. Facts

Facts: The Unaltered Truth Beyond Interpretation

Facts are the undeniable truths of reality, independent of personal beliefs or emotions. They exist outside of interpretation and are not influenced by past experiences or societal conditioning. True intelligence begins with the ability to observe and accept facts as they are, without distortion or bias. The mind, however, often distorts facts through its own conditioning, adding layers of interpretation, expectation, or personal desire. This distortion prevents us from seeing things clearly and leads to misunderstanding, conflict, and confusion.

One of the main reasons we struggle with seeing facts as they are is that emotions and preconceived notions often influence our perception. Fear, hope, and attachment can alter how we interpret reality, making us more likely to see facts through the lens of our desires or fears. Similarly, when we seek comfort in beliefs rather than confronting the raw reality, we allow opinions to replace facts, creating further distortions. These distortions can create inner and outer conflict, leading to superficial understanding and a failure to act with clarity.

To see facts without distortion requires the ability to observe reality without judgment or attachment. It is essential to let go of psychological biases and desires, and face facts without fear or resistance. Only when we drop our personal preferences and assumptions can we begin to see facts clearly, free from distortion. In doing so, we experience a profound understanding of life as it truly is—unfiltered by thought and free from conflict. This clarity is the foundation for intelligent action, where decisions are made based on truth, not on illusion.

279. What Is

What Is: The Only Truth That Exists in This Moment

"What is" refers to the pure reality of the present moment, without any interpretation or alteration. It is the raw, unfiltered experience of life as it occurs, free from the influence of past experiences or future expectations. However, the mind often struggles to accept "what is" because it is conditioned to seek "what should be"—an idealized version of reality that creates inner conflict. The desire to change, compare, or escape from the present moment makes it difficult to see things as they truly are.

The main reasons we struggle with accepting "what is" are rooted in the mind's habitual reactions. The mind constantly desires to change reality, avoiding unpleasant emotions or uncomfortable truths. We compare "what is" to ideals and expectations, which leads to dissatisfaction and conflict. Additionally, the mind tends to escape into thought, analyzing or justifying reality instead of experiencing it directly. This avoidance is often driven by the fear of facing ourselves, as "what is" includes acknowledging our thoughts, emotions, and limitations—truths we may not be ready to confront.

When we fully accept "what is," psychological conflict ends. The inner battle between how things are and how we want them to be dissolves, allowing clarity and peace. In this state of acceptance, intelligence and the right action arise naturally, without force. We are no longer trapped by illusions, beliefs, or false hopes. True freedom and understanding emerge from observing "what is" without judgment, labeling, or resistance. The mind becomes still and silent, allowing truth to reveal itself effortlessly. In this deep awareness, there is no struggle, just the pure perception of reality as it is.

280. Measurement

Measurement: The Comparison That Limits Understanding

Measurement is the act of comparing and evaluating things based on standards, whether in the physical world or in human relationships. While measurement is essential in areas such as science, technology, and practical living, it has little place when it comes to understanding oneself, love, or inner transformation. When we use measurement to define success, intelligence, or personal worth, we risk seeing ourselves and others only through the lens of comparison, which ultimately creates division, frustration, and a sense of inadequacy. The mind constantly measures, and this cycle of comparison keeps us trapped in a false sense of progress and validation.

The habit of measuring is ingrained in us by society, which teaches us to compare our worth with others. We measure ourselves against ideals and standards created by culture, religion, and society, which leads to a constant struggle for improvement. However, this drive to become "better" often creates internal conflict between "what is" and "what should be," leading to guilt, frustration, and feelings of insufficiency. Measurement also reinforces the illusion of the self, as the sense of identity is built upon comparison, and the pursuit of an ideal self keeps us perpetually unsatisfied. True growth and transformation are not linear or measurable, and love, awareness, and intelligence cannot be quantified or compared.

Living without psychological measurement requires the ability to observe oneself and the world without attaching labels or comparisons. When one stops measuring, progress becomes an organic process that happens in the present moment, rather than a goal to strive toward. True intelligence arises when one acts with awareness, free from the desire to "improve" oneself. By letting go of the habit of comparing and measuring, we experience life with clarity and intelligence, seeing the world as it truly is. In this freedom, there is no division between what we are and what we should be, only a direct, unfiltered experience of life.

281. Duality

Duality: The Illusion That Divides the Indivisible

Duality is the perception of opposites, such as good and bad, success and failure, self and other, which the mind uses to interpret and categorize life. It arises from the tendency of thought to divide experience into contrasting categories, creating an ongoing cycle of conflict and struggle. A mind trapped in duality lives in constant conflict, always striving to move from one state to another, seeking an ideal while rejecting what is. This fragmented thinking creates psychological tension, as the mind perpetually oscillates between desires, fears, and judgments.

The root of duality lies in the structure of thought itself. Thought operates by comparing, categorizing, and judging, creating an illusion of separation between 'me' and 'you,' 'self' and 'other.' This separation fosters inner division, and the ego, which thrives on such divisions, sees itself as distinct from the rest of existence. Dualistic thinking further entrenches fear, comparison, and conflict, as people constantly evaluate their lives in terms of opposites—success versus failure, right versus wrong, happiness versus sadness. These divisions distort reality, preventing direct understanding and wholeness.

Living without duality requires seeing beyond the mental constructs that categorize and divide experience. It involves observing life without judgment or comparison, allowing the mind to be free from the need to label or classify. Understanding that the observer and the observed are not separate dissolves the conflict inherent in dualistic thinking. True understanding transcends opposites, seeing reality as it is—whole and undivided. When duality ceases, there is no longer any struggle between 'this' and 'that'; instead, there is clarity, direct perception, and a profound sense of unity with life.

282. Opposites

Opposites: The Conflict Created by the Divided Mind

Opposites are the mental constructs created by thought—good and bad, success and failure, love and hate—that organize our experience. They divide reality into categories, creating the illusion that one state must be desired while the other must be avoided. A mind caught in opposites is in constant conflict, striving for one while rejecting the other. This division sustains inner tension, making life a perpetual battle between opposing forces. The mind is conditioned to see life in terms of these contrasts, and in doing so, it denies the possibility of perceiving life as a whole, undivided experience.

Opposites exist only in thought, not in reality. They arise from comparison and judgment, but in true perception, these divisions do not exist. Fear and courage, for example, are not separate but are two movements of thought within the same mental process. The pursuit of one while avoiding the other creates psychological conflict, making the mind incapable of seeing the present moment clearly. This division keeps us trapped in endless seeking and avoidance, perpetually chasing pleasure while running from pain, not realizing that both arise together. The ego strengthens itself through these opposites, defining itself by what it is not and living through comparison and struggle.

To live without opposites, one must first see them as mental constructs rather than inherent aspects of reality. When the mind stops labeling, comparing, and judging, opposites dissolve naturally. In deep observation, without division, one begins to perceive the wholeness of life as it truly is, without distortion. This state of perception does not depend on pursuing one side of a duality and rejecting the other—it is the natural flow of awareness. A mind free from opposites is free from conflict; it perceives directly, without division, and lives in the present moment with clarity, harmony, and undivided perception.

283. Uncertainty

Uncertainty: The Fear of Letting Go of the Known

Uncertainty is the state of not knowing what will happen in life—whether it's in relationships, career, health, or the world at large. It is a natural and inevitable part of existence that often creates anxiety and a strong desire for control. The mind craves predictability, seeking stability in jobs, relationships, and plans for the future. However, this need for certainty only leads to fear when the unpredictable nature of life is faced. We become dependent on beliefs, ideologies, or systems to give us the comfort of stability, but is this true security, or is it merely an illusion preventing us from embracing the fullness of life?

The pursuit of certainty can lead to psychological dependence, making us fearful of change and unwilling to step into the unknown. This need for control and predictability confines the mind and restricts exploration. By clinging to beliefs or following rigid systems, we avoid the discomfort of uncertainty, but in doing so, we miss out on the richness of new experiences and discoveries. Certainty, ultimately, is an illusion. Life is inherently uncertain—relationships evolve, jobs end, and the body ages. Seeking certainty only sets us up for disappointment, as we realize that nothing remains fixed or predictable.

To live without fear of uncertainty, we must accept it as a natural part of life, not something to be feared or avoided. True freedom comes from letting go of the illusion of control and allowing life to unfold without the need for preconceived answers or expectations. The key is to meet each moment with fresh awareness and clarity, not based on what we think should happen, but fully engaged with the present as it is. A mind that is deeply aware of the impermanence of all things remains stable without the need for external security or fixed beliefs. In embracing uncertainty, we find freedom—the freedom to explore, to grow, and to experience life fully in the now.

284. Beyond

Beyond: Stepping Into the Unknown Without Fear

Beyond is not a destination or a place; it is a state of freedom where limitations, concepts, and the known dissolve. It arises when the mind ceases to cling to the familiar, whether through beliefs, definitions, or memories. True freedom comes from the absence of mental, emotional, and conceptual boundaries. A mind caught in the idea of "beyond" still seeks escape or an achievement, but a mind that truly experiences "beyond" moves without effort, understanding that it is the absence of the barriers created by thought, not something to attain.

We struggle to go beyond because we are attached to the known—the safety of familiarity, past experiences, and concepts that provide a sense of stability. The mind continuously seeks something more, believing that a higher state of achievement or enlightenment will bring liberation. However, true beyond is the end of seeking itself, not a further step in the pursuit of more. Fear of letting go of the ego, identity, and attachment to the past keeps us bound within these limits. "Beyond" is not a future goal or something to be reached; it exists in the present moment when the mind is free from psychological time and the conditioning that keeps it bound to the past or future.

To go beyond without effort, one must see that it is not about striving or achieving, but about letting go of the psychological boundaries that create separation. The mind must stop looking for "beyond" in concepts, words, or theories and instead live in the present—fully engaged with reality as it is. In this state, beyond is not a destination but a continuous unfolding, a deeper awareness that comes with clarity and freedom. When the search ends and the mind is free from fear, attachment, and the ego, one lives in harmony with life, beyond limitations and illusions.

WAKE UP

14. Purpose & Direction

WAKE UP

WAKE UP

285. Focus

Focus: The Art of Seeing Without Distraction

Focus is the ability to direct attention fully to a particular object, thought, or experience without being distracted or divided. It is not about forcing the mind to concentrate, but about allowing natural, effortless attention to flow. True focus arises when there is no inner conflict—when the mind is at peace and fully engaged with the present moment. The difference between concentration and focus lies in the effort: concentration requires a deliberate blocking out of distractions, while focus is relaxed, allowing perception to unfold freely without resistance. A mind that is truly focused is one that is completely present, without any division between the observer and the observed.

The struggle with focus often arises from our tendency to force it. When we attempt to focus through sheer effort, we create resistance and frustration. The mind, conditioned to seek constant stimulation, is prone to distraction, particularly in an environment filled with external noise and constant information. Inner conflict, such as fear, doubt, or confusion, also fragments attention, making sustained focus difficult. Additionally, we often associate focus with achievement and external rewards, creating a conditional relationship with it. True focus, however, is independent of such conditions and arises naturally when we are genuinely interested in the present moment.

To focus without struggle, one must observe the movement of the mind without trying to control or suppress it. Allowing the mind to rest in curiosity and interest is key—when one is deeply engaged, focus happens effortlessly. Multitasking divides attention, weakening focus, so it is essential to give attention to one thing at a time. The key to sustained focus lies not in forceful discipline but in living with awareness. In this state, focus becomes a natural extension of clarity, presence, and deep engagement with the world, free from conflict, fear, and the need for external validation.

286. Goal

Goal: The Destination That Limits the Journey

A goal is a mental projection of a desired future state—something we want to achieve or become. It creates a division between 'what is' and 'what should be,' leading the mind to constantly strive and measure progress instead of fully experiencing the present moment. While goals can provide direction and motivation, they often create inner conflict, as they tie fulfillment to a future outcome that may never truly arrive. The pursuit of goals can lead to a life focused on achievement, leaving little room for awareness of the present and often resulting in frustration, anxiety, and the belief that fulfillment lies only in the future.

The struggle with goals arises from the belief that success or completion is what brings meaning to life. Society conditions people to think that life must be lived in pursuit of external markers of success—wealth, career, status—making individuals feel incomplete until they reach their goals. This conditioning attaches happiness and security to the achievement of external milestones, preventing a deeper engagement with life as it is. The more one clings to goals, the more one distances themselves from the richness of the present moment, as the mind constantly projects into the future and measures its progress.

To live without the burden of goals, one must recognize that life is not a path to somewhere, but an experience to be fully lived here and now. True action arises when one is present in the moment, not as a means to an end but as an expression of awareness. Fulfillment does not come from reaching an imagined destination—it comes from the depth of attention given to each moment. When the mind is free from the pressure of goals, life flows naturally, without struggle or striving, allowing true intelligence, love, and understanding to unfold without the need for future achievements.

287. Seeking

Seeking: The Endless Search That Prevents Discovery

Seeking is the movement of the mind toward an imagined goal or ideal, driven by the belief that something is missing or incomplete. It arises from the desire for happiness, success, truth, or inner peace, but the pursuit itself is often the barrier to discovering what one seeks. Seeking implies that fulfillment lies somewhere outside of the present moment, which keeps the mind constantly projecting into the future and avoiding the direct experience of what is. The act of seeking creates inner conflict, dissatisfaction, and a feeling of restlessness, because the mind is never fully content with the present.

The struggle with seeking arises from the belief that fulfillment is something that can be attained through effort, whether it's spiritual growth, knowledge, or success. Society and religion often reinforce this idea, teaching that there is a path, a goal, or a system to follow in order to reach an ideal state. However, true understanding, peace, and freedom are not found in the future or in external attainment—they exist only in the present moment, when the mind is free from the need to seek or strive. The constant seeking of something external keeps one trapped in psychological time, away from the immediacy of direct perception.

To live without seeking, one must recognize that the act of seeking itself is the problem. When the mind is not occupied with the desire for change, understanding and truth can emerge naturally. True perception occurs when one observes without trying to alter or label what is. By letting go of psychological time and living in the present, there is no need for seeking or striving. Action becomes effortless and complete when it is not driven by an expectation of a result. In the absence of seeking, the mind is free, fully engaged with life as it is, and there is no longer any feeling of lacking or wanting.

288. Will

Will: The Force That Either Frees or Binds

Will is the force that drives the mind to pursue goals, assert control, or resist unwanted experiences. Rooted in desire and fear, it is the manifestation of the self trying to shape life according to its expectations. While society glorifies willpower as a mark of strength and discipline, it often leads to inner conflict and division. The mind that is driven by will struggles against what is, creating endless tension between what is and what should be. It is through this struggle that will perpetuates the illusion of control, pushing the mind into psychological time—always projecting into the future, always striving to attain something.

The pursuit of will is inherently tied to desire. The stronger the desire, the more forceful the will becomes, leading to greater conflict and emotional suppression. Society conditions individuals to view will as the key to success, but this creates a cycle of effort and struggle. True intelligence and understanding do not arise from this forceful striving; they emerge from deep observation and awareness. Will, in its attempt to control, suppresses the natural flow of life, creating rigid patterns and expectations. It is only through letting go of the need for will that true, spontaneous action can occur.

To live without will is to live in awareness, free from the need to control or resist. When desire is understood and observed without attachment, the need for will diminishes. Action then flows effortlessly, arising from intelligence rather than struggle. The mind that is free from will is free from conflict and division, allowing it to move naturally, with clarity and harmony. In this state, there is no compulsion, no force—just deep intelligence and the effortless movement of life, unfolding in its own time.

289. Meaning of Life

Meaning of Life: A Question That Thought Cannot Answer

The search for meaning is a fundamental human impulse, driven by the mind's desire to understand life and find purpose. However, meaning is not something that can be grasped by thought, belief, or purpose. The mind often seeks to assign meaning to life through external measures like success, religion, or relationships, but these external sources do not bring lasting fulfillment. The true essence of life is not in its meaning or purpose, but in experiencing it fully, without interpretation or attachment to goals.

The mind seeks meaning due to psychological insecurity—the fear of uncertainty and the unknown. We cling to beliefs and concepts because they offer a sense of stability, but this stability is illusory. Thought's desire for continuity leads to the pursuit of meaning, but life is not a timeline; it is the present moment unfolding continuously. By focusing on seeking meaning or purpose, we miss the beauty and richness of the present, failing to see that life itself is enough, without the need for additional labels or constructs.

True freedom comes when one stops seeking meaning externally. Life, when lived in full attention, is the meaning in itself. When the mind ceases to search for purpose, it allows for complete immersion in each moment. The beauty of existence is revealed when we live without resistance, not needing to define life or explain it. In this state, the mind is free, and meaning ceases to be a question—it simply is.

290. Purpose

Purpose: The Mind's Attempt to Justify Existence

Purpose is the idea that life, action, and existence must have a defined goal to be meaningful. It arises from thought projecting itself into the future, seeking direction, achievement, or fulfillment. A mind caught in purpose is never fully present—it is always striving, waiting, or becoming, unable to see the depth of life as it is. Conditioned by society, education, and ambition, purpose becomes a psychological need, making one believe that without it, life is meaningless. This attachment to purpose creates inner struggle, as the mind measures itself against ideals, believing that significance comes only through accomplishment.

The pursuit of purpose strengthens psychological time, dividing the present from the imagined future. When action is driven by purpose, it is no longer spontaneous—it is calculated, controlled by expectation. This pursuit creates conflict, as there is always a gap between "what is" and "what should be." Even when a goal is achieved, the mind immediately moves to the next, never truly arriving at contentment. The need for purpose is rooted in insecurity—the fear of being directionless, of existing without structure. Instead of seeing that meaning is in direct living, the mind searches for validation through success, progress, or recognition.

Freedom from purpose is not in rejecting goals but in seeing that fulfillment is not in the future. When action is whole in itself, not seeking a result, it is complete, effortless, and intelligent. A mind that is fully attentive does not ask, "What is my purpose?"—it simply moves with life, without inner division. Letting go of the need for purpose does not make life empty; it reveals a richness that exists beyond seeking. In this state, action is not bound by ambition or expectation—it is pure, free, and deeply connected to the present. A life without purpose is not meaningless—it is beyond meaning, beyond seeking, and full of the vastness of direct experience.

WAKE UP

15. Time & Experience

WAKE UP

WAKE UP

291. Time

Time: The Illusion That Binds the Mind

Time, in its essence, is the measurement of movement—both chronological and psychological. Chronological time is useful for organizing our lives, helping us schedule, plan, and learn. Yet, psychological time, the mental construct of the past and future, creates an inner divide. It binds the mind to past regrets and future expectations, preventing one from fully living in the present moment. The mind, caught in this cycle of comparison between what is and what should be, struggles to be free of psychological conflict. It is in this struggle that time becomes a burden, not allowing true presence or clarity.

We live in psychological time because we are conditioned to define ourselves by the past and project our fulfillment into the future. Identity is constructed from past experiences—successes, failures, relationships—and the mind clings to these memories for a sense of continuity. Similarly, there is the constant hope for future fulfillment—happiness, success, love—promised as something that is always just out of reach. The fear of the present, of what is unknown and unpredictable, pushes us further into the illusions of the past and future, preventing us from experiencing life as it truly is.

However, the moment we stop identifying with the past and future, and begin to live fully in the present, psychological time fades. When we cease to chase future goals or rely on past memories for identity, we experience life in its entirety, as a whole. Living in the now means acting without seeking a future result, without striving for transformation, for it happens instantaneously when one sees truth. Freedom from psychological time is the liberation from the illusion of becoming, where life is no longer something to achieve but something to experience deeply, effortlessly. In this timeless awareness, life unfolds naturally, beyond the confines of past and future, in the purity of the present.

292. Continuity

Continuity: The Unbroken Chain of the Past Shaping the Present

Continuity is the mind's desire to maintain stability, identity, and permanence through memory, attachments, and expectations. It arises from the fear of change and the unknown, giving us a false sense of security and predictability. We cling to the past, hoping that what we hold dear—relationships, beliefs, personal identity—will remain unchanged. This attachment to continuity creates the illusion that we are a fixed, permanent "self," but is this self truly unchanging, or just a movement of thoughts and memories that change with time?

The search for continuity prevents real living. By holding onto past experiences and identities, we fail to experience life as it truly is, in the present moment. This fixation on the unchanging creates conflict—when life inevitably changes, we struggle to maintain what is fading, and in doing so, we create resistance. This resistance fosters fear: the fear of losing what we think we need to preserve. Psychological continuity strengthens this fear, binding us to the past and keeping us from embracing change, causing unnecessary suffering.

True freedom comes when we let go of the need for continuity. Life is in constant motion—everything changes, from our bodies to our relationships, to our ideas. The acceptance of impermanence allows us to live without the psychological burden of time, without constantly projecting into the future or holding onto the past. In doing so, we become free to experience life fully, in each moment, without the fear of endings. This freedom arises when we let go of the desire to possess, to preserve, or to continue, and instead allow life to flow as it is, unimpeded by the illusion of permanence.

293. Rebirth

Rebirth: The Cycle of Memory, Identity, and Conditioning

Rebirth is not a physical continuation or reincarnation but the psychological death of the past, allowing something new to emerge. It is the shedding of old patterns, identities, and attachments, making space for fresh perception and awareness. Most of us cling to the idea of reincarnation or an afterlife because the mind fears the finality of death, seeking comfort in continuity. However, this belief often perpetuates the illusion of a persistent self, rooted in memory and conditioning, rather than encouraging true transformation.

True rebirth occurs when one dies to the past—when attachment, fear, and identity are completely let go. Rebirth is not a distant future event but an immediate possibility in each moment. By letting go of psychological time, we open ourselves to the present moment, free from past burdens and future anxieties. When we stop identifying with societal labels and the psychological baggage of past experiences, we can experience life anew, fresh, and vibrant.

Living without accumulation or psychological attachment allows us to constantly renew our perception, and each moment becomes an opportunity for rebirth. This is not about clinging to beliefs or concepts about rebirth; rather, it is about experiencing a continual transformation of mind and perception. A mind that dies to past conditioning, each moment, is always in a state of renewal—alive, free, and fully present. True rebirth is found in the constant dissolution of the old and the ever-present birth of the new.

294. Change

Change: The Movement That Can Be Either Superficial or Profound

Change is often viewed as a gradual process of improvement, growth, or progress, but real transformation is something entirely different. True change is not the act of becoming better or striving for some future ideal—it is a radical shift in perception, an immediate ending of what is false. This change does not unfold over time, but happens instantaneously in the present moment, when the mind is free from the constraints of psychological time and the search for improvement.

The belief in gradual change is an illusion. Many people think that they will change over time through effort and discipline, but real change cannot be achieved through time—it occurs when the truth is seen instantly. The desire to "become" something— whether it's peaceful, successful, or enlightened—is still the continuation of the same old mind with new desires. True change happens when the mind stops trying to change, when it fully observes life and sees things as they are, without the filters of comparison, judgment, or desire.

Real change arises when one sees the false as false. This means observing emotions, desires, and attachments without trying to suppress or escape them. When fear, anger, or attachment is fully understood, they naturally dissolve. True change also involves the realization that the 'self' is an illusion—a collection of thoughts and conditioning. When one sees that the self is not a permanent entity, deep freedom arises. This shift in understanding does not require effort or time; it happens in the instant one sees clearly, when the search for change itself stops, and the mind becomes silent, present, and fully awake. In this state of awareness, life unfolds effortlessly, and change happens without struggle or resistance.

295. Evolution

Evolution: Progress or the Repetition of Patterns?

Evolution is commonly understood as the process of change and adaptation, whether it's biological, technological, or psychological. While biological evolution is an observable process in nature, psychological evolution is a concept created by the mind—a belief that the self can improve and evolve over time through knowledge, effort, and experience. However, this idea of psychological evolution raises the question: can the self, which is merely a construct of thought, truly evolve into something new, or does it simply modify itself while remaining essentially the same?

Biological evolution is a gradual process, but psychological evolution often presents itself as an illusion. The mind operates within psychological time, projecting the idea of "becoming"—an endless pursuit of improvement or enlightenment. However, true transformation does not happen through the passage of time or effort, but through instantaneous insight. The self, which seeks to evolve, is a product of accumulated memories, identities, and experiences—how can something that is built on past conditioning ever truly change? Striving for inner evolution only creates inner conflict, as the mind becomes trapped in the pursuit of an ideal future state, while real change can only happen when the illusion of "becoming" is seen and dropped in the present moment.

Though technological advancements have radically transformed the external world, human consciousness remains largely unchanged. We continue to struggle with the same issues—fear, greed, and conflict—that have plagued humanity for millennia. If psychological evolution were real, would these problems not have been solved by now? True transformation, whether personal or collective, does not unfold over time; it happens in the immediacy of the present moment. When the mind sees clearly, free from the need to improve or evolve, it is already transformed—no longer bound by the illusion of time, progress, or the self. In this clarity, there is no need for psychological evolution—there is simply awareness and freedom from the conditioning of thought.

296. Impermanence

Impermanence: The Truth That Thought Resists

Impermanence is the intrinsic quality of existence, where everything is in constant flux—our bodies, emotions, relationships, and even the world around us. The fundamental nature of life is change, and when one resists this truth, suffering arises. However, understanding impermanence can lead to freedom, as it enables us to move with life rather than against it. A mind that resists the flow of change, holding onto what is temporary, invites fear, loss, and disappointment. True liberation comes when one accepts impermanence, allowing the natural cycle of life to unfold.

The struggle with impermanence arises from the desire for permanence in a world that is in constant motion. People seek stability in relationships, possessions, and their identities, not realizing that these are also transient. The fear of loss and the unknown reinforces this attachment. However, impermanence also brings growth and renewal. It is through change that new possibilities emerge—every ending opens the door to a new beginning. Life cannot remain static, and the constant change allows for learning, transformation, and evolution.

To live with impermanence without fear, one must understand that clinging to anything creates suffering. True freedom comes from embracing change and living fully in the present. When we let go of our attachment to stability, we are free to flow with life as it moves, with clarity and ease. The fear of loss dissipates when we realize that death, endings, and changes are a natural part of existence, not personal failures. In this understanding, impermanence becomes a beautiful rhythm of life, where each moment is fully appreciated, and there is no fear of what is yet to come.

297. Past

Past: The Weight That Shapes Perception

The past is a collection of memories, experiences, and impressions that shape our thoughts, emotions, and identity. Though it exists only in memory, its influence is profound, affecting how we react, believe, and interact with the present. A mind trapped in the past cannot see the current moment clearly, as it views everything through the lens of what has already been. This attachment to the past creates a distorted sense of self, as individuals often define themselves by their past experiences and achievements, limiting their ability to see who they truly are in the present.

Living in the past prevents one from fully experiencing life as it unfolds. Memories are not static; they are altered by emotions, beliefs, and biases, causing us to reinterpret events and see them through a distorted lens. This can lead to emotional suffering, especially when painful memories or regrets are repeatedly replayed in the mind. Furthermore, the mind often seeks comfort in the known, choosing the familiarity of the past over the uncertainty of the present, even when that familiarity causes suffering or limits growth. This attachment to the past creates a cycle of psychological dependence, preventing individuals from embracing the unpredictability of life.

True freedom comes when one is able to release the past's grip. By recognizing that the past exists only as thought and memory, its influence begins to fade. Observing memory without identification allows the mind to be free from its conditioning, and living without the burden of psychological time enables one to engage fully with the present moment. A mind free from the past is not encumbered by past experiences, fears, or expectations. It moves with clarity, spontaneity, and openness, seeing life as it is, without distortion. In this freedom, each moment is fresh and new, unburdened by the shadows of yesterday.

298. Present

Present: The Moment That Thought Tries to Escape

The present is the only true reality—it is not a mere segment of time, but the state of being fully aware and engaged with life as it unfolds. The past and future are constructs of the mind; they are not real except in memory and anticipation. A mind that is caught in memories of what has been or projections of what might come cannot experience the present as it is. The present exists as pure awareness, free from the weight of psychological time, and it is where true living happens—without attachment to outcomes, rewards, or expectations.

The present is not merely a stepping stone to the future nor is it a fleeting moment of pleasure or distraction. It is the fullness of life as it is, when one is fully attentive and not consumed by desires or the search for fulfillment. Transformation and change do not happen in the future—they happen now, in this moment. Living fully in the present is to see, act, and understand without hesitation, relying on no past knowledge or future aspirations. It is a state of complete presence, where life is experienced directly and fully.

To live fully in the present requires letting go of the past and the future. One must observe life without the interference of memory, expectation, or psychological time. True perception happens when the mind is free from the need to categorize, label, or judge. In the now, everything that is essential—life, understanding, truth—exists. The mind that is free from time, free from the burden of "becoming," experiences life in its entirety. In this deep awareness of the present, clarity, freedom, and profound connection with life are naturally revealed.

299. Future

Future: The Projection of Desire and Fear

The future is a mental construct, a projection created by thought, shaped by our past experiences, desires, fears, and hopes. It is never a real entity but exists only in our imagination, always out of reach. The mind, however, continuously looks to the future, seeking security in an imagined tomorrow. We believe that happiness, success, or fulfillment will come "one day," but in reality, these are projections that prevent us from experiencing the fullness of the present moment. The future, with its promises of fulfillment, keeps us in a state of desire, preventing true contentment from arising in the now.

Living in the future creates several issues. We are conditioned to believe in progress over time, and society reinforces the idea that growth and fulfillment require patience and effort. However, true transformation does not need time; it happens instantly when one has clear insight. The future becomes an escape from the present, where we retreat into fantasies, hopes, or anxieties about what may come. This escape prevents us from confronting and engaging with the present moment, where true change and awareness lie. The future, therefore, is always an idea, never truly realized, and in constantly seeking it, we remain trapped in a cycle of desire, fear, and uncertainty.

To live fully, one must recognize the future for what it is: a mere projection of thought. When the mind is completely present and engaged in the now, the need for the future dissolves. Transformation is not a matter of waiting for something to happen later, but occurs the moment one sees the truth of the present. Living without the illusion that time brings understanding allows clarity to emerge immediately. True freedom comes when we drop the notion of becoming something in the future, embracing the present moment fully, where life unfolds effortlessly without the burden of anticipation, waiting, or illusion.

300. Tomorrow

Tomorrow: The Escape from 'What Is'

Tomorrow is nothing more than a mental projection—an idea that the mind creates based on its desires, fears, and expectations. It is never real; when it arrives, it is always now. The mind's attachment to the idea of tomorrow keeps it in a constant state of postponement, preventing full engagement with the present moment. Living in the illusion of tomorrow means the mind is often preoccupied with what is to come, rather than experiencing life as it is in the present. This creates a sense of delay, where transformation, understanding, or change is always deferred, never happening fully in the now.

The search for something better tomorrow is rooted in the mind's desire to control the unknown and to escape the discomfort of the present. By projecting hopes of future success, happiness, or fulfillment, the mind avoids facing the uncertainties and challenges of the current moment. Psychological time, created through the constant movement of desire and fear, keeps the mind trapped in an endless cycle of anticipation. However, real transformation does not reside in the future; it can only happen when one is fully present, when tomorrow is seen for what it truly is—just an idea, not something to wait for or strive towards.

Living without the illusion of tomorrow means recognizing that the future is only a mental construct, and when understood, the mind can stop postponing clarity and action. True freedom comes when the mind stops waiting for a 'better tomorrow' and instead acts fully in the present. When one observes life without expectation and lives without the habit of postponing, every moment becomes complete in itself. The idea of tomorrow fades away, leaving only the pure, undivided presence of life as it is, with no need for future promises or projections.

301. Now

Now: The Only Reality That Exists

Now is the only true reality, beyond thought and time. Everything else—the past and the future—exists only in the mind. The past is a collection of memories, and the future is merely an imagination. The present, or the now, is not a mere moment between two times, but the flow of life itself. A mind fully present in the now is undivided, free from distraction, and completely aware. It is the only place where action occurs, and it is the absence of psychological time, where there is no regret from the past or fear of the future.

We often avoid living in the now because the mind is conditioned to dwell on the past and anticipate the future. We fear the present because it calls for total engagement, without the comfort of memory or the projection of desire. The ego wants to preserve its continuity, and society pressures us to look ahead for future rewards, making the present seem insignificant. But the truth is, there is no future, only the now. The moment we stop seeking to 'become' or to 'do,' we experience the essence of life, which is always unfolding, free from measurement, attachment, or resistance.

Living in the now is not about capturing the present moment or intellectualizing it. It's about letting go of the burden of past memories and future desires and embracing each moment as it is. When we observe life without interference from thought— without naming, judging, or projecting—we experience life in its fullness. A mind in the now acts effortlessly, without delay or hesitation, free from conflict and fear. This is the natural state of being—alive, present, and fully engaged with life, beyond time and thought. When we let go of the illusion of becoming, we find the essence of life itself in the now.

302. Living

Living: The Art of Being Without Becoming

Living is not merely existing or going through the motions of daily routines—true living is a profound state of awareness and freedom. It is about being fully present in each moment, free from the constraints of habit, fear, and the constant search for pleasure or security. Most of us live mechanically, trapped in the past or future, constantly striving to fulfill desires or avoid discomfort. True living happens when the mind is free from these distractions, when one is fully engaged in the present moment, experiencing life as it unfolds.

The struggle to live fully arises when we are consumed by thoughts, anxieties, and attachments. Fear of failure, loss, and the desire for security create a barrier between us and the richness of life. We resist what is, constantly measuring our reality against what we think it should be. True living, however, happens when we stop resisting life, when we let go of our attachments and fears, and when we live without the need to control or possess. In this state of freedom, we can experience life deeply, with complete attention and presence.

To live fully, one must observe life without judgment or expectation, seeing things as they are. Living without the habit of "becoming" means no longer seeking fulfillment in the future but fully embracing the now. This is a life lived without fear, without seeking reward, and without the need to cling to the self.

When we let go of the psychological "I," the sense of identity bound by memory and expectation, we free ourselves from the struggle and allow life to flow naturally. True living is not about achieving or accumulating—it is about being fully awake, in total awareness, and fully immersed in the present moment.

303. Future of Humanity

Future of Humanity: Awakening or Further Division?

The future of humanity is not predetermined by external factors such as technology, politics, or economic systems. It is shaped by the collective psychological state of human beings and how we choose to live, think, and act in the present moment. The challenges we face—psychological division, greed, environmental destruction, and dependence on systems—are all symptoms of the conditioning that governs human thought. As long as we remain caught in conflict, separation, and fear, the future will merely be a continuation of the past, repeating the same patterns of division and struggle. However, transformation is possible if humanity begins to awaken to its conditioning, letting go of the illusions that perpetuate division and suffering.

The fundamental threat to humanity's future lies in our internal divisions and the endless cycle of greed and fear. Nationalism, religion, and ideology create artificial boundaries, leading to wars, competition, and exploitation. The pursuit of success, wealth, and power, driven by fear and insecurity, only deepens this divide, preventing us from seeing that all humans share the same fundamental desires and fears. Additionally, the destruction of the environment, fueled by overconsumption and profit-driven motives, threatens the very survival of the planet. Until humanity recognizes its interconnectedness with nature, and stops exploiting it for short-term gain, we risk our own existence.

True transformation can only occur within, not through external systems or technological advancements. The future of humanity depends on the awareness and understanding of the mind's conditioning. When individuals see their own fears, attachments, and limitations without resistance or escape, they begin to act with intelligence, love, and responsibility. If we continue to cling to division and illusion, the future will remain clouded by conflict. However, if humanity awakens to a deeper awareness, a new kind of collective consciousness can emerge—one that embraces unity, compassion, and clarity, paving the way for a future free from fear, greed, and suffering. The real question is not what the future holds, but whether we will choose to awaken and transform now, before it is too late.

304. Mechanical Living

Mechanical Living: The Repetition That Kills Awareness

Mechanical living is the unconscious repetition of thought, behavior, and routine without awareness. It emerges when life is guided by habit, conditioning, and social conformity rather than fresh perception. A mind caught in mechanical living operates like a machine—efficient yet unaware, active yet devoid of true essence. It is governed by the repetition of habit, reducing life to predictable and dull patterns, instead of vibrant, dynamic experiences.

The nature of mechanical living is deeply rooted in societal conditioning, where individuals are trained to follow established patterns. From childhood, we are conditioned to think and behave in particular ways, which then become automatic responses. This prevents the possibility of fresh insight, as life becomes a mere continuation of the past. The resulting stagnation creates boredom and dissatisfaction, with individuals continuously seeking superficial excitement to escape their habitual patterns.

Breaking free from mechanical living involves recognizing that habitual behavior is not true awareness. By observing without automatic reaction and letting go of psychological routines, one can begin to live with clarity and intelligence. Instead of following mindless repetition, engaging with life fully allows for a fresh and meaningful experience. Freedom from mechanical living begins when one steps out of the illusion of security in routine and embraces the spontaneity and creativity of living in the present.

WAKE UP

16. Deception & Illusion

WAKE UP

WAKE UP

305. False

False: The Unseen Lies We Live By

The false is any concept, belief, or perception created by thought that is mistaken for truth. It arises when the mind distorts reality through conditioning, authority, tradition, or psychological needs. When the mind holds onto the false, it lives in illusion, mistaking projections of thought for actual reality. This illusion can manifest in various forms—whether it is societal beliefs, personal identities, or ideologies that obscure truth and understanding.

The nature of the false is rooted in thought itself. Thought operates based on memory, which is always limited and conditioned. When thought projects these limitations as truth, the false is born. The false thrives on belief and assumption—accepting something without directly perceiving it. People cling to comforting illusions to avoid uncertainty, and in doing so, they reinforce ideas that may not be true. Psychological security, fueled by belief and authority, strengthens the false and perpetuates division and conflict.

To be free from the false, one must question everything without fear. Thought, being limited, cannot grasp the whole of reality—truth lies in direct perception. Letting go of the comfort of belief and observing without seeking a conclusion can expose the illusion. By living with full attention and not clinging to ideas or secondhand knowledge, one can see life as it truly is. When the false is discarded, there is clarity, and the mind moves with understanding, free from illusion and distortion.

306. Lie

Lie: The Escape from Truth That Distorts Reality

A lie is a deliberate distortion or concealment of truth, created for personal gain, protection, or to avoid undesirable consequences. It arises from a desire to safeguard an image, escape judgment, or manipulate a situation. A mind that lies lives in contradiction, projecting one version of reality while internally knowing the truth. The lie acts as an escape from facing reality, but this avoidance only creates internal conflict, as the truth does not change, no matter how the situation is manipulated through deception.

Lying is rooted in fear—fear of rejection, punishment, or discomfort. The desire to protect one's image often fuels the need to lie, as people want to appear stronger, more successful, or virtuous than they actually are. Lies can also be used to gain an advantage in situations, which may provide temporary benefits but ultimately lead to instability and distrust. Society often conditions individuals to lie, especially from childhood, teaching that dishonesty is sometimes necessary to avoid negative consequences. This conditioning makes lying feel natural, and over time, it becomes easier to justify, weakening one's ability to see things clearly.

Living without lying requires understanding that a lie does not change the reality of the situation. The facts remain the same regardless of how a lie is constructed. When fear is seen for what it is, the need to lie dissolves. True freedom from deception comes when one no longer seeks to protect an image or gain personal advantage through falsehood. Observing life with clarity and living transparently makes lies unnecessary. A mind that does not fear the truth operates with integrity, seeing and acting in the world without masks or distortions, grounded in honesty and complete alignment with reality.

307. Illusion

Illusion: The False Perception Created by Thought

Illusion is the mind's distortion of reality, where what is false is perceived as true. It arises when thought imposes beliefs, desires, or fears onto the present moment, shaping our perception of the world, ourselves, and others. Illusion does not only exist externally but is deeply embedded in how we see ourselves and the relationships we create. This distortion leads us to misunderstand the true nature of life and experience, often making us live in a cycle of conflict and dissatisfaction.

The mind creates illusions for various reasons. Desire plays a significant role in shaping our perception, as we see what we wish to see rather than what truly is. For example, in love, we may idealize someone, and in fear, we may perceive threats where there are none. Additionally, the mind seeks psychological security through beliefs, traditions, and ideologies that offer comfort, even if these beliefs are unfounded. Memory and past experiences also distort our perception, as thought projects old patterns onto new situations, preventing us from seeing the present clearly.

Living in illusion brings conflict, suffering, and a lack of true understanding. The gap between 'what is' and 'what should be' creates a constant sense of dissatisfaction. Illusion strengthens the ego, which survives through attachments, comparisons, and beliefs. To free ourselves from illusion, we must observe life without desire or fear, question every belief and assumption, and recognize that thought itself is the maker of illusion. When we see through the false, illusion fades, and true understanding naturally arises, bringing clarity and peace. In this clarity, reality is no longer something to be found—it is already present when we stop holding onto illusion.

308. Deception

Deception: The Art of Manipulating Perception

Deception is the act of intentionally misleading or distorting the truth to serve personal, psychological, or social interests. It arises from fear, self-preservation, or the desire to manipulate others' perceptions. A mind that operates through deception creates illusions that obscure both internal truths and external realities. However, a mind that sees clearly does not need to deceive, as it embraces truth without distortion. Deception manifests in many forms—not just as overt lies but through subtle manipulation of perception, whether through words, silence, or omission of facts. The root of deception lies in the mind's tendency to deceive itself first, which then leads to deceiving others.

People engage in deception for a variety of reasons. The fear of facing uncomfortable truths drives individuals to hide reality, as it may threaten their identity, relationships, or status. Many seek personal gain through falsehoods, such as power, influence, or financial advantage, only to face long-term consequences. Deception is often justified as harmless or for the greater good, but such rationalizations erode integrity. In modern society, people are conditioned to accept deception as a norm—through marketing, politics, or social expectations—making it an ingrained part of life. However, this continuous cycle of dishonesty breeds fear, insecurity, and weakens trust in both personal relationships and societal institutions.

Living without deception requires a deep understanding of its roots—primarily fear and the need to protect one's image or desires. To live truthfully, one must first be honest with themselves, acknowledging their own fears and illusions. When one ceases to deceive internally, external deception naturally fades. Living transparently, without hidden motives or agendas, becomes possible when fear no longer controls the mind. True freedom from deception is not about forcing honesty; it is about understanding why deception exists and eliminating the need for it altogether. A mind free from illusion and self-interest operates naturally in truth, without effort, distortion, or pretense. In this clarity, there is no longer a need to deceive, as reality is seen and lived fully, just as it is.

309. Self-Deception

Self-Deception: The Mind's Trick to Avoid Seeing

Self-deception is the mind's way of distorting reality to avoid facing uncomfortable truths. It arises when thought manipulates perception to align with desired beliefs, fears, or identities, creating an illusion that protects the self from confronting its contradictions. A person caught in self-deception lives in a world of illusion, refusing to see things as they truly are, thus avoiding transformation. This distortion is often driven by the conflict between reality and desire—when the mind wants life to be a certain way, it alters perception to make it conform to those desires, preventing genuine understanding.

At its core, self-deception strengthens the ego by protecting its sense of identity. The mind creates narratives that reinforce the ideal image of 'who I am,' resisting exposure to the reality of one's true nature. This false sense of identity prevents growth and deep self-awareness. People deceive themselves to maintain psychological comfort, hiding from truths that could be unsettling or cause inner conflict. Whether through justifications, excuses, or unconscious patterns, self-deception becomes a mechanism that blocks true change and prevents real transformation.

To be free from self-deception, one must see it clearly as the mind's protective mechanism. Instead of judging or excusing one's thoughts, it is essential to observe them without reaction, allowing awareness to naturally dissolve the falsehoods. By questioning assumptions and letting go of the need for self-approval or comforting beliefs, a person can begin to see life as it is, without distortion. True freedom from self-deception arises from deep clarity and understanding, where there is no need to maintain a false image or belief. In this state of awareness, the mind moves effortlessly, free from illusion, and attuned to the truth of the present moment.

310. Mask

Mask: The Identity We Wear to Hide Ourselves

A mask is the false identity that one constructs to protect themselves, gain acceptance, or seek advantage in society. It is shaped by societal expectations, fear, and the desire to be seen in a particular way, rather than revealing the true self. The mind that relies on wearing a mask lives in deception, appearing confident or composed on the outside, while harboring insecurity or discomfort inside. This creates a sense of division between one's outward persona and inner reality, leading to constant inner conflict. Over time, the mask can become so ingrained that it begins to replace the true self, making it difficult to distinguish between what is real and what is performed.

The mask functions as a defense mechanism, shielding the individual from judgment, rejection, or criticism. This defense may seem to offer security, but it only strengthens the illusion of stability, keeping the mind disconnected from authenticity. The person may wear different masks in various social contexts—at work, at home, or with friends—adapting to fit the expectations of each situation. Fear of being seen as weak, inadequate, or different often drives the maintenance of the mask, causing anxiety and self-doubt. Over time, the mask can become so deeply integrated into the person's identity that they forget it is just a construct, leading to a life of shallow connections and a lack of true self-awareness.

Living without a mask requires seeing that the mask is not the real self. By observing the motivations behind wearing a mask— such as the desire for approval or the fear of vulnerability—one can begin to dissolve the need for pretense. The mask is reinforced by the need for social acceptance, but true strength and confidence arise from self-understanding, not from the image projected to others. Vulnerability and honesty become key to forming deeper, more genuine connections, as there is no longer a need to hide behind a facade. A life lived without a mask is one of clarity and authenticity, where the inner and outer self align, and where freedom from fear and deception allows for true living.

311. Pretending

Pretending: The Fear of Facing 'What Is'

Pretending is the act of presenting a false image, emotion, or belief either to oneself or to others. It arises from a desire to avoid facing reality, often driven by fear, insecurity, or societal conditioning. A mind caught in pretending lives in self-deception, constructing false identities that mask the truth. This creates a division between who one truly is and the image they project, leading to inner conflict. The need to pretend often stems from the fear of judgment, rejection, or not fitting in, but a mind that is clear and aware has no need for pretense.

Pretending serves as an escape from reality. People often pretend to be happy, confident, or knowledgeable in order to hide their insecurities. However, pretending does not change the truth; it only delays its recognition. This is evident in both words and actions—some pretend through exaggerated speech, while others stay silent when honesty is required. Pretending creates an inner division between what is real and what is false, causing stress, anxiety, and an inability to be fully present. This division weakens one's connection with themselves and others, reinforcing the need for masks and creating an environment of deception.

To live without pretending, one must first recognize that pretense is rooted in fear. When this fear is understood and released, the need to hide or act inauthentically diminishes. Observing one's thoughts without creating an image or self-identity helps dismantle the habit of pretending. Living honestly, without seeking approval or validation, allows true freedom to emerge. When one drops the need to control how others perceive them, pretense naturally dissolves. A free mind does not need to create false images—it exists authentically, in simplicity, and without effort. In this space, there is no struggle to fit in, just the pure expression of truth.

312. Misleading

Misleading: The Distortion That Creates Illusion and Confusion

Misleading is the act of distorting or concealing the truth, either intentionally or unconsciously, in order to influence perception. It arises from various motivations such as self-interest, ignorance, or the desire to avoid revealing uncomfortable realities. A mind caught in misleading behavior often uses manipulation, half-truths, and deception to control others, but a mind that seeks truth has no need to distort reality. Whether through words, actions, or silence, misleading creates illusions that not only misguide others but also foster division and distrust in relationships, communities, and institutions.

The nature of misleading lies in its ability to distort the truth, whether through intentional deceit or unconscious misrepresentation. Presenting only partial truths or framing information to serve a particular agenda creates a misleading narrative. Misleading relies heavily on psychological influence, manipulating emotions, fears, and desires to craft false perceptions. People may mislead either to gain power, avoid responsibility, or protect their self-image. Over time, misleading becomes a habit, normalized by societal conditioning and external pressures, where half-truths and falsehoods go unchallenged, creating a world where trust is weakened and clarity is hard to find.

To live without misleading requires understanding that deception is rooted in fear—fear of the unknown, fear of consequences, or fear of losing control. When one no longer operates from fear, the need to mislead dissolves naturally. It is essential to observe thoughts without justification, recognizing when one rationalizes dishonesty or manipulation. A truthful mind that does not cling to illusions can live with transparency, no longer influenced by hidden motives. True freedom comes from deep self-awareness and honesty, where one does not need to protect an image or distort facts. In this state, there is no need to mislead—only clarity, openness, and the natural unfolding of truth.

313. Hypocrisy

Hypocrisy: The Contradiction Between Words and Actions

Hypocrisy arises when there is a disconnection between what one claims to believe and how one actually behaves. It occurs when an individual espouses ideals or virtues but fails to align their actions with those beliefs. This contradiction creates a form of self-deception, where a person may appear virtuous on the surface while acting in ways that contradict their declared values. Hypocrisy is a deep conflict between the ideal image one projects and the reality of their behavior, leading to inner turmoil and outward dishonesty. It manifests not only on a personal level but also within larger societal, religious, and political contexts where institutions may preach values they themselves fail to uphold.

The nature of hypocrisy is grounded in the division between the ideal and reality. Many people aspire to high moral values, but their actions often fall short of these ideals, creating a gap that fuels inner conflict. This divide is often driven by the desire to maintain a favorable self-image. The mind constructs an identity based on these ideals, but when one's actions don't align with the image they project, hypocrisy emerges. Hypocrisy is also often unconscious, with individuals rationalizing their behavior and distorting their perception to avoid confronting the truth of their contradictions. The societal pressure to conform and maintain appearances further perpetuates this behavior, reinforcing the need to appear virtuous while behaving otherwise.

Breaking free from hypocrisy involves observing and understanding the patterns of self-deception that drive this behavior. The mind, conditioned to seek approval and validation, must become aware of the contradictions it creates without judgment. Instead of building an ideal self or adhering to societal expectations, one must focus on living authentically in the present moment. True integrity is not about perfection but about aligning actions with words without pretense. Observing one's behavior honestly, acting without seeking validation, and living without masks dissolves hypocrisy naturally. In this state, there is no division between beliefs and actions—just a life lived with transparency, honesty, and self-awareness.

314. Gossip

Gossip: The Mind's Escape Through the Lives of Others

Gossip is the act of discussing others, often in a critical or exaggerated manner, and it serves various psychological needs such as entertainment, social bonding, or expressing hidden emotions like jealousy and resentment. Although gossip may appear harmless, it creates unnecessary divisions, strengthens the ego, and distorts reality. Instead of addressing its own issues, the mind uses gossip as a way to temporarily elevate itself by comparing and judging others. The mind becomes distracted from self-awareness, engaging in conversations that have no meaningful impact on personal growth or understanding. Ultimately, gossip distorts relationships and promotes misunderstanding, making it a habit that hinders deeper connections with others.

The reasons people gossip are rooted in psychological desires and insecurities. The need for entertainment arises when life feels dull or repetitive, and gossip provides a temporary sense of excitement or importance. This act often strengthens the ego, as discussing others' faults or mistakes can make the speaker feel superior, more knowledgeable, or morally right. Additionally, gossip creates a false sense of social connection by bonding individuals through shared criticism. However, the underlying motive often stems from hidden jealousy or competition, especially when someone else achieves success or admiration. Instead of confronting envy, the mind seeks to diminish others by highlighting their flaws through gossip.

Breaking free from gossip involves developing self-awareness and observing the reasons behind such behavior. Once the underlying motives, such as boredom, insecurity, or the desire to feel connected, are recognized, the compulsion to gossip weakens. Speaking with awareness and responsibility means asking whether the words are true, necessary, and conducive to understanding. Real communication, rooted in meaningful ideas and insights, replaces gossip, fostering a deeper sense of connection. A mind that is aware and interested in truth no longer finds comfort in idle talk. True intelligence comes from observing oneself and speaking with clarity, intelligence, and love, without resorting to judgment or gossip.

WAKE UP

WAKE UP

17. Inner World & Consciousness

WAKE UP

315. Being

Being: The Essence Beyond Thought and Identity

Being is the natural state of existence, a state free from effort, struggle, or the desire to become something else. It is not a goal to be attained or an idea to be understood—being is simply the direct perception of what is in the present moment. A mind caught in the pursuit of becoming seeks constant change, improvement, or achievement. In contrast, a mind in being is still, aware, and whole, moving with the flow of the present without resistance or desire for more.

Being is the absence of striving. The mind, conditioned to seek progress and constantly "become" something more, struggles against the simplicity of being. There is no movement toward a future goal in true being; it is the actuality of the present. This state is not an intellectual concept; it cannot be grasped through thought or mental constructs. A mind that attempts to understand being through ideas is still caught in the trap of becoming. Being is the direct experience of the present moment, beyond the confines of time, ego, and identity. It exists only when the mind is free from the past and future—only in the here and now.

The struggle to simply be arises because of conditioning, fear, and the illusion of progress. Society, education, and religion teach us that we must constantly improve, evolve, and attain something. This conditioning creates an inner conflict, making us believe that being is insufficient. We fear emptiness and seek to fill it with achievements, experiences, and future promises. But in reality, true being is not empty; it is a state of fullness, existing without dependency. The mind that is fully present, without the need to chase experiences or outcomes, moves with clarity, intelligence, and peace. True freedom comes not from striving or seeking, but from complete acceptance of the present moment, allowing life to unfold effortlessly.

316.Unconsciousness

Unconsciousness: The Hidden Layers of Conditioning

Emptying consciousness is the natural process of freeing the mind from psychological conditioning, not through suppression or force but by allowing past experiences, attachments, and beliefs to dissolve. This emptying is not about achieving a blank state but about the ending of psychological burdens, which then creates a space for fresh awareness and clarity. A mind that is empty is not dull or lifeless; it is alive, full of intelligence, and able to perceive without distortion. True emptiness arises when there is no interference from thought, when the mind is simply aware, without clinging to past memories or future projections.

The process of emptying consciousness cannot be forced through willpower. Effort only strengthens the inner conflict and attachment to the self. Instead, it happens when one observes thought without identification or resistance, allowing the mind to quiet naturally. The self, which is a collection of memories and identifications, naturally dissolves when one realizes that it is not a permanent entity but just a construct of thought. When one lets go of psychological time—of past regrets and future expectations—there is freedom from the burden of mental clutter, and the mind becomes capable of seeing things as they are.

The challenge lies in the mind's attachment to accumulation, whether it is knowledge, experiences, or self-identity. Society encourages this accumulation by reinforcing beliefs and traditions, creating a fear of emptiness. However, true freedom lies in letting go of these attachments and allowing emptiness to happen naturally. When one stops seeking, when there is no desire to become something or achieve a particular state, consciousness empties itself effortlessly. In this emptiness, there is no void—there is only pure perception, clarity, and intelligence. The mind becomes free, and life is experienced fully, without the burden of psychological accumulation.

317. Consciousness

Consciousness: The Content That Defines the Self

Consciousness is the total movement of thought, memory, experience, desire, fear, and awareness. It encompasses everything we know and do not know, both the surface thoughts and the deeper, hidden layers of the mind. Consciousness is inseparable from its content—it is made up of everything it contains. What we think, feel, and experience is not separate from consciousness, as it includes both the conscious and subconscious realms. Thus, consciousness is constantly shaping how we perceive the world and ourselves, often without full awareness.

The structure of consciousness can be divided into different layers. The superficial consciousness is the active, thinking part of the mind that we use in daily life—it functions through memory, analysis, and learned knowledge. On the other hand, the hidden consciousness or subconscious mind holds past experiences, fears, desires, and inherited beliefs that influence our reactions and behaviors, often without our conscious awareness. Additionally, there is the collective consciousness that all humans share, shaped by common fears, desires, and cultural conditioning across time. This collective layer is shared by humanity as a whole, impacting how we experience life in a shared reality.

Consciousness is shaped by the past, which is stored as memory and influences how we respond to life. This conditioning creates limitations, preventing us from seeing reality as it truly is. Consciousness constantly divides experience, creating conflict between 'me' and 'not me,' and the movement between fear and desire traps the mind in a cycle of craving and avoidance. To go beyond consciousness, one must understand that the observer is also part of consciousness itself, not separate from it. In the dissolution of the illusion of self, there is freedom and clarity. True observation involves watching thought without identification, allowing consciousness to empty itself naturally, bringing the possibility of touching something beyond thought, time, and limitation.

318. Emptying Consciousness

Emptying Consciousness: The Dissolution of the Past

Emptying consciousness is the natural process of freeing the mind from psychological conditioning, not through suppression or force but by allowing past experiences, attachments, and beliefs to dissolve. This emptying is not about achieving a blank state but about the ending of psychological burdens, which then creates a space for fresh awareness and clarity. A mind that is empty is not dull or lifeless; it is alive, full of intelligence, and able to perceive without distortion. True emptiness arises when there is no interference from thought, when the mind is simply aware, without clinging to past memories or future projections.

The process of emptying consciousness cannot be forced through willpower. Effort only strengthens the inner conflict and attachment to the self. Instead, it happens when one observes thought without identification or resistance, allowing the mind to quiet naturally. The self, which is a collection of memories and identifications, naturally dissolves when one realizes that it is not a permanent entity but just a construct of thought. When one lets go of psychological time—of past regrets and future expectations—there is freedom from the burden of mental clutter, and the mind becomes capable of seeing things as they are.

The challenge lies in the mind's attachment to accumulation, whether it is knowledge, experiences, or self-identity. Society encourages this accumulation by reinforcing beliefs and traditions, creating a fear of emptiness. However, true freedom lies in letting go of these attachments and allowing emptiness to happen naturally. When one stops seeking, when there is no desire to become something or achieve a particular state, consciousness empties itself effortlessly. In this emptiness, there is no void—there is only pure perception, clarity, and intelligence. The mind becomes free, and life is experienced fully, without the burden of psychological accumulation.

319. Emptiness

Emptiness: The Space Where True Seeing Begins

Emptiness is often misunderstood as a feeling of lack or meaninglessness, but it is actually the space where true freedom begins. It is the state where the mind is not consumed by thought, desire, or identity, and is free from the clutter of the self. While the ego fears emptiness because it threatens the continuity of its identity, true emptiness is not a void—it is the absence of psychological attachment, allowing clarity and deep awareness to emerge. The fear of emptiness arises from the mind's tendency to seek constant occupation and distraction, and from the ego's attachment to its own survival. Yet, in reality, emptiness is not a loss—it is a state of wholeness and freedom.

The nature of true emptiness is the absence of psychological clutter and attachment. It is not loneliness or a feeling of lacking something, but rather a state of pure awareness, free from the burdens of memory, desire, and ego. This absence of attachment creates an open space in which truth can be perceived without distortion. Emptiness is not to be filled or avoided—it is to be understood and embraced. When one stops trying to escape it or fill it with external distractions, the depth of emptiness reveals itself as a source of clarity and freedom. This understanding dissolves the illusion that emptiness is something negative and allows for the experience of life without psychological resistance.

Living in emptiness without fear requires letting go of attachments and the need for external validation. The mind conditioned by society to seek constant purpose, activity, and fulfillment finds it difficult to embrace stillness. However, true emptiness does not require the mind to seek a "state" or experience—it simply arises when the psychological burden is dropped. In this state, there is no fear, no desire to possess, and no struggle to attain. Instead, there is a profound sense of presence, clarity, and freedom, allowing life to unfold naturally. Far from being an absence, emptiness is a profound fullness, offering a clear perception of reality as it is—free from conflict and limitation.

320. Fragmentation

Fragmentation: The Division That Creates Conflict

Fragmentation is the division within the mind that separates thought, action, and perception into conflicting parts, creating psychological struggle. This division occurs when the mind distinguishes between self and others, desire and reality, and the past and the future. A fragmented mind constantly battles internal contradictions, confusion, and an endless cycle of psychological conflict. Thought, by nature, divides reality into concepts and categories, generating an illusion of separation. In fact, life is undivided, but the mind's tendency to compartmentalize leads to division, both within the self and in relationships with the world.

The consequences of fragmentation are far-reaching, not only causing inner conflict but also deepening fear and insecurity. Fragmentation strengthens the ego by creating psychological boundaries between people, groups, and ideas. When the mind perceives itself as separate from others, it fosters fear, comparison, and competition, which in turn further divides individuals and societies. The mind's conditioned habit of thinking in opposites, reinforced by societal values, contributes to a sense of separation. This false sense of division leads to unnecessary struggles and emotional turmoil, preventing real understanding or connection with others and the world around us.

To move beyond fragmentation, one must observe it without trying to escape or control it. True wholeness cannot be achieved through effort or mental analysis—it arises when the mind is free from labels, categories, and identification with past experiences. The mind must be present, attentive, and open to life as it is, not as it is perceived through the lens of thought. When one recognizes that fragmentation is an illusion, the mind becomes naturally whole, free from psychological borders and inner conflict. In this state of pure awareness, the mind flows effortlessly, in harmony with life, without division, without contradiction, and without effort.

321. Psyche

Psyche: The Inner Landscape of Thought and Emotion

The psyche is the total movement of thought, memory, emotion, and identity—the psychological structure that forms the 'self.' It is shaped by past experiences, fears, desires, beliefs, and conditioning. Over time, this accumulation of experiences builds the sense of 'I,' the center from which we perceive and react to life. However, is the psyche truly a fixed, independent entity, or is it just a series of conditioned responses? The answer lies in observing how the mind operates within the limits of this psychological structure, which constantly reinforces its own existence through thought and identity.

The psyche is formed through memory and experience, each moment leaving a mark that shapes our reactions, thoughts, and feelings. From birth, society and culture condition us to adopt specific beliefs, roles, and identities, which further solidify the ego. These external influences continue to shape how we see the world and ourselves, often without our conscious awareness. The psyche also creates psychological time, perpetuating a movement between the past, present, and future—always striving for improvement, security, or escape. This cycle of comparison and conflict sustains the psyche, but it often creates suffering, as we become attached to an image of self that is constantly at odds with reality.

True freedom from the psyche comes when we understand that the 'self' is merely a construct of thought, not a fixed reality. By observing our emotions, thoughts, and fears without identifying with them, we can begin to dissolve the illusion of the separate self. Letting go of the desire for psychological continuity, and the need to preserve an image of who we are, allows the mind to experience pure awareness—free from the burden of past conditioning. In this state, there is no struggle or conflict, only an intelligence that transcends thought, time, and the limitations of the psyche. When the psyche dissolves, we are left with a deeper, unconditioned awareness that is vast, silent, and immeasurable.

322. Known

Known: The Prison of Past Experience

The known is everything stored in memory—our experiences, beliefs, knowledge, conditioning, and past impressions. It includes facts, traditions, science, language, and personal identity. The mind operates primarily within the field of the known, continuously referencing memory to interpret reality. This reliance on the known provides psychological security, as it offers stability, familiarity, and a sense of control. The mind clings to beliefs, routines, and identities because they reduce the unpredictable nature of life, providing the comfort of certainty. However, this attachment to the known can create conflict, as it often limits perception and hinders true understanding of the present moment.

The unknown, on the other hand, encompasses everything that cannot be grasped by thought, memory, or experience. It is not a mystery to be solved or a distant future event, but rather exists beyond the limitations of the mind. Truth, love, beauty, and deep insight reside in the unknown because they cannot be captured by knowledge or thought. We fear the unknown because it cannot be controlled, defined, or predicted. To the mind, this uncertainty feels threatening, so we create beliefs, ideologies, and philosophies to structure the unknown and make it more manageable. But the unknown is not confined to time—it is present when thought is silent and the mind is free of past conditioning.

To enter the unknown, one must let go of attachment to the past, identity, and beliefs, living each moment as entirely fresh. Observing life without the filter of the known—without labeling, comparing, or interpreting through past experiences—opens the mind to direct contact with the unknown. True intelligence arises when thought recognizes its own limitations and quiets. The unknown is not something to be discovered in the future, but is found when the mind is fully present in the now. A mind free from the burden of psychological time, silent and aware, naturally moves into the unknown, where truth and love are revealed in their purest form.

323. Knowing

Knowing: The Movement That Prevents Discovery

Knowing is the accumulation of experience, facts, and conclusions that are stored in memory, helping us navigate daily life and make practical decisions. It is essential for learning skills, language, and understanding the world around us. However, psychological knowing becomes a limitation when it prevents fresh perception and reinforces existing conditioning. The mind that clings to what it knows is unable to approach new experiences with clarity, constantly filtering them through past knowledge, which distorts the true essence of reality.

The nature of knowing is that it is always tied to the past. Knowledge is based on what has already been learned, experienced, or remembered, meaning it can never fully embrace the new. This creates an illusion of psychological security, where the mind believes that knowing something brings control over life. Yet, life is constantly changing, and clinging to past knowledge only hinders the ability to perceive the present as it is. When the mind identifies with its knowledge, it becomes trapped in repetition, reinforcing the illusion of the 'self' and limiting true intelligence, which arises from perceiving without distortion.

To live without the burden of knowing, one must recognize that all knowing is incomplete and bound by the past. The key to freedom is not in accumulating more knowledge, but in observing the present without judgment or attachment to what has been known. Letting go of psychological dependence on knowledge allows the mind to move freely, unconditioned by past conclusions. Real truth is not found in knowledge—it is revealed when the mind is silent and fully aware in the present. A mind free from the burden of knowing experiences deep clarity, intelligence, and an openness to the vastness of perception.

324. Insight

Insight: The Light That Shatters Illusion

Insight is a sudden, direct understanding of reality, arising not from logic, analysis, or accumulated knowledge but from a state of complete mental stillness. It is a perception without distortion, and it has the power to transform consciousness instantly and without effort. True insight is not intellectual; it goes beyond thought, allowing the mind to directly perceive the truth without interference from past experiences or conditioning. Unlike intellectual conclusions that build over time, insight arises in a moment of clarity, allowing falsehoods to dissolve naturally as soon as they are seen for what they are.

Insight is immediate and instantaneous, not gradual. It cannot be achieved through practice or effort, but rather arises when struggle ends, and the mind is free from distraction. It is beyond the limits of thought, knowledge, and memory, and it brings clarity without the need for discipline or control. When one truly understands something deeply, like fear or attachment, the transformation is effortless—insight itself brings resolution. This sudden illumination is akin to turning on a light in a dark room, instantly dispelling confusion and revealing truth in its pure form.

To live with insight, one must be free from psychological accumulation, such as beliefs, judgments, and conclusions, which cloud direct perception. A mind that is burdened by past experiences cannot see clearly. Insight occurs when one is fully present in the moment, observing without expectation, seeking nothing, and allowing the truth to be seen instantly. It is not something that can be gained from external sources like teachers or books but arises within, through deep self-awareness. In this state, there is no struggle, only the pure light of understanding, transforming how one interacts with life and reality itself.

325. Wholeness

Wholeness: The Mind That Is Free of Division

Wholeness is the state of being where life is not divided into conflicting parts, and it is the natural condition of a mind free from contradiction. It is not an ideal to strive for, but a realization of the mind's true nature. A whole mind does not compartmentalize its life into categories like work, relationships, emotions, or spirituality—it sees life as a unified movement. Wholeness arises when there is no internal conflict, when the mind does not desire one thing while resisting another. The mind becomes complete when it aligns with what is, rather than opposing it.

The nature of wholeness lies in the absence of inner division. Most people live in contradiction, torn between desires and fears, aspirations and doubts. When there is no conflict between 'what is' and 'what should be,' the mind is whole. Wholeness is not merely an idea—it is the reality that comes from direct observation. Thought, being fragmented, cannot perceive the whole, and thus, a fragmented mind seeks unity through ideals, while true wholeness transcends thought. Wholeness also marks the end of psychological conflict, where there is no ambition, fear, or comparison, and the mind is free to observe without suppression or control.

Living in wholeness involves observing fragmentation without attempting to fix it. The more one tries to force wholeness, the more fragmented the mind becomes. Wholeness comes from letting go of psychological divisions—such as national, religious, or personal identities—and seeing humanity as one. A mind that no longer identifies with division becomes whole. Being completely present in every action, free from distraction, further deepens the experience of wholeness. It is not about achieving perfection, but about facing life without the division between the thinker and the thought. In this state, one lives without fear, conflict, or division, moving with complete awareness of life as it is.

326. Immeasurable

Immeasurable: That Which Thought Cannot Contain

The immeasurable is that which transcends all attempts at definition, comparison, or measurement. It cannot be contained within the framework of knowledge, nor can it be captured by thought or language. Thought operates within limits, analyzing and categorizing, but the immeasurable exists outside those boundaries, beyond time and mental constructs. This vastness cannot be grasped by the intellect, as it lies beyond the reach of conventional understanding. In the attempt to define or measure the immeasurable, we only limit its true nature, reducing it to something finite when it is inherently boundless.

The mind's instinctive desire to measure the immeasurable stems from a need for security and control. We seek to contain the unknown within the familiar, attempting to fit it into predefined ideas. Society and education reinforce this tendency, teaching us that knowledge equals truth, but the immeasurable cannot be understood through accumulation or intellectual effort. The ego, seeking to possess and experience the infinite, believes it can attain the immeasurable through effort. However, true perception of the immeasurable only arises when the striving ceases, and the mind is allowed to be still, free from the compulsion to define or grasp.

To perceive the immeasurable, one must abandon the need for measurement, comparison, or progress. The search for knowledge, spiritual growth, or understanding through the measurable only obscures the immeasurable, for it cannot be attained through effort or conceptualization. True perception arises in silence, where the mind is completely free from the distortion of thought. In this state, there is no self to measure or experience—only direct awareness of what is, beyond all division and limitation. The immeasurable exists naturally in this presence, untainted by the ego's desire to possess or control.

327. Aloneness

Aloneness: The State of Being Without Isolation

Aloneness is not to be confused with loneliness; it is the state of being whole within oneself, independent of external validation or psychological dependence. Unlike loneliness, which arises from a feeling of incompleteness and the desire for connection, aloneness is the freedom to be content and at peace with oneself. It is a state of inner fulfillment, where the mind is free from attachment and distraction. True aloneness allows the mind to be fully still and aware, experiencing life without the need for constant external engagement or fulfillment. In aloneness, there is no struggle or fear of emptiness, only a deep sense of presence and clarity.

Loneliness is rooted in dependence on others, seeking fulfillment outside of oneself, whereas aloneness is the embodiment of freedom from these needs. Loneliness is often an escape from facing one's true self, with the mind seeking distractions through relationships, entertainment, or ideologies. In contrast, aloneness is about facing oneself fully, without avoidance, and finding peace in the process. The fear that often accompanies loneliness stems from the discomfort of being with oneself, but in aloneness, the mind is free from this conflict, allowing for clarity, silence, and true understanding. The beauty of aloneness lies in its ability to bring deep inner peace, a state where the mind is not plagued by the need for approval or connection but is free to observe and experience reality as it is.

Living in a state of aloneness requires letting go of attachments and psychological dependencies. It is not about isolating oneself from the world, but rather being completely present without seeking external fulfillment. By observing oneself without reaction and embracing the silence of the mind, one can experience the intelligence, creativity, and love that arise from true aloneness. The ability to be alone without fear opens the door to self-discovery and profound understanding. Aloneness, therefore, is not about being isolated from others but about finding completeness within, without reliance on external sources for happiness. When one is free from the need for approval or attachment, the mind is able to experience life in its fullness, without distortion or dependence.

328. Self

Self: The Construct That Separates and Confines

The self is the image we have of ourselves, shaped by our thoughts, memories, and experiences. It is constructed from our beliefs, fears, desires, social identity, and attachments. We tend to think of the self as a permanent and individual entity, but upon closer inspection, we must ask: is the self truly real, or is it simply an illusion created by the mind? This image of the self is constantly influenced by our past and the expectations we have of our future, but in reality, the self is a fleeting construct, changing with every thought, perception, and experience.

The self is created and maintained through memory and identification. We define ourselves based on what we remember—our successes, failures, identities, and labels. Society further reinforces this construct by encouraging comparisons, creating a sense of ambition, competition, and jealousy. These comparisons divide us, making us feel superior or inferior to others. Additionally, the self thrives on attachment—whether to people, beliefs, possessions, or achievements. When these attachments are threatened, fear and suffering naturally follow. The movement of the self, caught between what was, what is, and what should be, is responsible for much of our inner conflict, as we constantly chase stability in a world that is inherently impermanent.

To be free from the self, one must first recognize that it is an illusion. The self is not a fixed entity but a collection of thoughts and conditioning. Once we observe the self without identifying with it, we begin to see its true nature and the illusion dissolves. Letting go of attachment to identity and seeking psychological security can lead to deep inner freedom. When the self is no longer dominant, there is no division or conflict—only pure awareness, love, and intelligence. A life free from the self is not one of emptiness but one of connection, wholeness, and a profound understanding of life as it truly is. Freedom from the self arises not by suppression but by seeing it clearly, and in that clarity, transformation happens naturally.

329. Self-Knowledge

Self-Knowledge: Understanding Without Accumulation

Self-knowledge is not about accumulating intellectual concepts or psychological theories regarding oneself. It is about observing oneself directly—seeing one's thoughts, emotions, desires, fears, and conditioning in action during everyday life. True self-knowledge is not a fixed understanding, but rather a continuous unfolding of awareness. It requires the ability to observe oneself without judgment or distortion, seeing oneself as one truly is, without clinging to an idealized version of the self. In this process, one becomes more attuned to their real nature, not defined by external labels or societal expectations.

Without self-knowledge, a person falls prey to self-deception, creating false images of who they are. These illusions—believing oneself to be kind, intelligent, or spiritual—serve to hide the contradictions and limitations inherent in one's psyche. The lack of self-awareness creates inner conflict and makes freedom impossible, as the mind remains controlled by unconscious fears, desires, and societal conditioning. True freedom, however, is found in the complete understanding of oneself, where the boundaries created by the self dissolve, leaving a mind that is clear, open, and unburdened by illusion.

The journey toward self-knowledge is not about analyzing the past or accumulating knowledge, but about being fully present with oneself in the moment. It is not about changing or improving, but about seeing clearly, without judgment or justification. The effort to change or improve oneself is just another form of the 'self' trying to assert control, but transformation occurs naturally when one deeply understands the truth of their being. A mind that is constantly observing itself, asking questions, and remaining open to its own discoveries is alive, awake, and free. This freedom comes not in some future event, but in the present, when one sees themselves clearly and without distortion.

330. Self-Image

Self-Image: The Identity Built by Thought

Self-image is the mental construct that individuals create about themselves, shaped by past experiences, opinions, and societal conditioning. It is formed through thought, sustained by memory, and reinforced through comparison with others. A mind caught in self-image becomes preoccupied with protecting, enhancing, or defending this constructed identity, leading to both internal and external conflict. Self-image is a fluid mental concept, changing with circumstances, yet individuals often cling to it as though it were permanent, creating a false sense of self that hinders genuine self-understanding.

The nature of self-image is such that it is a mental construct, not grounded in reality. Thought creates an identity based on external validation and past experiences, but this identity is constantly changing. The more the self-image is tied to comparison with others, the stronger the competition, insecurity, and psychological struggle. Praise and approval reinforce the self-image, while criticism threatens it, leaving the person vulnerable to fluctuating self-esteem. This attachment to a fixed self-image creates a gap between the "actual" self and the "ideal" self, creating constant tension and internal conflict. The fear of judgment and failure further exacerbates the problem, as the individual becomes defensive and anxious to protect their identity.

To be free from self-image, one must see that it is merely a collection of thoughts and ideas, not a true representation of the self. By observing thought without defending or enhancing the self, the mind can begin to detach from the illusions of self-image. Letting go of psychological comparison and labels allows the mind to move freely, unburdened by insecurities or false identities. True freedom comes not from building a better self-image but from recognizing that all self-images are illusions. When one acts without reference to "who I am," action becomes natural, effortless, and aligned with clarity and intelligence. In this state of freedom, the mind is free from fear, judgment, and attachment, simply living in the truth of the present.

331. Ego

Ego: The Illusion of a Separate Center

The ego is the sense of "I"—the psychological identity created by thought, memory, and experience. It is the idea that we are separate from others, from life, from the world. The ego exists through identification with name, nationality, religion, beliefs, status, possessions, and achievements. The mind remembers past experiences and builds an image of itself, which becomes the 'self'—a collection of memories, successes, failures, and desires. Society conditions us to compare ourselves with others, creating pride when we feel superior and suffering when we feel inferior. We cling to relationships, beliefs, and possessions, fearing their loss, and while attachment gives the illusion of stability, it also creates fear and suffering. Thought projects itself into the future through desire and ambition or into the past through regret and attachment, keeping the 'I' alive in psychological time.

The ego is the source of conflict, for the moment there is an 'I', there is the 'other'—this division creates competition, jealousy, war, and separation. Every personal, political, and religious conflict is rooted in the ego's desire to assert itself over others. The ego seeks permanence in an impermanent world, fearing loss, failure, rejection, and death, because it is always seeking security in what is unstable. It is never satisfied—it always wants more knowledge, more status, more validation, preventing real peace and inner stillness. The ego sees only through its own desires and fears, never reality as it is, distorting perception. Can one see clearly when looking through the filter of 'me' and 'mine'?

If the ego is just a bundle of thoughts and memories, is it real? When one deeply sees that the ego is only an image created by thought, its hold weakens naturally. Do not fight the ego or suppress it—watch how it moves, how it reacts, how it seeks validation. This awareness itself is the beginning of freedom. The observer—the one who says, "I must change, I must be better"—is itself the ego. When one realizes that the observer is not separate from thought, duality ends, and the mind is silent. If the ego exists through attachments, can one live without clinging to identity, belief, or security? A mind that lets go of all psychological possessions is completely free. The ego is not a real entity—it is the movement of thought, memory, and attachment. It creates division, fear, and endless struggle, preventing real understanding. Freedom from the ego is not through suppression, but through deep awareness—seeing its illusion, not identifying with it, and living without attachment.

When the ego is absent, there is only silence, clarity, and a deep sense of oneness with life.

332. Self-Interest

Self-Interest: The Root of Division and Isolation

Self-interest is the pursuit of personal gain, driven by the need for security, recognition, and fulfillment. It operates from a place of desire and fear, often disregarding the needs of others. When a mind is caught in self-interest, it acts from attachment to possessions, status, or relationships, always seeking to secure or enhance itself. This focus on "me" and "mine" creates division, both internally and externally, leading to competition, jealousy, and exploitation. While self-interest often masquerades as morality or compassion, it is, in reality, a subtle form of manipulation, where actions are motivated by personal benefit rather than true concern for others.

The nature of self-interest is rooted in psychological insecurity, with individuals seeking stability through material possessions, beliefs, or identities. Society glorifies ambition, success, and personal achievement, conditioning people to prioritize self-interest as a natural response to life. This creates a cycle of fear—fear of losing what one has, fear of being left behind. People justify self-interest through the desire to gain more—whether through wealth, status, or influence—often confusing self-interest with intelligence. However, true intelligence is not about personal gain; it is the ability to see clearly without distortion or selfish motives.

Living without self-interest is possible only when one sees that it does not provide true security. No amount of wealth, status, or power guarantees inner peace. A mind free from self-interest observes its impulses without justifying them, letting go of the fear that drives ambition. True freedom comes from acting without seeking personal gain or benefit. Such action, devoid of fear and calculation, is spontaneous, pure, and effortless. A free mind lives with clarity, love, and intelligence, understanding that no external pursuit of self-interest brings lasting fulfillment. In this state, self-interest dissolves naturally, as there is no longer a self to serve—only life unfolding with wholeness, without division.

333. Self-Centeredness

Self-Centeredness: The Limited View That Creates Suffering

Self-centeredness is the state in which the mind is continuously focused on its own desires, fears, and ambitions, viewing everything in terms of "me" and "mine." This state arises from deep conditioning and the need for security, leading to a fragmented sense of self. A mind that is self-centered is often driven by the need for validation and recognition, making it isolated and detached from true connection with others. Instead of seeing the world as interconnected, the self-centered mind views others as separate, leading to division, competition, and conflict.

The root of self-centeredness lies in the mind's attachment to its identity, formed by past experiences, beliefs, and memories. The self becomes an illusion, sustained by thought, which creates constant dissatisfaction and a desire for more. When the self is the focal point of life, every disappointment is personalized, and the pursuit of pleasure becomes endless. This craving for recognition further fuels insecurity, while the ego's attachment to control creates fear and anxiety. The more one seeks approval and validation, the more they are trapped in the illusion of separateness and self-importance.

To be free from self-centeredness, one must observe the mind without identifying with the "self." The key lies in recognizing that the "self" is a creation of thought, rather than a fixed, permanent entity. As one understands this truth, the grip of self-centeredness naturally fades. Freedom from the ego comes from letting go of the need for recognition, approval, and validation, and acting without self-interest. When one lives without the illusion of separation, the mind moves freely, without division or isolation. In this freedom, compassion, awareness, and connection with life flow effortlessly, allowing one to experience a life unburdened by the ego.

334. Self-Realization

Self-Realization: The Freedom from the Illusion of Self

Self-realization is the direct insight into one's true nature, beyond the identification with thought, identity, and personal conditioning. It arises when the mind sees through its own illusions, recognizing that the concept of the 'self' is a creation of thought, and thus, an illusion. In this realization, the mind is freed from psychological conflict. True self-realization is not about becoming or improving the self—it is the dissolution of the false self, a realization that goes beyond concepts, experiences, or the ego. It is an immediate, effortless seeing, where there is no separation between the observer and the observed, and all division ceases.

The nature of self-realization is rooted in the understanding that the 'self' is not something to be perfected or attained. It is a mental construct sustained by memory, experiences, and conditioning. Once the mind sees this clearly, the illusion of the self naturally dissolves. True realization is not a mystical experience or a goal to be achieved—it is an immediate perception of what is. There is no need for effort or time; insight comes naturally when the mind is still, free from seeking and attachment. Realization does not add anything to the mind—it is simply the removal of illusion and the recognition of what already is.

Many struggle with self-realization because they view it as a process of improvement or a distant goal to achieve. The ego, which is conditioned to see itself as a separate entity, fears its own dissolution. This fear prevents true understanding and keeps the mind trapped in illusion. The key to self-realization is not seeking or striving, but observing the self without identification. When the mind is fully present, free from psychological time and the need for validation, the illusion of self fades naturally. True freedom arises when there is no longer a need to become something, but simply to be, fully and completely, without effort, division, or illusion.

WAKE UP

WAKE UP

18. Attention & Awareness

WAKE UP

335. Attention

Attention: The Act of Seeing Without Distortion

Attention is the state of complete awareness, where the mind is fully present without distraction. Unlike concentration, which involves focusing on a single object while excluding everything else, attention is inclusive—it encompasses everything without division or preference. True attention is effortless; it arises naturally when the mind is relaxed, yet fully alert. In this state, there is no force or tension, only a flow of awareness that perceives the world without judgment, resistance, or the need for control. Attention is a holistic experience, where everything is noticed as it is, without the interference of thought.

The nature of true attention is that it exists in the present moment, free from the past and future. When the mind is attentive, there is no memory distorting the experience, and no anticipation clouding perception. Attention does not create a division between the observer and the observed; it is a state where the 'I' dissolves and there is only the experience itself. This pure attention allows for deep connection and understanding, as there is no inner conflict between 'what is' and 'what should be.' In the state of total attention, life is experienced fully and without distortion, leading to clarity and intelligence.

We often lose attention through distraction, effort, or psychological noise. Thought tends to pull us away, either by dwelling on the past or projecting into the future, and this creates mental clutter. Effort and control also disrupt attention, as they create inner conflict. To cultivate attention, one must observe without judgment, be fully present in every action, and drop psychological time—releasing the mind from the constraints of past regrets and future anxieties. True attention requires the experience to be free from the observer's judgment, allowing life to be seen clearly and fully. In this state, there is no conflict, only pure awareness.

336. Attention and Inattention

Attention and Inattention: The Movement Between Clarity and Confusion

Attention is the natural state of awareness where the mind is fully present and alive, without effort or division. Unlike concentration, which requires focus on a single object while excluding others, attention encompasses everything around and within us. True attention is choiceless and open—it does not limit itself to an object but instead remains aware of the entire experience. In this state, the mind connects deeply with the present moment, observing life without judgment or interference, allowing for clarity, insight, and understanding. This openness allows one to experience life fully and freely, without the distractions that often cloud perception.

Inattention, on the other hand, is the wandering of the mind— driven by thought, habit, and conditioning. It manifests as distraction, forgetfulness, or a mechanical way of going through the motions without truly experiencing the present moment. Inattention occurs when the mind is lost in memory, expectation, or worry, preventing true perception and connection with the now. It often arises from the habitual movement of thought between past regrets and future anxieties, pulling the mind away from the immediacy of life. This mental distraction drains energy, creating inner conflict, confusion, and missed opportunities for understanding.

The key to moving from inattention to attention lies in observing the mind without judgment or resistance. By recognizing when the mind is distracted, one can begin to shift towards full awareness. Attention is not something that can be forced—it naturally arises when the mind is free from resistance and external distractions. Living with awareness in every action, whether walking, talking, or working, brings clarity, energy, and a deeper connection to life. True attention is not just for special moments of reflection, but for every moment of existence, enabling a fuller, richer experience of reality without the burden of inattention.

337. Awareness

Awareness: The Light That Dispels Illusion

Awareness is the natural state of a mind that is completely present, observing without judgment or interference from thought. It is not about effort, concentration, or technique—it is simply the act of seeing reality as it is, without trying to alter or escape it. True awareness happens when the mind is silent, free from distraction, and open to the present moment. In this state, one perceives life without distortion, as there is no need to add interpretation, comparison, or labeling. Awareness is a pure and immediate perception of what is, without any judgment or preconceived notions.

The rarity of awareness stems from the constant movement of thought, which pulls attention away from the present moment. The mind is often preoccupied with the past or the future, leaving little space for direct perception of the now. Our cultural conditioning and personal beliefs shape the way we view the world, causing us to see things through a biased lens. Furthermore, fear and desire cloud our awareness, making it difficult to observe things as they truly are. Instead of directly experiencing life, we often name, analyze, or compare, thereby losing touch with the richness of the present moment.

True awareness brings an end to inner conflict, as it dissolves the gap between 'what is' and 'what should be.' In this state, there is no division between the observer and the observed—awareness simply is, without the interference of thought. It is through this pure awareness that psychological suffering ends, as it allows for the complete understanding of pain and emotions. A mind that is fully aware responds intelligently and immediately, acting from clarity rather than conditioning. Awareness is not a practice or a goal to achieve but a state that arises naturally when the mind is free from past accumulation, resistance, and psychological burdens.

338. Choiceless Awareness

Choiceless Awareness: Perceiving Without Preference or Judgment

Choiceless awareness is the ability to observe life without judgment, preference, or interference from thought. It is not achieved through effort or willpower but arises naturally when the mind is fully present and free from conditioning. In choiceless awareness, the observer and the observed become one—there is no separation, just pure seeing. This state allows one to witness thoughts, emotions, and experiences as they are, without imposing any labels or judgments, revealing the true nature of things as they unfold in the present moment.

In contrast, ordinary awareness is based on selection—it focuses on what we like or feel comfortable with and avoids discomfort or unpleasantness. This selective perception is influenced by desire, fear, and past experiences, leading to fragmented observation. Choiceless awareness, however, sees everything equally, without resistance or preference, and exists beyond the limits of time. It does not judge or label experiences as good or bad but simply observes them as they are, allowing for a deeper, more holistic understanding of life without the filters of personal biases or conditioning.

Living with choiceless awareness involves being fully present, observing thoughts and emotions without reaction, and letting go of the need to control or shape experiences. It requires dropping the attachment to the self and recognizing that thoughts and emotions are simply passing movements—not the essence of who we are. By observing life in this way, without seeking any particular experience, the mind becomes naturally clear, peaceful, and free. Choiceless awareness opens the door to a life of deep intelligence and understanding, where there is no conflict, only clarity and direct insight into the truth of existence.

339. Silence

Silence: The Space Where Truth Reveals Itself

Silence is not merely the absence of sound; it is the stillness of the mind, unburdened by conflict or endless thought. It is a natural state that arises when the mind is deeply attentive and free from distractions. True silence is full of awareness and clarity, not emptiness. It is in this state that deep intelligence and understanding can be found. The mind's rare ability to be silent is often hindered by the constant movement of thought—always analyzing, comparing, and projecting. This non-stop mental activity prevents the stillness needed for direct perception, leaving no space for the mind to rest and observe reality as it is.

The mind also fears silence because it fears the loss of the 'self.' The ego thrives on thought and mental activity, and when thought ceases, it feels as though the self ceases to exist. This fear creates a barrier to true silence, as the mind clings to thoughts and identities to maintain its sense of self. Additionally, our dependence on external stimulation, such as entertainment or social interactions, makes silence uncomfortable. It forces us to face ourselves, and often, we avoid this by filling our lives with distractions. Many try to achieve silence through meditation or isolation, but true silence cannot be forced—it happens naturally when the mind is fully present and free from resistance.

True silence is the absence of psychological time—when thought is not preoccupied with past memories or future desires. In this space, the mind perceives reality without distortion, allowing truth to be seen, felt, and understood directly. Silence brings deep love and intelligence because, in its stillness, there is no division between the observer and the observed. There is no self to interfere with perception; only pure awareness remains. One can come upon silence naturally by observing thought without trying to control it, living fully in the present moment, and letting go of psychological burdens. Silence is not something to achieve but is revealed when thought ceases to dominate. In this silence, there is freedom, clarity, and the profound beauty of existence.

340. Mindfulness

Mindfulness: The Art of Being Fully Present Without Effort

Mindfulness is the state of complete awareness, where the mind is fully attentive to the present moment without distraction. It arises when thought does not wander into the past or future but remains with what is happening now. A mind caught in mindfulness as a practice tries to achieve presence, while a mind that understands deeply is effortlessly aware. Many think mindfulness is about forcing the mind to focus, yet true mindfulness is effortless—it happens when there is no distraction by thought. The restless mind jumps between memories, worries, and expectations, but when one simply observes without interference, mindfulness arises naturally. The mind moves between past regret and future anxiety, missing the present, yet true mindfulness exists only now—where thought does not divide time.

Society teaches people to rely on memory, planning, and projection, keeping them trapped in thought rather than in direct awareness. Many try to 'train' the mind, yet effort only creates tension, for a free mind does not need control—it simply observes without resistance. People attempt to 'stay present,' believing mindfulness requires effort, yet when one stops trying, presence happens naturally. The mind is filled with endless thoughts, emotions, and desires, yet true mindfulness exists when one sees this noise without being controlled by it. Many think mindfulness is something to attain, but real awareness is not a goal—it is the natural state of a mind free from conflict. The more one tries to 'be mindful,' the more tension arises, yet true mindfulness happens when effort ceases.

Awareness is always present—it is thought that clouds it. When one stops interfering, mindfulness is already there. A mindful mind does not force itself to be present—it watches thought as it is, and when there is no reaction, awareness is naturally sharp. Mindfulness is not about controlling thought, but about not being caught in it, for a free mind does not live in 'before' or 'later'—it simply is. When one is fully aware, there is no need to remind oneself to be mindful. True presence is not a technique—it is the effortless unfolding of attention. Mindfulness is not a practice, a skill, or an achievement—it is the natural state of a mind fully present, free from distraction and psychological time. Many struggle with mindfulness because they try to force presence, seek techniques, or attach it to effort, yet true mindfulness is not in trying—it is in letting go. A mind free from effort, control, and inner struggle does not need to 'practice' mindfulness—it simply exists, perceives, and moves in deep awareness. In this freedom, mindfulness is no longer something to attain—it is the natural clarity of a mind that is completely present, alive, and untouched by the noise of thought.

19. Freedom & Liberation

WAKE UP

341. Choice

Choice: The Illusion of Freedom in Decision-Making

Choice is commonly regarded as a symbol of freedom, the act of selecting between various options. However, it often arises from uncertainty, where the mind is divided between desires, fears, and past influences. A mind caught in the act of choosing believes it is free, but in reality, it is merely operating within the limits of conditioning. True freedom lies in clarity, where the need for choice vanishes and action flows naturally without hesitation. The act of choosing creates inner conflict, as the mind struggles to weigh options, which ultimately prevents direct perception and wastes energy.

The nature of choice is rooted in confusion. When clarity is present, there is no need to deliberate—the right action is immediate. The mind only engages in choice when it is uncertain, unsure of what to do. This confusion is often influenced by past conditioning—memory, experiences, and societal influences shape every decision we make. The ego thrives on the illusion of control, feeling empowered when it makes a choice, but this control is merely a product of past influences, not true freedom. The desire to make the "right" choice further intensifies the illusion, leading to hesitation and mental paralysis.

Living without choice comes when the mind is no longer trapped in the cycle of comparison and judgment. When one fully understands a situation, there is no need to choose—the right action emerges effortlessly. This freedom from choice is not the absence of action, but the presence of total awareness. A mind that is free from psychological dependence on choice moves with clarity, without the burden of decision-making. True freedom is not in selecting options, but in seeing things clearly, beyond the limitations of thought and conditioning, where intelligence and action merge seamlessly into a natural flow.

342. Detachment

Detachment: Letting Go Without Indifference

Detachment is the state of freedom from psychological dependence on people, possessions, emotions, or outcomes. It arises naturally when one deeply understands the nature of attachment and how it leads to suffering, fear, and illusion. While many mistakenly believe that detachment is about emotional numbness or suppression, true detachment is not the rejection of life—it is the ability to engage fully with life without clinging to any aspect of it. The mind that practices detachment as an effort can create internal conflict, but when detachment arises from insight, it is effortless and natural. True detachment brings freedom from psychological time, allowing one to live in the present without regret or anticipation.

One of the key aspects of detachment is that it is not indifference or emotional withdrawal. True detachment is the absence of psychological possession—recognizing that nothing is truly "mine." It involves seeing life without the distortion of desire or fear, allowing us to observe things as they are, rather than how we wish them to be. Detachment does not involve suppressing emotions; rather, it arises naturally when we see the root causes of attachment. The mind, in its natural state of detachment, lives fully in the moment without clinging to past memories or future expectations. This way, detachment allows one to experience life more fully and freely, without the weight of attachment or control.

Detachment is not about denying the world but rather engaging with it without attachment or expectation. When one lets go of the fear of losing what they are attached to, true detachment follows. The ego's need for possession, control, and security creates conflict and suffering. The freedom from attachment allows love to flow freely, without possessiveness or the fear of loss. Living with detachment means experiencing life deeply—enjoying beauty, love, and success—without making them possessions. A detached mind acts without needing a result or reward. In this freedom, there is no conflict, no fear, only the deep peace and understanding that comes from living fully in the moment, free from the need for control or attachment.

343. Renunciation

Renunciation: The Illusion of Escaping the Self

Renunciation is often seen as the path to freedom, where one gives up material possessions, desires, and attachments in pursuit of something higher or more spiritual. Many people renounce worldly pleasures with the belief that letting go of external things will bring inner peace, clarity, or spiritual growth. However, true freedom is not found in renouncing the external but in understanding and seeing clearly that attachment itself creates suffering. Renunciation can easily become another form of attachment if the mind is still clinging to desires, beliefs, or the idea of attaining something. In essence, renunciation is not about giving up the world but about letting go of the psychological burdens that prevent true freedom.

People often renounce in the hope of escaping suffering, conflict, or responsibility, but escape is not the same as understanding. The desire for recognition, spiritual status, or simplicity also fuels many acts of renunciation, but these motives reveal that the ego is still present. True renunciation arises from deep understanding, not from an effort to attain a higher state or to gain something. A mind that seeks to renounce is still in conflict—still struggling between desires and ideals. Real freedom is not in the practice of renouncing; it is in the effortless letting go of what is unnecessary when the mind is clear.

True renunciation is the natural result of understanding the nature of attachment and desire. It does not involve suppression or force but comes from the realization that attachment leads to suffering. A mind that is free from attachment moves lightly, without the weight of psychological burdens, without clinging to beliefs, past experiences, or ambitions. It is not about rejecting the world but living in it with complete freedom—without the need to possess, control, or escape. When one sees clearly, there is no need for renunciation; the mind is already free, and in this freedom, there is no longer a struggle or division between what is and what could be.

344. Spontaneity

Spontaneity: The Action That Arises Without Effort

Spontaneity is the natural ability to act without calculation, hesitation, or fear, arising effortlessly in response to life's demands. It is not driven by impulse but by a deeper intelligence that enables immediate action, free from the distortions of thought, comparison, or conditioning. Unlike impulsive behavior, which can be rash and uncontrolled, true spontaneity is grounded in clarity, intelligence, and fluidity, allowing for a natural and harmonious flow of action. It is a state where the mind responds to the present moment with full engagement, without the burdens of overthinking or hesitation.

The rarity of spontaneity can be attributed to the conditioning that shapes the mind from a young age. Society teaches us to think before we act, to calculate consequences, and to fear mistakes, all of which create internal conflict and hesitation. This conditioning prevents the mind from responding naturally, making it difficult to act freely and effortlessly. Fear of judgment, insecurity, and the desire for control over outcomes only further stifles spontaneous action, making it hard to break free from mental patterns. Overthinking, in particular, kills spontaneity, as it transforms natural expression into a rigid, mechanical response, creating a barrier to immediate and intuitive action.

True spontaneity, however, is not chaotic—it is a form of creativity and intelligence in action. It is the ability to live fully in the present, free from the constraints of psychological time, past regrets, or future anxieties. In a state of spontaneity, there is no inner conflict; thought and action are in perfect harmony.

This state of being allows one to respond to situations with clarity and presence, without the burden of doubt or fear. Spontaneity is an expression of freedom, an intelligence that moves effortlessly and fluidly, without hesitation, and without the need for control. When one is truly spontaneous, the mind is liberated from past conditioning, and action flows naturally, responding to life's demands with deep understanding and presence.

345. Revolution

Revolution: The Outer Change Without Inner Transformation

Revolution is commonly viewed as the act of overthrowing an existing system—be it political, social, or ideological—to instigate change. It is often perceived as a necessary step for progress, justice, or freedom. However, the question arises: does revolution truly bring about transformation, or does it merely replace one system of control with another? Many revolutions, while creating external shifts in power, often fail to address the deeper psychological issues that underpin human suffering, leaving the fundamental problems unaddressed. While we may be dissatisfied with the current system, we must ask if a new system can truly solve the core issues of fear, greed, and division within human consciousness.

The desire for revolution often stems from dissatisfaction with the present system, particularly due to corruption, injustice, and inequality. However, is this desire for change merely a reflection of our frustration with the status quo, or does it stem from a deeper need for inner transformation? While external revolutions may replace one set of leaders or systems with another, they often perpetuate the same cycles of oppression and suffering. History has shown that revolutions, while creating change, often fail to solve the deeper issues that drive human conflict. A new system or ideology cannot bring real freedom if it does not address the fundamental conflict within human minds.

True revolution is not external; it is an inner transformation that dissolves psychological conflict. The real revolution occurs when we see beyond conditioning—when we drop all ideological attachments and beliefs that create division. True revolution is not a political movement but a shift in consciousness, where the mind is free from the psychological patterns of fear, greed, and desire. The only way to create real change in society is through individual awareness, not by implementing new laws or systems. When the mind is liberated from its conditioning, it naturally acts in harmony, and society, in turn, transforms. The true revolution, therefore, is an inward revolution—one where there is freedom from the self-imposed boundaries of thought, and where action arises naturally from clarity and awareness.

346. Yoga

Yoga: Beyond Postures—The Union of Mind and Awareness

Yoga is often seen as a physical practice focused on asanas, breathing exercises, and meditation, but its true essence goes beyond these elements. At its core, yoga is the union of body, mind, and consciousness. It is not simply a practice but a state of being where the mind is free from conflict and completely immersed in the present moment. True yoga involves the cessation of psychological noise, allowing one to experience peace, clarity, and freedom without effort or external validation. It is a holistic practice, uniting all aspects of life into a seamless flow of awareness and understanding.

Many misconceptions surround the concept of yoga. It is not merely a tool for physical health, nor is it a discipline rooted in control or willpower. While physical postures (asana) are part of the practice, they serve as a means to an end, not the end itself. The true goal of yoga is not enlightenment or an elevated state of consciousness, as these pursuits keep the mind tied to time and seeking. Yoga also does not belong to any specific tradition or method; it transcends prescribed systems, offering a direct experience of truth that does not rely on external authorities or rituals. True yoga occurs in the present moment when the mind is silent and fully attuned to the reality of 'what is.'

Real yoga is not a process of effort but the natural state of inner freedom. It is the ending of psychological conflict, the quieting of the mind, and the understanding that nothing needs to be attained. Through yoga, one discovers that all that is needed is presence and awareness. When the mind stops seeking, controlling, or striving, yoga happens effortlessly. Whether in postures, daily life, or stillness, yoga is experienced through complete awareness, free from the distractions of desire, fear, and comparison. It is the profound realization that true peace, clarity, and freedom arise not from achieving something but from simply being fully present and aware in the moment.

347. Radical Change

Radical Change: The Shift That Leaves Nothing Untouched

Radical change is not about gradual improvement or modification of existing patterns—it is a complete transformation that occurs instantly. It involves a shift in perception that ends the root of psychological conditioning. This type of change is not about becoming better or more advanced; rather, it is the act of seeing clearly, and in that moment of clarity, change unfolds naturally. Most efforts to change stem from dissatisfaction with the current state of affairs, a desire to improve ourselves or society, and the belief that gradual progress brings about transformation. But real transformation is not a slow, incremental process—it happens when we understand and see things as they truly are.

The reason change often does not happen is that people attempt to bring about transformation through willpower, struggle, or external systems. These efforts only reinforce inner conflict, keeping the mind trapped in the cycle of desire and dissatisfaction. Radical change happens when one understands that the self, with its attachments, beliefs, and identity, is the source of conflict. When thought recognizes its own limitations, it shifts beyond the old patterns. Change occurs when there is deep understanding of the present moment, not when we impose future expectations or wait for a better time.

Living in radical change means letting go of psychological time and the concept of 'becoming.' It requires being fully aware and observing thought without escaping or avoiding it. When one sees clearly, the struggle ends, and in that moment, the transformation is complete. Radical change is the ending of psychological conditioning, not the continuous modification of the old. A mind that is truly free does not need gradual progress, systems, or improvement—it is free now, and in that freedom, life becomes completely new, without the weight of past conditioning or struggle.

348. Transformation

Transformation: The Death of the Old Without Effort

Transformation is a radical shift in perception, not a gradual change or self-improvement. It involves the ending of conditioned thought and the emergence of clarity, happening not through time or effort but in the present moment. True transformation cannot be sought or forced—it occurs when one sees reality completely, without resistance. The mind must be free of the need to become or improve, and transformation arises when the individual fully engages with what is, letting go of the past and future.

Many seek transformation to escape the conflict and suffering they feel, hoping that by changing themselves, they will find peace. However, transformation is not about becoming something different; it is about seeing the truth of what is, fully and without distortion. Psychological time, the belief that change will come gradually or in the future, only postpones the possibility of true transformation. Real change happens instantly when one perceives life without the filters of thought, without striving for an ideal, and without the illusion of self.

To experience true transformation, one must observe thoughts, reactions, and emotions without judgment or interference. Transformation is not achieved through struggle or effort, as this only strengthens inner conflict. Instead, it is about seeing the false as false, letting go of what is no longer needed, and living fully in the present. When the mind is quiet and free from the need to control or change, transformation happens effortlessly. In this state, there is no division between the observer and the observed, and the mind is free, clear, and completely present. This is the true nature of transformation—instant, complete, and without the burden of past conditioning.

349. Freedom

Freedom: The State of Being Without Fear or Conflict

Freedom is not just a political or social condition—it is an internal state of being free from fear, conditioning, attachment, and authority. Many people equate freedom with the ability to make choices or act without restrictions, but true freedom is not rooted in choice or rebellion. It is the complete clarity of mind where there is no burden of fear or past conditioning. Real freedom arises when the mind is silent, unburdened, and fully aware of the present. When the mind is free from the weight of external pressures or internal anxieties, it moves with intelligence, understanding, and love.

The common illusions of freedom are often misunderstood. People think that freedom is merely about having choices, but choice itself arises from confusion—the mind that is truly free does not need to choose; it simply perceives the truth as it is. Similarly, freedom is not rebellion or escape from responsibility, but the ability to act from intelligence, without reacting against external authority or personal desires. A mind driven by fear, desire, or the need to escape is not free; it is simply reacting to external or internal stimuli, reinforcing inner conflict rather than resolving it. True freedom, therefore, comes when the mind is free of such distortions and acts effortlessly in the present moment.

To live in freedom, one must be fully aware of the conditioning that governs thoughts, emotions, and actions. Freedom begins with observing thoughts, emotions, and reactions without judgment, seeing them clearly without labeling them as good or bad. It requires questioning everything, not blindly accepting beliefs, ideologies, or societal norms. This deep inquiry dissolves attachments and the need for a fixed identity, allowing for a deeper understanding of life and oneself. When one understands that the 'self' is merely an illusion of thought, a profound freedom arises, unencumbered by fear, desire, or the passage of time. A mind that lives in such freedom is deeply aware, full of intelligence, and responds to life without resistance or attachment.

350. Liberation

Liberation: The Mind Unburdened by the Known

Liberation is not something to be pursued or achieved—it is the natural state of the mind when it is free from psychological conditioning, attachment, and inner conflict. Many confuse liberation with escape or retreat, but true liberation does not come from withdrawal; it arises from the understanding and dissolution of fear, belief, and the ego. When the mind is no longer bound by past experiences, memories, and societal conditioning, it is free to move with intelligence, clarity, and pure awareness. Liberation is not a future goal or something to be attained over time—it exists in the present moment, when the mind is silent, unburdened, and completely open.

The reasons we remain unfree are rooted in our attachments to beliefs, possessions, and the self. The mind clings to comfort, security, and the known, preventing true freedom from unfolding. Fear of the unknown and a dependency on external authority keep the mind trapped in its limitations. The ego seeks to protect itself through attachments, and even the search for liberation can become another form of desire, reinforcing the cycle of attachment. Liberation occurs when one stops seeking it, letting go of the illusion of the 'self' and embracing the present moment without judgment or expectation. It is the cessation of mental conflict, where the mind simply sees what is, without the interference of past conditioning or psychological time.

To live in liberation, one must observe the mind without judgment or control. This allows for a natural stillness to arise, free from the constant movement of thought. True freedom comes not from effort or discipline but from seeing clearly, without the distortion of attachment. A liberated mind does not struggle with the past or future—it is fully present, experiencing life as it unfolds. When one sees that liberation is not personal, that it is not 'my' freedom but the natural state of the mind, then there is no longer a search for it. In this state, life moves effortlessly, without the burden of fear, comparison, or the illusion of self.

20. Spirituality & Transcendence

WAKE UP

WAKE UP

351. Spirituality

Spirituality: The Journey Beyond Belief and Dogma

Spirituality is not confined to religious practices, meditation, or rituals—it is a deep and profound inquiry into the nature of existence, truth, and life itself. True spirituality is about being fully awake, fully aware, and free from the constraints of conditioning, beliefs, and ideologies. It is not about following a prescribed path or gaining spiritual experiences; it is a state of being that transcends the ego and seeks no escape. True spirituality is found in direct perception, where one sees reality as it is, without distortion or expectation.

Many misconceptions surround the concept of spirituality, including the belief that it is synonymous with religion or self-improvement. Spirituality is not about seeking higher experiences or escaping the mundane realities of life. It is not about becoming more peaceful or enlightened through effort or discipline—it is about understanding what is. Spirituality is not an escape but a full engagement with life, seeing it clearly and deeply, and acting with love and intelligence in the present moment. It requires freedom from conditioning, where one is not bound by religious dogma, social expectations, or personal desires.

True spirituality is about silence, deep awareness, and compassion. It is not found in thoughts or concepts about the divine but in the stillness where truth naturally reveals itself. A mind that is free from psychological attachment and belief sees life clearly, without filters or judgments. It acts with intelligence and love, free from the need to follow systems or seek external validation. Spirituality, in this sense, is a state of being that transcends the self, revealing a connection with life that is unbroken, undistorted, and deeply alive. In this deep awareness, there is no seeker—only a profound understanding of life as it is.

352. Meditation

Meditation: The Art of Silent Awareness

Meditation is not a practice or a goal to be achieved. It is the natural state of complete awareness and inner silence, where the mind is free from effort and conflict. True meditation happens when the mind is still, free from the distractions of past and future thoughts. It is not about controlling the mind, but simply observing it without interference or judgment. Meditation is not separate from life—it is an approach to perceiving life with total attention and clarity, whether in silence or daily activity. When the mind is unburdened by the need for achievement or escape, meditation unfolds effortlessly, revealing peace and truth.

True meditation goes beyond concentration or repetition of techniques. Concentration forces the mind to focus, creating tension, while meditation is a state of effortless awareness. Any attempt to achieve a particular experience, whether bliss or enlightenment, can interfere with the natural flow of meditation. When one seeks an experience, the mind is divided, which is the opposite of meditation. The essence of meditation lies in seeing life as it is, without illusions or distractions. It is a state of total awareness in the present moment, free from the noise of past conditioning or future expectations.

Meditation naturally happens when one observes their thoughts without reacting or seeking control. The mind becomes quiet not through force but through letting go of the need for results. It is about being fully present, not in the past or future, and allowing silence to arise naturally. True meditation is found not only in dedicated practices but also in the awareness brought to every action and interaction in daily life. When the mind is clear and free from the 'self,' there is no division between the observer and the observed, and in this stillness, clarity and understanding emerge effortlessly.

353. Religion

Religion: The Organized Belief That Divides and Binds

Religion, in its truest form, is the search for truth—a quest to discover what is sacred and beyond the limitations of thought and belief. However, organized religion has often become a structure that imposes authority, rituals, and dogmas, which can divide people and prevent true understanding. While temples, churches, and scriptures may provide guidance, the essence of true religion is found in the deep, personal inquiry into life, the self, and the nature of reality. It is not about adhering to prescribed beliefs but about awakening to the truth through direct experience.

The problem with organized religion lies in its emphasis on belief rather than personal discovery. Many religions promote faith in doctrines, rituals, and scriptures, but truth cannot be handed down from authority—it must be personally experienced. Religion often creates divisions between people, each religion claiming to hold the exclusive truth, leading to conflict and violence. True religion does not belong to any one sect or ideology; it is beyond labels and divisions. Furthermore, religion has often become a way to escape fear and suffering rather than a path to understanding. The reliance on rituals and prayers provides comfort but does not address the underlying fears and questions of life.

True religion, therefore, is not found in the external world but within. It is the state of a silent mind, free from fear, attachment, and the burden of belief. It is the realization that the sacred is not contained in rituals or scriptures but is discovered through direct awareness of life as it is. A truly religious mind does not seek comfort or security through faith—it is free, questioning, and fully present. Religion, in this sense, is not an external set of practices but a state of deep connection with life, where the mind is free from psychological dependency and open to the truth beyond all conditioning. In this freedom, there is no division, no seeking, only awareness and deep communion with what is sacred.

354. Guru

Guru: The Authority That Can Either Free or Enslave

A guru is traditionally seen as a teacher, a spiritual guide, or an enlightened master who leads others toward truth. Throughout history, people have sought gurus in religion, philosophy, and self-improvement. However, the question arises: does truth lie in another, or must it be discovered firsthand? The pursuit of truth through a guru often arises from the need for certainty, guidance, and security in the face of life's uncertainties and confusion. But is truth something that can be handed down, or must it be uncovered through direct perception, free from reliance on another?

The desire for certainty and guidance often leads individuals to seek a guru. Many people turn to gurus for answers, direction, and psychological security. However, this dependency creates a barrier to true understanding, as the seeker may believe that someone else has already found the truth and that they must follow them. The illusion that wisdom can be transferred through teaching, rituals, or secret knowledge prevents individuals from realizing that truth cannot be given; it must be discovered personally. The act of following a guru fosters dependence, weakening the seeker's ability to inquire independently and discover their own truth.

To be free of the need for a guru, one must see that no external authority can provide true understanding. While books, teachers, and practices can offer information, they cannot give direct truth. Understanding comes from deep self-awareness and direct perception. The moment one stops seeking externally and begins observing internally, they realize that truth exists within themselves, independent of any guru. When the mind is completely silent and free from fear or seeking, the light of truth emerges naturally, revealing that a guru is not necessary. True wisdom arises from clarity, awareness, and presence, making the search for an external guide obsolete.

355. Path

Path: The Search That Can Lead Nowhere

A path is typically seen as a structured route or journey leading to a goal, such as success, enlightenment, or personal achievement. It arises from the mind's desire for progression and security, giving a sense of direction and movement. However, a mind that is truly aware understands that truth has no path— there is no journey to be taken, no destination to reach. The idea of a path creates the illusion that we must progress to attain truth, while in reality, understanding is instant and available in the present moment.

Paths are products of thought and conditioning—whether they exist in religion, philosophy, career, or personal development. These paths are based on past experiences and mental projections, leading the mind to believe that truth or understanding can be gradually attained. The pursuit of a path implies that there is a right way to go, with the authority of teachers, systems, and beliefs dictating the steps. But truth is not something external; it is something to be directly perceived. When we stop seeking a path, we realize that the illusion of a journey is unnecessary—truth was always here, unchanging and present.

The desire for a path stems from the mind's conditioning to think in terms of progress and success. We are taught that knowledge, growth, and fulfillment require effort and steps forward. But in truth, these are merely mental constructs; real understanding arises from insight and direct perception, not gradual achievement. When one lets go of the need to follow a path or arrive at a destination, they experience true freedom in the present moment. A mind free from paths moves with clarity and awareness, without struggle or the illusion of progress.

356. Cause and Effect

Cause and Effect: The Chain That Shapes Thought and Action

Cause and effect is the principle that every action leads to a corresponding result, shaping both the physical world and human understanding. It provides order and predictability in science, psychology, and daily life. However, when applied to the psychological realm, cause and effect may be more of a mental construct than an absolute truth. The mind seeks explanations for everything, believing that every effect has a traceable cause. This desire for order creates a sense of security and control, reinforcing the idea that the future is determined by the past. As a result, people try to control outcomes, believing that success, happiness, or suffering can be directly managed through calculated actions. Society and religion further condition this belief, teaching that rewards and punishments are linked to past deeds. But is this psychological causality real, or is it just a framework created by thought?

The idea of cause and effect strengthens the illusion of a continuous 'self.' If every present experience is caused by the past, then identity becomes a product of accumulated history. However, true transformation does not happen through analyzing the past—it happens in the present. Thought operates within time, projecting past experiences into the future, making people believe they are bound by their previous actions. This creates patterns of guilt, regret, and expectation, reinforcing psychological suffering. But is every emotion, fear, or moment of joy truly caused by a single past event? When deeply observed, one sees that psychological states are not always the result of a linear cause—they arise, change, and dissolve beyond simple explanations.

To move beyond the illusion of psychological cause and effect, one must observe without immediately seeking reasons. Instead of asking, "Why am I suffering?" can one simply observe suffering directly, without judgment or analysis? The present moment is not bound to the past unless thought continuously revives it. True freedom exists not in controlling outcomes but in acting with deep awareness, without expecting future results. A mind free from psychological cause and effect does not live in the weight of past mistakes or future rewards—it moves effortlessly in the now, responding with clarity, intelligence, and deep perception. In this state, action is not dictated by fear, regret, or anticipation—it flows naturally, beyond the limitations of cause and effect.

357. Karma

Karma: The Burden of the Past That Shapes the Present

Karma is the idea that every action, whether physical or mental, produces consequences that shape our future experiences. It is often interpreted as a law of cause and effect, explaining success, suffering, and destiny. A mind caught in karma sees life through the lens of past actions, reinforcing the belief that our future is determined by our past deeds. This perception can lead to a constant cycle of reward and punishment, preventing one from experiencing life fully in the present.

The nature of karma lies in the psychological continuation of cause and effect. The mind constantly links past actions with present situations, creating a belief that suffering or success is the result of previous behavior. This leads to the justification of pain and hardship as consequences of past wrongs, making one accept suffering passively rather than actively understanding it. Karma often creates the illusion of moral balance, where good actions are thought to bring positive results and bad actions lead to suffering, but life doesn't always follow these predictable patterns.

To be free from karma, one must realize that it is not a fixed law but a psychological continuation. The mind remains bound to past actions as long as it clings to them. True freedom arises when one acts without the expectation of reward or the fear of punishment, living fully in the present. By letting go of the psychological burden of past actions and living without psychological time, karma loses its hold. True action comes from awareness, not from belief in a system of rewards and consequences. A mind that is free from the conditioning of karma acts with clarity and intelligence, unburdened by past or future.

358. Heaven and Hell

Heaven and Hell: The Projections of Fear and Desire

Heaven and hell are psychological constructs created by thought to define ultimate experiences of reward and punishment. These concepts often manifest in religious, cultural, and personal beliefs, where heaven represents a state of ultimate pleasure and security, while hell represents suffering and punishment. A mind caught in these notions lives in duality, acting out of fear or desire rather than a deep understanding of life. These ideas, though powerful, are based on imagined futures shaped by fear and longing, not reality. People experience their own versions of heaven and hell daily, depending on their state of mind— suffering and inner conflict can already be a psychological hell, while peace and clarity can be a form of heaven in the present moment.

The idea of heaven and hell serves as a tool for control, particularly within religious or societal frameworks. These concepts encourage obedience, with the fear of hell motivating submission and the hope for heaven encouraging attachment to specific beliefs. However, these notions are psychological projections rather than tangible truths. Every individual's perception of heaven and hell is influenced by conditioning, varying greatly across cultures, demonstrating that they are not universal, but products of thought and belief. The truth is that such beliefs distract from living fully in the present, where true peace and understanding reside. A mind free from these constructs moves naturally, with clarity and intelligence, unburdened by the need for reward or fear of punishment.

Belief in heaven and hell arises from deep fears—fear of death, the unknown, or the need for justice in life. Society and culture condition individuals from childhood to accept these ideas, making them difficult to question. The desire for meaning beyond life often drives people to search for security in the afterlife, leading to the hope of salvation or the fear of eternal punishment. However, true transformation comes not from belief in an afterlife, but from a deep understanding of life and suffering as they are. When one stops seeking escape through heaven or fearing punishment through hell, they can live fully in the present. A mind that is free from the illusion of heaven and hell is clear, aware, and connected to reality, moving beyond imagined futures and into direct experience.

359. Soul

Soul: The Eternal Question Without an Answer

The soul is often viewed as the eternal, unchanging essence of an individual, a concept shaped by religious, spiritual, and philosophical beliefs. It arises from the mind's desire for permanence in a world defined by impermanence. The idea of the soul provides comfort, offering the hope of continuity beyond death, but does it truly exist, or is it simply a psychological projection created by thought to avoid the fear of death? The mind, attached to this idea, seeks to find identity beyond the physical body, yet in reality, there is no clear distinction between the soul and the accumulated experiences, thoughts, and memories that define our sense of self.

The concept of the soul varies across cultures, with some seeing it as personal and individual, while others view it as part of a greater universal consciousness. This diversity reveals that the soul is not a universal truth but rather a belief shaped by cultural conditioning. The search for the soul often leads to a life of seeking—purifying, evolving, or saving the soul—while ignoring the deeper, more direct understanding of life as it truly is. Believing in the soul can prevent one from seeing that the desire for continuity, for permanence beyond death, is just a product of thought, masking the truth of impermanence.

True understanding comes when one observes the mind's desire for continuity and questions whether the soul is anything more than accumulated memory and experience. The search for the soul and immortality distracts from living fully in the present. Life is not about seeking something beyond death; it is about understanding the impermanence of the self and embracing life as it is. True freedom arises when the mind stops clinging to the idea of the soul, recognizing it as an illusion created by fear and desire. In this awareness, life is lived fully, without the burden of seeking continuity or immortality.

360. Reincarnation

Reincarnation: The Continuation of the Self or an Illusion?

Reincarnation is often seen as a way to address the fear of death and the desire for continuity. It is rooted in the belief that the soul or consciousness persists beyond death, taking on new forms in subsequent lives. This idea provides comfort and reassurance for those who fear the cessation of existence.

However, when examined deeply, reincarnation may simply be a projection of the mind's attachment to the self and the desire for permanence. The belief that life must continue in another form arises from the mind's inability to accept the impermanence of the self. The notion of reincarnation strengthens the illusion of continuity, further entangling individuals in the cycle of psychological time and reinforcing the ego's need for stability and security.

The problems with reincarnation arise from its focus on the continuation of the self. By believing that the "I" will persist through multiple lives, one avoids confronting the impermanence of thought and identity in the present. The idea of reincarnation also postpones the opportunity for true transformation. If one believes that spiritual growth requires many lifetimes, the urgency to awaken in this life is diminished. Instead of focusing on immediate change, the individual is encouraged to delay growth until the next incarnation. Furthermore, the future self projected through reincarnation remains a product of thought—an abstract idea, not a real, ongoing existence. This reinforces the illusion of self and prevents direct understanding of the present moment.

To live without the idea of reincarnation, one must see psychological continuity for what it is: an illusion created by thought. The fear of death and the need for continuity vanish when the mind fully understands the transient nature of the self. Real transformation happens in the present, not through the hope for another life. A mind free from belief in reincarnation is free from the limitations of thought, from the projection of future lives, and from the fear of death. In this freedom, the mind opens to the vastness of the present, beyond the need for a self, beyond the fear of death, and beyond the confines of time and rebirth.

The question of reincarnation becomes irrelevant because the mind is fully alive and awake in the now.

361. Sacred

Sacred: That Which Is Untouched by Thought

The sacred is not a concept, nor something that can be defined or grasped by the mind. It transcends rituals, symbols, and beliefs, and cannot be captured by human thought. The search for the sacred arises when the mind senses a deeper longing for something beyond the ordinary—the divine, the eternal. However, the very act of seeking the sacred can often obstruct its perception. We are conditioned by religious and cultural teachings to look for the sacred in external objects, practices, and doctrines. But can the sacred truly be found outside, or does it reveal itself when the mind ceases its constant striving, when thought quiets, and when the illusion of separation dissolves?

The problems with the search for the sacred stem from the mind's constant attempt to define or attain it. The sacred is not a thing that can be captured, manipulated, or even named. Thought can only create symbols, rituals, and beliefs that seem to represent the sacred, but these are mere reflections, not the reality. Seeking the sacred as an external object or through effort only brings the seeker further from it. The moment we pursue the sacred with desire or expectation, we are trapped in time and self-interest. To truly perceive the sacred, the mind must be free from attachment, from the need to define, and from all beliefs or preconceived notions. It must simply observe, without labeling or measuring.

To truly perceive the sacred, one must empty the mind of all thoughts, beliefs, and expectations. The sacred cannot be reached through striving, practice, or even experience—it arises when the mind is still, free from division. The sacred is not found in separation; it is in the unity of all things, in the present moment where life unfolds. When one perceives without fragmentation, seeing all of existence as one interconnected movement, the sacred is revealed. In the stillness of a silent mind, free from the ego's search, the sacred presence becomes apparent—not as something external to us, but as the totality of what is, immeasurable and beyond definition.

362. Light

Light: The Clarity That Dispels Darkness Within

Light is not simply a physical entity; it symbolizes clarity, awareness, and the ability to perceive without distortion. It arises when the mind is free from confusion, ignorance, and illusion. True light is not created through effort or accumulated knowledge; it naturally emerges when the mind is clear, without trying to achieve enlightenment. The search for light often arises from the desire to overcome darkness—whether that darkness is confusion, suffering, or ignorance. However, light is not opposed to darkness; it simply exists when confusion ends. In this state, there is no battle between light and darkness, as the mind no longer creates opposition. True clarity comes when the mind sees without distortion, without projection, and without the influence of past conditioning.

Our pursuit of light often stems from a misunderstanding of its nature. We associate light with external sources—teachers, religious teachings, or philosophies—believing they hold the key to our understanding. Yet true light does not come from these external sources, but from within. The mind is naturally equipped with the ability to see clearly when it is free from distortion. When one stops searching for illumination and instead observes what clouds the mind, clarity arises effortlessly. The search for light can itself create a sense of darkness because it implies the need to overcome something, reinforcing the duality of light and darkness. The true way to experience light is through deep attention, where the mind is silent and present with what is, without seeking, without fear, and without judgment.

The nature of light is such that it is not a product of effort, but the result of a mind that is free from conflict and separation. Light is awareness itself—pure perception that sees things as they are, without projecting or interpreting. When the mind is free from conditioning and the illusion of division between the observer and the observed, light is simply present. This light is not an external force that we need to seek, but an inherent quality of being that emerges naturally when the mind is in a state of true observation. In this space of pure perception, light is not a goal to attain—it is the natural state of a mind that has let go of distortion, fear, and attachment. It is boundless, effortless, and ever-present.

363. Enlightenment

Enlightenment: The Mind Free from Illusion

Enlightenment is not something to be achieved through effort, practice, or specific experiences. It is the ending of psychological conditioning, illusion, and internal conflict. The mind that is enlightened is free from division and confusion, existing fully in the present moment. It is not seeking anything or becoming something different; it is simply aware of what is, without interference from thought or attachment. This state of awareness reveals the true nature of reality, where there is no fear or distortion, and the mind moves naturally, effortlessly, and with intelligence.

Many seek enlightenment because they desire ultimate security, relief from suffering, or a permanent state of peace. However, this search often becomes an illusion in itself, as the pursuit of enlightenment becomes just another desire of the self—an ego-driven quest for something to attain or achieve. The mind, conditioned by religious or spiritual traditions, may believe that enlightenment is a mystical experience or an extraordinary mental state to be reached through practice. But true enlightenment is not a temporary experience, nor is it found in the accumulation of knowledge or the following of specific paths.

Real enlightenment is the complete ending of psychological time—the freedom from the past and future, where the mind exists fully in the now. It is not about expanding the self or becoming someone more profound, but about the dissolution of the 'I' that seeks, compares, or defines. Enlightenment happens when one stops seeking it, when one lives with awareness, attention, and without attachment to any specific goal. True freedom and clarity come from seeing life as it is, without distortion or division. It is not found in special retreats or places, but in the way one lives every moment, aware and present, free from fear, desire, and the psychological self.

364. God

God: The Unknown That Thought Tries to Define

The concept of God arises from the human need for meaning, security, and order. It represents the idea of a supreme being, force, or intelligence that governs existence and the unknown. While different religions define God in various ways, it is often seen as a source of comfort, authority, or salvation, providing answers to life's uncertainties. However, the idea of God can also become a barrier to direct understanding, as it is shaped by human beliefs, cultures, and interpretations. The mind caught in the idea of God may seek refuge in this concept rather than inquire deeply into the nature of existence itself.

God is a concept that is deeply influenced by belief and tradition. Each religion offers its own definition of God, ranging from a personal deity to an impersonal force or formless presence. These variations suggest that God is not an objective reality but a creation of human thought and culture. People often turn to God as an answer to the unknown, especially when reason or science cannot explain certain phenomena. However, the reliance on God to fill gaps in human understanding raises questions: is truth found in belief, or in direct inquiry and experience? The idea of

God can bring unity for some but also create division, as different interpretations often lead to conflict.

The human belief in God is often rooted in a desire for security, fear of death, and a search for meaning and purpose. People may cling to the idea of God to feel that life is guided by a higher power, providing stability and hope for an afterlife. This belief is often conditioned by society and tradition, making it difficult to question or deeply examine. However, true understanding of God lies not in belief or dogma but in direct perception and awareness of existence. When one frees the mind from the need for security or authority, the need to seek answers from external sources dissolves. Through deep awareness and observation, one can begin to see life and existence directly, beyond the limitations imposed by religious or philosophical ideas about God.

365. Truth

Truth: That Which Cannot Be Sought or Owned

Truth is not a concept, belief, or something that can be defined—it is the direct perception of reality as it is, free from distortion and thought. It is not personal or subjective, as many would believe; it is universal and beyond individual opinions. Truth cannot be discovered through intellectual pursuits or external authorities; it can only be realized when the mind is silent, unclouded by bias, and fully present in the moment. It is not something to be attained, but something that is always available when one's perception is free from the conditioning of thought and belief.

The mind seeks truth because it is caught in constant conflict, uncertainty, and fear. In an effort to find stability, people often turn to religions, philosophies, or ideologies, hoping they provide the answers and meaning to their existence. However, any truth that is dependent on authority or external validation is not true—it is merely a belief that we have accepted without question. The real truth cannot be found through external teachings, nor can it be understood through intellectual analysis—it exists only when the mind is free from attachment to any belief or framework.

The greatest obstacle to truth is belief and conditioning—our ingrained habits, opinions, and cultural perspectives shape how we view the world, often blinding us from seeing what is truly there. Truth is not something to be sought or found in the future—it exists in the present moment, and it is revealed when the mind is fully aware and free from fear. When thought, memory, and time cease to dominate, there is only pure perception, and in that perception, truth is naturally seen. In total awareness, where there is no judgment or expectation, truth unfolds effortlessly, timelessly, and without distortion.

A Note of Thanks

Thank you for choosing to read *Wake Up*. This book is the result of years of deep reflection, exploration, and dedication to uncovering the essence of awareness and transformation. I am truly grateful for your time, your curiosity, and your willingness to engage with these ideas. If this book has resonated with you, I encourage you to share its insights with those around you, for wisdom grows when it is shared.

Your support, feedback, and encouragement mean everything to me. They inspire me to continue this journey of writing, questioning, and seeking deeper truths. Every thought you reflect upon, every realization you embrace, and every change you make within yourself contributes to a world that is more conscious, more compassionate, and more awakened.

We all have the ability to break free from limitations.

We all have the potential to see beyond illusion.

We all have the strength to awaken to life's deeper realities.

Do not remain asleep to the patterns of conditioning.

Do not accept anything without questioning.

You are here to *Wake Up*—to see, to live, and to be free.

With gratitude,

Srinivas

WAKE UP

WAKE UP

About the Author

Srinivas Panaganti, known by his pen name ***Srinivart***, is a software engineer by profession and an artist at heart. His journey of creativity spans across multiple realms—digital art, painting, and writing—all of which serve as mediums for his deep introspection and exploration of human consciousness. Passionate about reading from an early age, he finds immense fulfillment in both absorbing wisdom and sharing it through his art and words.

After the success of his debut book, ***"Be the Best Version of Yourself"***, Srinivas now presents *Wake Up*, a thought-provoking work that challenges readers to break free from conditioned thinking and see life with absolute clarity. Through his writing, he aims to inspire awareness, transformation, and a deeper connection to truth. His mission is to leave an imprint in the hearts and minds of those who seek to understand life beyond the surface.

You can connect with him and explore his artworks through:

Instagram/YouTube: **@Srinivart**

Website: **www.srinivart.com**

LinkedIn: **Srinivas Panaganti**

Email: **Srinivart@gmail.com**

Srinivas welcomes your thoughts, reflections, and feedback. His journey of writing and art is an ongoing conversation with the world—one that he hopes will continue to inspire and awaken many.